MW00396878

Web Design with
HTML5 & CSS3

INTRODUCTORY

MINNICK | FRIEDRICHSEN   **Eighth Edition**

Web Design with
HTML5 & CSS3

INTRODUCTORY

MINNICK | FRIEDRICHSEN   **Eighth Edition**

CENGAGE
Learning·

Australia · Brazil · Mexico · Singapore · United Kingdom · United States

Web Design with HTML5 and CSS3, Introductory, Eighth Edition
Jessica Minnick, Lisa Friedrichsen

Product Director: Kathleen McMahon

Senior Product Manager: Jim Gish

Content Developer: Kate Mason

Senior Marketing Manager: Eric La Scola

Senior Content Project Manager: Matthew Hutchinson

Art Director: Heather Marshall, Lumina Datamatics, Inc.

Manufacturing Planner: Julio Esperas

IP Analyst: Amber Hosea

Senior IP Project Manager: Kathryn Kucharek

Production Service: Lumina Datamatics, Inc.

Compositor: Lumina Datamatics, Inc.

Cover Images:
    Background image: iStockPhoto.com/ virusowy
    Computers: iStockPhoto.com/scyther5

Unless otherwise stated, all screenshots courtesy of Microsoft Corporation. Microsoft and the Office logo are either registered trademarks or trademarks of Microsoft Corporation in the United States and/or other countries. Cengage Learning is an independent entity from the Microsoft Corporation, and not affiliated with Microsoft in any manner.

© 2016, 2013 Cengage Learning

WCN: 01-100-101

ALL RIGHTS RESERVED. No part of this work covered by the copyright herein may be reproduced, transmitted, stored or used in any form or by any means graphic, electronic, or mechanical, including but not limited to photocopying, recording, scanning, digitizing, taping, Web distribution, information networks, or information storage and retrieval systems, except as permitted under Section 107 or 108 of the 1976 United States Copyright Act, without the prior written permission of the publisher.

For product information and technology assistance, contact us at
Cengage Learning Customer & Sales Support, 1-800-354-9706
For permission to use material from this text or product,
submit all requests online at **cengage.com/permissions**
Further permissions questions can be emailed to
permissionrequest@cengage.com

Library of Congress Control Number: 2015935389

Student Edition:
ISBN: 978-1-305-58576-8

Cengage Learning
20 Channel Center Street
Boston, MA 02210
USA

Cengage Learning is a leading provider of customized learning solutions with employees residing in nearly 40 different countries and sales in more than 125 countries around the world. Find your local representative at **www.cengage.com**.

Cengage Learning products are represented in Canada by Nelson Education, Ltd.

To learn more about Course Learning Solutions, visit **www.cengage.com**.

Purchase any of our products at your local college store or at our preferred online store **www.cengagebrain.com**

Printed in the United States of America
Print Number: 01   Print Year: 2015

Web Design with HTML5 & CSS3

INTRODUCTORY   Eighth Edition

Contents

Web Design with HTML5 and CSS3

Appendices

Preface

The Shelly Cashman Series® offers the finest textbooks in computer education. We are proud that our previous web design and development books have been so well received. With each new edition of our HTML and CSS books, we make significant improvements based on web technology and comments made by instructors and students. For *Web Design with HTML5 and CSS3, Eighth Edition*, the Shelly Cashman Series development team carefully reviewed our pedagogy and analyzed its effectiveness in teaching today's student. Contemporary students read less, but need to retain more. As they develop and perform skills, students must know how to apply the skills to different settings. Today's students need to be continually engaged and challenged to retain what they're learning.

With this web design book, we continue our commitment to focusing on the user and how they learn best.

Objectives of This Textbook

Web Design with HTML5 and CSS3, Eighth Edition, is intended for a first course that offers an introduction to HTML, CSS, and basic web design techniques. No experience with webpage development or computer programming is required. The objectives of this book are:

- To teach the fundamentals of how to plan and organize the webpages for a new website

- To thoroughly apply two fundamental webpage technologies to realistic case studies: HTML for structure and CSS for style and layout

- To provide an exercise-oriented approach that reinforces learning by doing

- To introduce students to new web technologies and trends

- To promote curiosity and independent exploration of web resources

- To support current, professional webpage development best practices

- To encourage independent study and support distance learners

The Shelly Cashman Approach

Proven Pedagogy with an Emphasis on Project Planning

Each chapter presents a practical problem to be solved, within a project planning framework. The project orientation is strengthened by the use of the Roadmap, which provides a visual guide for the project. Step-by-step instructions with supporting screens guide students through the steps. Instructional steps are supported by the Q&A, Other Ways, Experimental Steps, and BTW features.

Visually Engaging Book That Maintains Student Interest

The step-by-step tasks with supporting figures create a rich visual experience for the student. Callouts on the screens that present both explanatory and navigational information provide students with information they need when they need to know it.

Supporting Reference Materials (Appendices)

The appendices provide additional information about the details of HTML and CSS so that students can quickly look up information about web design terms, HTML elements, attributes, and valid values as well as CSS properties and values.

End-of-Chapter Student Activities

Extensive end-of-chapter activities provide a variety of reinforcement opportunities for students where they can apply and expand their skills. To complete some of these assignments, you will be required to use the Data Files for Students. Visit www .cengagebrain.com for detailed access instructions or contact your instructor for information about accessing the required files.

New to This Edition

Fresh, Industry-Leading Website Design Practices

For this edition, the development team made a huge leap forward in bringing up-to-date, forward-thinking website development practices into focus and application.

Semantic Wireframe

The webpage development process starts with a semantic wireframe, which uses the structural elements new to HTML5 to efficiently organize the regions of a webpage.

Focus on Responsive Design and Fluid Layout

Design a single website that responds to the screen displays of desktop and laptop computers, tablets, smartphones, and other mobile devices.

HTML5 and CSS3 Features

The chapter project and exercises incorporate the latest additions to HTML and CSS, including new HTML5 elements, CSS3 properties, and syntax recommended by the World Wide Web Consortium (W3C). Every chapter validates documents using online tools for HTML5 and CSS3.

All New Projects

This edition contains a wealth of contemporary projects that logically build in complexity and probe for understanding. Our goal is not only to help you teach valid HTML and CSS, but to reveal deeper conceptual issues essential to the field of web development. Using the technologies of today's web developers results in websites that are worthy candidates for an electronic portfolio.

Professional Best Practices

With the advent of today's powerful content management systems and website builder tools, do you still need to learn how to create HTML and CSS files from scratch in a text editor? Professionals in the field answer that question with a united, enthusiastic yes! Mastering these technologies is essential to all web-related careers.

Instructor Resources

The Instructor Resources include both teaching and testing aids and can be accessed via www.cengage.com/login.

Instructor's Manual Includes lecture notes summarizing the chapter sections, figures, and boxed elements found in every chapter, teacher tips, classroom activities, lab activities, and quick quizzes in Microsoft® Word® files.

Syllabus Easily customizable sample syllabus covers policies, assignments, exams, and other course information.

Figure Files Illustrations for every figure in the textbook in electronic form.

PowerPoint Presentations A multimedia lecture presentation system that provides slides for each chapter. Presentations are based on chapter objectives.

Data Files for Students Includes all the files that are required by students to complete the exercises.

Solutions to Exercises Includes solutions for all end-of-chapter exercises and chapter reinforcement exercises.

Test Bank & Test Engine Test banks include questions for every chapter, featuring objective-based and critical thinking question types. Cengage Learning Testing Powered by Cognero is a flexible, online system that allows you to:

- author, edit, and manage test bank content from multiple Cengage Learning solutions
- create multiple test versions in an instant
- deliver tests from your LMS, your classroom, or wherever you want

Learn Online

CengageBrain.com is the premier destination for purchasing or renting Cengage Learning textbooks, eBooks, eChapters, and study tools at a significant discount (eBooks up to 50% off Print). In addition, CengageBrain.com provides direct access to all digital products including eBooks, eChapters, and digital solutions, regardless of where purchased.

course|notes™
quick reference guide

CourseNotes

CourseNotes are six-panel quick reference cards that reinforce the most important and widely used features of a software application in a visual and user-friendly format. CourseNotes serve as a great reference tool during and after the student completes the course. CourseNotes are available for software applications such as Microsoft Office 2013, Windows 8, and HTML. Topic-based CourseNotes, including Best Practices in Social Networking, Hot Topics in Technology, and Leverage the Internet for Your Career Search, are also available. Visit www.cengagebrain.com to learn more!

Textbook Walk-Through

The Shelly Cashman Series Pedagogy: Project-Based — Step-by-Step — Variety of Assessments

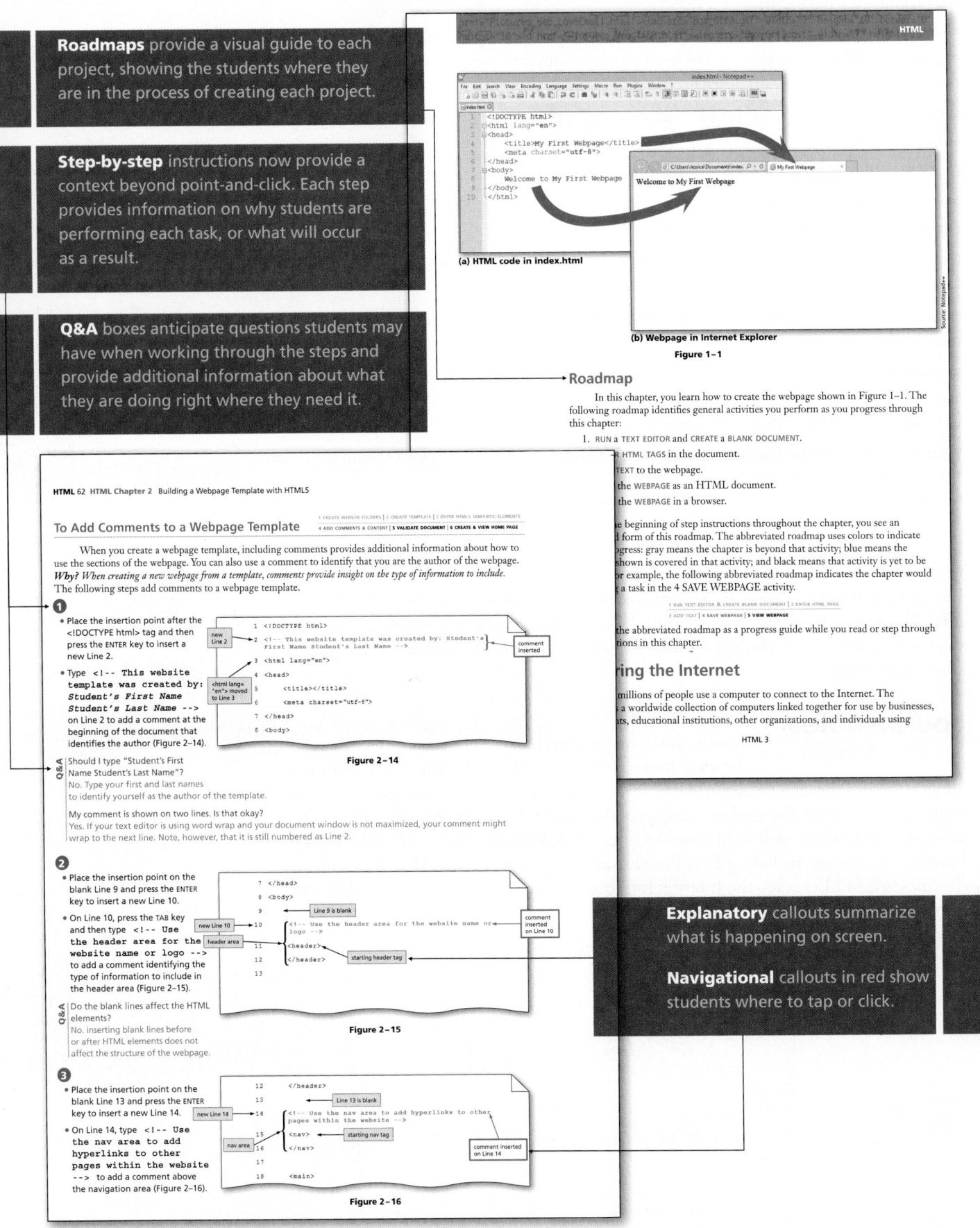

Roadmaps provide a visual guide to each project, showing the students where they are in the process of creating each project.

Step-by-step instructions now provide a context beyond point-and-click. Each step provides information on why students are performing each task, or what will occur as a result.

Q&A boxes anticipate questions students may have when working through the steps and provide additional information about what they are doing right where they need it.

(a) HTML code in index.html

(b) Webpage in Internet Explorer

Figure 1–1

Roadmap

In this chapter, you learn how to create the webpage shown in Figure 1–1. The following roadmap identifies general activities you perform as you progress through this chapter:

1. RUN A TEXT EDITOR and CREATE A BLANK DOCUMENT.
2. [EN]TER HTML TAGS in the document.
3. [ADD] TEXT to the webpage.
4. [SAVE] the WEBPAGE as an HTML document.
5. [VIEW] the WEBPAGE in a browser.

[At th]e beginning of step instructions throughout the chapter, you see an [abbreviate]d form of this roadmap. The abbreviated roadmap uses colors to indicate [your pro]gress: gray means the chapter is beyond that activity; blue means the [task is] shown is covered in that activity; and black means that activity is yet to be [covered. F]or example, the following abbreviated roadmap indicates the chapter would [be coverin]g a task in the 4 SAVE WEBPAGE activity.

1 RUN TEXT EDITOR & CREATE BLANK DOCUMENT | 2 ENTER HTML TAGS
3 ADD TEXT | **4 SAVE WEBPAGE** | 5 VIEW WEBPAGE

[Use] the abbreviated roadmap as a progress guide while you read or step through [the instruc]tions in this chapter.

[Explo]ring the Internet

[Today,] millions of people use a computer to connect to the Internet. The [Internet i]s a worldwide collection of computers linked together for use by businesses, [governmen]ts, educational institutions, other organizations, and individuals using

HTML 3

HTML 62 HTML Chapter 2 Building a Webpage Template with HTML5

To Add Comments to a Webpage Template

1 CREATE WEBSITE FOLDERS | 2 CREATE TEMPLATE | 3 ENTER HTML5 SEMANTIC ELEMENTS
4 ADD COMMENTS & CONTENT | 5 VALIDATE DOCUMENT | 6 CREATE & VIEW HOME PAGE

When you create a webpage template, including comments provides additional information about how to use the sections of the webpage. You can also use a comment to identify that you are the author of the webpage. *Why? When creating a new webpage from a template, comments provide insight on the type of information to include.* The following steps add comments to a webpage template.

❶
- Place the insertion point after the <!DOCTYPE html> tag and then press the ENTER key to insert a new Line 2.

- Type <!-- **This website template was created by:** *Student's First Name Student's Last Name* --> on Line 2 to add a comment at the beginning of the document that identifies the author (Figure 2–14).

```
1  <!DOCTYPE html>
2  <!-- This website template was created by: Student's
   First Name Student's Last Name -->
3  <html lang="en">
4  <head>
5      <title></title>
6      <meta charset="utf-8">
7  </head>
8  <body>
```
new Line 2

<html lang="en"> moved to Line 3

comment inserted

Figure 2–14

Q&A Should I type "Student's First Name Student's Last Name"?
No. Type your first and last names to identify yourself as the author of the template.

My comment is shown on two lines. Is that okay?
Yes. If your text editor is using word wrap and your document window is not maximized, your comment might wrap to the next line. Note, however, that it is still numbered as Line 2.

❷
- Place the insertion point on the blank Line 9 and press the ENTER key to insert a new Line 10.

- On Line 10, press the TAB key and then type <!-- **Use the header area for the website name or logo** --> to add a comment identifying the type of information to include in the header area (Figure 2–15).

```
7   </head>
8   <body>
9
10      <!-- Use the header area for the website name or
    logo -->
11      <header>
12      </header>
13
```
Line 9 is blank

new Line 10

header area

comment inserted on Line 10

starting header tag

Figure 2–15

Q&A Do the blank lines affect the HTML elements?
No. inserting blank lines before or after HTML elements does not affect the structure of the webpage.

❸
- Place the insertion point on the blank Line 13 and press the ENTER key to insert a new Line 14.

- On Line 14, type <!-- **Use the nav area to add hyperlinks to other pages within the website** --> to add a comment above the navigation area (Figure 2–16).

```
12      </header>
13
14      <!-- Use the nav area to add hyperlinks to other
    pages within the website -->
15      <nav>
16      </nav>
17
18      <main>
```
Line 13 is blank

new Line 14

nav area

starting nav tag

comment inserted on Line 14

Figure 2–16

Explanatory callouts summarize what is happening on screen.

Navigational callouts in red show students where to tap or click.

Experiment Steps within the step-by-step instructions encourage students to explore, experiment, and take advantage of web technologies. These steps are not necessary to complete the projects, but are designed to increase confidence and problem-solving skills.

Consider This boxes pose thought-provoking questions with answers throughout each chapter, promoting critical thought along with immediate feedback.

HTML 94 **HTML Chapter 3** Enhancing a Website with Links and Images

1 ADD HYPERLINKS | 2 ADD IMAGES | 3 ADD DIV ELEMENTS | 4 ADD HEADINGS & LISTS
5 VIEW WEBSITE IN BROWSER & TEST LINKS | 6 VALIDATE PAGES

To Add an Email Link in the Home Page

Next, add an email link to the email address in the footer area of the home page. *Why? Although you added an email link in the footer of the template, you still need to add an email link to the home page to match the website template.* The following steps add an email link to the home page.

1

- Place your insertion point before forwardfitness@club.net on Line 38, located within the footer area, to prepare to insert an email anchor tag.

- Type `<a href="mailto: forwardfitness@club.net">` to insert a starting anchor tag that links to an email address.

- Place the insertion point after the email address on Line 38 to prepare to insert an ending anchor tag.

- Type `</a>` to insert an ending anchor tag (Figure 3–23).

```
36  <footer>
37      &copy; Copyright 2015. All Rights Reserved.<br>
38      <a href="mailto:forwardfitness@club.net">forwardfitness@club.net</a>
39  </footer>
```

Figure 3–23

2

- Tap or click the Save button on the toolbar to save your changes.

- Open File Explorer (Windows) or Finder (Mac), navigate to the index.html file in the fitness folder, and then double-tap or double-click the file to open it in your default browser (Figure 3–24).

Figure 3–24

Experiment

- Tap or click the Home link and the email link, and then close the window for the new email message and close the browser.

BTW
Overusing Images
Be cautious about overusing images on a webpage. Using too many images may give your webpage a cluttered look or distract the visitor from the purpose of the webpage. An image should have a purpose, such as to convey content, visually organize a page, provide a hyperlink, or serve another function.

Adding Images to a Website

Images include photos, drawings, diagrams, charts, and other graphics that convey visual information. On a webpage, they help break up text and contribute to the design and aesthetics of a website. However, rather than merely decorate a webpage, images should support the purpose of the page or illustrate content. Images can also provide visual representations of a company's products and services. When determining what images to use within your website, choose those that relate directly to the content. Images that do not support the content can be distracting or confusing. For

---

CONSIDER THIS

Can I redesign a desktop-only website for multiplatform displa
Yes. If your audience is accustomed to the desktop-only website, retrofitting 1
makes sense because the site remains familiar to users. You also avoid buildi
vantage of design decisions such as color scheme and use media you have al
content and number of pages, redesigning may be a time-consuming proces

Wireframe

Before web designers actually start crea
they sketch the design using a wireframe. A **w**
clearly identifies the location of main webpag
organization logo, content areas, and images.
your webpages, use lines and boxes as shown
plenty of white space within your design to i
distinguish among the areas on the webpage.
active white space and passive white space. **Ac**
that is intentionally left blank. Typically, the g
the design of an asymmetrical page. **Passive**
areas. Passive white space helps a user focus on one part of the page. Proper use of white
space makes webpage content easy to read and brings focus to page elements.

Figure 1–12

© 2016 Cengage Learning®

Site Map

A **site map** is a planning tool that lists or displays all the pages on a website and indicates how they are related to each other. In other words, a site map shows the structure of a website. Begin defining the structure of a website by identifying the information to provide and then organize that information into divisions using the organizing method that makes the most sense for the content. For example, if the website offers three types of products for sale, organize the site by product category. If the website provides training, organize the site in a step-by-step sequence.

Next, arrange the webpages according to a logical structure. A website can use several types of structures, including linear, hierarchical, and webbed. Each structure connects the webpages in a different way to define how users navigate the site and view

Textbook Walk-Through

Chapter Summary lists the tasks completed in the chapter, grouped into major task categories in an outline format.

TextWrangler

```
TextWrangler   File   Edit   Text   View   Search   Go   Window   #!   ⏚   Help
                                      index.html
T.   ⬡   File Path ▾ : ~/Documents/index.html                                    ✎ ⚙ ▤
     ◀ ▶ index.html      ⬡ (no symbol selected)
  1   <!DOCTYPE html>
  2 ▼ <html lang="en">
  3 ▼ <head>
  4       <title>Webpage Example</title>
  5       <meta charset="utf-8">
  6 ⌐ </head>
  7 ▼ <body>
  8       Welcome to My First Webpage
  9 ⌐ </body>
 10 ⌐ </html>
 11
```
Source: TextWrangler

Figure 1–43

Chapter Summary

In this chapter, you learned about the Internet, the web, and associated technologies, including web servers and web browsers. You learned the essential role of HTML in creating webpages and reviewed tools used to create HTML documents. You also learned how to create a basic HTML webpage. The items listed below include all the new concepts and skills you have learned in this chapter, with the tasks grouped by activity.

Creating a Basic Webpage
  Start Notepad++ and Create a Blank Document (HTML 30)
  Add Basic HTML Tags to a Document (HTML 31)
  Add a Title and Text to a Webpage (HTML 32)
  Save a Webpage (HTML 33)
  View a Webpage in a Browser (HTML 34)

Exploring the Internet
  Describe the Internet (HTML 3)
  Describe the World Wide Web (HTML 4)
  Define Protocols (HTML 6)
  Discuss Web Browsers (HTML 7)
  Identify Types of Websites (HTML 9)

Planning a Website
  Identify the Purpose and Audience of the Website (HTML 11–12)

Design for Multiplatform Display (HTML 13)
  Describe a Wireframe and a Site Map (HTML 14)
  Consider Graphics, Navigation, Typography, and Color (HTML 17–19)
  Design for Accessibility (HTML 20)

Understanding the Basics of HTML
  Define Hypertext Markup Language (HTML 21)
  Describe HTML Elements (HTML 21)
  List Useful HTML Practices (HTML 22)
  Identify Technologies Related to HTML (HTML 23)
  Explain the Role of Other Web Programming Languages (HTML 23)

Using Web Authoring Tools
  Identify Text Editors (HTML 24)
  Download and Install a Text Editor (HTML 27)
  Describe WYSIWYG Editors (HTML 27)

CONSIDER THIS

What decisions will you need to make when creating your next webpage?
Use these guidelines as you complete the assignments in this chapter and create your own webpages outside of this class.

1. Plan the website.
   a. Identify the purpose of the website.
   b. Identify the users of the website.
   c. Recognize the computing environments of the users.
   d. Design a wireframe and a site map.
2. Choose the design components.
   a. Identify possible graphics for the website.
   b. Determine the types of navigation tools and typography to use.
   c. Select a color scheme.
   d. Consider accessibility.

Continued >

Consider This: Plan Ahead box presents a single master planning guide that students can use as they create webpages on their own.

Apply Your Knowledge exercise usually requires students to open and manipulate a file to practice the activities learned in the chapter.

Enhancing a Website

Apply Your Knowledge

Reinforce the skills and apply the concepts you learned in thi

Creating a Page with Links, Images, Lists, and Headings
Instructions: In this exercise, you will use your HTML editor to er
to create a template for the pages for a new website as well as the h
Jewelry and Gem Shop. The completed home page is shown in Fig
as well as the HTML5 tags required to insert an image, headings, li
information for this page. You will also use professional web develo
space, validate, and check the spelling of your work.

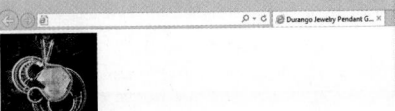

Durango Jewelry and Gem Shop

Distinguished wire-wrapped jewelry, pendants, and gems

Classics Specials Gems Contact Me

Durango Jewelry and Gem Shop pampers you with one-of-a-kind, high-quality wire-wrapped pendants and gems. Our works of art are inspired by natural geometries and the vast beauty of mother nature.

The featured pendant provides these characteristics:

  • gemstone is "Smoky quartz" also called a "Soulmate Crystal"
  • gemstone is over two carats
  • wire is a mixture of antique colored copper and .930 pure silver
  • high-quality silver alloy requires very little polishing
  • pendant is approximately 4cm x 3cm

Come to Durango Jewelry and Gem Shop to make your stay in Durango a life-time treasure.

Durango Jewelry and Gem Shop, 10101 Main Street, Durango, CO

Established 1979

Contact us through email

Photo courtesy of Kelsey Friedrichsen

Figure 3–67

Perform the following tasks:

1. Open your HTML editor and then open the apply03.html file from the Data Files for Students. Use the File Save As feature to save the webpage in the chapter03\apply folder with the name **index.html** to create the home page.

2. Modify the comment at the top of the page to include your name and today's date.

3. Enter **Durango Jewelry Pendant Gem** in the <title> tags. Recall that content in the title tags appears in the tab at the top of the browser and is also used by search engines.

4. In the **header** section, enter the following content, each on its own line in the HTML editor.
   a. An image element coded as follows:
   ```
   <img src="wirewrap01.jpg" alt="smoky quartz pendant" width="171"
   height="171">
   ```

Continued >

11. Submit the `index.html` file in a format specified by your instructor.

12. ⊛ In this exercise, you were instructed to use the <div id="main"> tag instead of the HTML5 <main> tag to mark up the main content in the body of the webpage. Because browsers are constantly changing and improving, it's important to make sure that the audience you are trying to reach supports the HTML5 elements and attributes you are using on your website. Find two websites that address the issue of HTML5 browser compatibility. Paste those links and a screenshot of the webpage into a document. (*Hint:* To take a screenshot of the webpage, press the PrtSc or Print Screen key on your keyboard, tap or click your document, and then tap or click the Paste button.)

Use your research to answer these questions:

a. When is the div element used within a webpage written with HTML5 tags?

b. What are the HTML5 semantic tags?

c. What is the primary advantage and the primary disadvantage of using the <main> tag versus <div id="main">?

Extend Your Knowledge

Extend the skills you learned in this chapter and experiment with new skills. You may need to use additional resources to complete the assignment.

Inserting Links

Instructions: In this exercise, you will use your HTML editor to enter the needed tags and content to create several different types of links. The completed page is shown in Figure 3–68. The starting file contains comments to note the location of links you will add to the page. You will also use professional web development best practices to indent, space, validate, and check the spelling of your work.

Perform the following tasks:

1. Open the `ski03.html` file from the Data Files for Students and then modify the comment at the top of the page to include your name and today's date.

2. After the <!--Insert an image with a link--> comment, insert an <img> tag as follows:

```
<img src="ski.jpg" alt="happy skiers" height="
```

3. Make the image a link to `http://www.breckenridge.co`

4. Make each word in the <nav> section a link to another page or own line for readability as follows:

```
<a href="events.html">Events</a> |
<a href="lessons.html">Lessons</a> |
<a href="snowreports.html">Snow Reports</a> |
<a href="employment.html">Employment</a>
```

5. In the <div id="content"> section, make the phone number, link to that number. (*Hint:* The letters SKI translate to the n keypad.)

6. Make the text "Write to Kent" an email link to `kent@ilove`

7. In the `footer`, make the text "snow.com" a link to `http:`

8. To make it easier for users to navigate the home page, add two will quickly take the user back to the top and main areas of the

---

Extend Your Knowledge projects at the end of each chapter allow students to extend and expand on the skills learned within the chapter. Students use critical thinking to experiment with new skills to complete each project.

Analyze, Correct, Improve projects call on students to analyze a file, discover errors in it, fix the errors, and then improve the file using the skills they learned in the chapter.

Perform the following tasks:

1. HTML comments are inserted into a webpage using special tags with the following syntax:

<!-- comment goes here -->

A comment may be placed anywhere in the HTML document after the opening <!DOCTYPE html> statement and may be one or more lines long as needed. The only requirement is that the comment opens with the same four characters <!--, and ends with the same three characters, -->. In ski01.html, enter a comment after the opening <!DOCTYPE html> declaration statement that includes your name and the current date as shown in Figure 1–51a.

2. Enter the remaining tags and text shown in Figure 1–51a without any indents or blank lines. Save the file and open it in a browser. In a Word document named `ski01.docx`, answer these questions:

a. How do HTML comments appear on the webpage when it is opened in a browser?

b. How does the content within the <p> … </p> tags appear in a browser?

3. Return to your HTML editor and add blank lines and indents as shown in Figure 1–51a. Save the HTML file and refresh it in your browser to see the changes. In your Word document, answer these questions:

a. What is the purpose of adding extra lines and indents in the HTML editor?

b. How do the extra lines and indents change the way the webpage appears in the browser?

4. Add <p>, </p>, and <br> tags as shown in Figure 1–51a so that the content is rendered in the browser on multiple lines. In your Word document, answer these questions:

a. What is the purpose of adding the <p> and </p> tags?

b. What is the purpose of adding the <br> tags?

5. Save the HTML file and refresh it in your browser to see the changes. Compare Figure 1–51a and Figure 1–51b. In your Word document, identify how the following two lines use white space in the HTML editor and compare that to how the browser reads and displays the same line.

a. "Our ski and snowboard…"

b. "Phone: 1-800…"

6. Submit your assignment in the format specified by your instructor.

7. ⊛ What would happen if webpage developers did not use comments, indents, and white space? Identify a potential problem associated with each.

Analyze, Correct, Improve

Analyze a webpage, correct all errors, and improve it.

Correcting HTML Errors

Note: To complete this assignment, you will be required to use the Data Files for Students. Visit www.cengage.com/ct/studentdownload for detailed instructions or contact your instructor for information about accessing the required files.

Instructions: Open your HTML editor and then open the analyze01.html file provided in the Data Files for Students. This document lists 10 HTML5 best practices in its body section. You will follow these 10 guidelines to correct the webpage as instructed. Save the page as `practices01.html` in the same location and view it in a browser. Figure 1–52a shows the completed HTML document in Notepad++ and Figure 1–52b shows the completed webpage in a browser.

Continued >

Textbook Walk-Through

Analyze, Correct, Improve *continued*

   c. Change the <p>...</p> tags that surround the HTML5 best practices title to <h1>...</h1> tags. The <h1> (heading level 1) tag is more meaningful (semantic) for this content than the <p> (paragraph) tag.

   d. Find and correct the two spelling errors. (*Hint:* The word *lowercase* and *inline* are spelled correctly in this context.)

   e. Replace the placeholder text in the comment with your own name and the current date.

3. Submit the analyze02.html file in a format specified by your instructor.

4. ⊙ After reflecting on this exercise and using outside resources if needed, answer these questions.

   a. Identify three types of errors the W3C validator helps you find and correct.

   b. Identify three types of errors that the W3C validator will *not* help you find and correct.

   c. Identify three reasons it is a good practice to validate all webpages.

> **In the Lab** Three in-depth assignments in each chapter require students to apply the chapter concepts and techniques to solve problems. One Lab is devoted to special topics in web development.

In the Lab

Labs 1 and 2, which increase in difficulty, require you to create webpages based on what you learned in the chapter; Lab 3 requires you to dive deeper into a topic covered in the chapter.

Lab 1: Creating a Home Page for City Farmer

Problem: You work for a local but rapidly growing gardening supply company called City Farmer that specializes in products that support food self-sufficiency. The company has identified a small number of extremely successful products that they want to market through a website and have hired you to get started. Create the webpage shown in Figure 2–36 that contains the textual content that City Farmer wants on their home page.

Instructions: Perform the following tasks:

1. If you created the cityfarmer.html file in the Lab 1 exercise from Chapter 1, open the file and then save it with the name `cityfarmer02.html`. If you did not create the cityfarmer.html file, enter the required HTML tags as shown in Figure 2–36 and save the file with the name [...].

   ...</title> tags contain the text `City Farmer Home Page`.

   ...content in the body section, and add the content in the <header>, <nav>, [...] <footer> sections as shown in Figure 2–36a.

   ...content within the `head` and `body` sections to make each section [...].

   ...comment after the opening <!DOCTYPE html> statement to contain your [...] date.

   ...and fix any errors.

   ...the text so it matches the code in Figure 2–36a, which shows the file in [...] appearance varies if you are using a different HTML editor).

   ...age within a browser as shown in Figure 2–36b.

   ...ent in the format specified by your instructor.

3. Using the web server documentation provided by your instructor or school, fill out the right column of the table to identify the pieces of information needed to publish your webpages. A sample solution is provided in webpublishing.docx that applies to students at Johnson County Community College in Overland Park, Kansas.

4. Use the web to research three inexpensive web server alternatives.

5. Open the webserveralternatives.docx document from the Data Files for Students.

6. Using the information you found in Step 4, complete the table in the webserveralternatives. docx document to compare three web server alternatives. You may be asked to share and compare this information with the rest of the class.

7. Confirm if and how your instructor wants you to publish your webpages, as well as how your work will be submitted for grading purposes.

8. ⊙ Some web hosting companies offer *free* web hosting services. However, all businesses need to generate revenue in order to survive. Using your favorite search engine, identify three ways *free* web hosting companies generate revenue.

⊛ Consider This: Your Turn

Apply your creative thinking and problem-solving skills to design and implement a solution.

Note: To complete this assignment, you will be required to use the Data Files for Students. Visit www.cengage.com/ct/studentdownload for detailed instructions or contact your instructor for information about accessing the required files.

1. Design and Create a Personal Portfolio Website

Personal

Part 1: As in almost every field, the job market for the best jobs in web development are competitive. One way to give yourself a big edge in a job search is to create an appropriate personal portfolio website to showcase your skills. Plan the website by completing the table in the portfolio.docx document in the Data Files for Students. Answer the questions with thoughtful, realistic responses. Be sure to sketch the wireframe for your home page on the last page. Submit your assignment in the format specified by your instructor.

Part 2: ⊙ What do you want this website to accomplish?

2. Design and Create a Website for a Web Development and Consulting Business

Professional

Part 1: When you are finished with college, you plan to join a web development and consulting firm to gain experience in the field. Your long-term goal is to start and own a web development and consulting firm. You decide to begin by designing a website you would eventually like to build for the firm. Start planning the website by completing the table in the webdevelopment.docx document in the Data Files for Students. Answer the questions with thoughtful, realistic responses. Be sure to sketch the wireframe for your home page on the last page. Submit your assignment in the format specified by your instructor.

Part 2: ⊙ What are some general characteristics of any successful small business that you want this website to portray? What are some characteristics of a successful web development consulting firm that you want this website to portray?

Continued >

> **Consider This: Your Turn** exercises call on students to apply creative-thinking and problem-solving skills to design and implement a solution.

Web Design with
HTML5 & CSS3

INTRODUCTORY

MINNICK | FRIEDRICHSEN

Eighth Edition

1 | Introduction to the Internet and Web Design

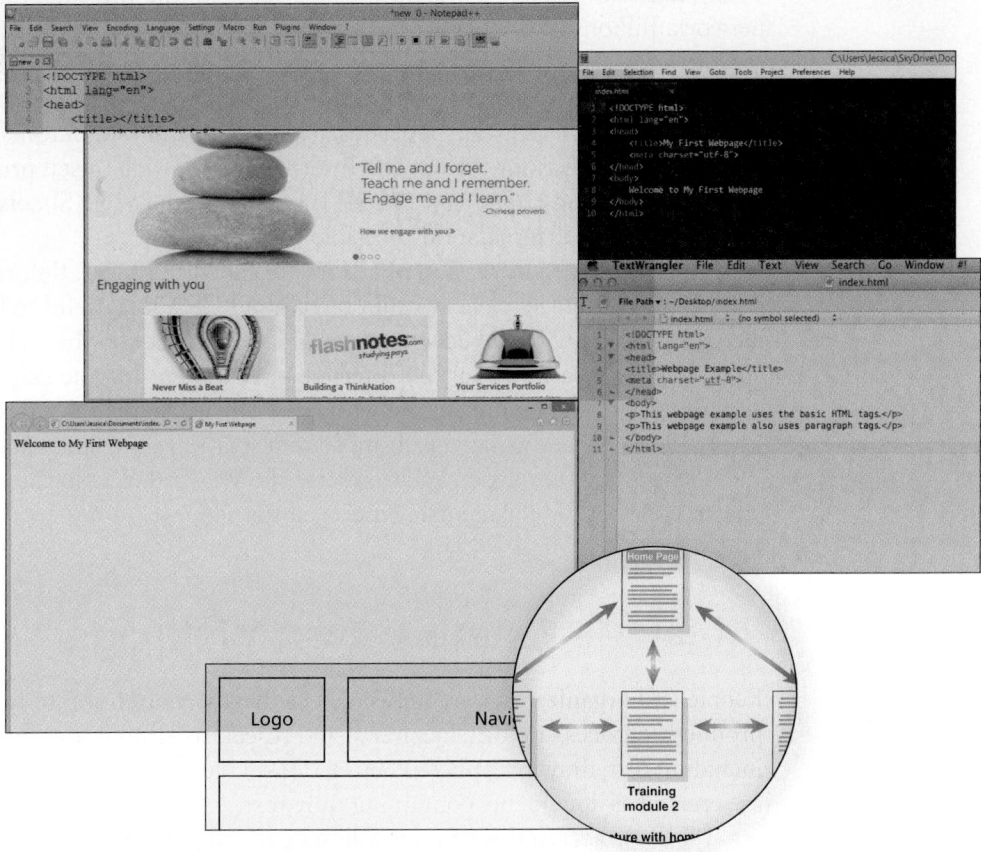

Objectives

You will have mastered the material in this chapter when you can:

- Define the Internet and associated key terms
- Recognize Internet protocols
- Discuss web browsers and identify their main features
- Describe the types and purposes of websites
- Plan a website for a target audience
- Define a wireframe and a site map
- Explain how websites use graphics, navigation tools, typography, and color

- Design for accessibility and multiplatform display
- Define Hypertext Markup Language (HTML) and HTML elements
- Recognize HTML versions and web programming languages
- Identify web authoring tools
- Download and use a web authoring tool
- Create and view a basic HTML webpage

1 | Introduction to the Internet and Web Design

Introduction

Today, millions of people worldwide have access to the Internet, the world's largest network. Billions of webpages providing information on any subject you can imagine are currently available on the web. People use the Internet to search for information, to communicate with others around the world, and to seek entertainment. Students use the Internet to register for classes, pay tuition, and find out final grades. Businesses and other organizations rely on the Internet and the web to sell products and services. Hypertext Markup Language (HTML) and Cascading Style Sheets (CSS) are two of the technologies that make this possible.

The most recent version of HTML is called HTML5. Before exploring the details of creating webpages with HTML5 and CSS, it is useful to look at how these technologies relate to the development of the Internet and the web. In this chapter, you learn some basics about the Internet and the web, and the rules both follow to allow computers to communicate with each other. You review types of websites and learn how to properly plan a website so that it is appealing and useful to your target audience. You also explore web browsers, HTML, and its associated key terms. Lastly, you create a basic webpage using a text editor.

Project — Create a Basic Webpage

People and organizations create webpages to attract attention to information such as products, services, multimedia, news, and research. Although webpages display content including text, drawings, photos, animations, videos, and links to other webpages, they are created as documents containing only text.

The project in this chapter follows general guidelines and uses a text editor to create the webpage shown in Figure 1–1. Figure 1–1a shows the **code**, meaningful combinations of text and symbols that a web browser interprets to display the webpage shown in Figure 1–1b. The content includes two lines of text. Other parts of the code indicate that one line of text should be displayed as the webpage title, which appears in the browser on a webpage tab. Code also specifies that the other line of text should appear as a paragraph of body text.

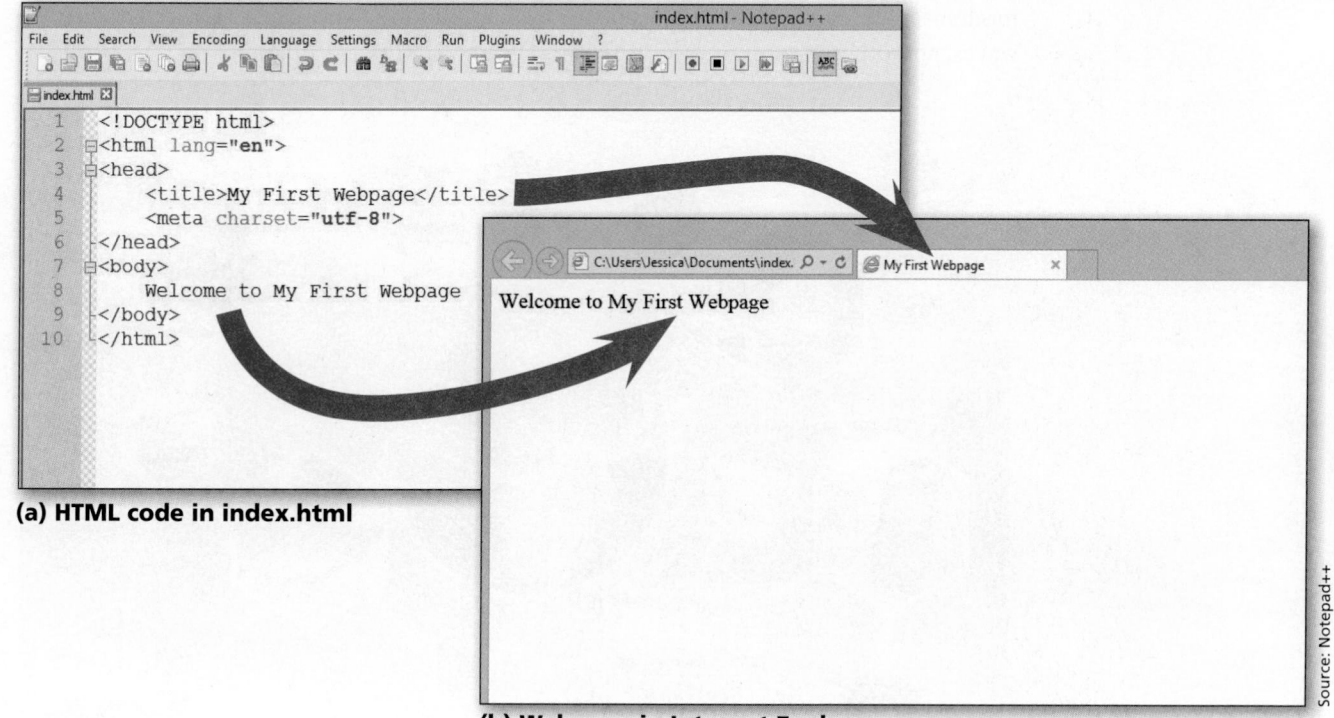

(a) HTML code in index.html

(b) Webpage in Internet Explorer

Source: Notepad++

Figure 1–1

Roadmap

In this chapter, you learn how to create the webpage shown in Figure 1–1. The following roadmap identifies general activities you perform as you progress through this chapter:

1. RUN a TEXT EDITOR and CREATE a BLANK DOCUMENT.

2. ENTER HTML TAGS in the document.

3. ADD TEXT to the webpage.

4. SAVE the WEBPAGE as an HTML document.

5. VIEW the WEBPAGE in a browser.

At the beginning of step instructions throughout the chapter, you see an abbreviated form of this roadmap. The abbreviated roadmap uses colors to indicate chapter progress: gray means the chapter is beyond that activity; blue means the task being shown is covered in that activity; and black means that activity is yet to be covered. For example, the following abbreviated roadmap indicates the chapter would be showing a task in the 4 SAVE WEBPAGE activity.

1 RUN TEXT EDITOR & CREATE BLANK DOCUMENT | 2 ENTER HTML TAGS

3 ADD TEXT | **4 SAVE WEBPAGE** | **5 VIEW WEBPAGE**

Use the abbreviated roadmap as a progress guide while you read or step through the instructions in this chapter.

Exploring the Internet

Every day, millions of people use a computer to connect to the Internet. The **Internet** is a worldwide collection of computers linked together for use by businesses, governments, educational institutions, other organizations, and individuals using modems, phone lines, television cables, satellite links, fiber-optic connections, radio waves, and other communications devices and media (Figure 1–2).

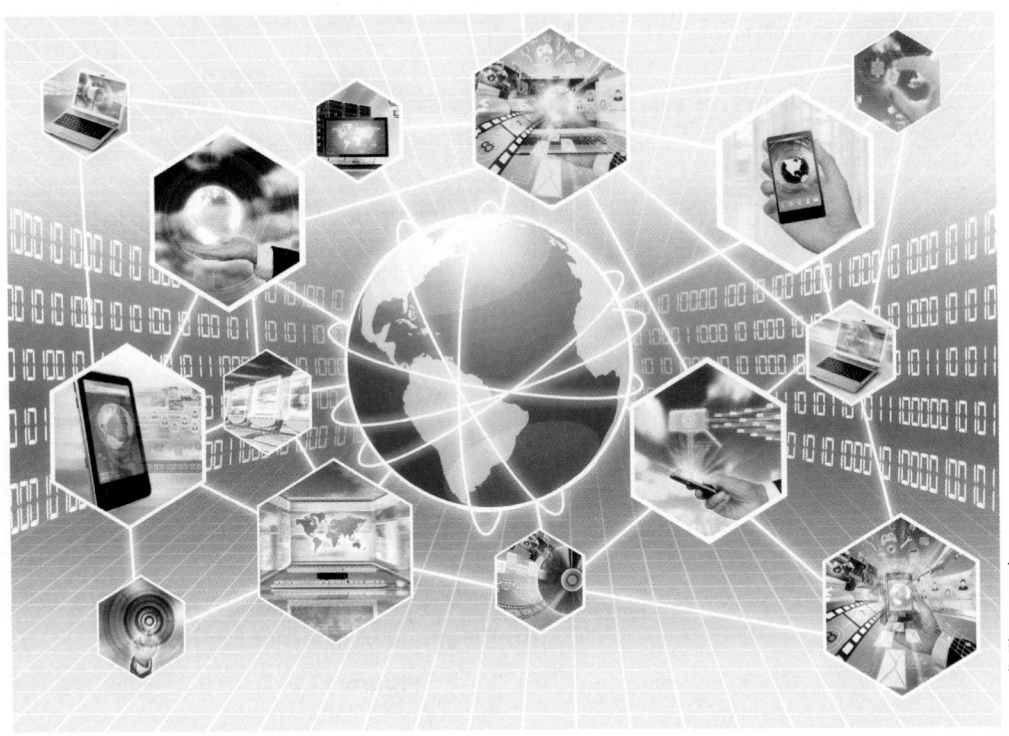

© nmedia/Shutterstock.com

Figure 1–2

The Internet was developed in the 1960s by the Department of Defense Advanced Research Projects Agency (ARPA). ARPANET (as the Internet was originally called) had only four nodes and sent its first message in 1969. A **node** is any device, such as a computer, tablet, or smartphone, connected to a **network**, which is a collection of two or more computers linked together to share resources and information. The Internet has billions of nodes on millions of networks. The **Internet of Things** is a term used to describe the ever-growing number of devices connecting to a network, including televisions and appliances. Today, high-, medium-, and low-speed data lines connect networks. These **data lines** allow data (including text, graphical images, audio, and video) to move from one computer to another. The **Internet backbone** is a collection of high-speed data lines that link major computer systems located around the world. An **Internet service provider (ISP)** is a company that has a permanent connection to the Internet backbone. ISPs use high- or medium-speed data lines to allow personal and business computer users to connect to the backbone for access to the Internet. A home Internet connection is generally provided through a cable or fiber-optic line that connects to an ISP.

Billions of people in most countries around the world connect to the Internet using computers in their homes, offices, schools, and public locations such as libraries. In fact, the Internet was designed to be a place in which people could share information and collaborate. Users with computers connected to the Internet can access a variety of popular services, including email, social networking, and the web.

World Wide Web

Many people use the terms Internet and World Wide Web interchangeably, but these terms have different meanings. The Internet is the infrastructure, or the physical networks of computers. The **World Wide Web**, also called the **web**, is the service that provides access to information stored on web servers, the high-capacity, high-performance computers that power the web. The web consists of a collection of linked files known as **webpages**, or pages for short. Because the web supports text, graphics, audio, and video, a webpage can display any of these multimedia elements in a browser.

A **website**, or site for short, is a related collection of webpages created and maintained by a person, company, educational institution, or other organization, such as the U.S. Department of Education (Figure 1–3). Each website contains a **home page**, which is the main page and the first document users see when they access the website. The home page typically provides information about the website's purpose and content, often by including a list of links to other webpages on the website.

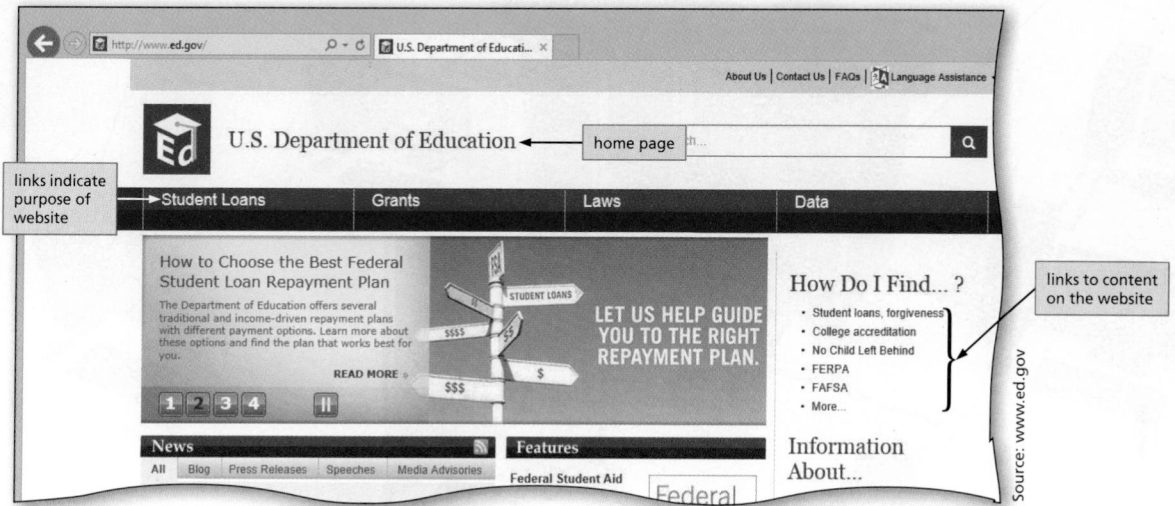

Figure 1–3

Hyperlinks are an essential part of the web. A **hyperlink**, more commonly called a **link**, is an element that connects one webpage to another webpage on the same server or to any other web server in the world. Tapping or clicking a link allows you to move quickly from one webpage to another without being concerned about where the webpages reside. You can also tap or click links to move to a different section of the same webpage.

With hyperlinks, you do not necessarily have to view information in a linear way. Instead, you can tap or click the available links to view the information in a variety of ways, as described later in this chapter. Many webpage components, including text, graphics, and animations, can serve as links. Figure 1–4 shows examples of several webpage components used as hyperlinks.

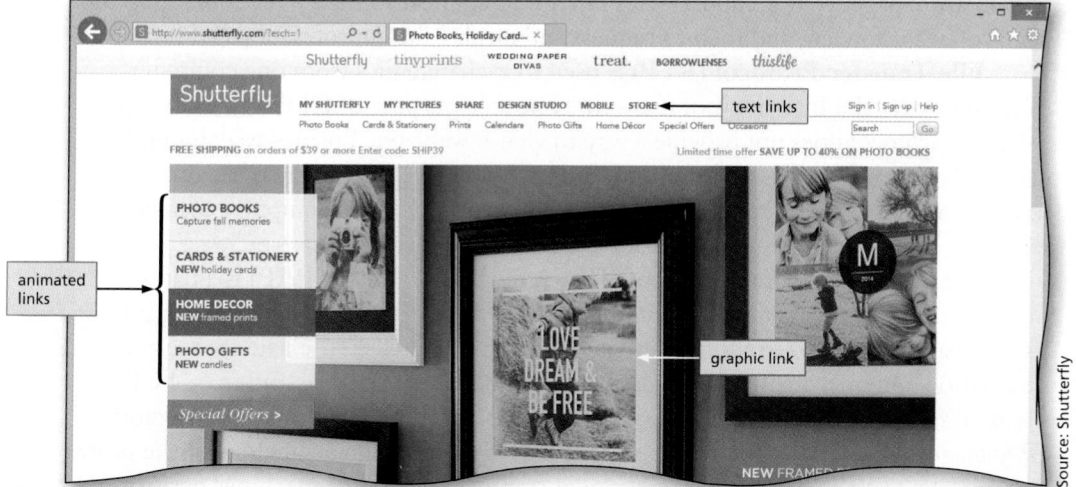

Figure 1–4

Protocols

A computer is also referred to as a client workstation. Client workstations connect to the Internet through the use of a protocol. A **protocol** is a set of rules that defines how a client workstation can communicate with a server. A client workstation uses a protocol to request a connection to a server. The **server** is the host computer that stores resources and files for websites (Figure 1–5).

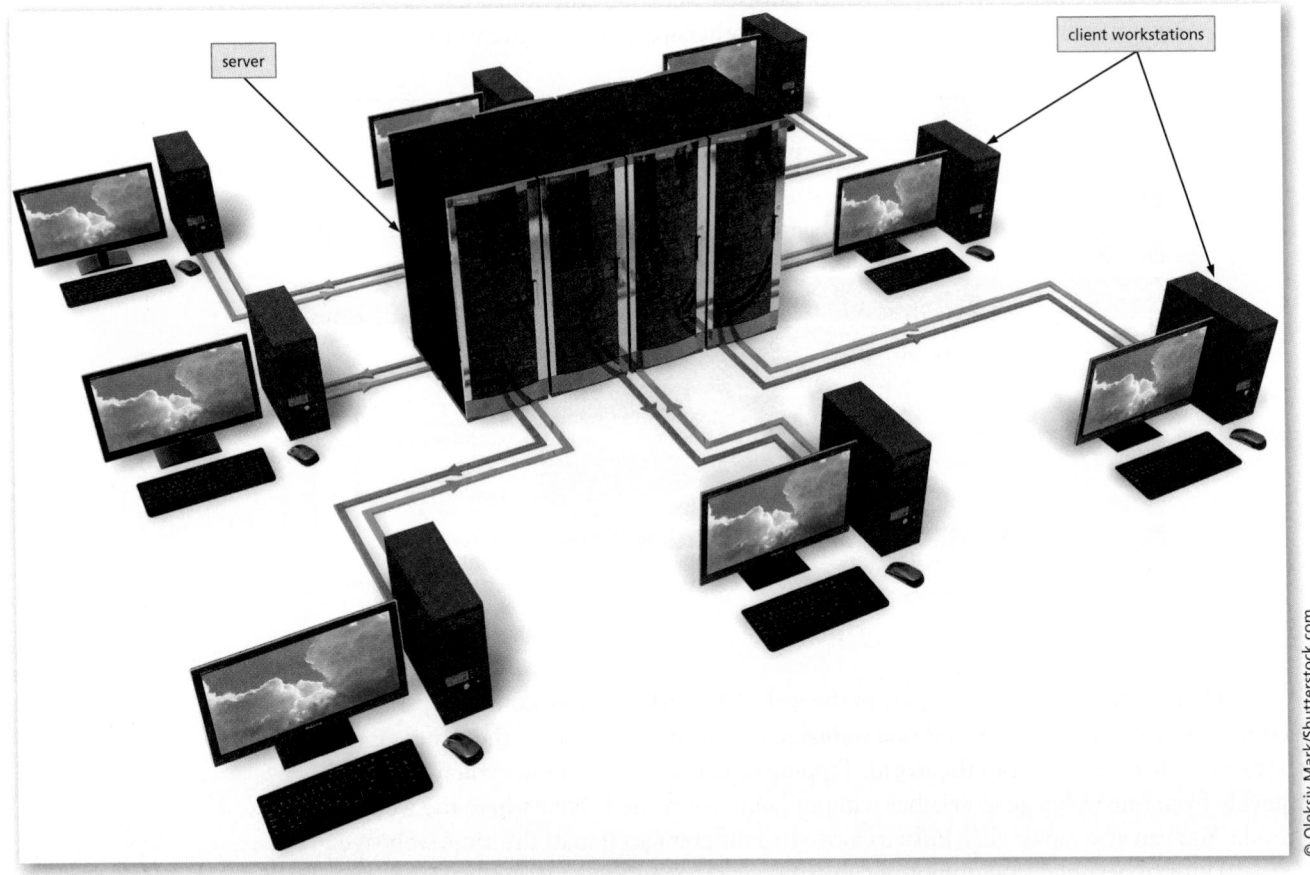

Figure 1–5

© Oleksiy Mark/Shutterstock.com

Hypertext Transfer Protocol (HTTP) is the fundamental protocol used on the web to exchange and transfer webpages. HTTP is a set of rules for exchanging text, graphics, audio, video, and other multimedia files on the web. When you tap or click a link on a webpage, your computer uses HTTP to connect to the server containing the page you want to view, and then to request and display the appropriate page.

File Transfer Protocol (FTP) is used to exchange files from one computer to another over the Internet (not the web). The sole purpose of FTP is to exchange files; this protocol does not provide a way to view a webpage. Businesses commonly use FTP to exchange files with vendors and suppliers. Web designers often use FTP to transfer updated website content to a web hosting server, the computer that stores webpages and other related content for a website.

Transmission Control Protocol/Internet Protocol (TCP/IP) is a pair of protocols used to transfer data efficiently over the Internet by properly routing it to its destination. TCP oversees the network connection between the data source and destination and micromanages the data. When data is sent over the Internet, TCP breaks the data into packets. Each packet contains addressing information, which the IP manages. One way to better understand TCP/IP is through an analogy of the postal system. The tasks TCP performs are similar to those workers or machines perform when handling a bundle of packages in a post office. In this analogy, the packages are addressed to one destination, but are too large to send as a single bundle. TCP breaks up the bundle into manageable pieces and then sends them out for delivery. When each piece arrives at the destination, TCP reassembles the bundle of packages.

Internet Protocol (IP) ensures data is sent to the correct location. In the postal system analogy, the IP part of TCP/IP refers to the street address and zip code to route a piece of mail. Just as people have a unique mailing address, every client workstation and server on the Internet has a unique IP address. An example of an IP address is 192.168.1.5. Every website has a unique IP address, which makes it easy for computers to find websites. However, most people have difficulty remembering and using IP addresses to access websites. The **Domain Name System (DNS)** was created to resolve this issue. The DNS associates an IP address with a domain name. For example, the DNS associates the IP address 204.79.197.200 with the domain name bing.com.

Web Browsers

To access a website and display a webpage, a computer, tablet, or mobile device must have a web browser. A **web browser**, also called a **browser**, is a program that interprets and displays webpages so you can view and interact with them. Computing devices such as smartphones, tablets, laptops, and desktops include their own default browser, but you also have the option to download and use the browser of your choice. Microsoft Internet Explorer, Mozilla Firefox, Google Chrome, Apple Safari, and Opera (Figure 1–6) are popular browsers. You use a browser to locate websites, to link from one webpage to another, to add a favorite or bookmark a webpage, and to choose security settings.

(a) Internet Explorer

(b) Google Chrome

Source: Google

Source: Opera

(d) Opera

Source: Mozilla

(c) Mozilla Firefox

Source: Apple

(e) Apple Safari

Figure 1–6

Besides varying by publisher, browsers vary by version. Most browsers do not display webpages identically. In fact, older versions of some browsers do not support the most recent HTML5 standards. As you are designing your website, you must view it using various browsers to ensure that it looks and functions as you intended.

Internet Explorer (Figure 1-7) is the default browser provided with the Windows 8.1 operating system and provides tools for visiting webpages and an array of options to customize settings. As with all browsers, you can use Internet Explorer to enter a website address in the address bar to display a particular webpage, designate a specific webpage or set of webpage tabs to display when you run the browser, and bookmark frequently visited websites as favorites for easy access. Important features of Internet Explorer are summarized in Table 1–1.

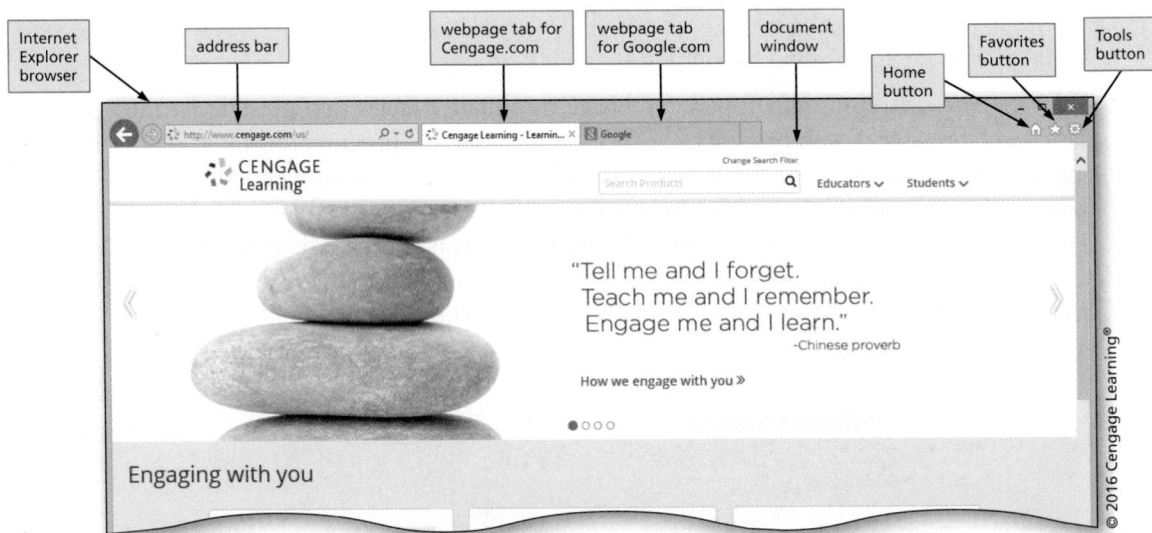

Figure 1–7

Table 1–1 Features of Internet Explorer 11

Feature	Description
Address bar	Displays the website address of the webpage you are viewing
Webpage tab	Displays the title of the webpage; you can open multiple tabs to view multiple webpages
Home button	Opens the browser's designated home page or default webpage, which can be customized on the General tab of the Internet Options dialog box
Favorites button	Allows you to save and view your favorite webpages
Tools button	Provides access to print, zoom, and safety features and lets you view downloads and manage add-ons
Document window	Displays the current webpage content

CONSIDER THIS

What is the difference between a website's home page and a web browser's home page?

A website's home page is the default page displayed when you enter a web address such as www.cengage.com into the address bar of a browser. As mentioned earlier, this type of home page is the introductory page of a website and provides links to access other parts of the site. A browser also has a home page, which appears when you open a browser or tap or click the Home button in the browser window. You can specify any webpage as the default home page of a browser.

A web address, or **Uniform Resource Locator (URL)**, is the address of a document or other file accessible on the Internet and identifies the network location of a website, such as www.bing.com. To access a website using a browser, you type the webpage's URL in the browser's address bar (Figure 1–8).

Figure 1–8

The URL in Figure 1–8 indicates to the browser to use the HTTP communications protocol to locate the index.html webpage in the shop folder on the cengagebrain.com server or domain. A **domain** is an area of the Internet a particular organization or person manages. In this case, cengagebrain.com is the name of the domain, with the .com indicating it is registered as a commercial enterprise. The www part of the URL is short for World Wide Web and is a common subdomain used in a URL. The www is not required and can be omitted or replaced with another meaningful name for the subdomain. You can find webpage URLs in a wide range of places, including school catalogs, business cards, product packaging, and advertisements.

How do you use a subdomain within a URL?

A subdomain further identifies an area of content. For example, the URL support.microsoft.com indicates that support is a subdomain name used in the microsoft.com domain or server. This subdomain contains helpful information to support Microsoft products.

CONSIDER THIS

Types of Websites

An **Internet site** is another term for a website that is generally available to anyone with an Internet connection. Other types of websites include intranets and extranets, which also use Internet technology, but limit access to specified groups. An **intranet** is a private network that uses Internet technologies to share company information among employees. An intranet is contained within an organization's network, which makes it private and available only to those who need access. Organizations often distribute documents such as policy and procedure manuals, employee directories, company newsletters, product catalogs, and training manuals on an intranet.

An **extranet** is a private network that uses Internet technologies to share business information with select corporate partners or key customers. Companies and other organizations can use an extranet to share product manuals, training modules, inventory status, and order information. An extranet might also allow retailers to purchase inventory directly from their suppliers or to pay bills online.

Companies use websites to advertise or sell their products and services worldwide, as well as to provide technical and product support for their customers. Many company websites also support **electronic commerce (e-commerce)**, which is the buying and selling of goods and services on the Internet. Using e-commerce technologies, these websites allow customers to browse product catalogs, compare products and services, and order goods online. Figure 1–9a shows wayfair.com, a company that uses an e-commerce website to sell and distribute home furnishings. Many e-commerce websites also provide links to order status information, customer service, news releases, and customer feedback tools to solicit comments from their customers.

(a) Wayfair

(b) LMS

(c) Facebook

(c) Blog

Figure 1–9

Colleges, universities, and other schools use websites to distribute information about areas of study, provide course information, and register students for classes online. Many educational institutions use a **Learning Management System (LMS)** to simplify course management. An LMS is a web-based software application designed to facilitate online learning. Instructors use the LMS to communicate announcements, post questions on reading material, list contact information, and provide access to lecture slides and videos. Students use the LMS to find information related to their courses, including project instructions and grades. Many LMS tools allow instructors to write their own webpage content that provides further information for their students. For example, the LMS webpage in Figure 1–9b is an HTML page written by an instructor to provide an assignment schedule to students.

While organizations create commercial and academic websites, individuals might create personal websites to share information with family and friends. Families and other groups can exchange photographs, video and audio clips, stories, schedules, or other information through websites. Many individual websites allow password protection, which creates a safer environment for sharing information. Another popular type of website is a social media site, such as Facebook, Twitter, or LinkedIn (Figure 1–9c). These websites encourage their users to share information, pictures, videos, and job-related skills. Many business websites also include links to their social media pages.

People use search engine websites to research topics. Popular search engine sites include Google, Bing, and Yahoo!. A news website provides information about current events. Another type of common website is a blog, which is short for weblog. A single person or small group creates and oversees a blog, which typically reflects the author's point of view on a particular topic (Figure 1–9d).

Planning a Website

When visiting a physical retail store, visitors are more likely to make a purchase if the store is clean and well organized and offers quality products and services. Likewise, computer users have several expectations when visiting a website. They expect the website to load quickly in the browser. If a website takes more than a few seconds to load, a visitor is likely to leave and find another site, possibly belonging to a competitor. Website visitors also expect an attractive design and color scheme that enhances the experience of visiting the site and makes it easy to read and view information. They expect a clear navigation system that helps them quickly find the products, services, or information they are seeking. A poor design, distracting color scheme, or confusing website navigation tools also prompt visitors to switch to another website. An attractive, useful, and well-organized website is not created by accident. Building a successful website starts with a solid strategic plan.

Web designers begin planning activities by meeting with key business personnel to ask several important questions to understand the purpose of the website and the goals of the business. If you are a web designer working as a consultant or contractor, you meet with your clients to plan the website. If you are a web designer providing services within an organization, you meet with decision makers and others who are sponsoring the web design project. In either case, you begin by identifying the purpose of the website and goals of the business to help shape the design and type of website you are developing.

Purpose of the Website

The purpose of a commercial business website is related to the goal of selling products or services. A business can take a direct approach and use a website to sell products and services through e-commerce or through information that prompts website users to visit a physical location such as a store or restaurant. As an alternative, a business can take an indirect approach and use a website to generate leads to potential customers, promote the expertise of the business, raise the public profile of the business, or inform and educate its customers. Each purpose demands a different type of website and design. For example, if the purpose of a website is to serve as an online store, the website should allow easy access to product information, reviews, and e-commerce tools. If the purpose of the website is to build a company's reputation, the website should feature articles about the company, its employees, and its products and integrate with social media sites such as Facebook.

Every business needs to have a mission statement that clearly addresses the purpose and goal of the business. For example, the mission statement of a bank might be "Our mission is to provide world-class service while helping our customers achieve their financial goals." The business website should promote the mission statement. Web designers often ask their clients for a copy of the mission statement and use it as the foundation for the website plan. The more you know about the purpose of the website, the more likely you are to be successful with a web development project.

Target Audience

In addition to understanding the website's purpose, you should understand the people who will use the website, also known as the target audience. Knowing the makeup of your target audience — including age, gender, general demographic background, and level of computer literacy — helps you design a website appropriate for them. Figure 1–10 shows the website for Michaels, an arts and crafts store. Its target audience includes creative people who enjoy making decorations and other items. The home page displays an image customized for the year-end holiday season and offers special savings to further entice its target audience to make a purchase. The simple navigation bar near the top of the page makes it easy for a customer to shop, discover a new project, or find inspiration. A search tool above the navigation bar provides quick access to products. Knowing the information that your target audience is searching for means you can design the site to focus on that information, which enhances the shopping and purchasing experience of your audience.

Figure 1–10

Multiplatform Display

Today, users can access a website with computing devices ranging from desktop computers to laptops, tablets, and smartphones. In fact, people are rapidly increasing their use of a tablet or smartphone to access websites. According to Pew Research, the number of mobile (or smartphone) Internet users increased by 100 percent from 2009 to 2014. Today, more than 55 percent of Americans own a smartphone, and more than 50 percent of smartphone owners use their phone to access the Internet. In addition, more than 30 percent of those who access the Internet do so exclusively with their smartphones. These trends are only expected to increase. Yet most webpages are designed for a large display screen on a desktop or laptop and do not translate well to the smaller screen of a tablet or smartphone. This problem leads to another question web developers must ask: "How do I consistently reach the people in my target audience when they are using so many difference devices?" The solution is to use **responsive design**, which allows you to create one website that provides an optimal viewing experience across a range of devices. The website itself responds and adapts to the size of screen on the visitor's device. For example, Figure 1–11 shows the responsive design of angieslist.com in desktop, tablet, and mobile screen sizes. Chapter 5 provides much more information about responsive design.

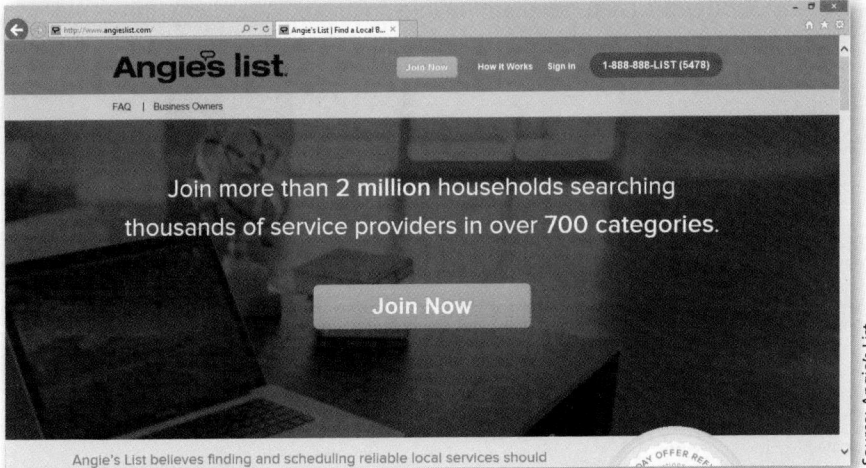

(a) Desktop Display

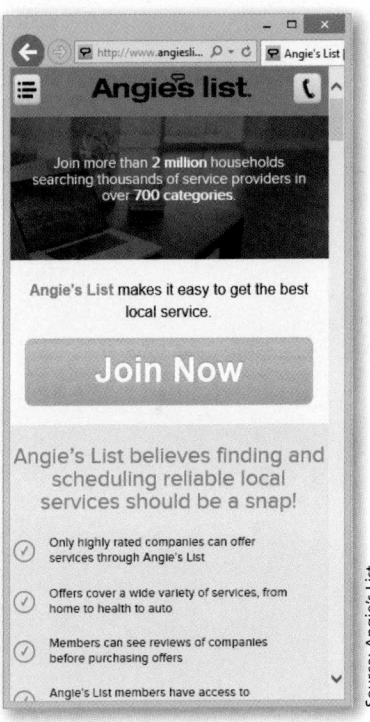

(c) Mobile Display

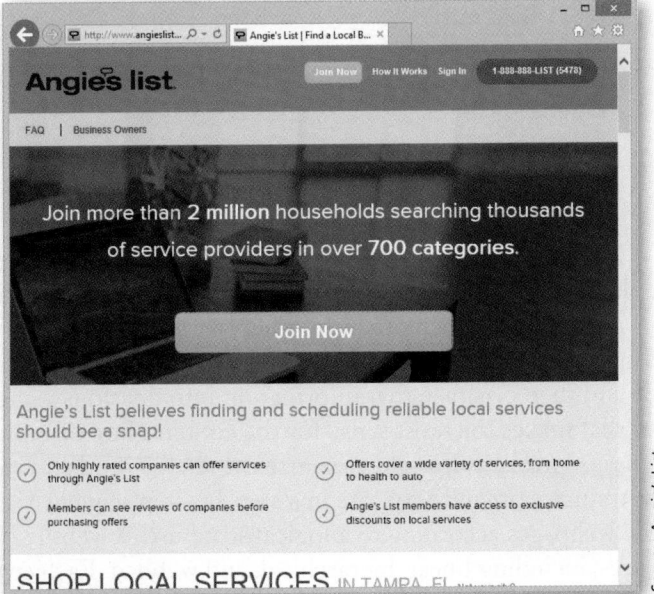

(b) Tablet Display

Source: Angie's List

Figure 1–11

CONSIDER THIS

Can I redesign a desktop-only website for multiplatform display?

Yes. If your audience is accustomed to the desktop-only website, retrofitting the website for tablet and mobile display screens makes sense because the site remains familiar to users. You also avoid building a new site from scratch and you can take advantage of design decisions such as color scheme and use media you have already acquired. However, depending on the site content and number of pages, redesigning may be a time-consuming process.

Wireframe

Before web designers actually start creating the first webpage for a website, they sketch the design using a wireframe. A **wireframe** is a simple, visual guide that clearly identifies the location of main webpage elements, such as the navigation area, organization logo, content areas, and images. When you create a wireframe sketch for your webpages, use lines and boxes as shown in Figure 1–12. Also be sure to incorporate plenty of white space within your design to improve readability and to clearly distinguish among the areas on the webpage. You can use two types of white space: active white space and passive white space. **Active white space** is an area on the page that is intentionally left blank. Typically, the goal of active white space is to help balance the design of an asymmetrical page. **Passive white space** is the space between content areas. Passive white space helps a user focus on one part of the page. Proper use of white space makes webpage content easy to read and brings focus to page elements.

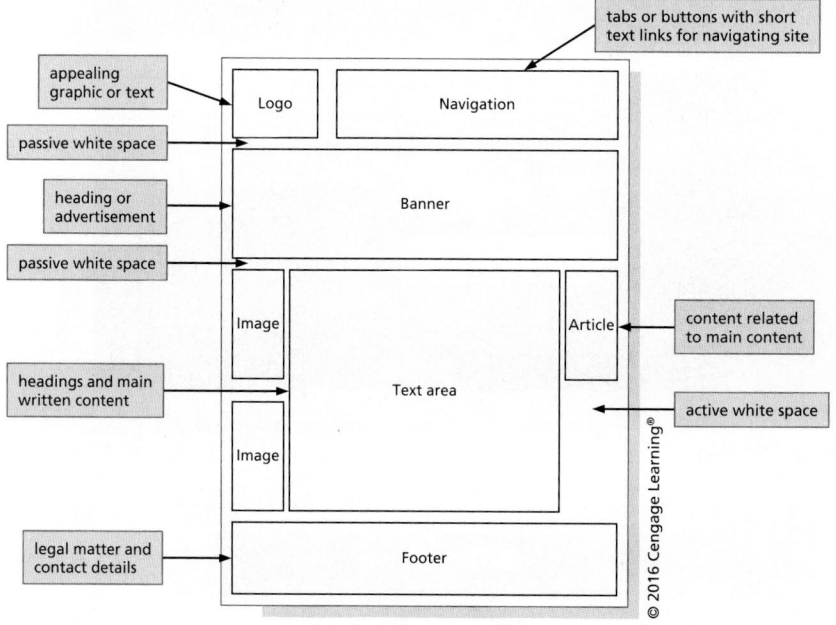

Figure 1–12

Site Map

A **site map** is a planning tool that lists or displays all the pages on a website and indicates how they are related to each other. In other words, a site map shows the structure of a website. Begin defining the structure of a website by identifying the information to provide and then organize that information into divisions using the organizing method that makes the most sense for the content. For example, if the website offers three types of products for sale, organize the site by product category. If the website provides training, organize the site in a step-by-step sequence.

Next, arrange the webpages according to a logical structure. A website can use several types of structures, including linear, hierarchical, and webbed. Each structure connects the webpages in a different way to define how users navigate the site and view the webpages. You should select a structure for the website based on how you want users to navigate the site and view the content.

A **linear** website structure connects webpages in a straight line, as shown in Figure 1–13. Each page includes a link to the next webpage and another link to the previous webpage. A linear website structure is appropriate if visitors should view the webpages in a specific order, as in the case of training material in which users need to complete Training module 1 before attempting Training module 2. If the information on the first webpage is necessary for understanding information on the second webpage, you should use a linear structure.

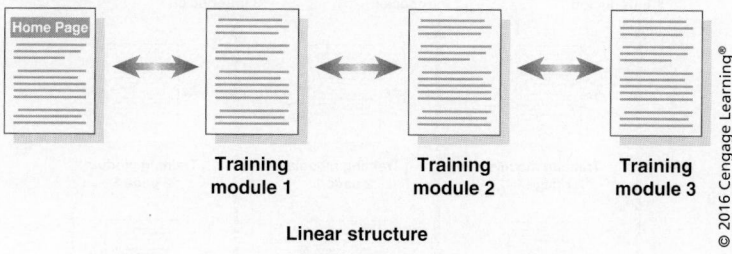

Linear structure

Figure 1–13

In a variation of a linear website structure, each page can include a link to the home page of the website, as shown in Figure 1–14. For some websites, moving from one page to the next page is still important, but you also want to provide users with easy access to the home page at any time. To meet these goals, you provide links from each page to the previous, next, and home pages. In this way, users do not have to tap or click the previous link multiple times to get back to the home page. The home page also includes links to all the pages in the site so users can quickly return to a page.

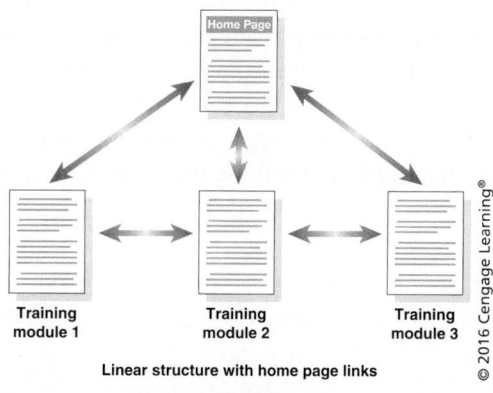

Linear structure with home page links

Figure 1–14

A **hierarchical** website connects webpages in a treelike structure, as shown in Figure 1–15. This structure works well on a site with a main index or table of contents page that links to all other webpages. With this structure, the main index page displays general information and secondary pages include more detailed information. Notice how logically the information in Figure 1–15 is organized. A webpage visitor can go from the home page to any of the three modules. In addition, the visitor can easily find the first page of Training module 3 by way of the Training module 3 link. One of the inherent problems with this structure and the two linear structures, however, is the inability to move easily from one section of pages to another. As an example, to move from Training module 1, page 2, to Training module 3, visitors must tap or click a link to return to Training module 1, introduction, tap or click another link to return to the home page, and then tap or click the Training module 3 link. This is moderately annoying for a site with two webpages, but think what it would be like if Training module 1 had 100 webpages.

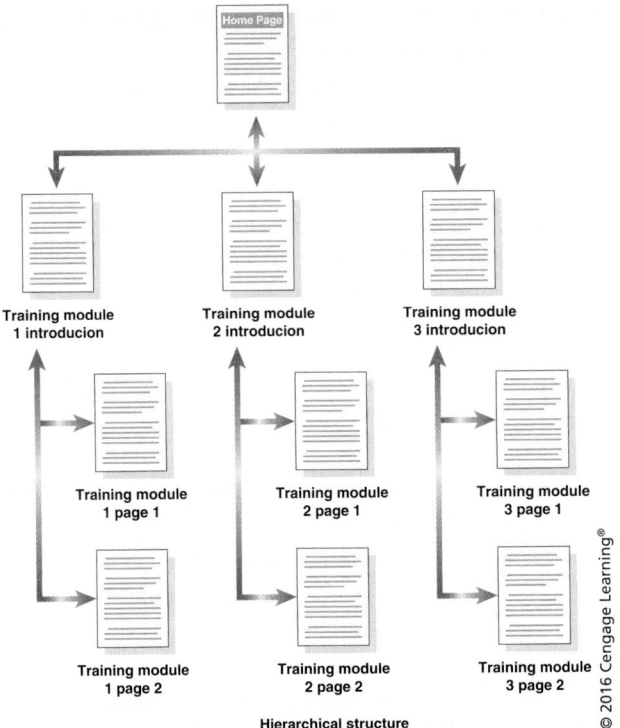

Hierarchical structure

Figure 1–15

To circumvent the problems with the hierarchical model, you can use a webbed model. A **webbed** website structure has no set organization, as shown in Figure 1–16. Visitors can move easily between pages, even if the pages are located in different sections of the website. A webbed structure works best on sites with information that does not need to be read in a specific order and pages that provide many navigation options. The web itself uses a webbed structure, so users can navigate among webpages in any order they choose. With this model, you most often provide a link to the home page from each page. Many websites use a graphical image (usually the organization's logo) in the upper-left corner of each webpage as the home page link. You will use that technique later in the book.

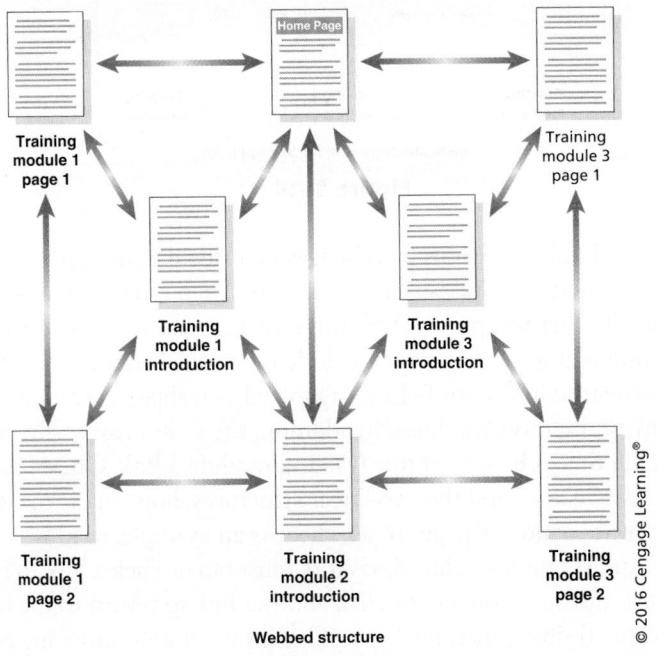

Webbed structure

Figure 1–16

Most websites use a combination of linear, hierarchical, and webbed structures. Some information on the website might be organized hierarchically from an index page, other information might be accessible from all areas of the site, and still other information might be organized in a linear structure to be read in a specific order. Using a combination of the three structures is appropriate if it helps users navigate the site easily. The goal is to get the right information to the users in the most efficient way possible.

Graphics

Graphics add visual appeal to a webpage and enhance the visitor's perception of your products and services. Be sure to use appropriate graphics on your site, those that communicate your brand, products, and services. For example, the website for Pret A Manger shown in Figure 1–17 displays a new product that serves as the focal point on the website. The graphic communicates to the user that the new dish is fresh and hot, right out of the oven. The smaller graphics below the primary graphic offer additional visual stimulation and provide an aesthetically pleasing balance to the page. These graphics are simple, yet effective in catching the user's attention.

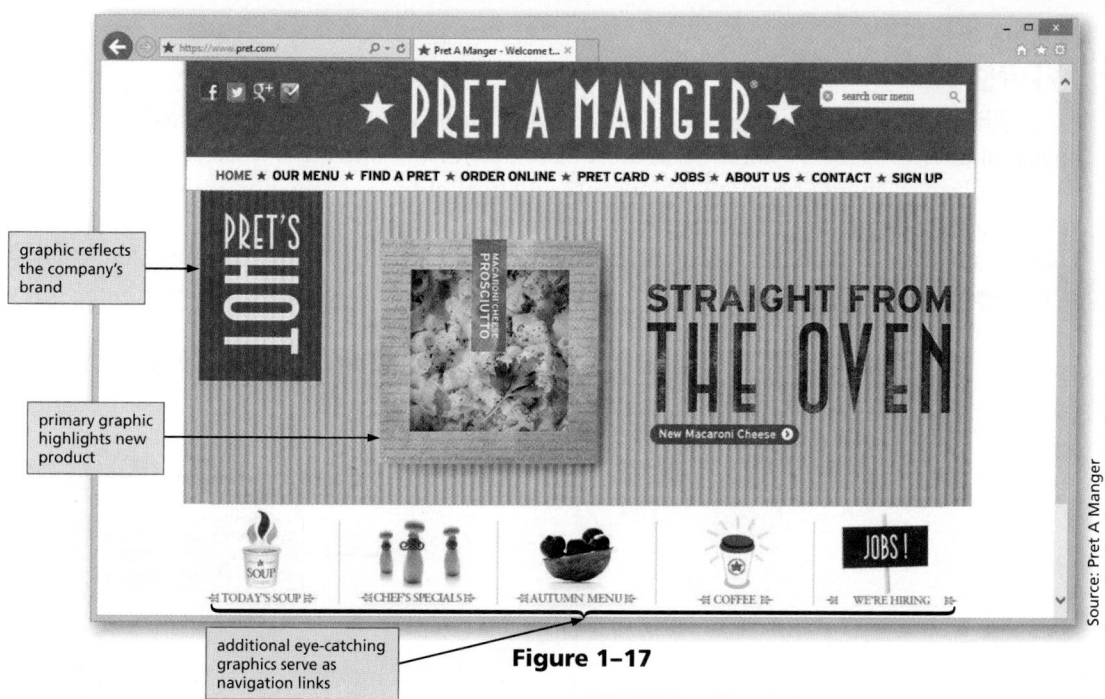

graphic reflects the company's brand

primary graphic highlights new product

additional eye-catching graphics serve as navigation links

Source: Pret A Manger

Figure 1–17

Navigation

As mentioned previously, the navigation of your website should be clear and concise. Each webpage should have a designated navigation area with links to other pages in the site, as shown in Figure 1–18. The navigation area should be prominent and easy to use. Incorporating a search box near the navigation area provides another avenue for customers to find the item they want.

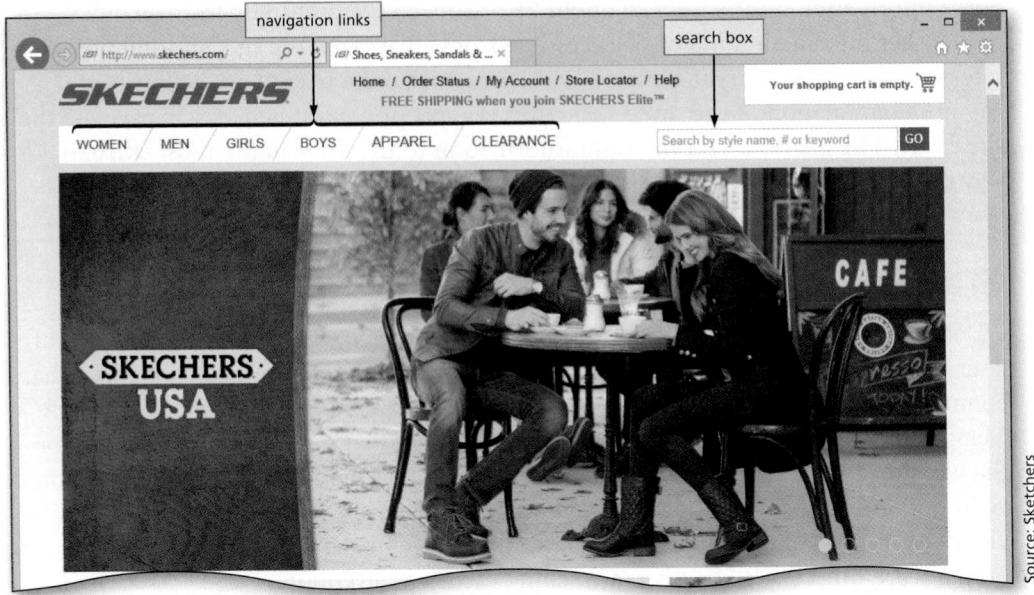

Figure 1–18

Typography

The use of effective typography, or fonts and font styles, enhances the visual appeal of a website. Above all, the text must be legible or the website is useless. Typography also should promote the purpose and goal of the website. For example, review the wedding photography website shown in Figure 1–19. The style of the text conveys an attitude of practical elegance mixed with fun. The typography of the title at the top of the page is elegant and whimsical, while the typography of the navigation links is uncluttered and easy to read.

Figure 1–19

Color

All websites use color, even if the colors are black and white. Select a limited number of coordinated colors that help promote your purpose and brand. The combination of colors, also called a color scheme, contributes to the appeal and legibility of the website. Font and background colors must provide high color contrast for readability, so use dark text on a light background or light text on a dark background. Likewise, avoid a color combination such as a primary red background with yellow text, which is hard on the eyes. Aim to strike a balance among the background color, text color, and the color that represents your brand. Many successful color schemes have one main color, such as medium blue, and add at least one lighter and darker shade of the same color, such as sky blue and navy. Even a single shade can serve as a color scheme. Figure 1–20 displays the home page for the grocery store Publix. The store's logo is green. The site reinforces its brand by integrating the same shade of green throughout the site.

Figure 1–20

Colors convey meanings. For example, green is associated with things that are friendly, fresh, and healthy. Table 1–2 lists colors and their common meanings.

Table 1–2 Common Color Meanings	
Color	**Common Meaning**
Red	Love, romance, anger, energy
Blue	Trust, loyalty, integrity, honesty, dependability
Green	Freshness, friendliness, health, safety, strength
Yellow	Warmth, cheer, joy, excitement, humor
Orange	Energy, warmth, health
Brown	Nature, wholesomeness, simplicity, friendliness
Black	Elegance, tradition, sophistication, formality
White	Purity, honesty, sincerity, cleanliness

Accessibility

Finally, address accessibility and localization issues. A web designer should create pages for viewing by a diverse audience, including people with physical impairments and global users. Consider the software used by those with physical impairments to work with some web features. For instance, for each graphic you include on the website, always include alternative text so people with sight limitations can use screen-reading software to identify the visual content. To support an international audience, use generic icons that can be understood globally, avoid slang expressions in the content, and build simple pages that load quickly over low-speed connections.

In 1998, the Rehabilitation Act was amended with Section 508, which requires that any information technology created or bought by a government agency be accessible to persons with disabilities. Information technology includes websites, which means web designers must consider users with visual, auditory, motor, and cognitive disabilities in their website designs. Visit www.section508.gov for more information.

The **World Wide Web Consortium (W3C)** develops and maintains web standards, language specifications, and accessibility recommendations. Several companies that use web technologies participate in work groups with the W3C to develop standards and guidelines for the web. The website for W3C is www.w3.org.

BTW
W3C
The mission of the W3C is "to lead the World Wide Web to its full potential by developing protocols and guidelines that ensure the long-term growth of the Web." Information about the membership process is available at www.w3.org /consortium/membership.

Planning Checklist

The planning items just discussed are only a few of the basic webpage design issues that you need to consider when developing a website. A more sophisticated website requires additional design considerations and research of the business, its competition, and a complete business analysis. Throughout this book, design issues will be addressed as they relate to the chapter project.

The rest of the chapters in this book employ professional web design practices in addition to the development of webpages. You will learn many design and development techniques, including how to add links, styles, layout, graphics, tables, forms, and multimedia to your webpages.

Table 1–3 serves as a checklist of items to consider when planning a website.

Table 1–3 Checklist for Planning a Website	
Topic	**Web Designer Questions**
Purpose of the website	What is the purpose and goal of the website? What is the organization's mission statement?
Target audience	Describe the target audience (age, gender, demographics). What information is most pertinent to the users?
Multiplatform display	Will you design for display on multiple platforms or focus only on a desktop or mobile design?
Site map	How many webpages will be included in the website? How will the webpages be organized? What type of website structure is appropriate for the content?
Wireframe	What features will be displayed on each webpage?
Graphics	What graphics will you use on the website?
Color	What colors will you use within the site to enhance the purpose and brand?
Typography	What font styles will you use within the website?
Accessibility	How will the website accommodate people with disabilities?

Break Point: If you want to take a break, this is a good place to do so. To resume at a later time, continue reading the text from this location forward.

Understanding the Basics of HTML

Webpages are created using **Hypertext Markup Language (HTML)**, which is an authoring language used to create documents for the web. HTML consists of a set of special instructions called **tags** to define the structure and layout of content in a webpage. A browser reads the HTML tags to determine how to display the webpage content on a screen. Because the HTML tags define or "mark up" the content on the webpage, HTML is considered a **markup language** rather than a traditional programming language. HTML has evolved through several versions from the initial public release of HTML 1.0 in 1989 to the current version, HTML5. Each version has expanded the capabilities of the language.

HTML Elements and Attributes

A webpage is a text file that contains both content and HTML tags and is saved as an HTML document. HTML tags mark the text to define how it should appear when viewed in a browser. HTML includes dozens of tags that describe the structure of webpages and create links to other content. For instance, the HTML tags <nav> and </nav> mark the start and end of a navigation area, while <html> and </html> indicate the start and end of a webpage. An **HTML element** consists of everything from the start tag to the end tag, including content, and represents a distinct part of a webpage such as a paragraph or heading. For example, <title> Webpage Example </title> is an HTML element that sets the title of a webpage. In common usage, when web designers say "Use a p element to define a paragraph," or something similar, they mean to use a starting <p> tag to mark the beginning of the paragraph and an ending </p> tag to mark the end of the paragraph.

You can enhance HTML elements by using **attributes**, which define additional characteristics, or properties, of the element such as the width and height of an image. An attribute includes a name, such as width, and can also include a value, such as 300px, which sets the width of an element in pixels. Attributes are included within the element's start tag. Figure 1–21 shows the anatomy of HTML elements in Notepad++, which uses color coding to distinguish parts of the code. For example, Notepad++ displays tags in blue, attribute names in red, attribute values in purple, and content in black.

BTW

Lowercase HTML Tags
Although most browsers interpret a tag such as <nav> the same way it interprets <NAV>, the convention for HTML5 is to use all lowercase tags. Using lowercase tags means your HTML documents conform to the current W3C standard.

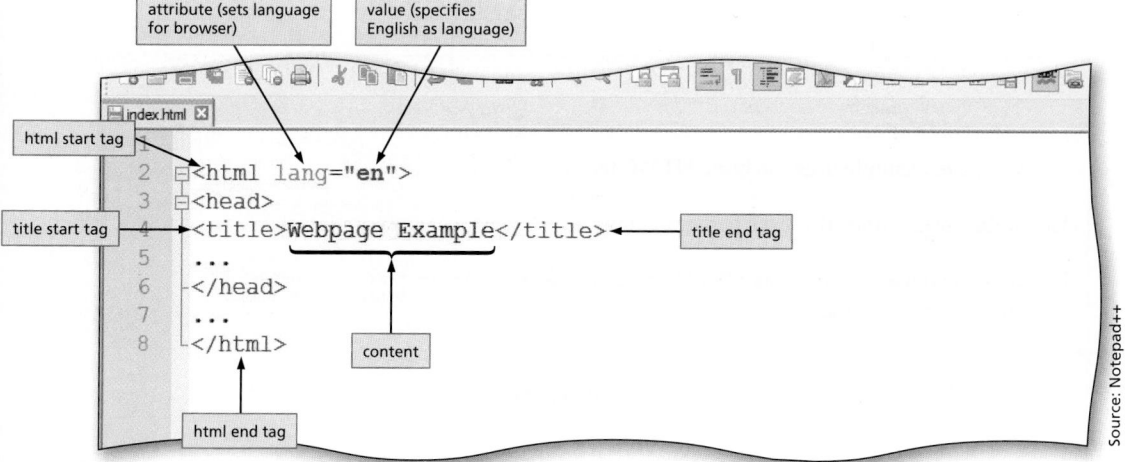

Figure 1–21

HTML combines tags and descriptive attributes that define how a document should appear in a web browser. HTML elements include headings, paragraphs, hyperlinks, lists, and images. Most HTML elements have a start tag and an end tag and follow the same rules, or **syntax**, which determine how the elements should be written so they are interpreted correctly by the browser. These HTML elements are called **paired** tags and use the syntax *<start tag> content </end tag>*, which has the following meaning:

- HTML elements begin with a start tag, or opening tag, such as <title>.
- HTML elements finish with an end tag, or closing tag, such as </title>.
- Content is inserted between the start and end tags. In Figure 1–21, the content for the title tags is Webpage Example.

Some HTML elements are void of content. They are called **empty**, or **void**, tags. Examples of empty tags are <br> for a line break and <hr> for a horizontal line, or rule. The syntax for empty tags is *<tag>*.

Figure 1–22 shows the HTML code and content needed to create the webpage shown in Figure 1–23.

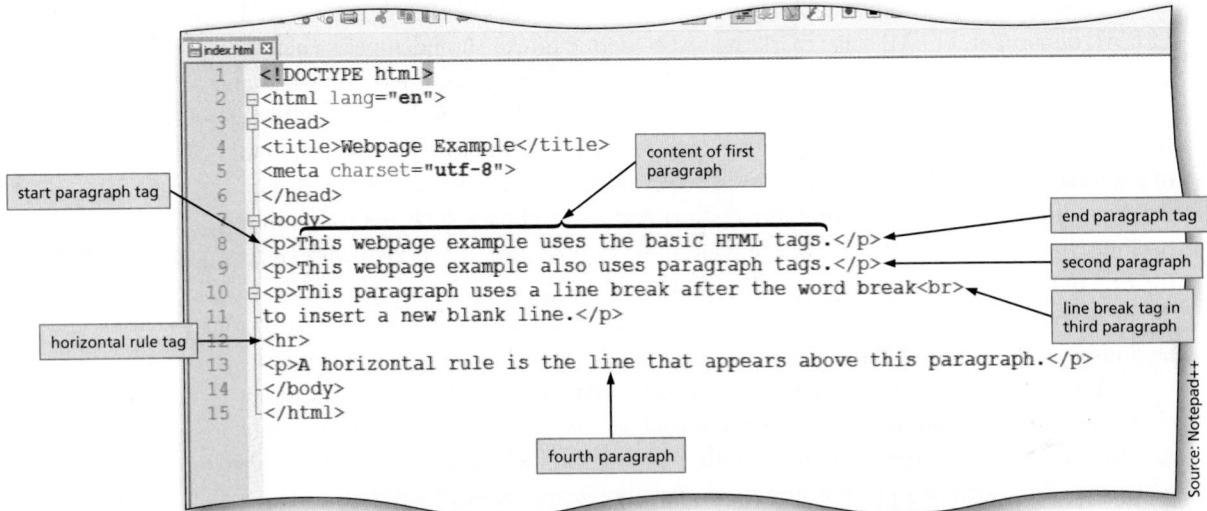

Figure 1–22

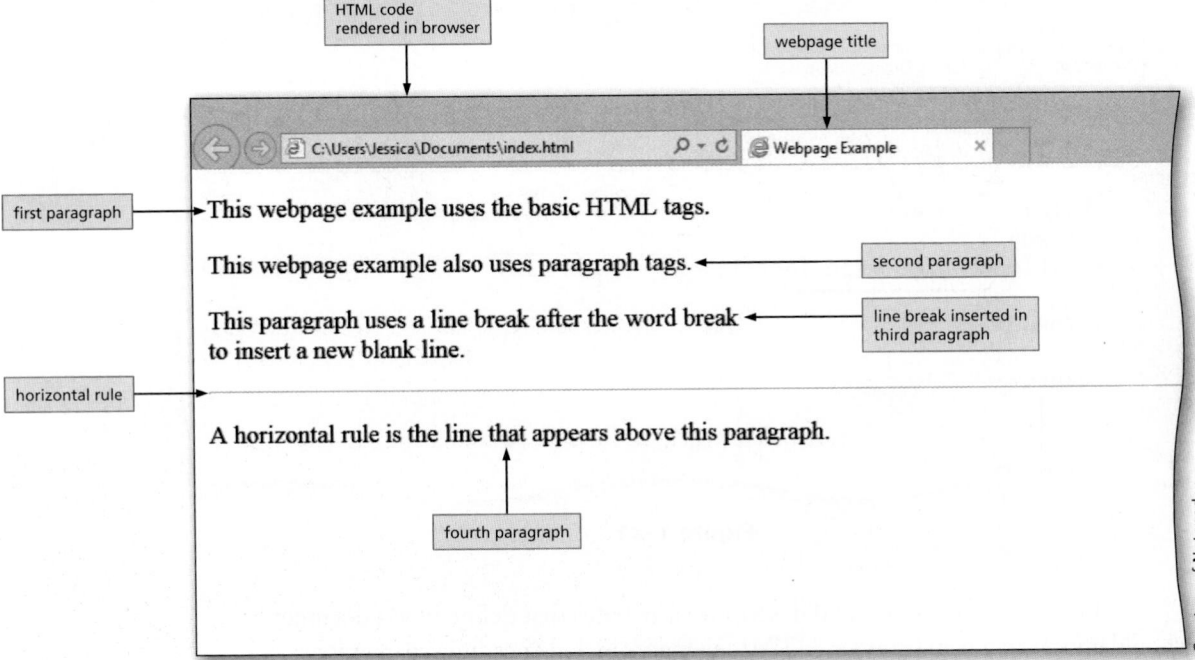

Figure 1–23

Technologies Related to HTML

Several technologies, listed as follows, have been developed since the introduction of HTML to extend its capabilities. These technologies also use tags to mark up content in a text document.

- **XML** — The W3C introduced **XML (Extensible Markup Language)** in 1998 to exchange and transport data. It does not replace HTML, but rather, can work with HTML by transporting web data obtained through an HTML webpage.

- **XHTML** — **XHTML (Extensible Hypertext Markup Language)** is a rewritten version of HTML using XML and was developed in 2000. Its primary benefit is that it is more widely accepted on mobile device platforms.

- **DHTML** — **DHTML (Dynamic Hypertext Markup Language)** is a term that refers to a combination of web technologies, such as HTML, CSS, and JavaScript to create interactive and dynamic webpage content. DHTML was introduced in the mid-1990s.

HTML5

With its debut in 2008, HTML5 is the most recent version of HTML. HTML5 introduces several new elements such as header, nav, main, and footer to better define the areas of a webpage. They are classified as structural elements because they define the structure of a webpage. These new elements also are considered semantic HTML elements because they provide meaning about the content of the tags. (The term *semantic* refers to the meaning of words or ideas.) For example, <header> is a semantic tag because it defines content that appears at the top of a webpage. The name and purpose of the <header> tag reflect its meaning. On the other hand, <b>, for bold, is not a semantic tag because it defines only how content should look, not what it means.

HTML5 also provides a more flexible approach to web development. For instance, with HTML5, you can incorporate audio and video with the use of <audio> and <video> tags. These new features reduce the need for browser plugins, which are small programs that let webpages play sounds or videos, for example. This book shows HTML5 tags and attributes that are currently supported by modern browsers.

Understanding the Role of Other Web Programming Languages

In addition to HTML, web developers use other web programming languages such as JavaScript and PHP to add interactivity and functionality. Although you can create websites without these languages, they are useful when you need to include features beyond the scope of HTML. You should be aware of these languages as you begin learning about web development.

JavaScript

JavaScript is a popular scripting language used to create interactivity within a web browser. Common uses for JavaScript include creating popup windows and alert messages, displaying the current date, and validating form data. JavaScript is a **client-side scripting language**, which means that the browser processes it on the client computer. Webpages that contain JavaScript are named with an .htm or .html extension, just like a webpage without JavaScript.

jQuery

jQuery is a library of JavaScript programs designed for easy integration onto a webpage. jQuery makes it easy for web developers to add JavaScript to a webpage. The jQuery Foundation (https://jquery.org) is a group of web developers that work together to create open-source projects. Their mission is to "improve the open web, making it accessible for everyone, through the development and support of open-source software, and collaboration with the development community."

PHP

PHP (Hypertext Preprocessor) is an open-source scripting language often used for common tasks such as writing to or querying a database located on a central server. PHP is a **server-side scripting language**, which means that the PHP script is processed at the server. The result of the PHP script is often an HTML webpage that is sent back to the client. Pages that contain PHP scripts must have file names that end with the file extension .php.

ASP

ASP (Active Server Pages) is a server-side scripting technology from Microsoft used to accomplish many of the same server-side processing tasks as PHP. Pages that contain ASP scripts must have file names that end with the file extension .asp.

Using Web Authoring Tools

You can create webpages using HTML with a simple text editor, such as Notepad, Notepad++, Sublime, Programmer's Notepad, TextEdit, and TextWrangler. Notepad comes installed with the Windows operating system, and TextEdit comes installed with the Mac OS X operating system. TextWrangler also runs only on Mac OS X, while the other text editors run on Windows. A **text editor** is a program that allows you to enter, change, save, and print text, which includes HTML tags. Text editors do not typically have many advanced features, but they do allow you to develop HTML documents easily. An HTML editor or code editor is a program that provides basic text-editing functions, as well as more advanced features such as color-coding for various HTML tags, menus to insert HTML tags, and a spelling checker. HTML is **platform independent**, meaning you can create, or code, an HTML file in Windows or Mac and then view it on any browser.

Text Editors

Notepad++ is a free, open-source text editor. You can use it to create files in several markup, scripting, and programming languages, including HTML, CSS, JavaScript, PHP, Java, C#, and Visual Basic. Notepad++ runs on Windows computers; go to http://notepad-plus-plus.org to download the program. Figure 1–24 displays the Notepad++ user interface.

Notepad++
application

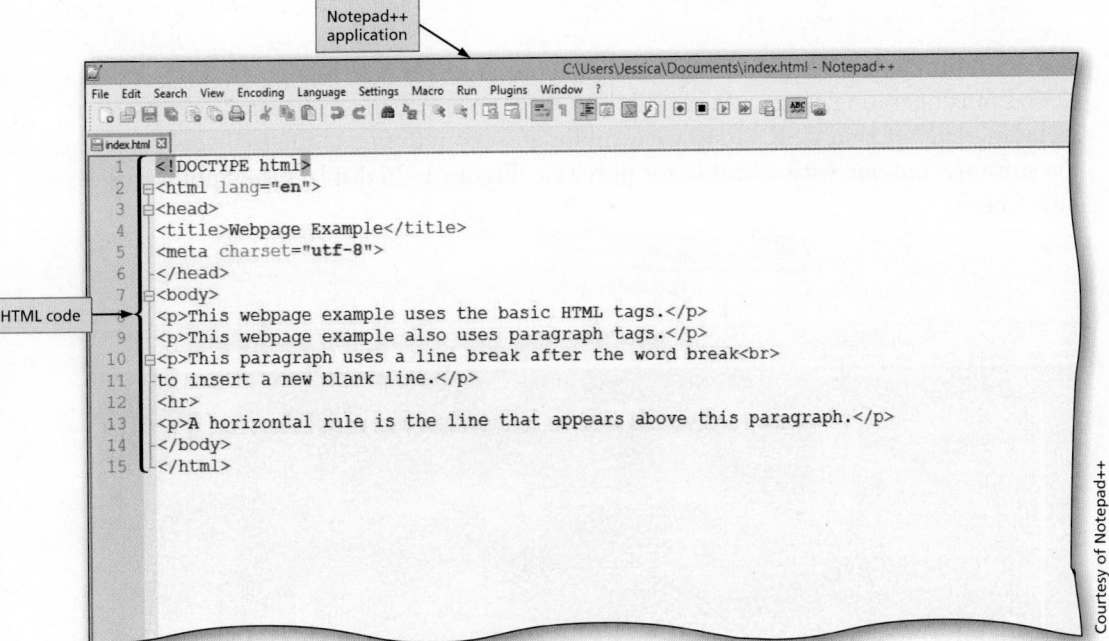

HTML code

Courtesy of Notepad++

Figure 1–24

Programmer's Notepad is another free, open-source text editor you can use to create webpages. Like Notepad++, you can use Programmer's Notepad to create files in several markup, scripting, and programming languages as well. Programmer's Notepad runs on Windows; go to www.pnotepad.org to download the program. Figure 1–25 displays the Programmer's Notepad user interface.

Programmer's
Notepad application

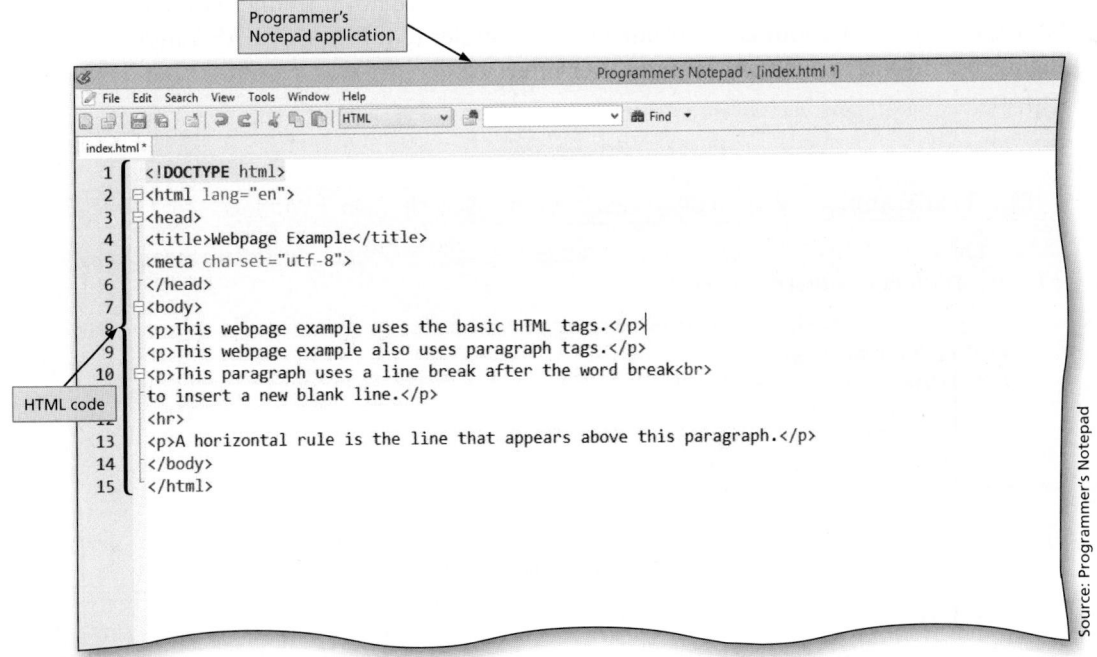

HTML code

Source: Programmer's Notepad

Figure 1–25

Sublime is a cross-platform text editor you can use on the Windows, Mac OS X, or Linux operating system. With Sublime, you can create files in several formats, including HTML and CSS. Go to www.sublimetext.com to find a free trial version of the software and one with a license for purchase. Figure 1–26 displays the Sublime user interface.

Figure 1–26

TextWrangler is a free, open-source text editor available for Mac OS X 10.6.8 or a later version. You can use it to create files in many formats, including HTML and CSS. Go to www.barebones.com/products/textwrangler to download TextWrangler. Figure 1–27 displays the TextWrangler user interface.

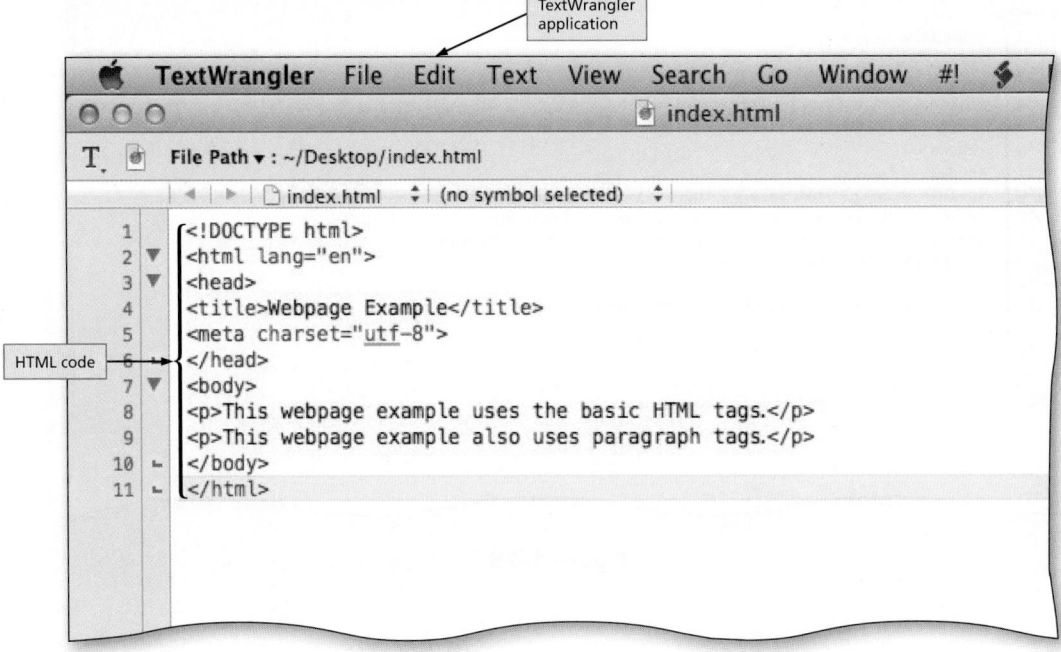

Figure 1–27

To Download and Install a Text Editor

Before you can create your first webpage, you must select a text editor that you will use to create your webpages. Begin by asking whether your instructor has a preferred text editor to use in the course. If not, use a text editor provided by your operating system (such as Notepad or TextEdit) or download one of the HTML text editors previously discussed. If you want to download and install an HTML text editor, you would perform the following steps.

1. Use your browser to access the website for Notepad++, Programmer's Notepad, Sublime, or TextWrangler.

   - Notepad++: http://notepad-plus-plus.org
   - Programmer's Notepad: www.pnotepad.org
   - Sublime: www.sublimetext.com
   - TextWrangler (Mac OS X only): www.barebones.com/products /textwrangler

2. Navigate the text editor's website to locate the download link.

3. Tap or click the link to download the software.

4. When the download is complete, open the downloaded file to begin the installation.

5. Follow the instructions in the setup wizard to complete the installation.

6. Run the text editor when finished.

WYSIWYG Editors

Many popular software applications also provide features that enable you to develop webpages easily. Microsoft Word and Excel, for example, have a Save As Web Page option that converts a document into an HTML file by automatically adding HTML tags to the document. Using Microsoft Access, you can create a webpage that allows you to view data from a database. Adobe Acrobat also has an export feature that creates HTML files. While these programs provide the capability to save as a webpage, they do not substitute the use of a text editor or a WYSIWYG editor. **WYSIWYG** stands for What You See Is What You Get. WYSIWYG editors provide a graphical user interface to design a webpage, as opposed to the blank page provided in a text editor used to write code. The WYSIWYG editor allows you to drag HTML elements onto the page while the editor writes the code for you. While these editors can be useful in developing webpages, understanding the code means you have the control and flexibility to create webpages that meet your needs.

Adobe Dreamweaver is a popular WYSIWYG editor used by many people and businesses around the world for web development. Several types of web file formats can be developed with Dreamweaver, including HTML, CSS, JavaScript, and PHP. Dreamweaver can be installed on a computer running Windows or Mac OS X. Dreamweaver provides several views for working with a webpage file, including Design view, Code view, Split view, and Live view. Design view shows the design of the webpage, while Code view is similar to a text editor. Split view provides a side-by-side view of the webpage design and code. Live view mimics a browser display. Figure 1–28 shows an example of Dreamweaver in Split view. Dreamweaver is part of Adobe Creative Cloud and is available for purchase as a monthly or annual subscription. Visit www.adobe.com for more information about Adobe Dreamweaver Creative Cloud.

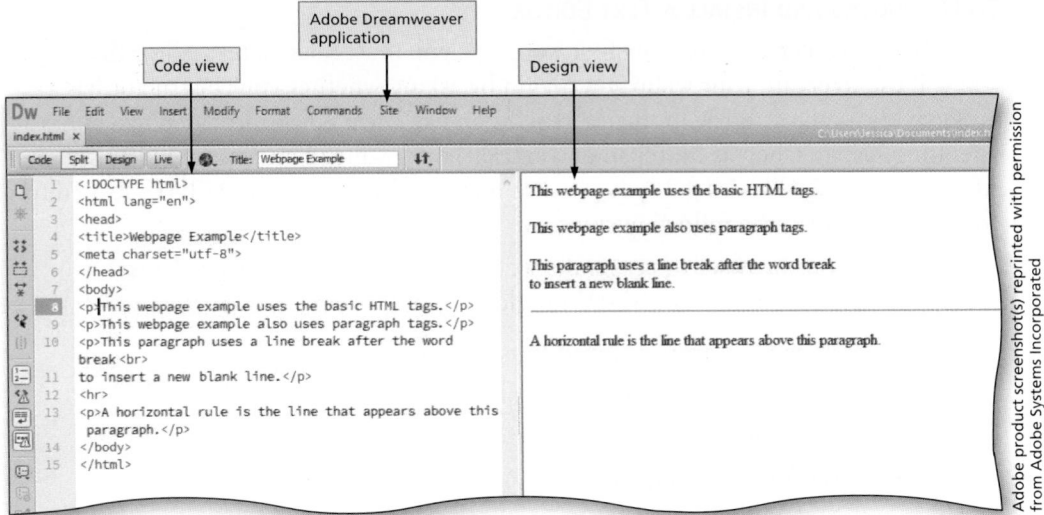

Figure 1–28

Adobe product screenshot(s) reprinted with permission from Adobe Systems Incorporated

Microsoft Expression Web 4 is a WYSIWYG webpage editor from Microsoft. Expression Web 4 is the final version of the software and is shown in Figure 1–29. Expression Web is available as a free download on the Microsoft website. To replace Expression Web, Microsoft is currently directing customers to use its Visual Studio Express 2013 for Web; however, this is a text editor and not a WYSIWYG editor. Visual Studio Express 2013 for Web is shown in Figure 1–30.

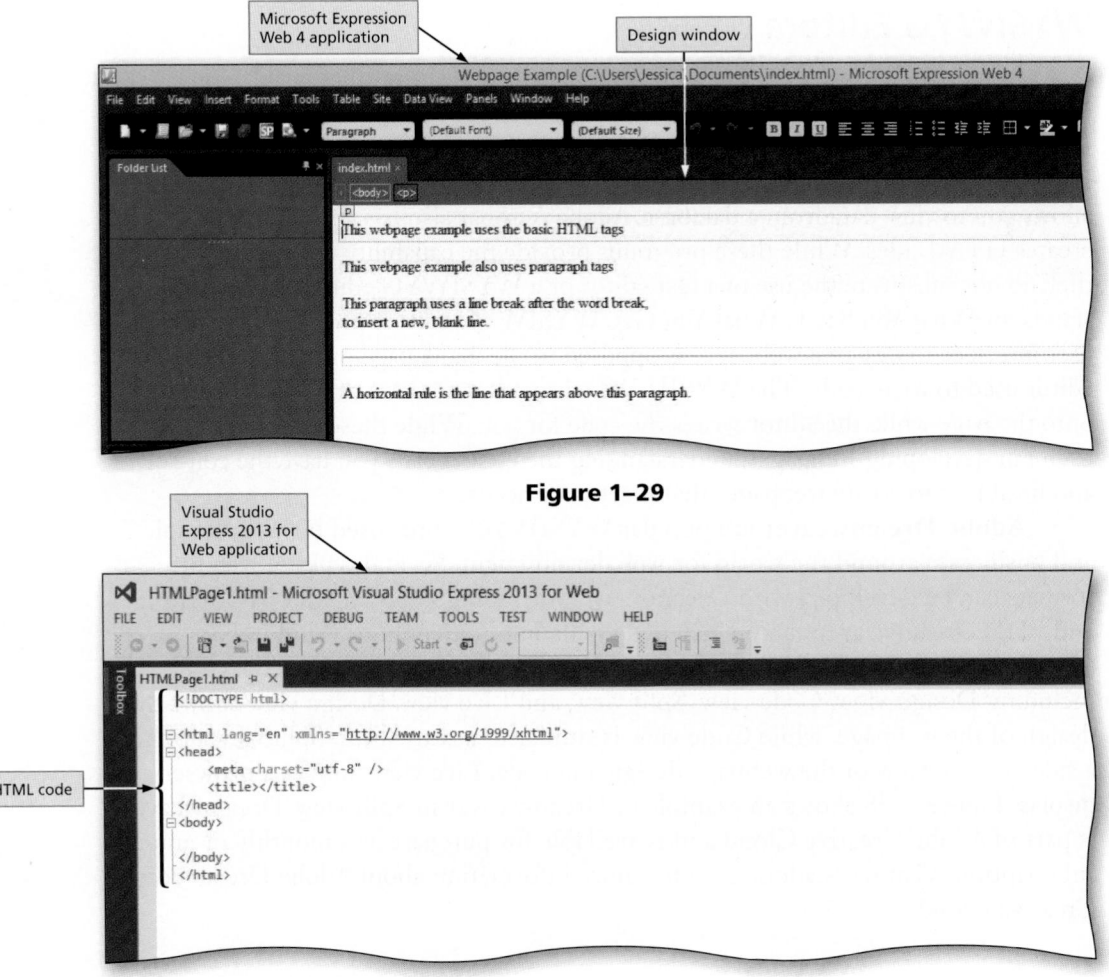

Figure 1–29

Figure 1–30

Creating a Basic Webpage

Every HTML webpage includes the basic HTML tags shown in Figure 1–31.

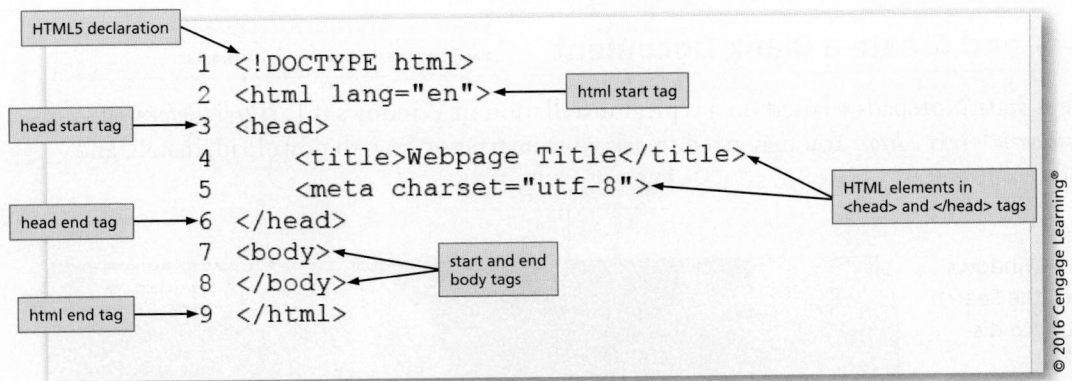

```
1  <!DOCTYPE html>
2  <html lang="en">
3  <head>
4      <title>Webpage Title</title>
5      <meta charset="utf-8">
6  </head>
7  <body>
8  </body>
9  </html>
```

HTML5 declaration

html start tag

head start tag

HTML elements in <head> and </head> tags

head end tag

start and end body tags

html end tag

© 2016 Cengage Learning®

Figure 1–31

The numbers on the left represent line numbers for each line of HTML code. Line 1 shows the tag for declaring an HTML5 webpage. All HTML5 webpages must begin with the HTML element **<!DOCTYPE html>**. This is the first line of HTML code for all of your HTML webpages.

Line 2 shows the HTML tag needed to begin an HTML document. The basic opening tag is **<html>** and the closing tag is **</html>**, which always appears on the last line of the webpage. The lang="en" contained within the opening html tag is an attribute that defines the type of language used (English).

Line 3 shows the head tag, which contains the webpage title and other information about the webpage. The opening head tag is **<head>** and the closing tag is **</head>**.

Line 4 shows the webpage title tags, **<title>** and **</title>**. The text contained between these tags is displayed within the web browser tab. The title tags belong within the opening and closing head tags. To make the head section easier to read, web developers customarily indent the tags in the head section, such as the title and meta tags.

Line 5 shows the meta tag. A **meta** tag contains information about the data on the webpage. In this instance, the meta tag designates the type of character set the browser should use, charset="utf-8". The charset is an attribute within the meta tag that specifies the character encoding to be used for the webpage. The **Unicode Transformation Format (UTF)** is a compressed format that allows computers to display and manipulate text. When the browser encounters this meta tag, it displays the webpage properly. UTF-8 is standard for HTML5 pages and is the preferred encoding standard for email and other applications. The encoding chosen is also important when validating the webpage, which you will do in Chapter 2. Note that the meta tag is a single tag element without opening and closing tags making it an empty element. The meta tag belongs within the opening and closing head tags.

Lines 7 and 8 show the **<body>** and **</body>** tags. All text, images, links, and other content displayed on the webpage are included within the <body> and </body> tags.

BTW
<!DOCTYPE>
Statement
Because the web includes billions of documents, a browser refers to the HTML version and type in the <!DOCTYPE> statement to display a webpage correctly. Previous versions of HTML had complicated <!DOCTYPE> statements.

Do I have to indent certain lines of HTML code?
Indenting lines of code is not required, but it helps improve the readability of the webpage. In Figure 1–31, Lines 4 and 5 are indented to clearly show the tags contained in the <head> and </head> tags. If the code included elements between the <body> and </body> tags, those lines could also be indented to make them easier to read. Using indents is a good web design practice.

CONSIDER THIS

Now that you have learned the basic HTML tag elements, it is time to create your first webpage. The following steps use Notepad++ to create an HTML document. You may complete these steps using a text editor other than Notepad++, but your screens will not match those in the book and your line numbers may vary slightly.

To Start Notepad++ and Create a Blank Document

1 RUN TEXT EDITOR & CREATE BLANK DOCUMENT | 2 ENTER HTML TAGS
3 ADD TEXT | 4 SAVE WEBPAGE | 5 VIEW WEBPAGE

The following steps start Notepad++ based on a typical installation in Windows 8.1. *Why? Before you can create a webpage, you must open a text editor.* You may need to ask your instructor how to download, install, and start Notepad++ for your computer.

1

- Open the Charms bar in Windows 8.1 and then tap or click the Search charm on the Charms bar to display the Search menu.

- Type **Notepad++** in the Search text box and watch the search results appear in the Apps list (Figure 1–32).

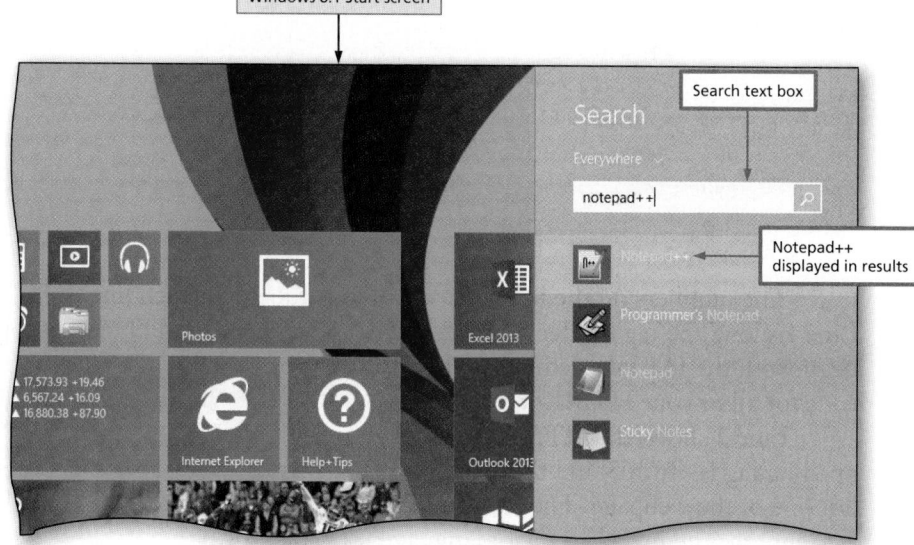

Figure 1–32

2

- Tap or click Notepad++ in the search results to start Notepad++ and display a new blank page.

- If the Notepad++ window is not maximized, tap or click the Maximize button next to the Close button on the title bar to maximize the window (Figure 1–33).

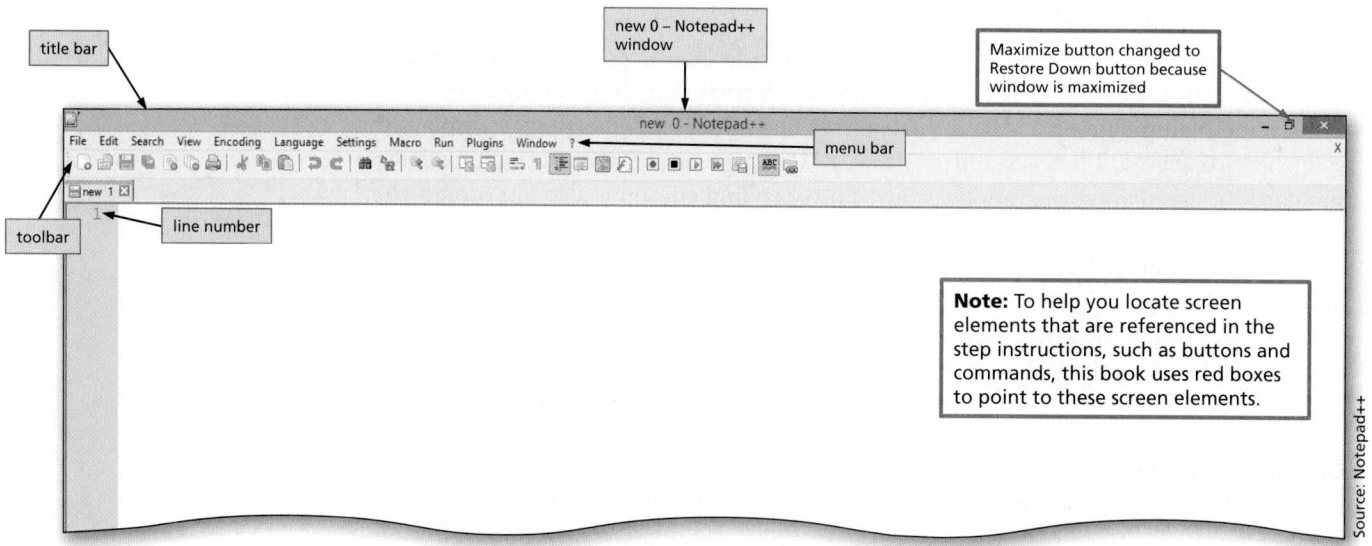

Note: To help you locate screen elements that are referenced in the step instructions, such as buttons and commands, this book uses red boxes to point to these screen elements.

Source: Notepad++

Figure 1–33

Other Ways

1. Double-tap or double-click Notepad++ icon on desktop

CONSIDER THIS

How do I use the touch keyboard with a touch screen?
To display the on-screen touch keyboard, tap the Touch Keyboard button on the Windows taskbar. When finished using the touch keyboard, tap the X button on the touch keyboard to close the keyboard.

To Add Basic HTML Tags to a Document

1 RUN TEXT EDITOR & CREATE BLANK DOCUMENT | 2 ENTER HTML TAGS
3 ADD TEXT | 4 SAVE WEBPAGE | 5 VIEW WEBPAGE

Create your first webpage beginning with the required minimum HTML tags. *Why? An HTML webpage requires several basic HTML tags so it can be displayed properly on a web browser.* The following steps add the required HTML tags to a document.

- On Line 1, type `<!DOCTYPE html>` to declare an HTML5 document.

- Press the ENTER key and then type `<html lang="en">` to add the opening html tag on Line 2.

- Press the ENTER key and then type `<head>` to add the opening head tag on Line 3 (Figure 1–34).

Q&A Why is the text "lang" underlined with a wavy red line?
The wavy red line indicates a possible spelling error. Because "lang" is the correct spelling for the language attribute, you can ignore this error.

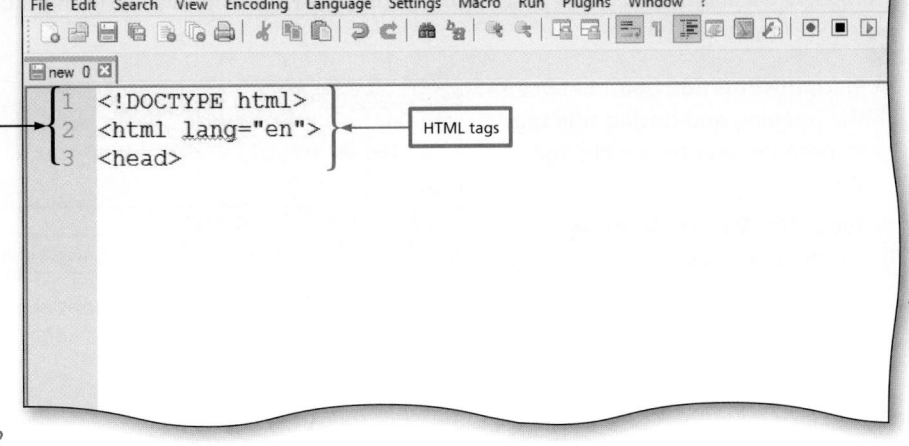

Figure 1–34

- Press the ENTER key and enter the lines of code as listed in Table 1–4 to add the remaining basic HTML tags (Figure 1–35).

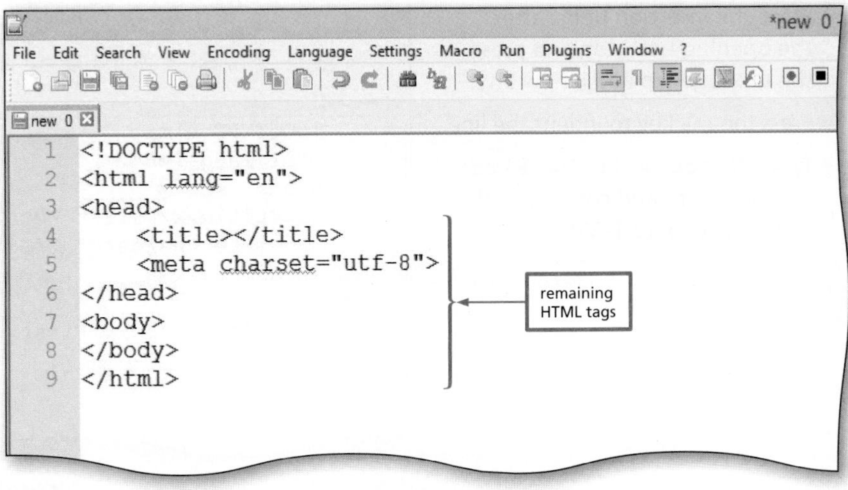

Q&A How should I move from one line to another in the document?
Press the ENTER key after each line to continue to the next line.

Should I indent any lines of code?
Yes. Indent Lines 4 and 5 by pressing the TAB key. Press the SHIFT+TAB keys to return the insertion point to the left margin.

Figure 1–35

Table 1–4 HTML Tags	
Line Number	HTML Tag
4	<title></title>
5	<meta charset="utf-8">
6	</head>
7	<body>
8	</body>
9	</html>

To Add a Title and Text to a Webpage

1 RUN TEXT EDITOR & CREATE BLANK DOCUMENT | 2 ENTER HTML TAGS
3 ADD TEXT | 4 SAVE WEBPAGE | 5 VIEW WEBPAGE

Now that you have added required HTML tags, you are ready to designate a title and add content to the page. *Why?* *A webpage title appears on the browser tab and usually displays the name of the webpage. After titling a webpage, you add content to the body section.* The following steps add a title and content to the webpage.

- Place the insertion point between the opening and closing title tags to prepare to enter a webpage title.
- Type **My First Webpage** to add a webpage title (Figure 1–36).

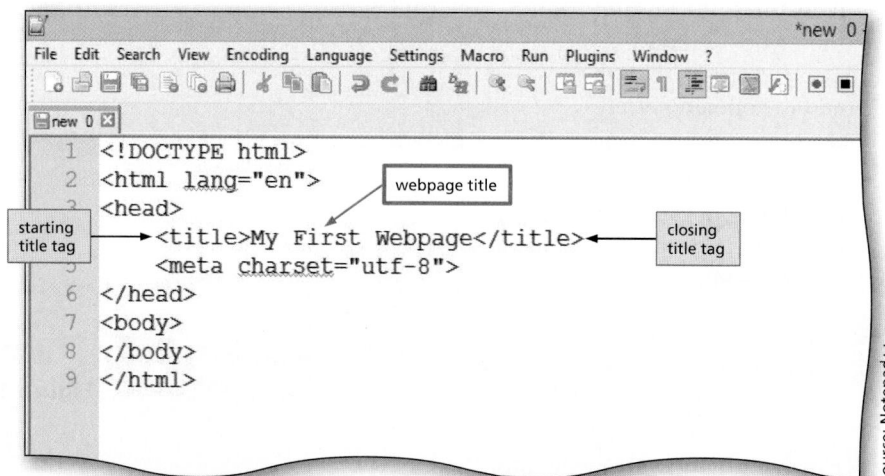

Figure 1–36

2

- Place the insertion point after the opening body tag and press the ENTER key to add a new line.
- Press the TAB key to indent the line.
- Type **Welcome to My First Webpage** to add content to the webpage (Figure 1–37).

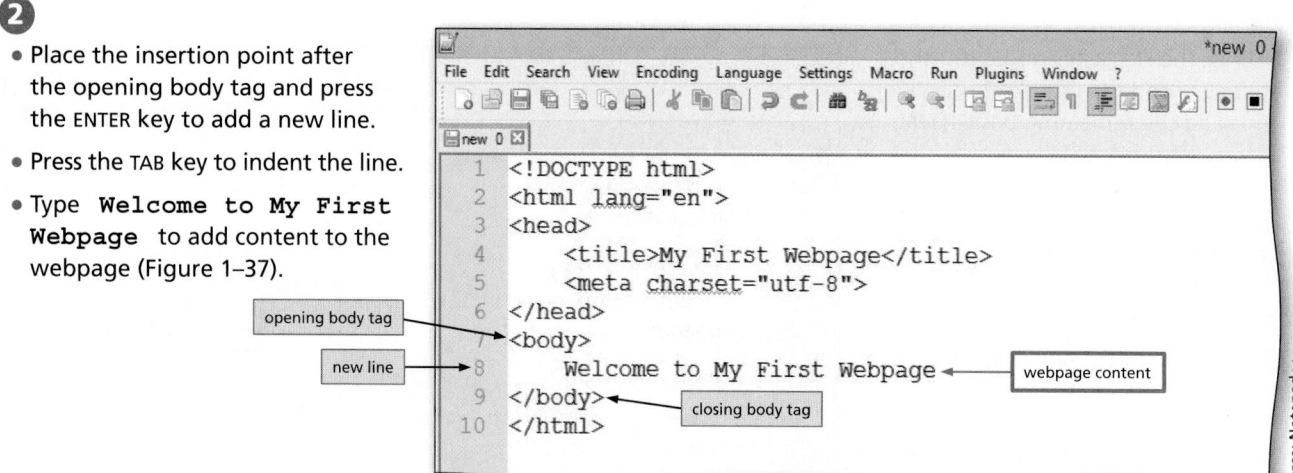

Figure 1–37

To Save a Webpage

After creating a webpage, you must save it as an HTML file. *Why? A text editor can be used to create many types of files; therefore, you must specify that this is an HTML file so a browser can display it as a webpage.* The following steps save the document as an HTML file.

- Tap or click File on the menu bar to display the File menu options.

- Tap or click Save As on the File menu to display the Save As dialog box (Figure 1–38).

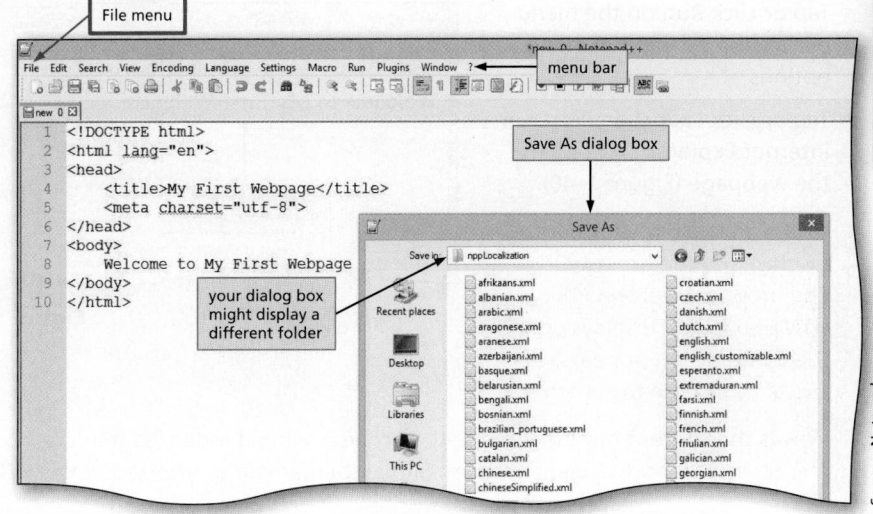

Figure 1–38

Source: Notepad++

- Tap or click the Save in list box and then navigate to your Documents folder.

Q&A Can I save the file in another location on my hard drive or on my flash drive?
Yes. If your instructor specified a different location, use that instead of the Documents folder. You learn about managing website files in Chapter 2.

- In the File name text box, delete the existing text and then type **index** to name the file.

Q&A Why am I using index as the file name?
The file name *index* is the standard name of a home page.

Why am I using all lowercase letters for the file name?
The current convention in web development is to use all lowercase letters for folder and file names.

- Tap or click the Save as type list box and then tap or click Hyper Text Markup Language file to select the HTML file type (Figure 1–39).

Figure 1–39

Source: Notepad++

- Tap or click the Save button to save the HTML document.

Other Ways

1. Press CTRL+S

To View a Webpage in a Browser

After saving an HTML document, you can view it as a webpage in a web browser. *Why? A web browser reads the HTML code and displays the webpage content.* The following steps display a webpage in a browser.

- Tap or click Run on the menu bar to display the Run menu options.

- Tap or click Launch in IE to run Internet Explorer and display the webpage (Figure 1–40).

Q&A Why are the HTML tags not displayed in the browser?
The browser interprets the HTML code and displays only the content that appears within the tags, not the tags themselves.

Why is the content not indented in the browser when I indented it in the text editor?
The browser ignores indents, spaces, and extra blank lines inserted in the HTML file to improve readability.

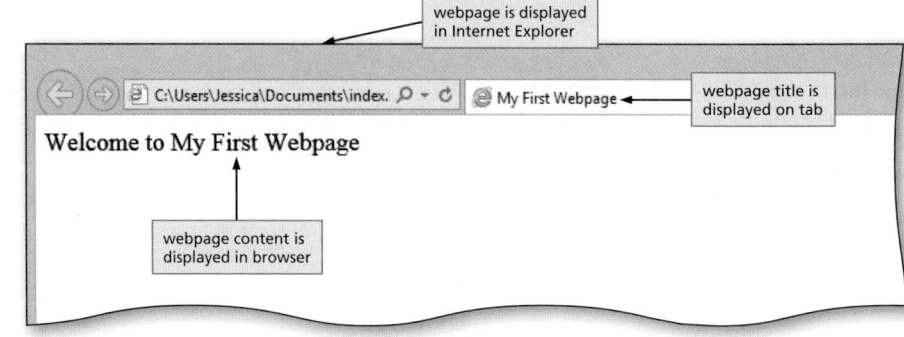

Figure 1–40

Using a Different Text Editor

If you completed the previous steps with a text editor other than Notepad++, your screen will look similar to Figure 1–41 for Programmer's Notepad, to Figure 1–42 for Sublime, and to Figure 1–43 for TextWrangler.

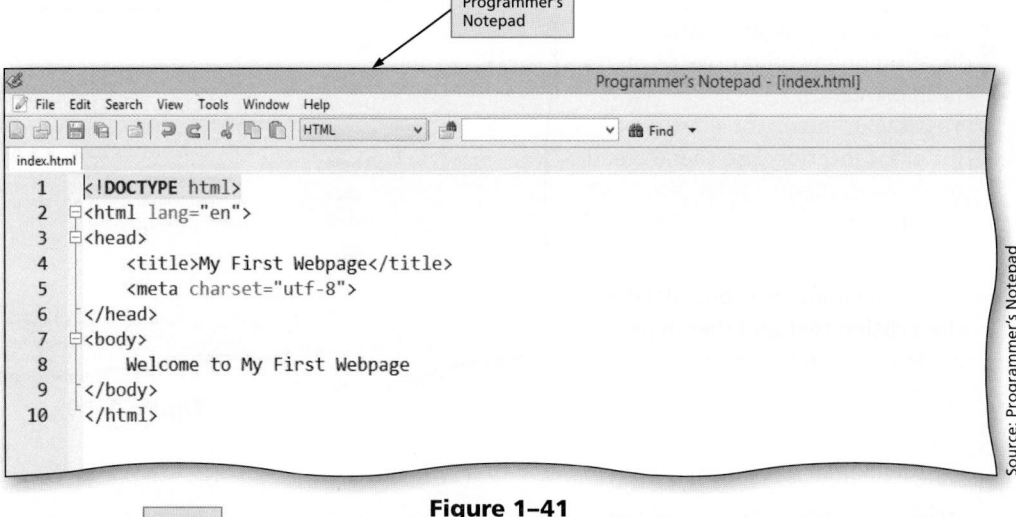

Figure 1–41

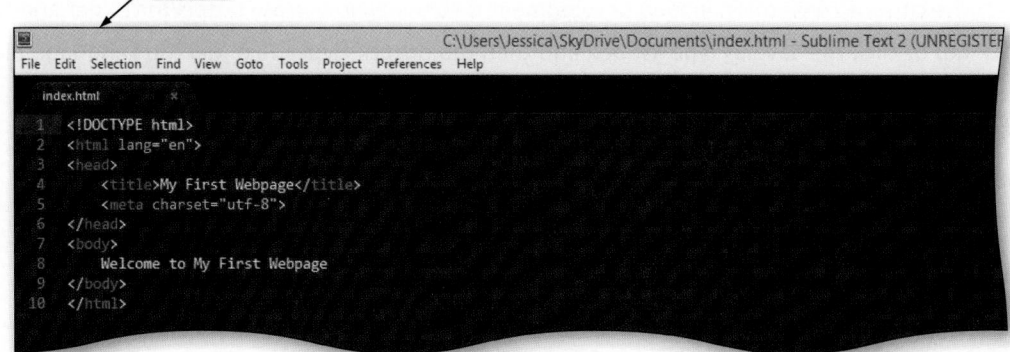

Figure 1–42

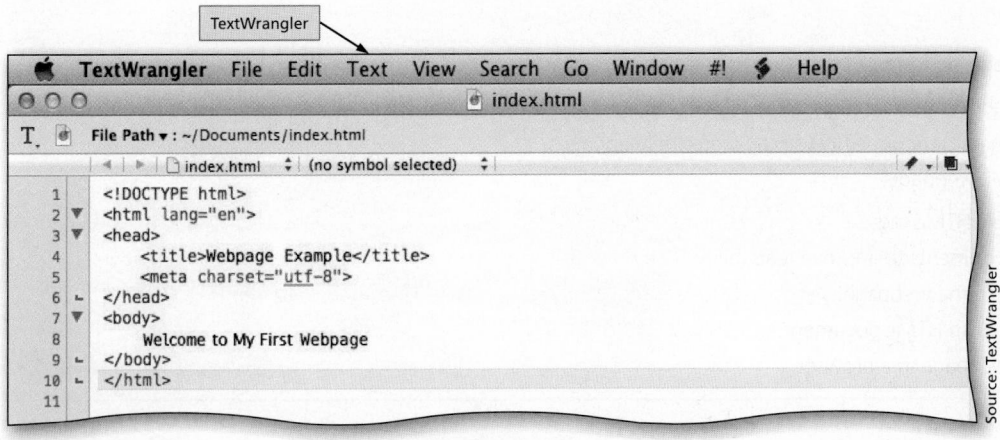

Figure 1–43

Chapter Summary

In this chapter, you learned about the Internet, the web, and associated technologies, including web servers and web browsers. You learned the essential role of HTML in creating webpages and reviewed tools used to create HTML documents. You also learned how to create a basic HTML webpage. The items listed below include all the new concepts and skills you have learned in this chapter, with the tasks grouped by activity.

Creating a Basic Webpage
Start Notepad++ and Create a Blank Document (HTML 30)
Add Basic HTML Tags to a Document (HTML 31)
Add a Title and Text to a Webpage (HTML 32)
Save a Webpage (HTML 33)
View a Webpage in a Browser (HTML 34)

Exploring the Internet
Describe the Internet (HTML 3)
Describe the World Wide Web (HTML 4)
Define Protocols (HTML 6)
Discuss Web Browsers (HTML 7)
Identify Types of Websites (HTML 9)

Planning a Website
Identify the Purpose and Audience of the Website (HTML 11–12)

Design for Multiplatform Display (HTML 13)
Describe a Wireframe and a Site Map (HTML 14)
Consider Graphics, Navigation, Typography, and Color (HTML 17–19)
Design for Accessibility (HTML 20)

Understanding the Basics of HTML
Define Hypertext Markup Language (HTML 21)
Describe HTML Elements (HTML 21)
List Useful HTML Practices (HTML 22)
Identify Technologies Related to HTML (HTML 23)
Explain the Role of Other Web Programming Languages (HTML 23)

Using Web Authoring Tools
Identify Text Editors (HTML 24)
Download and Install a Text Editor (HTML 27)
Describe WYSIWYG Editors (HTML 27)

CONSIDER THIS

What decisions will you need to make when creating your next webpage?
Use these guidelines as you complete the assignments in this chapter and create your own webpages outside of this class.

1. Plan the website.

   a. Identify the purpose of the website.

   b. Identify the users of the website.

   c. Recognize the computing environments of the users.

   d. Design a wireframe and a site map.

2. Choose the design components.

   a. Identify possible graphics for the website.

   b. Determine the types of navigation tools and typography to use.

   c. Select a color scheme.

   d. Consider accessibility.

Continued >

CONSIDER THIS *continued*

3. Select a webpage authoring tool.

   a. Review available authoring tools.

   b. Determine an authoring tool to use to create the webpages.

4. Create a basic HTML webpage.

   a. Insert the basic HTML tags.

   b. Indent some elements to improve readability.

   c. Add content to the webpage.

   d. Save the file as an HTML document.

   e. Display the webpage in a browser.

How should you submit solutions to questions in the assignments identified with a ❋ symbol?

Every assignment in this book contains one or more questions identified with a ❋ symbol. These questions require you to think beyond the assigned presentation. Present your solutions to the questions in the format required by your instructor. Possible formats may include one or more of these options: write the answer; create a document that contains the answer; present your answer to the class; discuss your answer in a group; record the answer as audio or video using a webcam, smartphone, or portable media player; or post answers on a blog, wiki, or website.

Apply Your Knowledge

Reinforce the skills and apply the concepts you learned in this chapter.

Creating a Basic HTML Webpage

Instructions: The page shown in Figure 1–44 contains the required HTML5 tags for all webpages. In your HTML editor, you will enter these required HTML tags and save the file as an HTML document that can serve as the model, or template, for other HTML documents. You will make a copy of the HTML template and insert the paragraph content to create and personalize a page to introduce yourself, your major, and your goals for the class. The figures in this exercise use Notepad++ (Windows) and TextWrangler (Mac) as HTML editors, but you can complete the exercises in this book using any HTML editor such as Sublime, Programmer's Notepad, KompZer, HTML Kit, CoffeeCup, Aptana, UltraEdit, or Microsoft WebMatrix, to mention a few.

Perform the following tasks:

1. Open your HTML editor, and enter the required HTML tags as shown in Figure 1–44. In this figure, the tags within the <head> section are indented to visually separate the <head> section from the <body> section. Adding spaces, indents, or extra blank lines to an HTML document does not change the way the page looks in the browser. Professional webpage developers use indents and blank space to make the code easier to read and maintain.

```
new 0
 1  <!DOCTYPE html>
 2  <html lang="en">
 3  <head>
 4      <title></title>
 5      <meta charset="utf-8">
 6  </head>
 7  <body>
 8
 9
10  </body>
11  </html>
```

Source: Notepad++

Figure 1–44

2. Save the file as a Hyper Text Markup Language file with the name `template01` in the chapter01\apply folder provided with the Data Files for Students. (*Hint*: If you are using TextWrangler, enter the entire file name and extension of `template01.html` to save the file as an HTML file). Both Notepad++ and TextWrangler save HTML files with an html file name extension and apply color coding.

3. Tap or click the opening <html> tag. Examine the HTML document shown in Figure 1–45, which displays the code in Notepad++. In a Word document, answer the following questions:

   a. In what color does Notepad++ display HTML tags?

   b. What color are HTML attributes?

   c. What color are HTML attribute values?

   d. When you tap or click the start or end tag of a set of paired tags, what background color is used to highlight the pair?

Source: Notepad++

Figure 1–45

4. Examine the HTML document shown in Figure 1–46, which displays the code in TextWrangler. In a Word document, answer the following questions:

   a. In what color does TextWrangler display HTML tags?

   b. What color are HTML attributes?

   c. What color are HTML attribute values?

   d. In what background color is the current line highlighted?

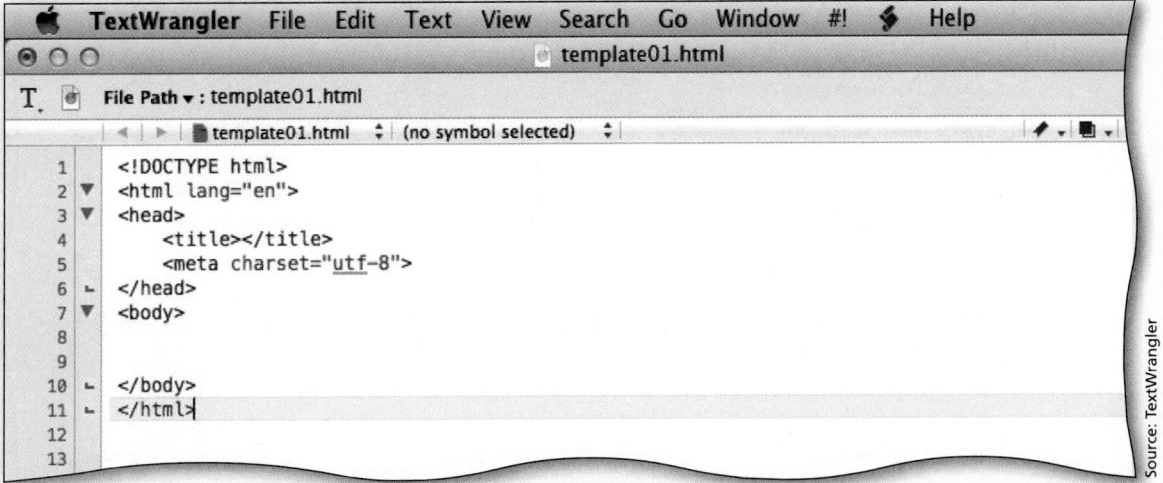

Source: TextWrangler

Figure 1–46

Continued >

Apply Your Knowledge *continued*

If you are using a plain text editor such as Notepad (Windows) or TextEdit (Mac), all of the code and content is black, as shown in Figure 1–47.

```
                                        template01.html - Notepad

File Edit Format View Help
<!DOCTYPE html>
<html lang="en">
<head>
        <title></title>
        <meta charset="utf-8">
</head>
<body>


</body>
</html>
```

Figure 1–47

5. Delete the closing quotation mark in the <meta charset="utf-8"> tag and observe how the colors change on the screen. In a Word document, explain how the colors changed on the screen. Replace the missing quotation mark. Observing how the colors work in your HTML editor helps you productively find and correct errors.

6. Save the template01.html file with the name **intro.html** in the chapter01\apply folder provided with the Data Files for Students. Given all HTML5 pages start with the same required tags, a productive way to create a new file is to open the template01.html file and then save it with a new name as a starting point for the new page.

7. Enter the paragraph tags, horizontal rule tags, and content as shown in Figure 1–48 (Notepad++) and Figure 1–49 (TextWrangler). Modify the content within the paragraph <p> ... </p> tags to introduce yourself in this page. Use indents as desired to make the page easy to read.

```
intro.html
1    <!DOCTYPE html>
2    <html lang="en">
3    <head>
4        <title>Introduction</title>
5        <meta charset="utf-8">
6    </head>
7    <body>
8        <p>Insert your name</p>
9        <p>Insert the current date</p>
10       <p>Insert the name of the course</p>
11       <p>Insert your instructor's name</p>
12       <hr>
13
14       <p>Insert the degree or certificate you are working toward<p>
15       <p>Insert any relevant work experience or webpage development experience</p>
16       <p>Insert a fun fact about yourself</p>
17       <hr>
18
19       <p>Insert any questions you have at this time.</p>
20
21   </body>
22   </html>
23
24
25
```

Source: Notepad++

Figure 1–48

```
1    <!DOCTYPE html>
2  ▼ <html lang="en">
3  ▼ <head>
4    <title></title>
5    <meta charset="utf-8">
6  ∟ </head>
7  ▼ <body>
8        <p>Insert your name</p>
9        <p>Insert the current date</p>
10 ∟      <p>Insert the name of the course</p>
11 ∟      <p>Insert your instructor's name</p>
12       <hr>
13
14       <p>Insert the degree or certificate you are working toward</p>
15       <p>Insert any relevant work experience or webpage development experience</p>
16       <p>Insert a fun fact about yourself</p>
17       <hr>
18
19       <p>Insert any questions you have at this time.</p>
20
21    </body>
22    </html>
23
```

Source: TextWrangler

Figure 1–49

8. Save intro.html and then open the file in a current browser. A sample solution is shown in Figure 1–50.

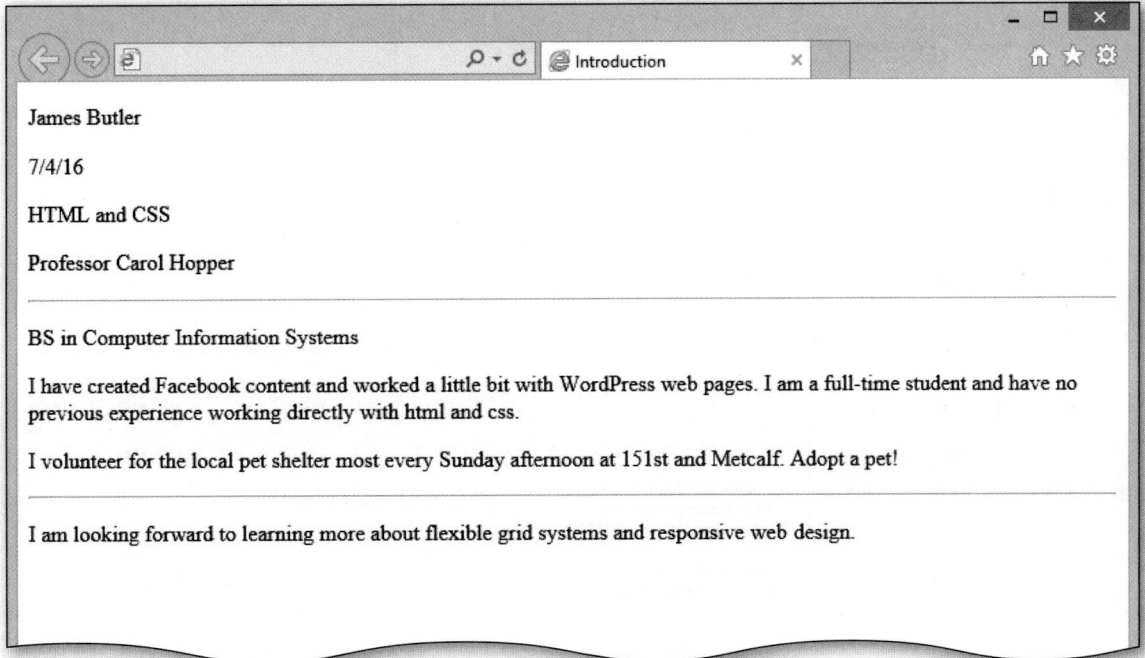

James Butler

7/4/16

HTML and CSS

Professor Carol Hopper

___

BS in Computer Information Systems

I have created Facebook content and worked a little bit with WordPress web pages. I am a full-time student and have no previous experience working directly with html and css.

I volunteer for the local pet shelter most every Sunday afternoon at 151st and Metcalf. Adopt a pet!

___

I am looking forward to learning more about flexible grid systems and responsive web design.

Figure 1–50

9. Submit the files you created in this exercise in a format specified by your instructor. You may be asked to electronically submit the files as an email attachment or drop-box attachment. You may be asked to publish the pages to a web server. See Lab 3 in this chapter and Chapter 12 for more information on publishing pages to web servers.

10. ✹ In Step 2, you saved a text file as an HTML file. At that point, an HTML editor will provide color-coded visual support. Identify three different ways that the color supports productive web development skills. Also, identify the HTML editor you are using, and note three different color codes applied by that editor.

STUDENT ASSIGNMENTS

Extend Your Knowledge

Extend the skills you learned in this chapter and experiment with new skills. You may need to use additional resources to complete the assignment.

Adding Comments to an HTML Document

Note: To complete this assignment, you will be required to use the Data Files for Students. Visit www.cengage.com/ct/studentdownload for detailed instructions or contact your instructor for information about accessing the required files.

Instructions: Open your HTML editor and then open the extend01.html file provided in the Data Files for Students. Add the HTML tags, text, indents, blank lines, and comments as instructed. Save the page as **ski01.html** in the same location and view it in a browser. Figure 1–51a shows the completed HTML document in Notepad++ and Figure 1–51b shows the completed webpage in a browser.

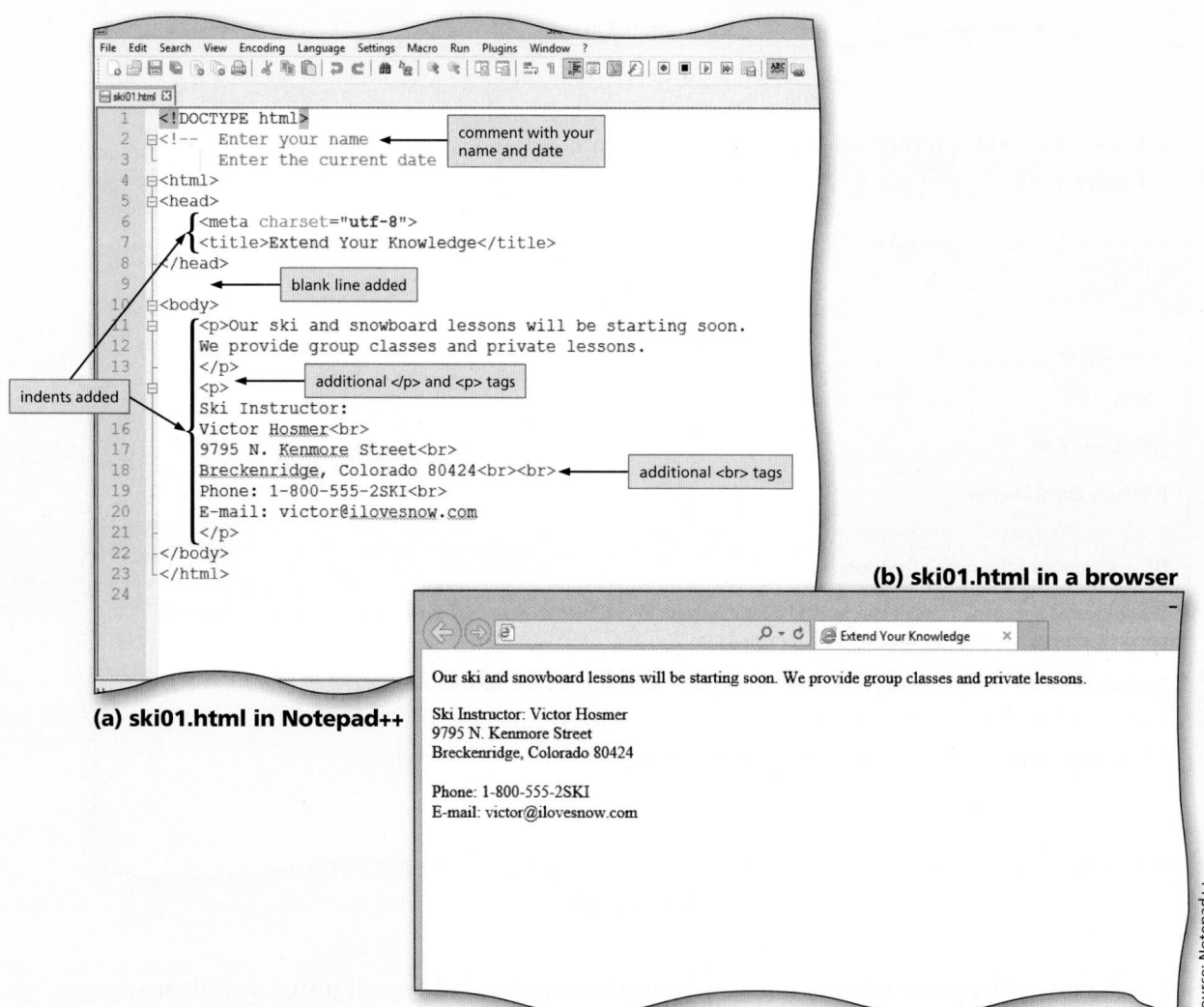

(a) ski01.html in Notepad++

(b) ski01.html in a browser

Source: Notepad++

Figure 1–51

Perform the following tasks:

1. HTML comments are inserted into a webpage using special tags with the following syntax:

   <!-- comment goes here -->

   A comment may be placed anywhere in the HTML document after the opening <!DOCTYPE html> statement and may be one or more lines long as needed. The only requirement is that the comment opens with the same four characters <!--, and ends with the same three characters, -->. In ski01.html, enter a comment after the opening <!DOCTYPE html> declaration statement that includes your name and the current date as shown in Figure 1–51a.

2. Enter the remaining tags and text shown in Figure 1–51a without any indents or blank lines. Save the file and open it in a browser. In a Word document named **ski01.docx**, answer these questions:

   a. How do HTML comments appear on the webpage when it is opened in a browser?

   b. How does the content within the <p> … </p> tags appear in a browser?

3. Return to your HTML editor and add blank lines and indents as shown in Figure 1–51a. Save the HTML file and refresh it in your browser to see the changes. In your Word document, answer these questions:

   a. What is the purpose of adding extra lines and indents in the HTML editor?

   b. How do the extra lines and indents change the way the webpage appears in the browser?

4. Add <p>, </p>, and <br> tags as shown in Figure 1–51a so that the content is rendered in the browser on multiple lines. In your Word document, answer these questions:

   a. What is the purpose of adding the <p> and </p> tags?

   b. What is the purpose of adding the <br> tags?

5. Save the HTML file and refresh it in your browser to see the changes. Compare Figure 1–51a and Figure 1–51b. In your Word document, identify how the following two lines use white space in the HTML editor and compare that to how the browser reads and displays the same line.

   a. "Our ski and snowboard…"

   b. "Phone: 1-800…"

6. Submit your assignment in the format specified by your instructor.

7. ✳ What would happen if webpage developers did not use comments, indents, and white space? Identify a potential problem associated with each.

Analyze, Correct, Improve

Analyze a webpage, correct all errors, and improve it.

Correcting HTML Errors

Note: To complete this assignment, you will be required to use the Data Files for Students. Visit www.cengage.com/ct/studentdownload for detailed instructions or contact your instructor for information about accessing the required files.

Instructions: Open your HTML editor and then open the analyze01.html file provided in the Data Files for Students. This document lists 10 HTML5 best practices in its body section. You will follow these 10 guidelines to correct the webpage as instructed. Save the page as **practices01.html**   in the same location and view it in a browser. Figure 1–52a shows the completed HTML document in Notepad++ and Figure 1–52b shows the completed webpage in a browser.

Continued >

STUDENT ASSIGNMENTS

Analyze, Correct, and Improve *continued*

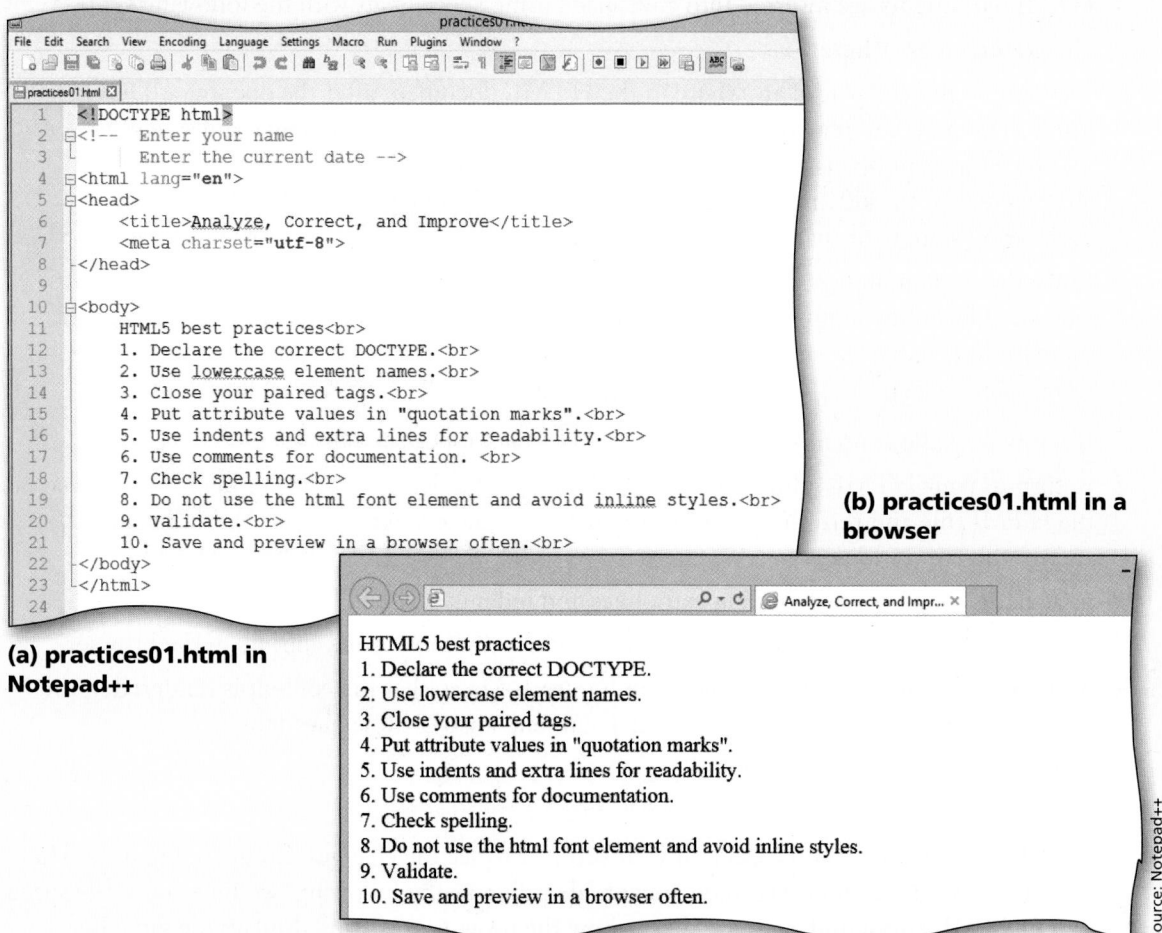

(a) practices01.html in Notepad++

(b) practices01.html in a browser

Source: Notepad++

Figure 1–52

1. **Correct**

   a. Replace the existing HTML4 DOCTYPE statement with the correct DOCTYPE statement for an HTML5 webpage.

   b. Go through the page and change all uppercase element and attribute names in the tags to lowercase.

   c. Go through the page and make sure all paired elements end with a closing slash (/) such as </title> or </head>.

   d. Go through the page and make sure all attribute values are surrounded by "quotation marks".

   e. Go through the page and add indents and extra lines for readability.

   f. Check the comments to make sure they start with <!-- and end with -->. Change the generic text in the comment to include *your* name and the current date.

   g. Select the content within the <body> . . . </body> tags and then check the spelling. Your HTML editor may have a spelling checker, or you may need to copy and paste the content into another program with a spelling checker such as Word. Fix any spelling errors you find.

   h. By completing Steps a–g, you have followed HTML5 best practices 1–7. You will learn about styles and validation in future chapters. Skip ahead to best practice 10 to save and view your webpage in a browser.

2. Improve

 a. In future chapters you will learn how to create an ordered list that automatically numbers each item in the list. For now, add a <br> tag after "HTML5 best practices" and after each item in the list to place the title and each item on the list on its own line.

 b. Save and preview the webpage.

 c. Submit your assignment in the format specified by your instructor.

3. ✳ Which error identified in Steps 1a–1g was the most difficult to find and correct? Use specific HTML terminology in your answer.

In the Labs

Labs 1 and 2, which increase in difficulty, require you to create webpages based on what you learned in the chapter. Lab 3 requires you to dive deeper into a topic covered in the chapter.

Lab 1: **Creating a Webpage from a Template and Using Placeholder Text**

Problem: You work for a local but rapidly growing gardening supply company that specializes in products to support food self-sufficiency. The company has identified a small number of extremely successful products that they want to market through a website and have hired you to get started. Create the webpage shown in Figure 1–53b that identifies the type of content you want to include on the company's home page. In later chapters, you will replace the placeholders with actual text and images.

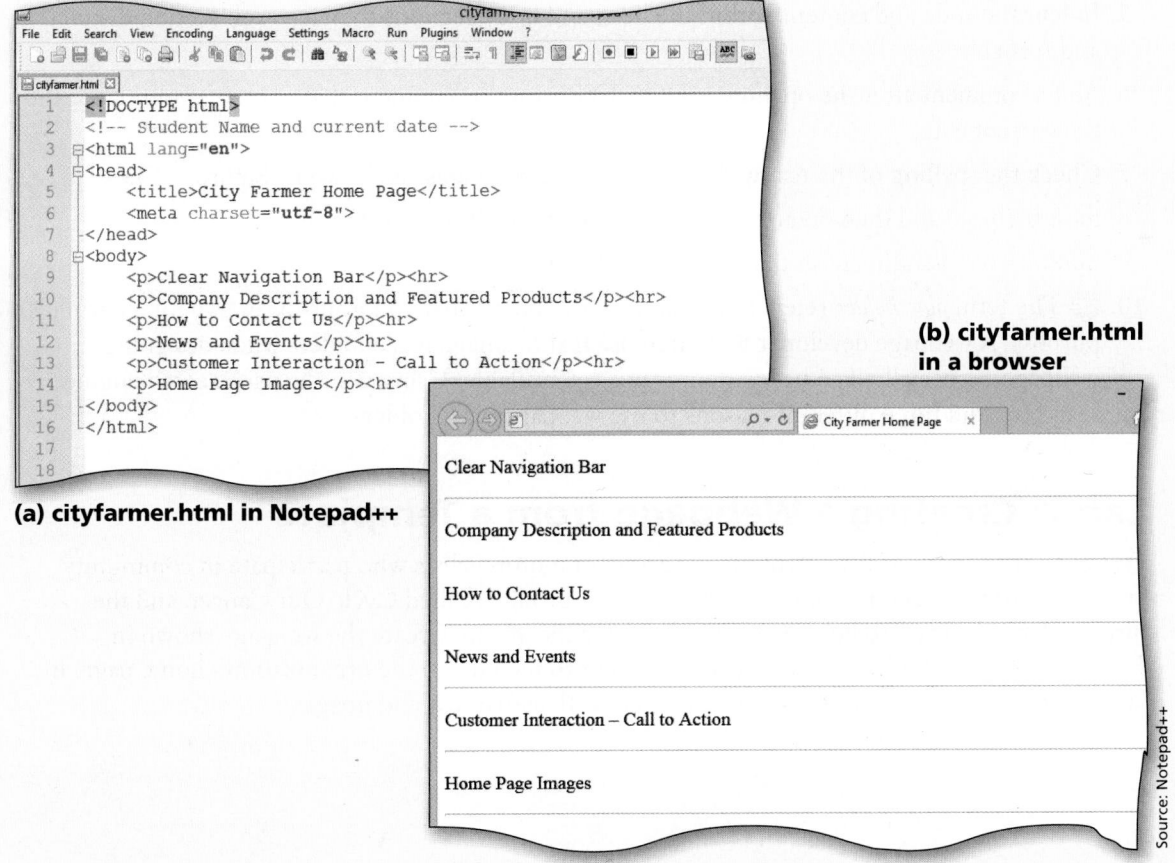

(a) cityfarmer.html in Notepad++

(b) cityfarmer.html in a browser

Source: Notepad++

Figure 1–53

Continued >

In the Labs *continued*

Instructions: Perform the following tasks:

1. If you created the template01.html file in the Apply Your Knowledge exercise in this chapter, open template01.html and then save it with the name `cityfarmer.html` in the chapter01\ lab1 folder provided with the Data Files for Students.

   If you did not create the template01.html file, enter the required HTML tags as shown in Figure 1–53a and then save the file with the name `cityfarmer.html` in the chapter01\ lab1 folder provided with the Data Files for Students.

2. Enter the text `City Farmer Home Page` within the <title> … </title> tags.

3. Within the body section, add the following content using six sets of paragraph tags. At this point, the content consists of six placeholder paragraphs that you will replace with actual webpage content in a later chapter.

```
<p>Clear Navigation Bar</p>

<p>Company Description and Featured Products</p>

<p>How to Contact Us</p>

<p>News and Events</p>

<p>Customer Interaction - Call to Action</p>

<p>Home Page Images</p>
```

4. Add an <hr> tag after each of the closing paragraph tags to insert a horizontal line after each paragraph.

5. Indent the code and content within the head and body sections to make each section distinct and readable.

6. Add a comment after the opening <!DOCTYPE html> statement that contains your name and the current date.

7. Check the spelling of the text within the title and body tags, as shown in Figure 1–53a.

8. Save the page and then open it in a browser, as shown in Figure 1–53b.

9. Submit your assignment in the format specified by your instructor.

10. ✳ The term *placeholder* refers to any area of a webpage that you want to reserve for a particular purpose. A webpage developer will often use text or image placeholders when designing webpages, especially if actual content is not yet available. Using your favorite search engine, search to find three different reasons to use webpage placeholders.

Lab 2: **Creating a Webpage from a Template**

Problem: You are part of a philanthropic group of motorcyclists who participate in community events and parades to raise cancer awareness. Your group is called Cycle Out Cancer, and the director has asked you to help create a website for the group. Create the webpage shown in Figure 1–54b, which identifies the type of content to include on the organization's home page. In later chapters, you will replace the placeholders with actual text and images.

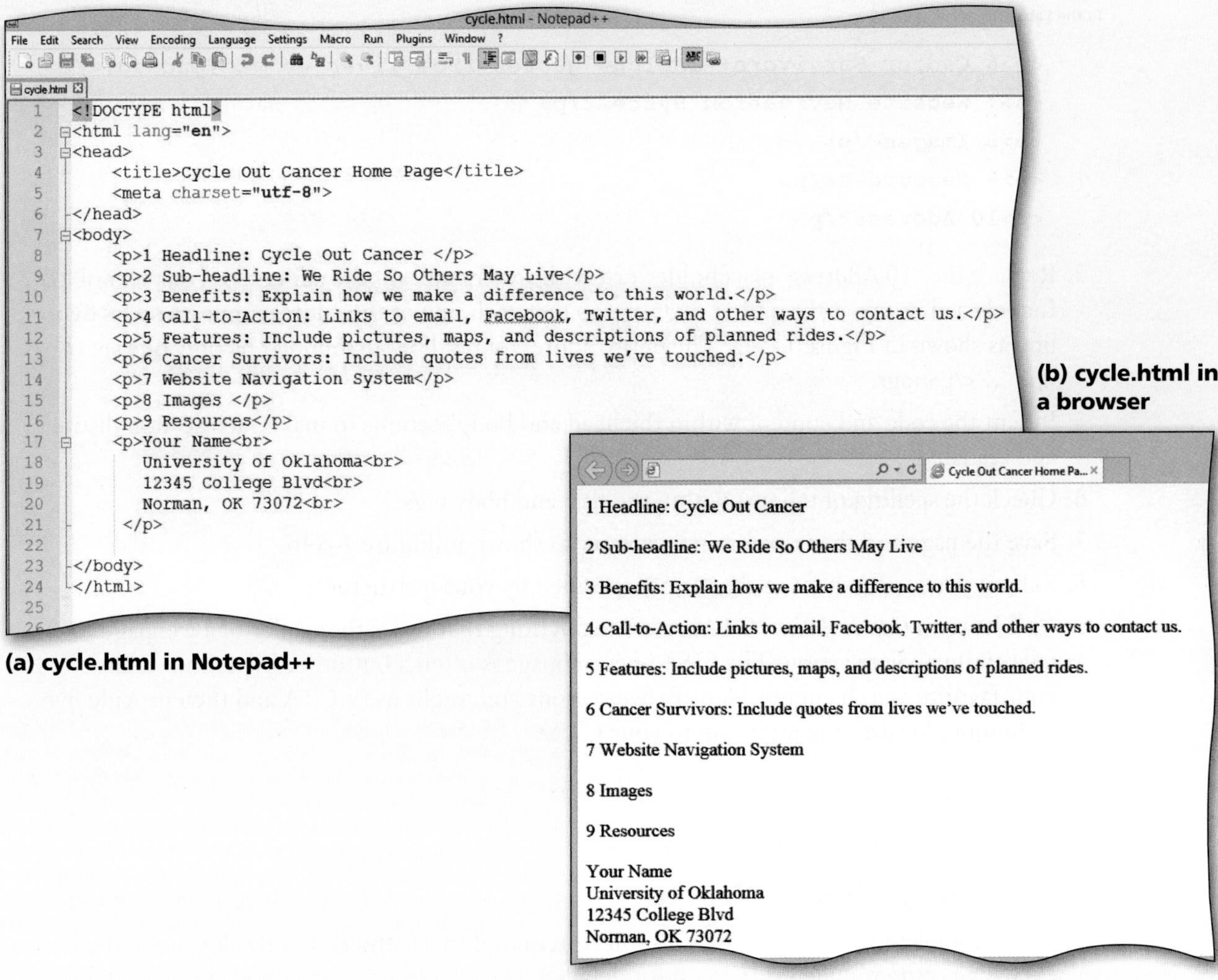

```
      cycle.html - Notepad++
File  Edit  Search  View  Encoding  Language  Settings  Macro  Run  Plugins  Window  ?

cycle.html

 1   <!DOCTYPE html>
 2   <html lang="en">
 3   <head>
 4       <title>Cycle Out Cancer Home Page</title>
 5       <meta charset="utf-8">
 6   </head>
 7   <body>
 8       <p>1 Headline: Cycle Out Cancer </p>
 9       <p>2 Sub-headline: We Ride So Others May Live</p>
10       <p>3 Benefits: Explain how we make a difference to this world.</p>
11       <p>4 Call-to-Action: Links to email, Facebook, Twitter, and other ways to contact us.</p>
12       <p>5 Features: Include pictures, maps, and descriptions of planned rides.</p>
13       <p>6 Cancer Survivors: Include quotes from lives we've touched.</p>
14       <p>7 Website Navigation System</p>
15       <p>8 Images </p>
16       <p>9 Resources</p>
17       <p>Your Name<br>
18       University of Oklahoma<br>
19       12345 College Blvd<br>
20       Norman, OK 73072<br>
21       </p>
22
23   </body>
24   </html>
25
26
```

(a) cycle.html in Notepad++

(b) cycle.html in a browser

Cycle Out Cancer Home Pa...

1 Headline: Cycle Out Cancer

2 Sub-headline: We Ride So Others May Live

3 Benefits: Explain how we make a difference to this world.

4 Call-to-Action: Links to email, Facebook, Twitter, and other ways to contact us.

5 Features: Include pictures, maps, and descriptions of planned rides.

6 Cancer Survivors: Include quotes from lives we've touched.

7 Website Navigation System

8 Images

9 Resources

Your Name
University of Oklahoma
12345 College Blvd
Norman, OK 73072

Source: Notepad++

Figure 1–54

Instructions: Perform the following tasks:

1. If you created the template01.html file in the Apply Your Knowledge exercise in this chapter, open template01.html and then save it with the name **cycle.html** in the chapter01\lab2 folder provided with the Data Files for Students.

   If you did not create the template01.html file, enter the required HTML tags as shown in Figure 1–54a and then save the file with the name **cycle.html** in the chapter01\lab2 folder provided with the Data Files for Students.

2. Enter the text **Cycle Out Cancer Home Page** within the <title> … </title> tags.

3. Within the body section, add the following content using 10 sets of paragraph tags. At this point, the content consists of 10 placeholder paragraphs that you will replace with actual webpage content in later chapters.

```
<p>1 Headline: Cycle Out Cancer</p>

<p>2 Sub-headline: We Ride So Others May Live</p>

<p>3 Benefits: Explain how we make a difference to this world.</p>

<p>4 Call-to-Action: Links to email, Facebook, Twitter, and other
ways to contact us.</p>

<p>5 Features: Include pictures, maps, and descriptions of planned
rides.</p>
```

Continued >

In the Labs *continued*

```
<p>6 Cancer Survivors: Include quotes from lives we've touched.</p>
<p>7 Website Navigation System</p>
<p>8 Images</p>
<p>9 Resources</p>
<p>10 Address</p>
```

4. Replace the "10 Address" placeholder text with *your* name and the address of your school. Include a <br> tag at the end of each line so that each line of the address appears on its own line as shown in Figure 1–54a. The entire address should be surrounded by only one set of <p> ... </p> tags.

5. Indent the code and content within the head and body sections to make each section distinct and readable.

6. Check the spelling of the text within the title and body tags.

7. Save the page and then open it in a browser as shown in Figure 1–54b.

8. Submit your assignment in the format specified by your instructor.

9. ✸ The term *Call to Action* (CTA) refers to anything that urges the reader of a webpage to take an immediate action. The CTA on a webpage is often a button or hyperlink. Using your favorite search engine, identify five reasons you might use a CTA and then provide five techniques for drawing attention to your CTAs.

Lab 3: Expand Your World
Publishing to a Website

Note: To complete this assignment, you will be required to use the Data Files for Students. Visit www.cengage.com/ct/studentdownload for detailed instructions or contact your instructor for information about accessing the required files.

Problem: If you want your webpages to be viewed by anyone connected to the Internet, you must store the pages on a web server. Transferring webpage files from your local computer to a web server is called publishing. Once your webpages are published on the web server, the server creates an http:// address that allows others to find and view your pages using any browser connected to the Internet.

Several key pieces of information and permissions need to be in place before you can successfully publish your webpages to a web server. This exercise will help you find and record the information you need to publish your webpages to your school's web server. If your school does not provide free web server space to students, this exercise will help you find free or inexpensive web server space where you can publish your webpages. (*Note:* Always check with your instructor regarding whether your webpages are to be published. Each school is set up differently, but this exercise helps you collect the necessary information.)

Instructions:

1. Ask your instructor if you are going to publish your webpages to a school web server and if any supporting documentation is available.

2. Open the webpublishing.docx document from the Data Files for Students.

3. Using the web server documentation provided by your instructor or school, fill out the right column of the table to identify the pieces of information needed to publish your webpages. A sample solution is provided in webpublishing.docx that applies to students at Johnson County Community College in Overland Park, Kansas.

4. Use the web to research three inexpensive web server alternatives.

5. Open the webserveralternatives.docx document from the Data Files for Students.

6. Using the information you found in Step 4, complete the table in the webserveralternatives. docx document to compare three web server alternatives. You may be asked to share and compare this information with the rest of the class.

7. Confirm if and how your instructor wants you to publish your webpages, as well as how your work will be submitted for grading purposes.

8. ✳ Some web hosting companies offer *free* web hosting services. However, all businesses need to generate revenue in order to survive. Using your favorite search engine, identify three ways *free* web hosting companies generate revenue.

✳ Consider This: Your Turn

Apply your creative thinking and problem-solving skills to design and implement a solution.

Note: To complete this assignment, you will be required to use the Data Files for Students. Visit www.cengage.com/ct/studentdownload for detailed instructions or contact your instructor for information about accessing the required files.

1. Design and Create a Personal Portfolio Website

Personal

Part 1: As in almost every field, the job market for the best jobs in web development are competitive. One way to give yourself a big edge in a job search is to create an appropriate personal portfolio website to showcase your skills. Plan the website by completing the table in the portfolio.docx document in the Data Files for Students. Answer the questions with thoughtful, realistic responses. Be sure to sketch the wireframe for your home page on the last page. Submit your assignment in the format specified by your instructor.

Part 2: ✳ What do you want this website to accomplish?

2. Design and Create a Website for a Web Development and Consulting Business

Professional

Part 1: When you are finished with college, you plan to join a web development and consulting firm to gain experience in the field. Your long-term goal is to start and own a web development and consulting firm. You decide to begin by designing a website you would eventually like to build for the firm. Start planning the website by completing the table in the webdevelopment.docx document in the Data Files for Students. Answer the questions with thoughtful, realistic responses. Be sure to sketch the wireframe for your home page on the last page. Submit your assignment in the format specified by your instructor.

Part 2: ✳ What are some general characteristics of any successful small business that you want this website to portray? What are some characteristics of a successful web development consulting firm that you want this website to portray?

Continued >

Consider This: Your Turn *continued*

3. Design and Create a Website for the Dog Hall of Fame

Research and Collaboration

Part 1: Dogs add an enormous amount of joy and happiness to a family. Some dogs guard and protect. Others fetch, herd, search, or hunt. Almost all pets provide loving companionship and unconditional acceptance. Because dogs play such a major role in the lives of their owners, your class has been approached by a retired veterinarian to help him build a website, the "Dog Hall of Fame," that honors three special dogs each year. The three award categories will include working dog, hero dog, and companion dog.

Your first order of business is to organize a group of three or four peers in your class to plan the website by completing the table in the doghalloffame.docx document in the Data Files for Students. Answer the questions with thoughtful, realistic responses. Be sure to sketch the wireframe for your home page on the last page. Submit your assignment in the format specified by your instructor.

Part 2: ✷ You made several decisions while planning the website for this assignment. Which two or three of the questions did you find the most difficult to answer and why? What additional information would be helpful in planning this website?

2 Building a Webpage Template with HTML5

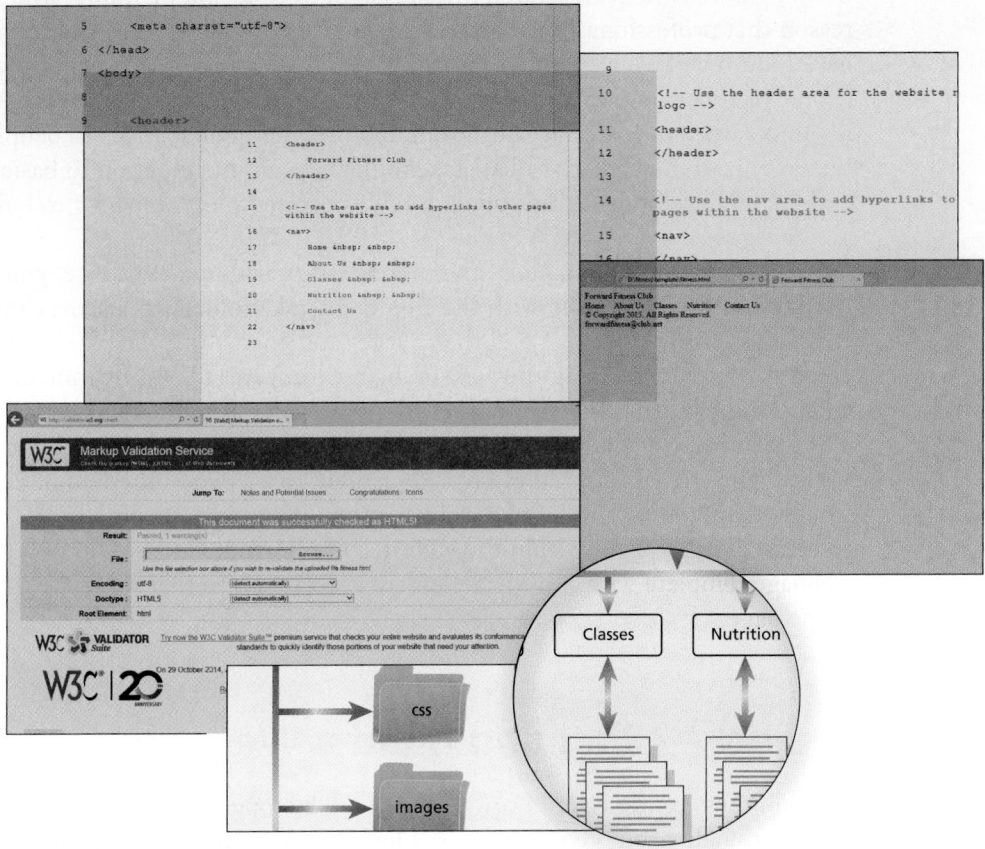

Objectives

You will have mastered the material in this chapter when you can:

- Explain how to manage website files

- Describe and use HTML5 semantic elements

- Determine the elements to use when setting the structure of a webpage

- Design and build a semantic wireframe

- Create a webpage template

- Insert comments in an HTML document

- Add static content to a webpage template

- Insert symbol codes and other character entities

- Describe the benefits of validating web documents

- Validate an HTML template

- Create a home page from an HTML template

- Add unique content to a webpage

2 | Building a Webpage Template with HTML5

Introduction

Building a website from scratch involves a lot of time and planning, which is one reason that professional web design services are in high demand. Some web designers have their own business and provide their services on contract to clients, who are people or other businesses that want to build or redesign a website. Other web designers work in larger organizations and provide their services to people within the organization, who are called stakeholders. As an introduction to basic website design and development, this book provides a foundation on which to build your web design skills.

As discussed in Chapter 1, before you start building a website, you must plan it, which includes meeting with the clients or stakeholders to discover their needs, the purpose of the website, and their target audience. After developing a plan, you can start constructing the website by creating an HTML document and then adding the required basic HTML elements so visitors can display the webpage in a browser. Next, include HTML5 elements to define the specific sections or areas of the webpage. This initial HTML document can serve as the template for the site. A **template** is a predefined webpage that contains a specific HTML structure to be used by all pages within the website. This chapter focuses on how to build a webpage template with HTML5 elements and then use that template to create a home page.

Project — Plan and Build a Website

A local fitness center called Forward Fitness Club opened recently and needs a website to help promote its business. The business owner wants the website to showcase the club's equipment, group fitness classes, nutrition information, and contact information. The owner hired you to plan and design the Forward Fitness Club website.

The project in this chapter follows generally accepted guidelines for planning and building the webpage template shown in Figure 2–1a to produce the home page shown in Figure 2–1b. The template contains code and text including the document title, header, navigation area, and footer, which is repeated on each page of the Forward Fitness Club website. The template also includes comments to remind the web designer about the purpose of each section.

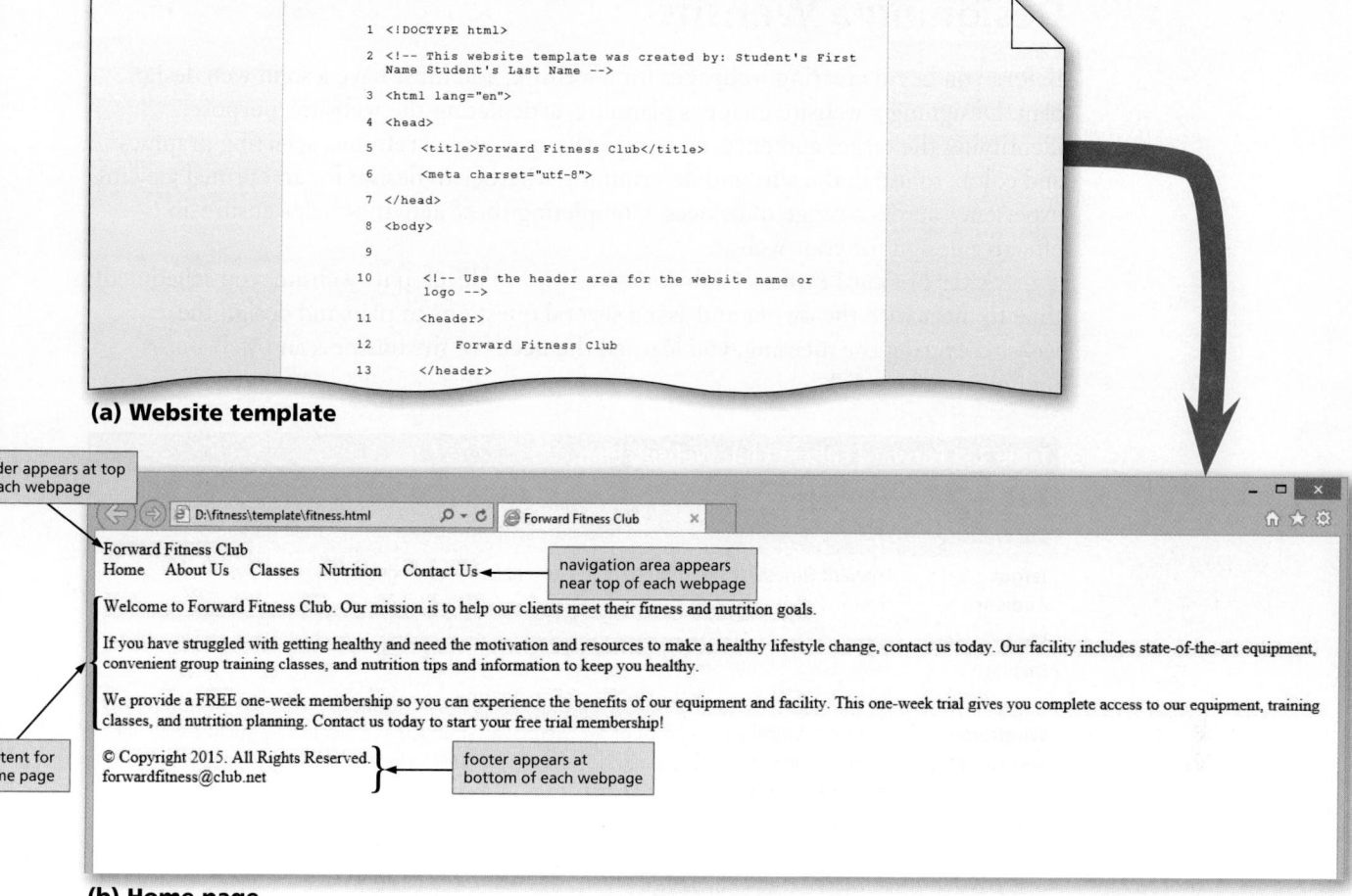

(a) Website template

header appears at top each webpage

navigation area appears near top of each webpage

content for home page

footer appears at bottom of each webpage

(b) Home page

Figure 2–1

Roadmap

In this chapter, you will learn how to create the webpage shown in Figure 2–1. The following roadmap identifies general activities you will perform as you progress through this chapter:

1. CREATE WEBSITE FOLDERS to organize files.
2. CREATE a TEMPLATE.
3. ENTER HTML5 SEMANTIC ELEMENTS in the document.
4. ADD COMMENTS AND CONTENT to the document.
5. VALIDATE the DOCUMENT.
6. CREATE AND VIEW the HOME PAGE.

At the beginning of step instructions throughout the chapter, you will see an abbreviated form of this roadmap. The abbreviated roadmap uses colors to indicate chapter progress: gray means the chapter is beyond that activity; blue means the task being shown is covered in that activity, and black means that activity is yet to be covered. For example, the following abbreviated roadmap indicates the chapter would be showing a task in the 4 ADD COMMENTS & CONTENT activity.

1 CREATE WEBSITE FOLDERS | 2 CREATE TEMPLATE | 3 ENTER HTML5 SEMANTIC ELEMENTS
4 ADD COMMENTS & CONTENT | 5 VALIDATE DOCUMENT | 6 CREATE & VIEW HOME PAGE

Use this abbreviated roadmap as a progress guide while you read or step through the instructions in this chapter.

Designing a Website

Before you begin creating webpages for a website, you must have a solid web design plan. Designing a website includes planning, articulating the website's purpose, identifying the target audience, creating a site map and wireframe, selecting graphics and colors to use in the site, and determining whether to design for an optimal viewing experience across a range of devices. Completing these activities helps ensure an effective design for your website.

After Forward Fitness Club contacted you to develop its website, you scheduled time to meet with the owner and asked several questions to plan and design the website. During the meeting, you learned the needs of the business and website, as outlined in Table 2–1.

Table 2–1 Forward Fitness Club Website Plan	
Purpose of the Website	To promote fitness services and gain new clients. The Forward Fitness Club mission: to facilitate a healthy lifestyle and help our clients meet their fitness and nutrition goals.
Target Audience	Forward Fitness Club customers are adults between the ages of 18 and 50 within the local community.
Multiplatform Display	Forward Fitness Club recognizes the growth in smartphone and tablet usage and wants a single website that provides an optimal viewing experience regardless of whether visitors are using a desktop, laptop, tablet, or smartphone.
Wireframe and Site Map	The initial website will consist of five webpages arranged in a hierarchal structure with links to the home page on every page. Each webpage will include a header area, navigation area, main content area, and footer area.
Graphics	Forward Fitness Club wants to display its fitness equipment and logo to help with local branding. Photos of the facility, members, and staff will increase visual appeal.
Color	Forward Fitness Club wants to use its logo colors, green and yellow, to promote health, strength, and a bright future.
Typography	To make the content easy to read, the website will use a serif font style for paragraphs, lists, and other body content, while providing contrast by using a sans serif font style for headings.
Accessibility	Standard accessibility attributes, such as alternative text for graphics, will be used to address accessibility. See Appendix D for an accessibility reference list.

Site Map

Recall that a site map indicates how the pages in a website relate to each other. To create a site map, you first need to know how many pages to include in the website. The owner of Forward Fitness Club has many ideas for the website, including some ambitious ones. To keep the website simple for now while allowing room for growth, you and the owner agree that the initial website will have a total of five webpages titled Home, About Us, Classes, Nutrition, and Contact Us. Because each page will contain links to all pages and accommodate future growth, the website will use a modified hierarchal structure. The webpages will include the following content:

- Home page: Introduces the fitness center and its mission statement
- About Us page: Showcases the facility's equipment and services
- Classes page: Includes a schedule of available group training and fitness classes
- Nutrition page: Provides nutrition tips and simple meal plans
- Contact Us page: Provides a phone number, email address, physical address, and form for potential clients to request additional information about the fitness center's services

Figure 2–2 depicts the site map for the Forward Fitness Club website.

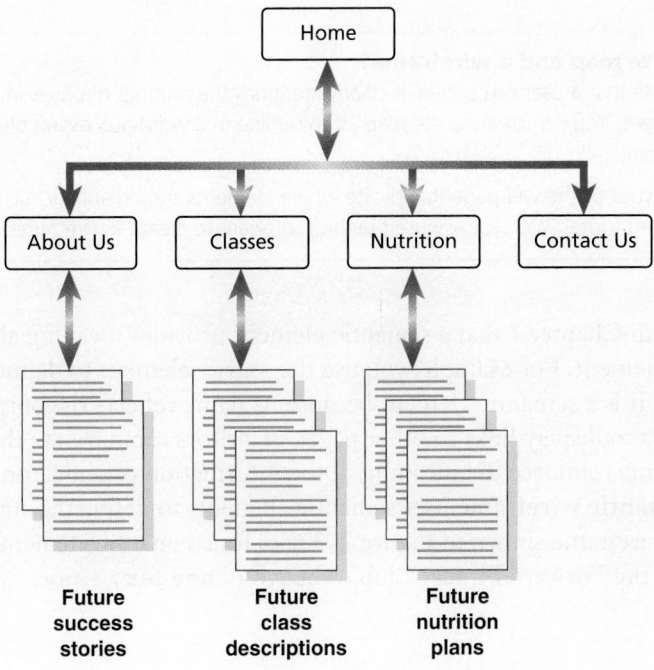

Figure 2–2

Wireframe

In addition to the site map for the Forward Fitness Club website, you have sketched out a webpage wireframe. Recall that a wireframe depicts the layout of a webpage, including its major content areas. Forward Fitness Club wants to promote its brand by including its logo, so each page will contain a designated area called the header for the logo. The header is located at the top of a webpage and identifies the site, often by displaying the business name or logo. For easy navigation, each page also will have a horizontal list of links to the other pages in the site. These page links will appear below the header in the navigation area. The primary page content, or the main content area, will follow the navigation area and will contain information that applies to the page, including headings, paragraphs of text, and images. Lastly, the footer will be located below the primary page content and will contain copyright and contact information. Figure 2–3 shows the proposed wireframe with these major content areas.

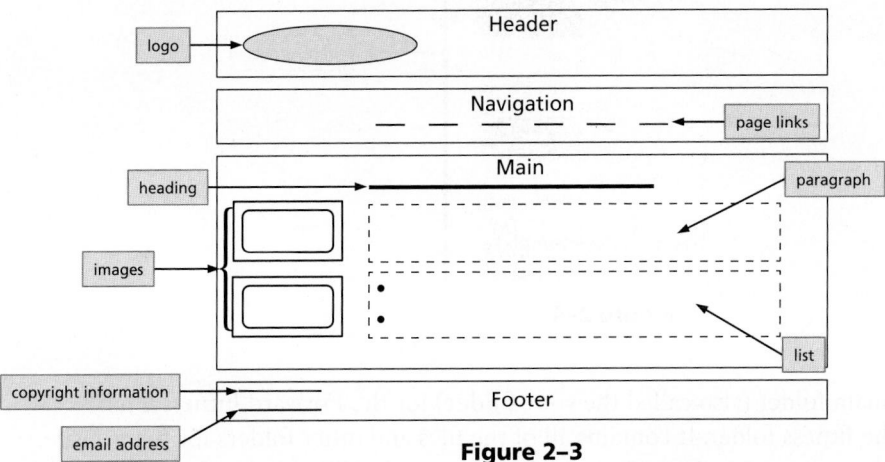

Figure 2–3

What is the difference between a site map and a wireframe?

A site map lists all the webpages in a website that a user can access. It clearly identifies the number of pages in the website and shows how each page is linked to other pages. You can create a site map as an outline in a word processing document or as an image using flowcharting or graphics software.

In contrast, a wireframe shows the visual layout of the webpage to indicate where elements should appear such as the logo, search box, navigation bar, main content, and footer. You typically use graphics software to create a wireframe.

Recall from Chapter 1 that a semantic element provides meaning about the content of the element. For example, you use the `nav` element to define the navigation area. It is a semantic element because its name reflects the purpose of its content, which is to display links to other pages so visitors can navigate the website. Semantic elements reinforce the meaning of the information provided on the webpage. A **semantic wireframe** uses semantic elements to define the structure of a webpage. The wireframe shown in Figure 2–3 uses four semantic elements to define the structure of the Forward Fitness Club webpages: `header, nav, main,` and `footer`.

File Management

Websites use several types of files, including HTML files, image files, media such as audio and video files, and CSS files, which you learn about in Chapter 4. Even a simple website might use hundreds of files. Therefore, each site must follow a systematic method to organize its files. Before you begin to create your first HTML page, start by creating a folder and subfolders to contain and organize your website files as shown in Figure 2–4.

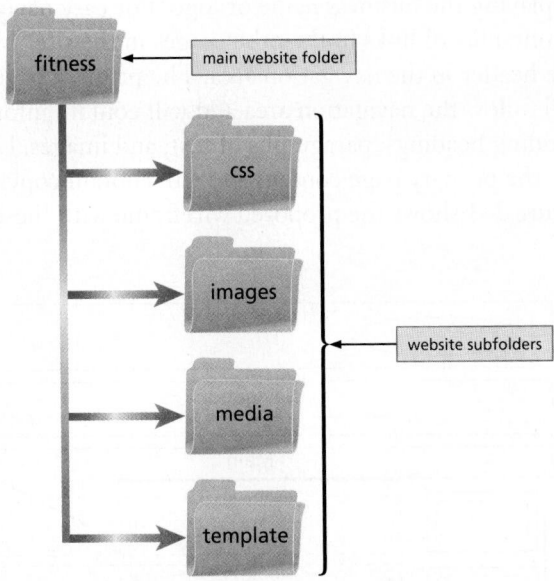

Figure 2–4

The main folder (also called the **root folder**) for the Forward Fitness Club website is the fitness folder. It contains all of the files and other folders for the website. The css folder will contain CSS files, which you create in Chapter 4 to format a webpage and its elements. The images folder will contain the Forward Fitness Club logo, photos, and other images to display on the webpages. The media folder will contain audio and video files, which you add in Chapter 9. The template folder contains the template document for the site's webpages, which you create in this chapter.

To Create a Website Folder and Subfolders

The following steps, which assume Windows 8.1 is running, create a folder and subfolders for the fitness website. *Why? Before you can create a website, you should create a folder for the website files.* You may need to ask your instructor whether you should create the website folder on a portable storage device, such as a USB flash drive.

- If necessary, tap or click the Desktop tile on the Windows 8.1 Start screen to display the desktop.
- Tap or click the File Explorer app button on the taskbar to display the File Explorer window.
- Navigate to the desired location for the website folder, such as the Documents folder or your USB flash drive, to prepare to create a new folder.
- Tap or click the New folder button on the Quick Access toolbar to create a new folder.
- Type **fitness** and then press the ENTER key to name the folder (Figure 2–5).

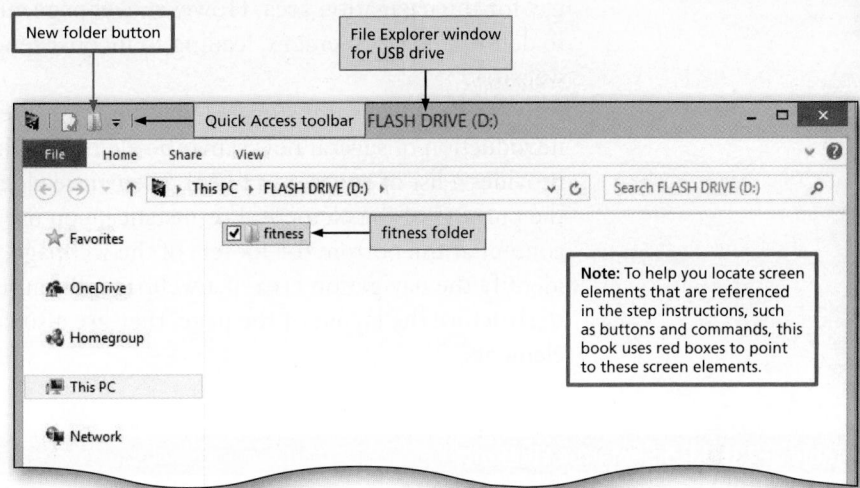

Figure 2–5

- Double-tap or double-click the fitness folder to open it.
- Tap or click the New folder button on the Quick Access toolbar to create a new folder.
- Name the new folder **css**.
- Tap or click the New folder button on the Quick Access toolbar to create a new folder.
- Name the new folder **images**.
- Tap or click the New folder button on the Quick Access toolbar to create a new folder.
- Name the new folder **media**.
- Tap or click the New folder button on the Quick Access toolbar to create a new folder.
- Name the new folder **template** (Figure 2–6).

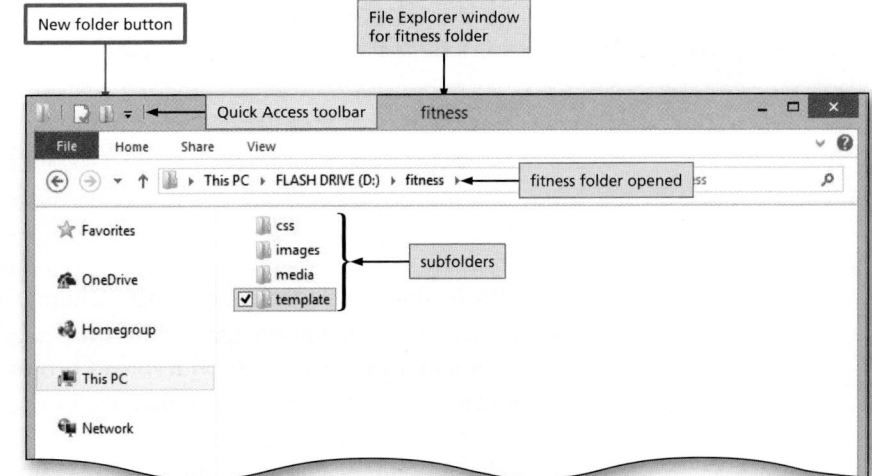

Figure 2–6

Other Ways

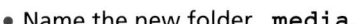

1 Tap or click New folder button (Home tab | New group)
2 Press CTRL+SHIFT+N
3 Press and hold or right-click blank spot in window, tap or click New, tap or click Folder

Using HTML5 Semantic Elements

As you learned in Chapter 1, you begin a new HTML document by adding the basic required HTML elements to it, such as the `html, head,` and `body` elements. Within the `body` element, you next add HTML elements that define the structure of the page. HTML 4.01 introduced the `div` element (with the <div> and </div> tags) to divide a page into separate sections. Each `div` element has a unique name to distinguish it from other `div` elements on the page. For example, you might use a `div` element named header for the header area and another `div` element named nav for the navigation area. However, webpage authors can use any name they like to define a `div` element, leading to inconsistency among naming conventions for websites.

HTML5 has transformed and improved website development with the introduction of several new semantic elements with standardized names. Table 2–2 provides a list of common HTML5 semantic elements. The name of each tag reflects the purpose of the element. For instance, you use the `footer` element to display content at the bottom (or footer) of the webpage. You use the `nav` element to identify the navigation area of a webpage. Because many of the semantic elements help to structure the layout of the page, they are also called structural elements or layout elements.

Table 2–2 HTML5 Semantic Elements	
Element	**Description**
<header>…</header>	Indicates the header information on the webpage. Header content typically consists of a business name or logo and is commonly positioned immediately after the opening <body> tag.
<nav>…</nav>	Indicates the start and end of a navigation area within the webpage. The `nav` element contains hyperlinks to other webpages within a website and is commonly positioned immediately after the closing </header> tag.
<main>…</main>	Indicates the start and end of the main content area of a webpage. Contains the primary content of the webpage. Only one main element can appear on a page.
<footer>…</footer>	Indicates the start and end of the footer area of a webpage. Contains the footer content of the webpage.
<section>…</section>	Indicates the start and end of a section area of a webpage. Contains a specific grouping of content on the webpage.
<article>…</article>	Indicates the start and end of an article area of a webpage. Contains content such as forum or blog posts.
<aside>…</aside>	Indicates the start and end of an aside area of a webpage. Contains information about nearby content and is typically displayed as a sidebar.

Professional web designers debate whether to use the `div` element or the `main` element to define the main content area of a webpage. Those who favor the `div` element argue that it has widespread browser support. The W3C introduced the `main` element after other semantic elements, and not all browsers or text editors recognize it yet.

Web designers who favor the `main` element do so because `main` is a semantic element while `div` is not. In other words, the name of the `main` element describes its purpose and function. The `div` element relies on its id attribute to provide meaning.

After discussing the pros and cons of the `main` and `div` elements with the owner of the Forward Fitness Club, you decide to use the `main` element for the fitness website. Because it is a new site that does not have to incorporate webpages created with earlier versions of HTML, it will use the new HTML5 structural elements, including `header`, `nav`, `main`, and `footer`, to lay out the webpages. Although the `div` element achieves the same results in layout, the future of web development includes using the new HTML5 layout tags, and Forward Fitness wants to create a foundation for this future. Using the semantic HTML5 elements standardizes naming conventions, making webpages more universal, accessible, and meaningful to search engines.

CONSIDER THIS

How can I find out whether my browser supports the new HTML5 elements?
Most major browsers have embraced several of the new HTML5 semantic tags. To know whether your preferred browser supports specific tags, visit caniuse.com and enter the name of the semantic element. The site lists the browsers and versions that support the element you entered. This site also provides information about the global usage of major browsers and their share of the market. Currently, the main element is not fully supported by Internet Explorer 11 or earlier.

Another good resource for up-to-date information on HTML5 is html5rocks.com. This site provides links to several HTML5 resources, including a timeline of HTML5 browser support of specific elements.

Header Element

The `header` element structurally defines the header area of a webpage. The `header` element starts with a <header> tag and ends with a </header> tag. Content placed between these tags appears on the webpage as part of the `header` element. Web designers often place a business name or logo within the `header` element.

Nav Element

The nav element structurally defines the navigation area of a webpage. The `nav` element starts with a <nav> tag and ends with a </nav> tag. The `nav` element usually includes links to other pages within the website.

Main Element

The `main` element structurally defines the `main` content area of a webpage. The main element starts with a <main> tag and ends with a </main> tag. Each page can have only one `main` element because its content should be unique to each page. At the time this book was written, all major browsers supported the `main` element, with the exception of Internet Explorer 11 and earlier versions. While Internet Explorer 11 will display content within the `main` element, it does not fully support the element. For example, Internet Explorer 11 might not correctly display formatting applied to the `main` element.

Footer Element

The `footer` element structurally defines the bottom, or footer area, of a webpage. The footer element starts with a <footer> tag and ends with a </footer> tag. Common content found within a webpage footer includes copyright information, contact information, and page links.

Figure 2–7 identifies the relationship between a coded webpage template with **header, nav, main,** and **footer** elements and the conceptual wireframe design of a webpage.

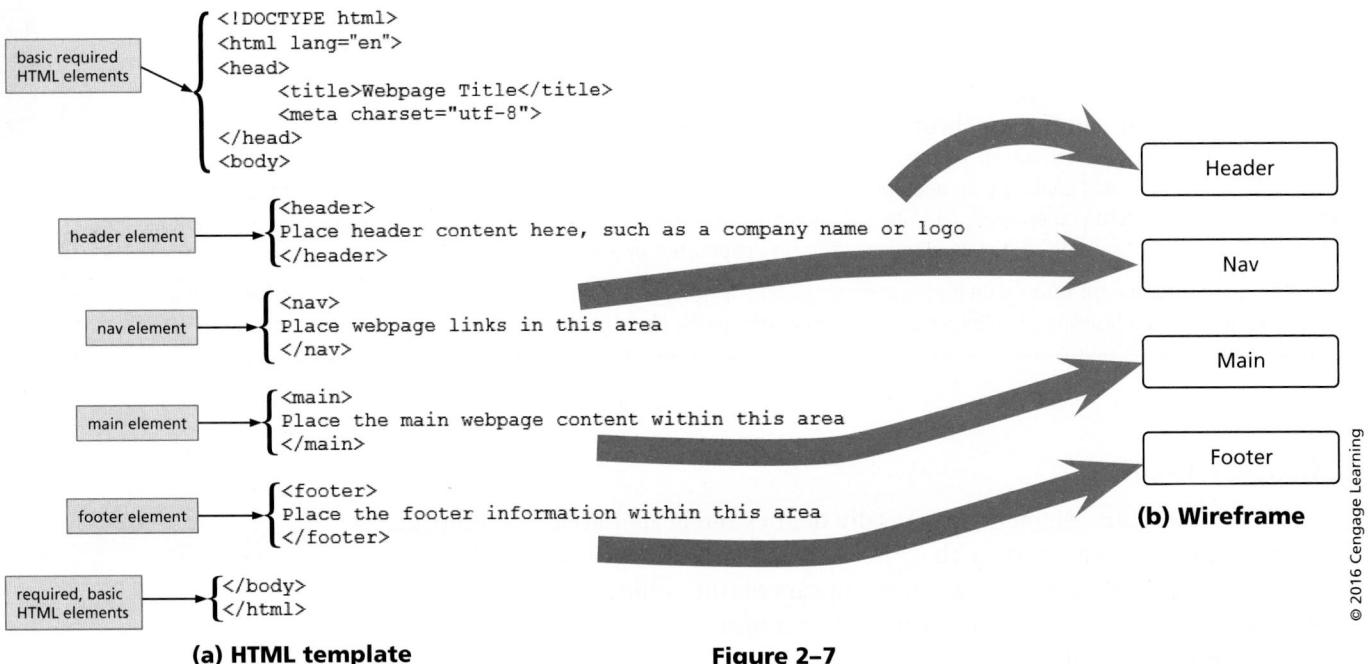

(a) HTML template

Figure 2–7

© 2016 Cengage Learning

Creating a Webpage Template

A hallmark of a well-designed website is that its webpages have the same look and feel. In other words, most pages have the same layout and all the pages share the same color scheme, typography, and style of graphics. In addition, elements work the same way on each page. For example, the navigation bar appears in the same position on each page and uses the same colors, fonts, and font styles. Visitors select a link on the navigation bar the same way, such as by tapping or clicking a page name. The selected link then appears in a contrasting color.

To make sure the webpages in a site share a standard layout, you can create a template, an HTML document that contains elements that should appear on each page. Instead of creating a webpage from scratch, open the template document in a text editor and save it using the name of the new webpage. You can then concentrate on adding content for that particular page rather than re-creating the basic required HTML elements and the structural elements.

For the fitness website, you can create a template that includes the basic required HTML elements (the DOCTYPE declaration and the **html, head, title, meta,** and **body** elements) and the four HTML structural semantic elements identified in the webpage wireframe shown in Figure 2–3: **header, nav, main,** and **footer.**

BTW
Saving Your Work
It is a good idea to save your HTML file periodically as you are working to avoid the risk of losing your work.

To Create a Webpage Template Document

To create a webpage template, you create an HTML document with the HTML elements that define the webpage structure. Use your preferred text editor to create the template or ask your instructor which text editor to use. The following steps create a basic webpage template.

1

- Open your text editor, tap or click File on the menu bar, and then tap or click New if you need to open a new blank document.
- Tap or click File on the menu bar and then tap or click Save As to display the Save As dialog box.
- Navigate to your fitness folder and then double-tap or double-click the template folder to open it.
- In the File name box, type **fitness** to name the file.

Q&A Why is the new file named fitness instead of index?
Fitness is the name of the template file you use to create webpages for this website. Use index as the file name for the home page.

- Tap or click the Save as type button and then tap or click Hyper Text Markup Language to select the file format.
- Tap or click the Save button to save the template in the template folder.
- On Line 1 of the text editor, type **<!DOCTYPE html>** to define a new HTML5 document (Figure 2–8).

Q&A Why does the <!DOCTYPE html> text appear in bold and red in Figure 2–8?
Throughout the book, the new text you add to a file in the current step is shown in bold and red in the accompanying figure.

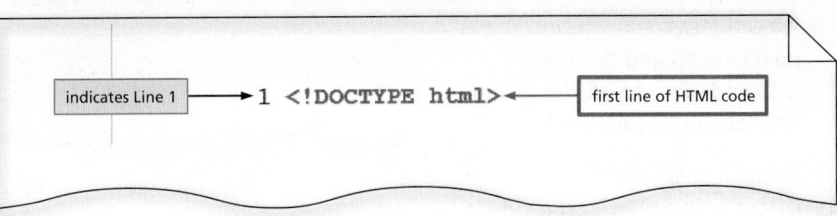

Figure 2–8

2

- Press the ENTER key to add Line 2 and then type **<html lang="en">** to add a starting <html> tag that defines the language as English.

- Press the ENTER key to add Line 3 and then type **<head>** to add a starting <head> tag (Figure 2–9).

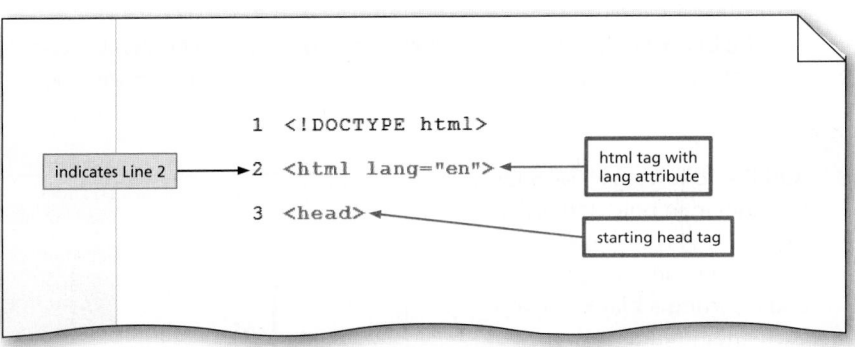

Figure 2–9

3

- Add the following HTML elements, also shown in bold and red in Figure 2–10, to complete the template, using the SPACEBAR or TAB key to indent Lines 4 and 5 and using the SHIFT+TAB keys to stop indenting.

```
<title></title>
<meta charset="utf-8">
</head>
<body>
</body>
</html>
```

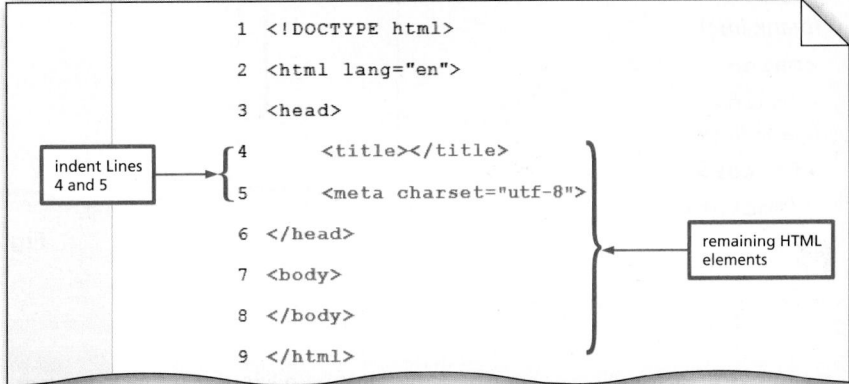

Figure 2–10

4

- Save your changes.

To Add HTML5 Semantic Elements to a Webpage Template

The wireframe in Figure 2–3 defines four areas to display content for the website. To define these content areas, insert the following HTML5 tags between the <body> and </body> tags: <header> </header>, <nav> </nav>, <main> </main>, and <footer> </footer>. Recall that the HTML5 **header** element defines the header area of the webpage. The **nav** element defines the navigation area of the webpage. The **main** element defines the primary content area of the webpage. The **footer** element defines the footer area of the webpage. The following steps insert HTML5 structural elements within the body tags.

- Place your insertion point after the beginning <body> tag and press the ENTER key twice to insert new Lines 8 and 9.

- On Line 9, press the TAB key and then type **<header>** to add a starting header tag.

- Press the ENTER key to insert a new Line 10 and then type **</header>** to add an ending header tag (Figure 2–11).

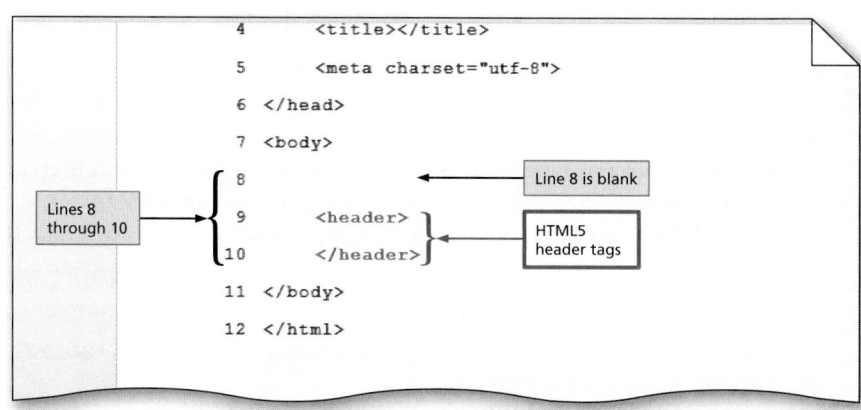

Figure 2–11

Q&A ◁ Why is Line 8 blank?
Line 8 is intentionally left blank to improve readability. As you add more HTML elements to a page, including white space helps to clearly identify the areas of a page. Using blank lines between HTML elements is a good design practice.

Will the blank line be noticeable when the page is displayed in a browser?
No. Browsers ignore blank lines when interpreting the code on the page.

- Add the following HTML5 tags, also shown in bold and red in Figure 2–12, to complete the wireframe, indenting each line and inserting a blank line after each ending tag.

<nav>

</nav>
(blank line)

<main>

</main>
(blank line)

<footer>

</footer>

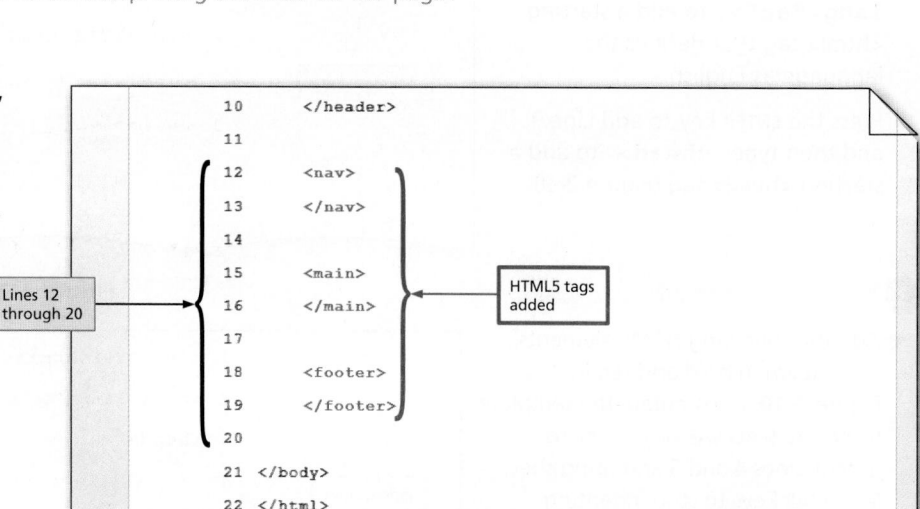

Figure 2–12

③

- Save your changes.

Q&A ◁ In Notepad++, why are the **main** tags not blue like the **header, nav,** and **footer** tags?
Because the **main** element is not completely supported by the current version of Internet Explorer (Internet Explorer 11), one of the most widely used browsers, the **main** element is not color-coded. However, Notepad++ still recognizes the main tags and pairs them together when you tap or click a tag.

To Add a Title to a Webpage Template

Recall that when a webpage is displayed in a browser, the browser tab displays the document title. To add a document title, type the title text between the starting and ending title tags. The following steps add a webpage title to a template.

- Place your insertion point after the beginning <title> tag and type **Forward Fitness Club** to add a webpage title.

- Save your changes and then view the page in a browser to display the webpage title (Figure 2–13).

Q&A

How do I display the webpage in a browser?
Recall from Chapter 1 that you can use a command in your HTML text editor to display a webpage. For example, in Notepad++, you can tap or click Run on the menu bar and then tap or click Launch in IE.

Why is the webpage blank when displayed in a browser?
You are creating a webpage template that will be used to create pages for the website. The subsequent webpages will contain content, but you have not added any content yet.

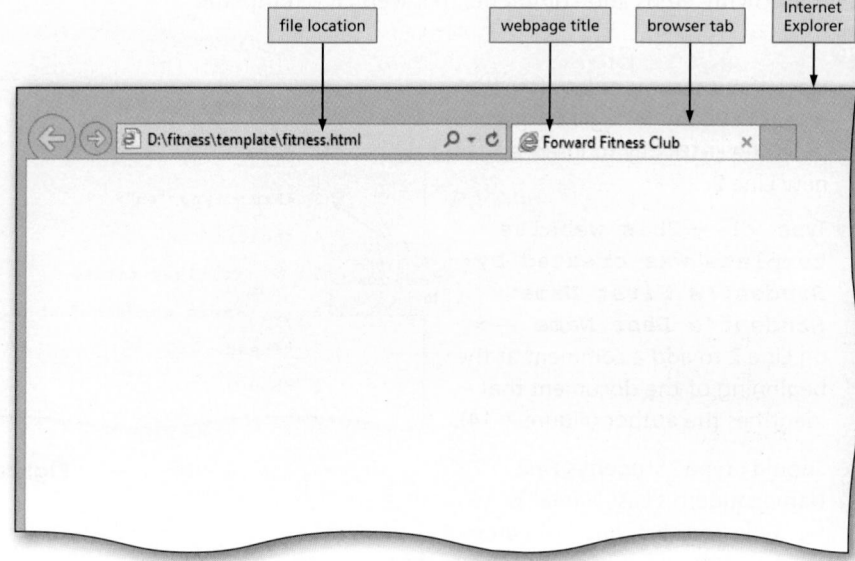

Figure 2–13

Comments

As you create a webpage template, include comments about the HTML elements you use to define the areas within the webpage. Comments can provide additional information about these areas and the type of information they include, which is especially helpful if you stop working on a partially completed page and then return to it later. Add a comment before a tag using the following syntax:

```
<!-- Place your comment here -->
```

The comment syntax uses the angle brackets, similar to the HTML tags. The next character is an exclamation mark followed by two dashes (--). Add the comment text after the first set of dashes. For example, you use comments to give instructions on how to use the template or to identify the author of the website. Close the comment by adding two dashes, followed by a closing angle bracket.

If you are using Notepad++, the text you enter scrolls continuously to the right unless you turn on the word wrap feature. **Word wrap** causes text lines to break at the right edge of the window and appear on a new line, so all entered text is visible in the Notepad++ window. When word wrap is enabled, a paragraph of text is assigned a single logical line number even though it may be displayed on multiple physical lines in Notepad++. Word wrap does not affect the way text prints.

BTW

Auto-Fill and Highlighting Features
If you are using Notepad++ or Sublime, you can use the auto-fill feature by starting to type the name of a tag and letting the text editor complete the tag for you. If you are using Notepad++, tap or click the starting <body> tag to highlight the starting and ending tags so you can easily identify them.

BTW

Turning on Word Wrap
To turn on word wrap in Notepad++, select View on the menu bar and then select Word wrap.

To Add Comments to a Webpage Template

When you create a webpage template, including comments provides additional information about how to use the sections of the webpage. You can also use a comment to identify that you are the author of the webpage. *Why? When creating a new webpage from a template, comments provide insight on the type of information to include.* The following steps add comments to a webpage template.

1

• Place the insertion point after the <!DOCTYPE html> tag and then press the ENTER key to insert a new Line 2.

• Type `<!-- This website template was created by: Student's First Name Student's Last Name -->` on Line 2 to add a comment at the beginning of the document that identifies the author (Figure 2–14).

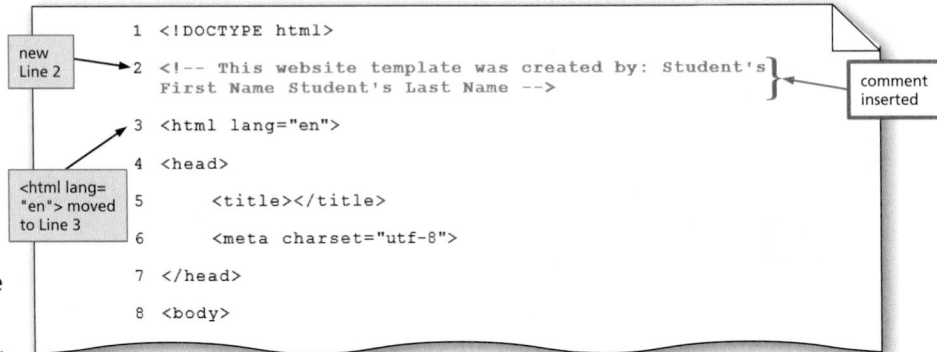

Figure 2–14

Q&A Should I type "Student's First Name Student's Last Name"?
No. Type your first and last names to identify yourself as the author of the template.

My comment is shown on two lines. Is that okay?
Yes. If your text editor is using word wrap and your document window is not maximized, your comment might wrap to the next line. Note, however, that it is still numbered as Line 2.

2

• Place the insertion point on the blank Line 9 and press the ENTER key to insert a new Line 10.

• On Line 10, press the TAB key and then type `<!-- Use the header area for the website name or logo -->` to add a comment identifying the type of information to include in the header area (Figure 2–15).

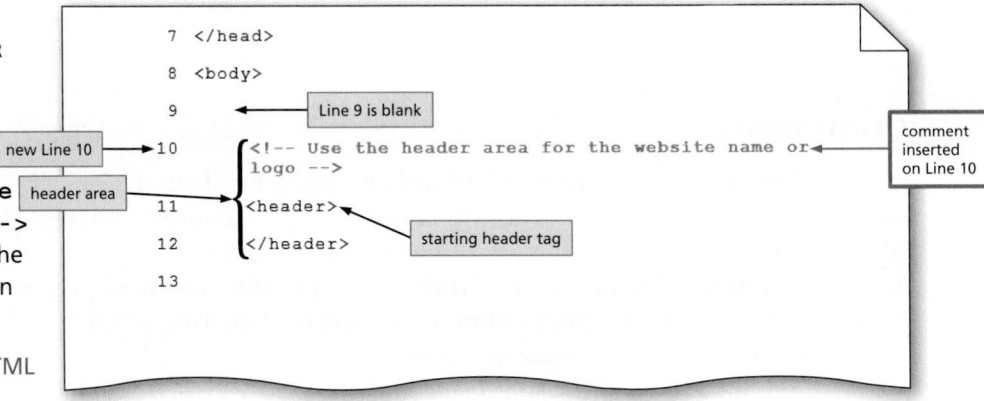

Figure 2–15

Q&A Do the blank lines affect the HTML elements?
No. inserting blank lines before or after HTML elements does not affect the structure of the webpage.

3

• Place the insertion point on the blank Line 13 and press the ENTER key to insert a new Line 14.

• On Line 14, type `<!-- Use the nav area to add hyperlinks to other pages within the website -->` to add a comment above the navigation area (Figure 2–16).

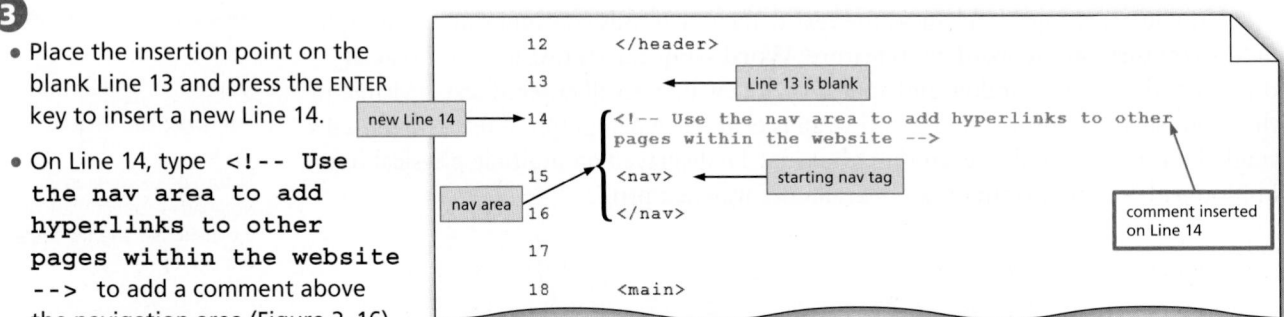

Figure 2–16

4

- Place the insertion point on the blank Line 17 and press the ENTER key to insert a new Line 18.

- On Line 18, type `<!-- Use the main area to add the main content of the webpage -->` to add a comment above the main area.

- Place the insertion point on the blank Line 21 and press the ENTER key to insert a new Line 22.

- On Line 22, type `<!-- Use the footer area to add webpage footer content -->` to add a comment above the footer area (Figure 2–17).

5

- Save your changes.

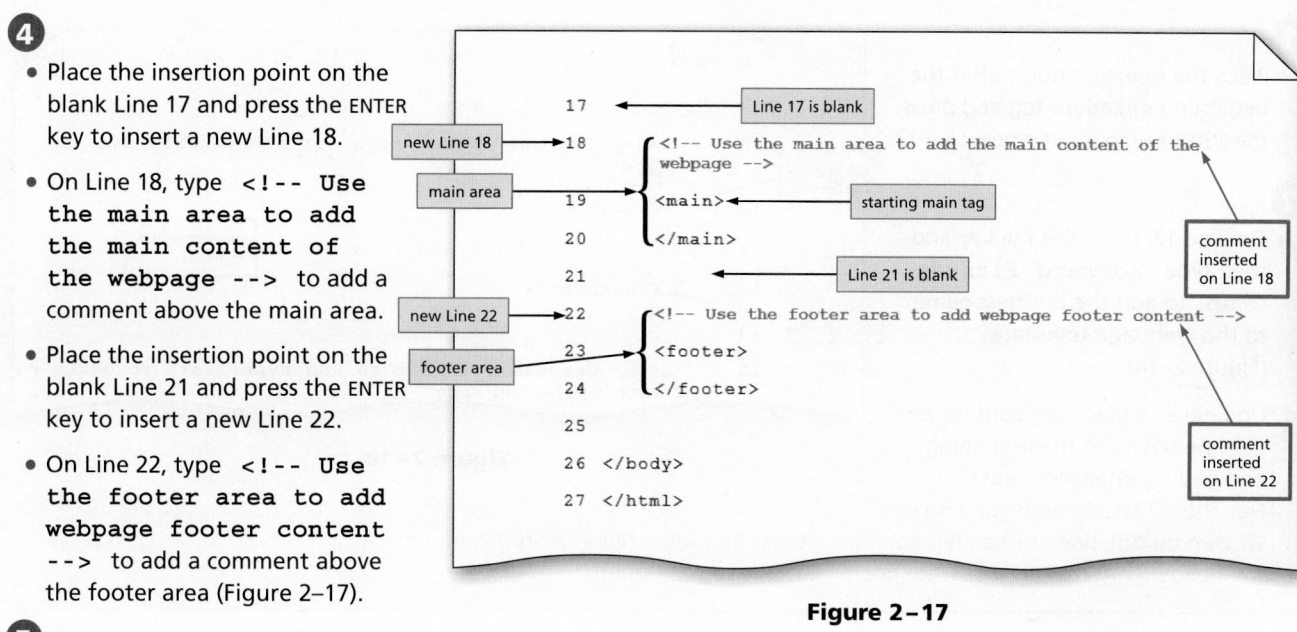

Figure 2–17

Break Point: If you want to take a break, this is a good place to do so. You can exit the text editor now. To resume at a later time, run your text editor, open the file called fitness.html, and continue following the steps from this location forward.

Webpage Content

After inserting the HTML tags and comments for a webpage template, add static content or content that will appear on every webpage, such as the business name or logo, the webpage links, and the footer information. Content is the text or other item that is displayed in a browser. Place content between the starting and ending tags. Following is an example of content added between header tags:

`<header>Forward Fitness Club</header>`

For the Forward Fitness Club website, the header area contains the business name, which will appear at the top of every page. (In Chapter 3, you replace the text with a graphic logo.) Other tags that contain static content include the nav area, which contains links to all pages within the website and will remain the same on each page. In addition, the footer area, which contains the copyright notice and an email address, will remain the same throughout the website.

Adding static content to a template saves time. Remember that the template will be used to create the webpages for the website. Because this content is meant to be displayed on each page, add it to the template once rather than to each page many times.

To Add Content to the Header Section

Now that the webpage template structure is complete, you can add static content that will appear on each webpage within the website. The header of each webpage in the fitness website should display the name of the business, Forward Fitness Club. For now, you enter the business name as text. In Chapter 3, you insert an image that displays the business logo, including a graphic and the business name. The following steps add content to the header area of a webpage template.

1

- Place the insertion point after the beginning <header> tag and press the ENTER key to insert a new Line 12.

2

- On Line 12, press the TAB key and then type **Forward Fitness Club** to add the business name to the webpage template (Figure 2–18).

Q&A Do I have to place the content on the line between the beginning and ending <header> tags?
No. This HTML element can also be written on one line as <header>Forward Fitness Club</header>. In Step 2, you place the header content on a separate line for improved readability.

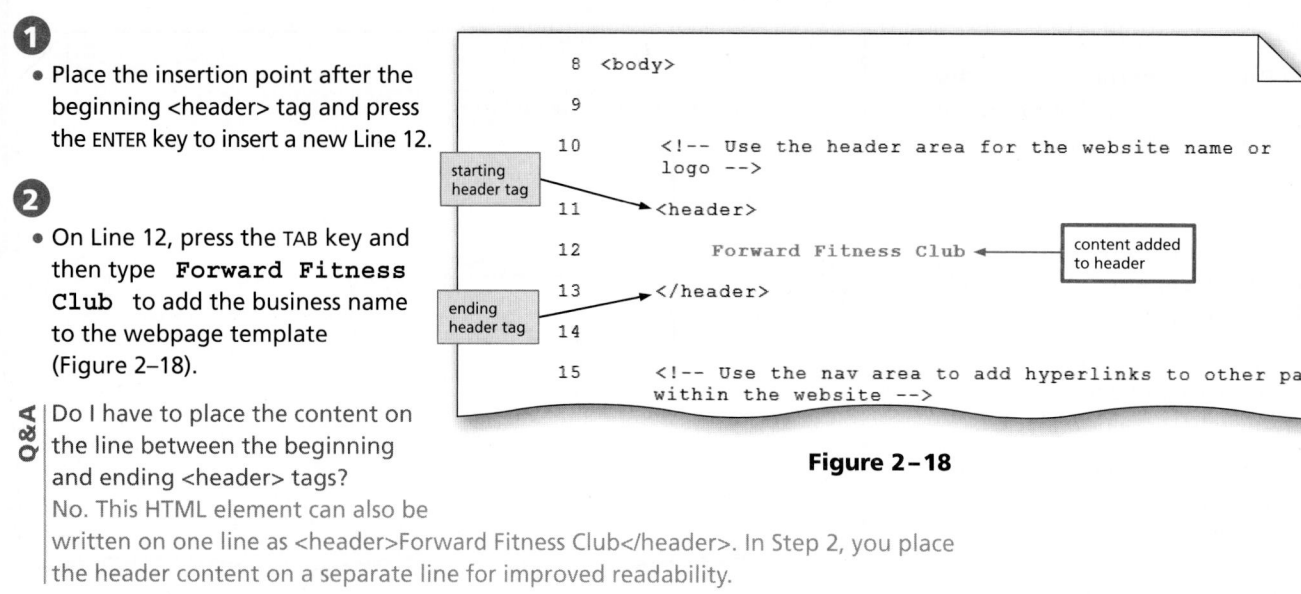

```
 8  <body>

 9

10      <!-- Use the header area for the website name or
         logo -->

11      <header>

12          Forward Fitness Club

13      </header>

14

15      <!-- Use the nav area to add hyperlinks to other pa
         within the website -->
```

Figure 2–18

Using Symbol Entities

When adding content to a webpage, you often need to insert symbols, such as a copyright symbol, ©. Some symbols such as less than (<) or greater than (>) are reserved for other uses, such as signifying the start and end of HTML tags. Other symbols such as © or € are not included on standard keyboards. Rather than inserting reserved symbols directly or avoiding other special symbols, you can insert a symbol on an HTML webpage by typing its HTML entity name or entity number. Inserting an **HTML character entity** in the code displays a reserved HTML character on the webpage. All character entities start with an ampersand (&) and end with a semicolon (;) to signal to the browser that everything in between is an entity representing a symbol. An **entity name** is an abbreviated name, and an **entity number** is a combination of the pound sign (#) and a numeric code. For example, the entity name for the copyright symbol is `&copy;` and the entity number for the copyright symbol is `&#169;`. You can use either an entity's name or number in your HTML code. An entity name is easier to remember than an entity number, though more browsers support entity numbers than names.

Table 2–3 lists common symbols along with their entity names and numbers.

Table 2–3 Common Symbol Entities			
Character	Description	Entity Name	Entity Number
©	Copyright symbol	&copy;	&#169;
®	Registered trademark	&reg;	&#174;
€	Euro	&euro;	&#8364;
&	Ampersand	&amp;	&#38;
<	Less than	&lt;	&#60;
>	Greater than	&gt;	&#62;
	Nonbreaking space		

A commonly used character is a nonbreaking space ` `, which forces browsers to display a blank space. You can insert indents, extra spaces, and paragraph breaks to make HTML code easier to read and maintain. When a browser displays the webpage, however, it ignores this extra white space, treating multiple spaces, indents, and paragraph breaks as a single space. For example, when you press the TAB key or use the SPACEBAR to indent header tags and content in the HTML code, a browser displays the header content on the left margin of the webpage with no indent. Likewise, if you insert two spaces between the page names in the nav area, a browser removes the extra spaces when it displays the webpage so only one space appears between the page names. What can you do if you want to display the extra spaces in a browser? You use the nonbreaking space character entity as in the following code:

```
Home     About Us
```

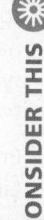

CONSIDER THIS

What is the purpose of the UTF-8 character set?

Computers can read many types of character sets. The Unicode Consortium developed Unicode Transformation Format (UTF)-8 to create a standard character set. The UTF-8 has been widely accepted and is the preferred character set for several types of web programming languages, such as HTML, JavaScript, and XML.

To Add Text and Nonbreaking Spaces to the Nav Section

1 CREATE WEBSITE FOLDERS | 2 CREATE TEMPLATE | 3 ENTER HTML5 SEMANTIC ELEMENTS
4 ADD COMMENTS & CONTENT | **5 VALIDATE DOCUMENT** | **6 CREATE & VIEW HOME PAGE**

Next, between the beginning and ending nav tags, add the name of the links to the other pages. *Why? The nav area is designed to contain hyperlinks to other pages within the website.* To insert two spaces between each page name, use the nonbreaking space character entity ` `. The following steps add content to the nav area of a webpage template.

1

- Place the insertion point after the beginning <nav> tag and press the ENTER key to insert a new Line 17.

- On Line 17, press the TAB key and then type **Home** to add the first webpage link name.

- Press the SPACEBAR once and then type **   ** to add two nonbreaking spaces (Figure 2–19).

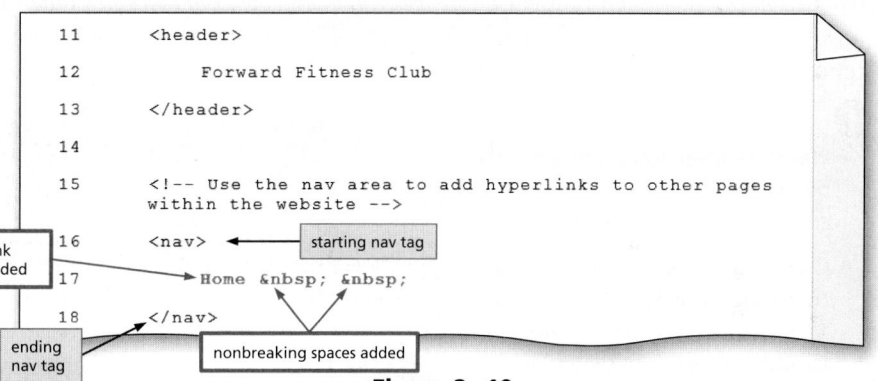

Figure 2–19

Q&A Do I have to place the link names on the line between the beginning and ending <nav> tags?
No. This HTML element can also be written on one line as `<nav>Home    </nav>`. In this case, you place the name of the link on a separate line to improve readability.

2

- Press the ENTER key to insert a new Line 18.
- On Line 18, type **About Us** to add the second webpage link name.
- Press the SPACEBAR once and then type **   ** to add two nonbreaking spaces (Figure 2–20).

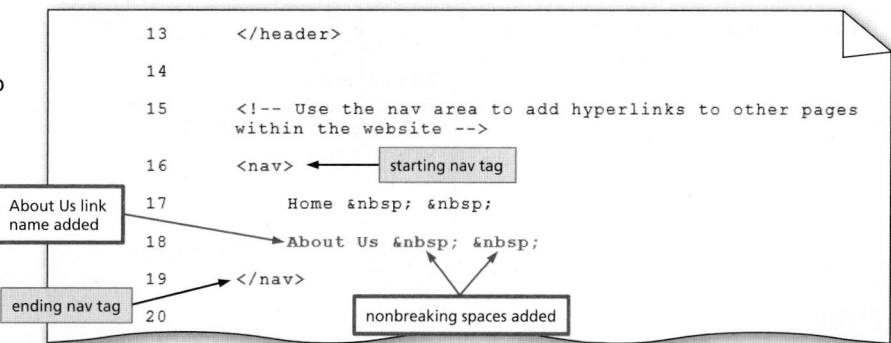

Figure 2–20

- Press the ENTER key to insert a new Line 19, type **Classes** to add the third webpage link name, press the SPACEBAR, and then type **   ** to add two nonbreaking spaces.

- Press the ENTER key to insert a new Line 20, type **Nutrition** to add the fourth webpage link name, press the SPACEBAR, and then type **   ** to add two nonbreaking spaces.

- Press the ENTER key to insert a new Line 21 and then type **Contact Us** to add the fifth webpage link name (Figure 2–21).

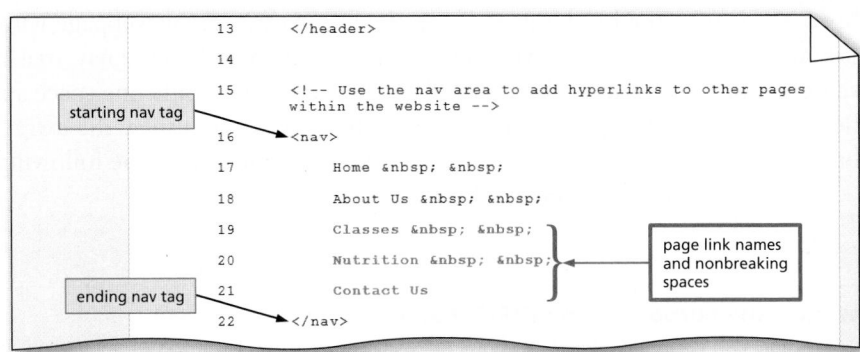

Figure 2–21

- Save your changes.

To Add Content and a Symbol to the Footer Section

1 CREATE WEBSITE FOLDERS | 2 CREATE TEMPLATE | 3 ENTER HTML5 SEMANTIC ELEMENTS
4 ADD COMMENTS & CONTENT | 5 VALIDATE DOCUMENT | 6 CREATE & VIEW HOME PAGE

The footer section of the website contains a copyright symbol and an email address. *Why? Legal notices and contact information usually appear in the footer of a webpage. You add this content to the footer in the template file so that the content appears on all webpages in the website.* The following steps add content to the footer area of a webpage template.

- Place the insertion point after the beginning <footer> tag and press the ENTER key to insert a new Line 30.

- On Line 30, press the TAB key and then type **© Copyright 2015. All Rights Reserved.** to add the copyright symbol and additional copyright information.

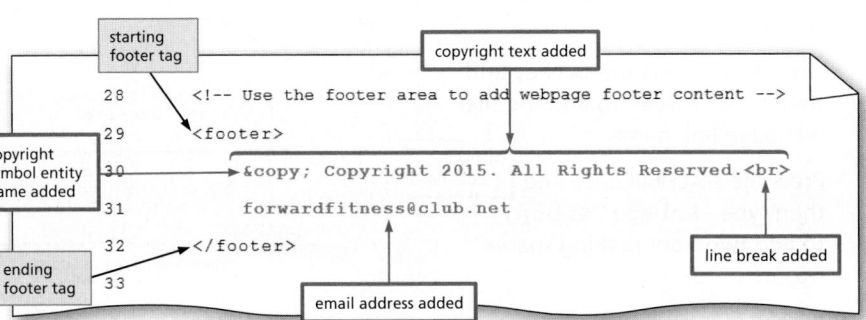

Figure 2–22

- Type **
** to insert a line break.

- Press the ENTER key to insert a new Line 31 and then type **forwardfitness@club.net** to add an email address to the footer section (Figure 2–22).

- Save your changes and then view the page in a browser to display the webpage template (Figure 2–23).

Q&A Why are the header, nav, and footer content areas so close to each other?
To format these areas and add space between each area, you use CSS styles, which you define in Chapter 4.

Where is the main area?
The main area is located after the navigation area and before the footer. Because the main area does not currently have any content, it is not displayed in the browser.

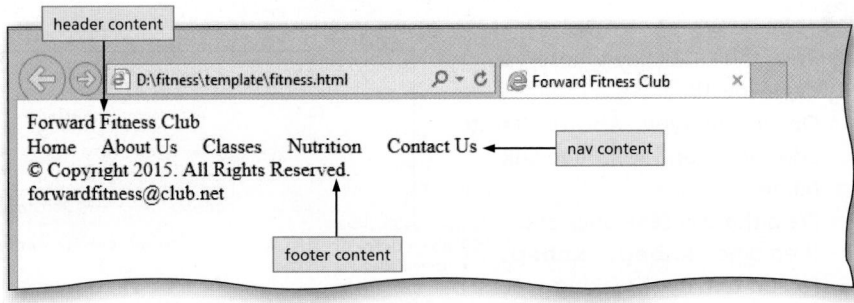

Figure 2–23

Validating HTML Documents

After creating an HTML file, you **validate** the document to verify the validity of the HTML code. When you validate an HTML document, you confirm that all of the code is correct and follows the established rules set by the W3C, the organization that sets the standards for HTML. The W3C recommends validating all HTML documents and making validation part of your webpage testing.

Many validation services are available on the web; you can use any of them to make sure that your HTML code follows standards and is free of errors. Some check only for errors, while others flag errors and suggest how to correct them. The W3C has a free online validator that checks for errors, indicates where they are located, and suggests corrections. Keep in mind that a validator looks for coding errors; it cannot make sure that browsers will display the webpage as you intend. To test the design of a webpage, you must display it in all of the popular browsers.

This book uses the online W3C Markup Validation Service (validator.w3.org). This validator checks the markup validity of web documents in HTML and XHTML, along with some other markup languages. The validator scans the DOCTYPE statement to see which version of HTML or XHTML you are using, and then checks to see if the code is valid for that version. You **upload** your HTML file to the validator, which means you transfer a copy of the document to the validation website. The validator reviews each line of code and locates any errors.

If the validator detects an error in your HTML code, it displays a warning such as "Errors found while checking this document as HTML5!" The W3C validator displays this warning in red in the header bar. A Result line below the header bar shows the number of errors in the document. You can scroll down the page or tap or click the Jump To: Validation Output link to see detailed comments on each error.

BTW

Common Validation Errors
Common validation errors include not spelling tags or attributes correctly and using uppercase letters (except for DOCTYPE). A single coding error can cause many lines of errors during validation.

BTW

Byte-Order Mark (BOM) Warning
In a common result, the validator finds a BOM in a file encoded for UTF-8. This is a warning rather than an error and does not need to be corrected. However, you can adjust the preferences in your text editor to use UTF-8 without BOM to avoid this warning.

To Validate the Webpage Template

1 CREATE WEBSITE FOLDERS | 2 CREATE TEMPLATE | 3 ENTER HTML5 SEMANTIC ELEMENTS
4 ADD COMMENTS & CONTENT | 5 VALIDATE DOCUMENT | **6 CREATE & VIEW HOME PAGE**

Before you use the webpage template to create the necessary webpages for the fitness website, run the template through the W3C validator to check the document for errors. ***Why?*** *If the document has any errors, validating gives you a chance to identify and correct them before using the template to create a webpage.* The following steps validate an HTML document.

1

- Open your browser and type `http://validator.w3.org/` in the address bar to display the W3C Markup Validation Service page.

- Tap or click the Validate by File Upload tab to display the Validate by File Upload information.

- Tap or click the Browse button to display the Choose File to Upload dialog box.

Q&A I do not see a Browse button, but I do have a Choose File button. Should I select the Choose File button instead?
Yes. The button names and other options may vary slightly depending on your browser.

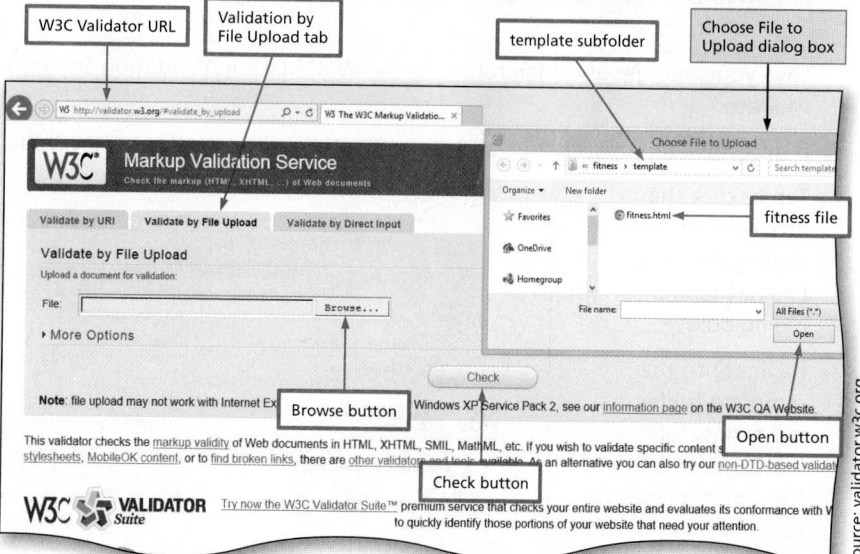

Figure 2–24

Source: validator.w3.org

- Navigate to your webpage template folder to find the fitness.html file (Figure 2–24).

- Tap or click the fitness.html document to select it.

- Tap or click the Open button to upload the selected file to the W3C validator.

- Tap or click the Check button to send the document through the validator and display the validation results page (Figure 2–25).

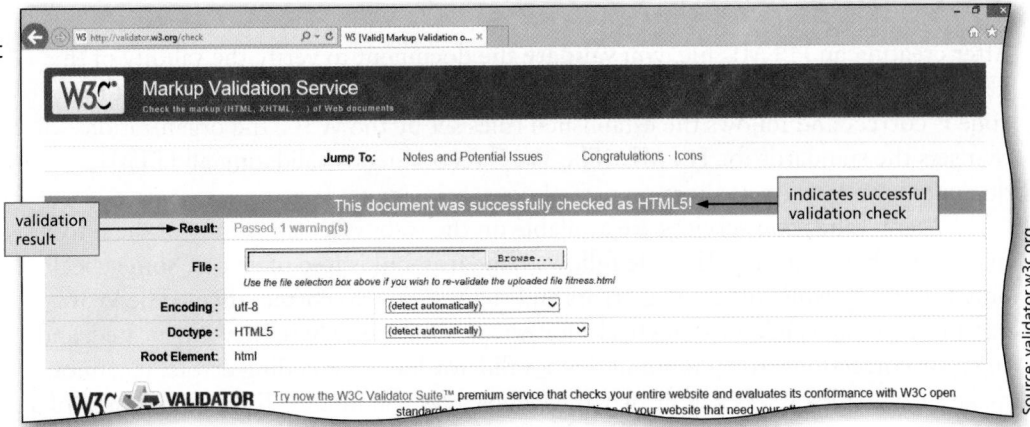

Figure 2–25

Q&A Why does the result show "Passed, 1 warning"?

The warning advises you that the validator checked the file with an experimental feature, the HTML5 conformance check. This message means the document does not contain errors and no corrections are necessary. You can scroll down to display the Notes and Potential Issues section, which explains this warning.

My results show errors. How do I correct them?

Scroll down the page to display the Notes and Potential Issues section. Review the errors listed below the validation output. Any line number that contains an error is shown in this section.

To Validate an HTML Document with Errors

1 CREATE WEBSITE FOLDERS | 2 CREATE TEMPLATE | 3 ENTER HTML5 SEMANTIC ELEMENTS
4 ADD COMMENTS & CONTENT | 5 VALIDATE DOCUMENT | 6 CREATE & VIEW HOME PAGE

If the webpage template was created successfully, you should not receive any errors, but you can review what the validator provides when a document with errors is uploaded to the validator. *Why? When errors are detected on a webpage, the validator provides information about the location of the error so you can identify and correct them.* The following steps insert an error in the fitness document and then validate the document with the W3C validator.

- Return to the fitness document in your text editor and delete html on Line 1 to remove "html" from the DOCTYPE declaration.

- Save your changes and then return to the W3C Markup Validation Service page in your browser to display the W3C validator.

- If necessary, tap or click the Validate by File Upload tab to display the Validate by File Upload information.

- Tap or click the Browse button to display the Choose File to Upload dialog box.

- Navigate to the template folder in the fitness folder, select the fitness.html file, and then tap or click the Open button to upload the file.

- Scroll down to display the Revalidate button (Figure 2–26).

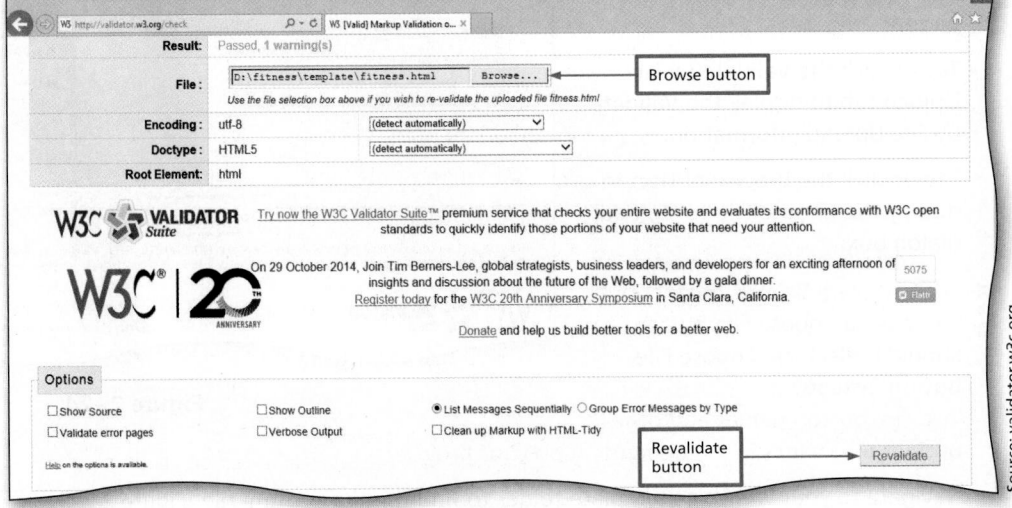

Figure 2–26

- Tap or click the Revalidate button to send the revised document through the validator and display the validation results (Figure 2–27).

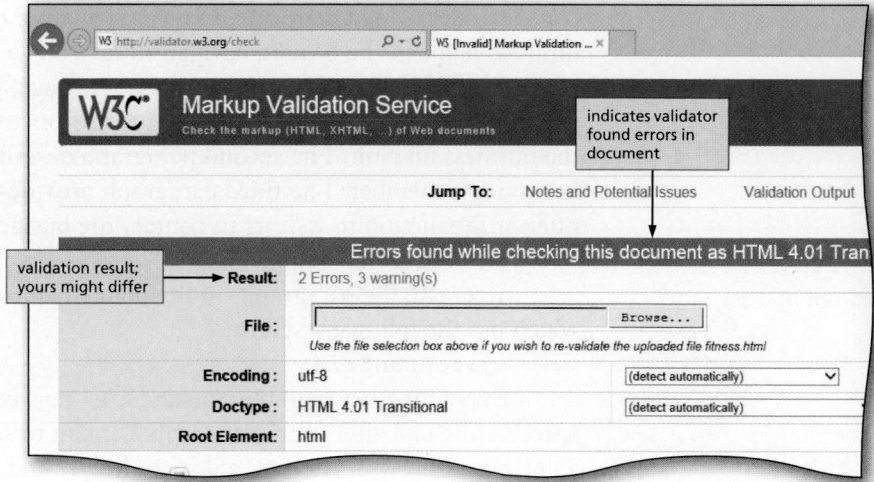

Figure 2–27

- Scroll down to display the Validation Output Errors.
- Review the errors and note the line numbers of the errors in the document (Figure 2–28).

- Return to your text editor and type `html` after the <!DOCTYPE declaration on Line 1 to correct the error.
- Save your changes and validate the document again to confirm it does not contain any errors.

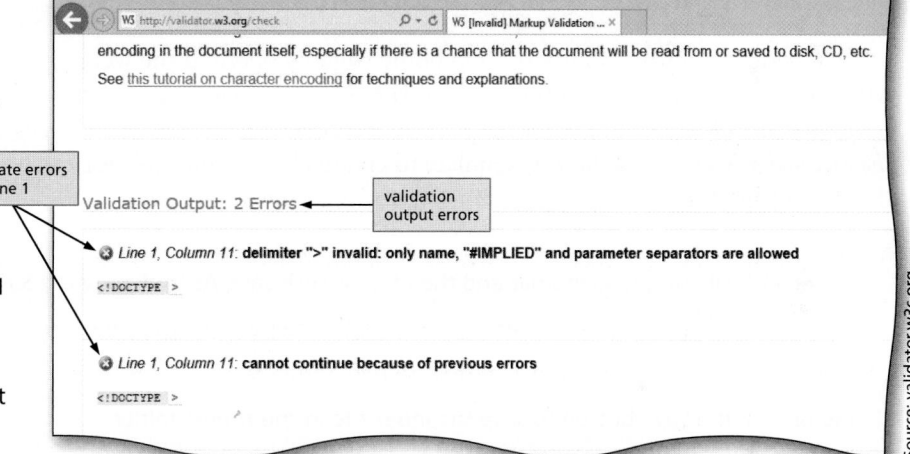

Figure 2–28

Creating a Home Page Using a Webpage Template

After creating a template for a website, you can save time by using the template to create the webpages in the site. The advantage of starting with a template is that it includes content and HTML elements that appear on every page. By opening the template and then saving it with a new name that corresponds to a page on the site, you save time, ensure consistency across the website, and avoid having to re-create repeating elements such as navigation bars. In the new webpage document, you can focus on developing the parts that are unique to that page.

Now that you have created a template for the Forward Fitness Club website, use it to create the website home page. Recall from Chapter 1 that the home page of a website is usually named index.html. Website home pages use this name for a practical reason. If someone uses a browser to enter a URL that includes the site's domain but does not end with a file name, the browser looks for and displays the index.html page automatically.

When you create the Forward Fitness Club home page from a template, the page includes a document title, HTML structural elements to organize the page, the business name in the header, navigation text, and a copyright notice and business email address in the footer. To complete the home page, you add three paragraphs to the main area. The first paragraph welcomes visitors to Forward Fitness Club and restates the business mission. The second paragraph describes the facility and the benefits of becoming a member. The third paragraph provides a strong call to action, which is an offer or instruction to visitors to contact the business to take advantage of a free one-week trial membership.

To create the paragraphs in the main area, you use the paragraph (<p>) element, which has the following syntax:

`<p>content</p>`

Everything between the <p> and </p> tags is a single paragraph. Browsers add space before and after each paragraph element to separate paragraphs. In contrast, for a line break, browsers do not add space before and after the <br> tag.

To Create a Home Page Using a Webpage Template and Add Content

1 CREATE WEBSITE FOLDERS | 2 CREATE TEMPLATE | 3 ENTER HTML5 SEMANTIC ELEMENTS
4 ADD COMMENTS & CONTENT | 5 VALIDATE DOCUMENT | **6 CREATE & VIEW HOME PAGE**

Create the Forward Fitness Club home page by opening the webpage template and then saving the page with a new name in the root fitness folder. *Why? Using a template saves time in coding because the basic wireframe for the page is already established in the template. As a document for one of the main pages of the site, the home page belongs in the root folder.* You use the fitness template to create all the webpages for the website. The following steps create the home page for the fitness website using the webpage template.

- Tap or click File on the menu bar and then tap or click Save As to display the Save As dialog box.

- Tap or click the Up One Level button to display the contents of the fitness folder.

- In the File name text box, type `index` to name the file.

- Tap or click the Save button to save the index file in the fitness folder.

- Place your insertion point after the beginning <main> tag and press the ENTER key twice to insert two new lines, in this case, Lines 26 and 27.

- On Line 27, press the TAB key and then type `<p>Welcome to Forward Fitness Club. Our mission is to help our clients meet their fitness and nutrition goals.</p>` to add paragraph tags and content to the page (Figure 2–29).

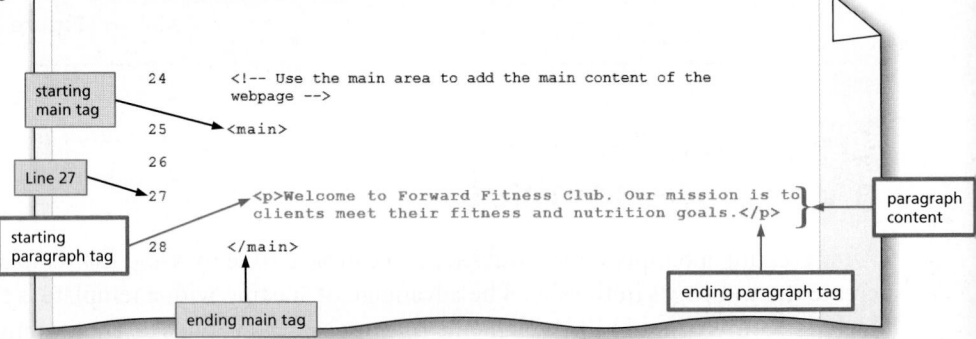

Figure 2–29

2

- Press the ENTER key two times to insert two new lines and then type `<p>If you have struggled with getting healthy and need the motivation and resources to make a healthy lifestyle change, contact us today. Our facility includes state-of-the-art equipment, convenient group training classes, and nutrition tips and information to keep you healthy.</p>` on Line 29 to add a second paragraph to the page.

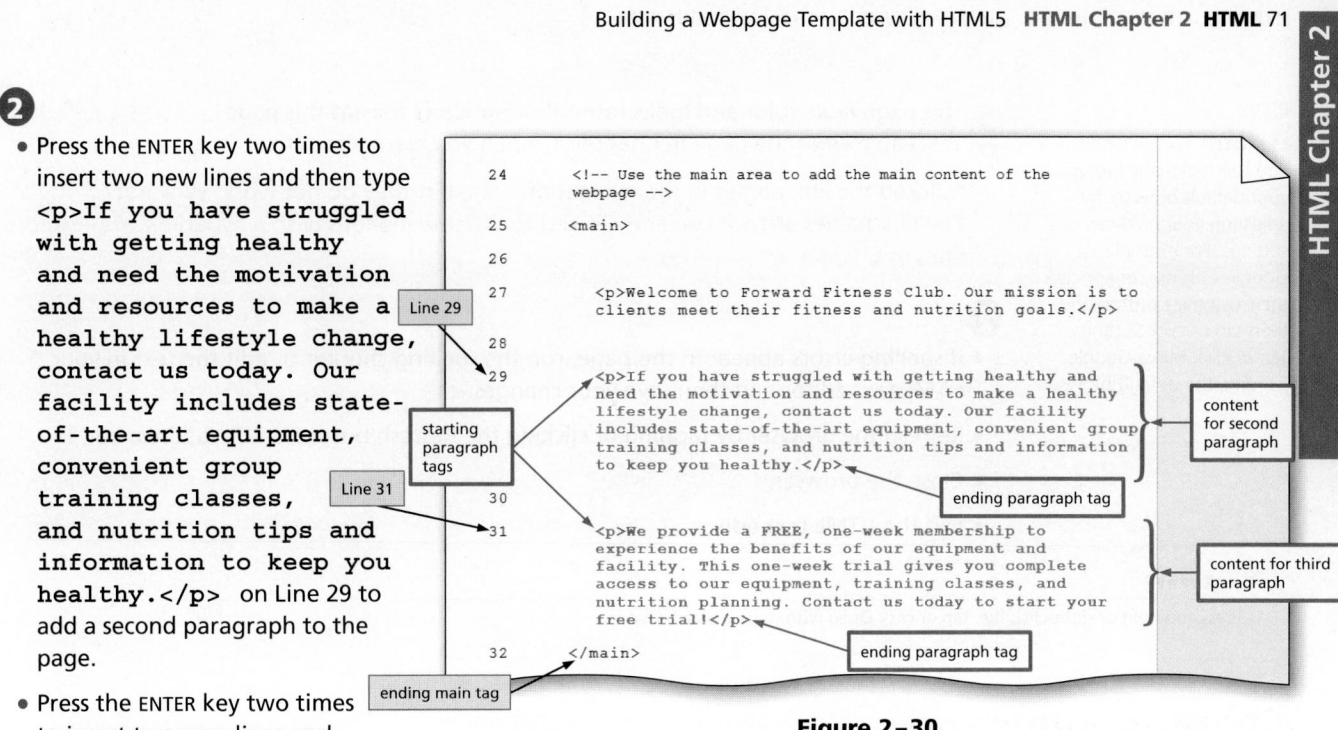

- Press the ENTER key two times to insert two new lines and then type `<p>We provide a FREE one-week membership so you can experience the benefits of our equipment and facility. This one-week trial gives you complete access to our equipment, training classes, and nutrition planning. Contact us today to start your free trial!</p>` on Line 31 to add a third paragraph to the page (Figure 2–30).

Figure 2–30

3

- Press the ENTER key to insert a new blank line above the ending </main> tag.

- Check the spelling of your document and save your changes.

To Display a Home Page in the Default Browser

1 CREATE WEBSITE FOLDERS | 2 CREATE TEMPLATE | 3 ENTER HTML5 SEMANTIC ELEMENTS
4 ADD COMMENTS & CONTENT | 5 VALIDATE DOCUMENT | **6 CREATE & VIEW HOME PAGE**

After creating the home page or any other page of the website and adding content to it, display it in a browser to view the completed page. *Why? You should view every page you create in a browser.* Besides using a command in an HTML editor, such as the Launch in IE command on the Run menu in Notepad++, you can open an HTML file from a file viewer such as File Explorer or Finder. When you double-tap or double-click an HTML file, it opens in the default browser on your computer. If you want to open the file in a different browser, you can press and hold or right-click the HTML file, tap or click Open with, and then tap or click an alternate browser. The following steps display the Forward Fitness Club home page in the default browser.

1

- Run File Explorer and navigate to the fitness folder to display the index .html page.

- Double-tap or double-click the index.html file to display the page in the default browser on your computer (Figure 2–31).

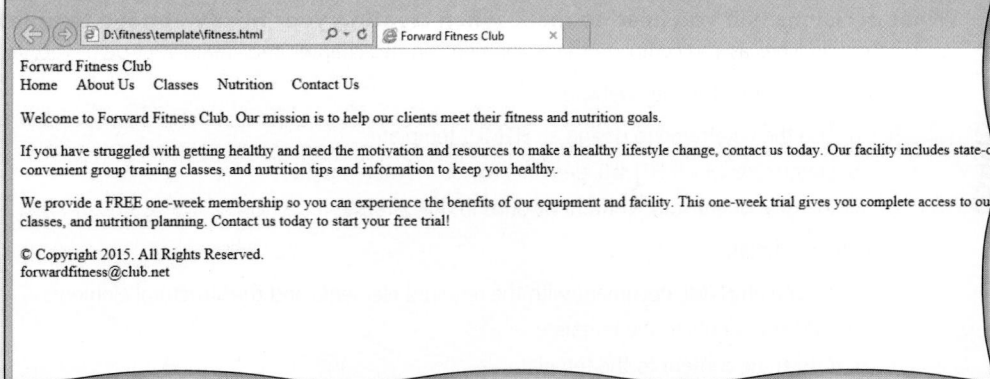

Figure 2–31

BTW
Default Browsers
You can make any browser your default browser by adjusting your browser settings. For example, in Google Chrome, tap or click the Customize button and then tap or click Settings. Tap or click Make Google Chrome the default browser.

Q&A This page lacks color and looks rather boring. Can I format this page?
Yes, you format the page in Chapter 4, when you learn about CSS.

I clicked the link names in the navigation area, but they do not work. Why not?
The link names are not currently linked to other webpages with a hyperlink. You explore links in Chapter 3.

- If spelling errors appear in the page, run the spelling checker or edit the text in your HTML text editor and then save your changes.
- Refresh the browser by tapping or clicking the Refresh button on the address bar.
- Close the browser.
- Exit the HTML text editor.

Other Ways

1 Press and hold or right-click file, tap or click Open with, tap or click browser

Chapter Summary

In this chapter, you learned how to prepare a website by organizing folders for the webpage files, using HTML5 structural elements to create a webpage template, validating the template, and then creating the home page. The items listed below include all the new concepts and skills you have learned in this chapter, with the tasks grouped by activity.

Designing a Website
Examine the Site Map (HTML 53)
Review the Wireframe (HTML 53)
Create a Website Folder and Subfolders (HTML 55)

Using HTML5 Semantic Elements
Use the Header Element (HTML 57)
Include the Nav Element (HTML 57)
Use the Main Element (HTML 57)
Insert the Footer Element (HTML 57)

Creating a Webpage Template
Create a Webpage Template Document (HTML 59)
Add HTML5 Semantic Elements to a Webpage Template (HTML 60)
Add Comments to a Webpage Template (HTML 62)

Using Symbol Entities
Add Text and Nonbreaking Spaces to the Nav Section (HTML 65)
Add Content and a Symbol to the Footer Section (HTML 66)

Validating HTML Documents
Validate the Webpage Template (HTML 67)
Validate an HTML Document with Errors (HTML 68)

Creating a Home Page
Create a Home Page Using a Webpage Template and Add Content (HTML 70)
Display a Home Page in the Default Browser (HTML 71)

CONSIDER THIS

What decisions will you need to make when creating your next webpage template?
Use these guidelines as you complete the assignments in this chapter and create your own websites outside of this class.

1. Build a wireframe for your website.

   a. Use the wireframe to design an HTML5 template.

   b. Determine which HTML5 elements to use in the template.

   c. Identify where static content belongs in the wireframe.

2. Create a template.

   a. Create an HTML document with the required elements and the structural elements.

   b. Add comments to the template.

   c. Add static content to the template.

   d. Validate your template and correct any errors.

3. Use the template to create the home page for your website.

    a. Add content to the main area and other areas that do not contain static content.

    b. Validate the home page to confirm that it does not contain any errors.

    c. View the home page in more than one browser.

    d. Identify any changes you need to make.

4. Depending on the structure of your website, determine whether you need to create additional templates to accommodate multiple wireframes.

How should you submit solutions to questions in the assignments identified with a ✳ symbol? Every assignment in this book contains one or more questions identified with a ✳ symbol. These questions require you to think beyond the assigned presentation. Present your solutions to the questions in the format required by your instructor. Possible formats may include one or more of these options: create a document that contains the answer; present your answer to the class; discuss your answer in a group; record the answer as audio or video using a webcam, smartphone, or portable media player; or post answers on a blog, wiki, or website.

Apply Your Knowledge

Reinforce the skills and apply the concepts you learned in this chapter.

Creating a Template with a Semantic Wireframe

Instructions: The page shown in Figure 2–31 contains the required HTML5 tags for all webpages as well as HTML5 structural tags for a basic, semantic wireframe. As you add content to your webpages, you should understand what each area of the wireframe represents and what type of content each section contains. In this exercise, you will use your HTML editor to enter the required HTML tags and semantic HTML5 structural tags to create a webpage template with a standard webpage wireframe. You will also use HTML comments to document where each section of the wireframe will appear on the webpage, as well as the type of content that is added to each section.

Perform the following tasks:

1. Open your HTML editor and enter the required HTML tags as shown in Lines 1–8 and Lines 25–26 in Figure 2–32. (Do not enter the comments.) Be sure to add indents as shown to make your code easy to read.

```
1   <!DOCTYPE html>
2   <html lang="en">
3   <head>
4       <title><!--Where does this content appear?
5               What is typically contained in this section?--></title>
6       <meta charset="utf-8">
7   </head>
8   <body>
9       <header>
10          <!-- Where does this section appear on the web page?
11              What is typically contained in this section? -->
12      </header>
13      <nav>
14          <!-- Where does this section appear on the web page?
15              What is typically contained in this section? -->
16      </nav>
17      <main>
18          <!-- Where does this section appear on the web page?
19              What is typically contained in this section? -->
20      </main>
21      <footer>
22          <!-- Where does this section appear on the web page?
23              What is typically contained in this section? -->
24      </footer>
25  </body>
26  </html>
27
```

Source: Notepad++

Figure 2–32

Continued >

STUDENT ASSIGNMENTS

Apply Your Knowledge *continued*

2. Save the file as a Hyper Text Markup Language file with the name `template02.html`.

3. Using your favorite search engine, research the `title` element to answer the questions posed as a comment between the <title>…</title> tags shown in Figure 2–32.

4. Replace the comment between the <title>…</title> tags in the template02.html file with the answer to those two questions. Enter the answer as an HTML comment. A sample answer for the <title>…</title> tags is shown in Figure 2–33. Use or modify that answer for your page.

```
1   <!DOCTYPE html>
2   <html lang="en">
3   <head>
4       <title><!--Shown in the webpage tab.
5                  Contains keywords for SEO, search engine optimization.--></title>
6       <meta charset="utf-8">
7   </head>
8   <body>
9       <header>
10          <!-- Shown at the top of the page.
11              Contains introductory content typically found on each page.
12              The company logo, name, and tagline often go here. -->
13      </header>
14      <nav>
15          <!-- Shown at the top of each page, right after the header.
```

Figure 2–33

Source: Notepad++

5. Open the `apply02.docx` Word document from the Data Files for Students, copy the address of the webpage you used to research the `title` element, and then paste it into the table. (A sample answer is already provided for the `title` element in the apply02 document as a guide. Replace it with the address you used.)

6. Repeat Steps 3, 4, and 5 to research the `header, nav, main,` and `footer` elements, the elements used to define the semantic wireframe.

   a. In the template02.html document, replace the questions posed as comments for the `header, nav, main,` and `footer` elements with answers to the questions. Be sure that your answers are also coded as comments.

   b. In the apply02.docx document, save the website address links used to answer each question.

7. In the template02.html document, review and check the spelling of your comments. Note that two questions are posed for each set of tags, so make sure that you have answered both questions. Also make sure that all of your answers are coded as HTML comments.

8. Validate the template02.html document using the W3C validator at validator.w3.org and fix any errors the validator identifies. Validation is complete when the validator returns the message "This document was successfully checked as HTML5!" in a green bar near the top of the webpage.

9. Submit the template02.html file in a format specified by your instructor.

10. ✳ In Steps 3, 4, 5, and 6, you researched the required `title` element as well as the semantic wireframe `header, nav, main,` and `footer` elements. Using your favorite search engine, research these questions that further explore the new semantic HTML5 elements:

   a. What is the definition of "semantic html?"

   b. What are the benefits of "semantic html?"

   c. What are the new, HTML5 semantic elements?

   d. What is the primary advantage and the primary disadvantage of using the <main> element vs. <div id="main">?

Extend Your Knowledge

Extend the skills you learned in this chapter and experiment with new skills. You may need to use additional resources to complete the assignment.

Converting an Old Template to a Semantic Wireframe

Instructions: Open your HTML editor and create the webpage with the wireframe and content shown in Figure 2–34. The starting data file contains many `div` tags that you will replace with more meaningful, semantic HTML5 elements.

Perform the following tasks:

1. Open the `ski02.html` file from the Data Files for Students and then modify the HTML code to update it to semantic HTML5 as shown in Figure 2–34. Be sure to make the following updates:

    a. Change the DOCTYPE statement. The HTML5 DOCTYPE statement is different and greatly simplified from any version of the HTML4 DOCTYPE statement.

    b. Replace the <div id="*name*">…</div> tags with their semantic HTML5 counterparts.

    c. Add all of the content including two headings in the <header>…</header> section and the <p>…</p> paragraph content in the <nav>, <main>, and <footer> sections. The company name in the <header> section should be marked up with <h1> tags. The tagline "Let it snow, let it snow, let it snow" should be marked up with <h2> tags.

    d. To mark up and duplicate the line spacing in the <main> section, insert a beginning paragraph tag before the "Ski Instructor:" text and insert an ending paragraph tag after the zip code. insert line break tags after the instructor's name and the street address. Mark up the phone and email lines each as their own paragraph. Enter a line break tag after the phone number.

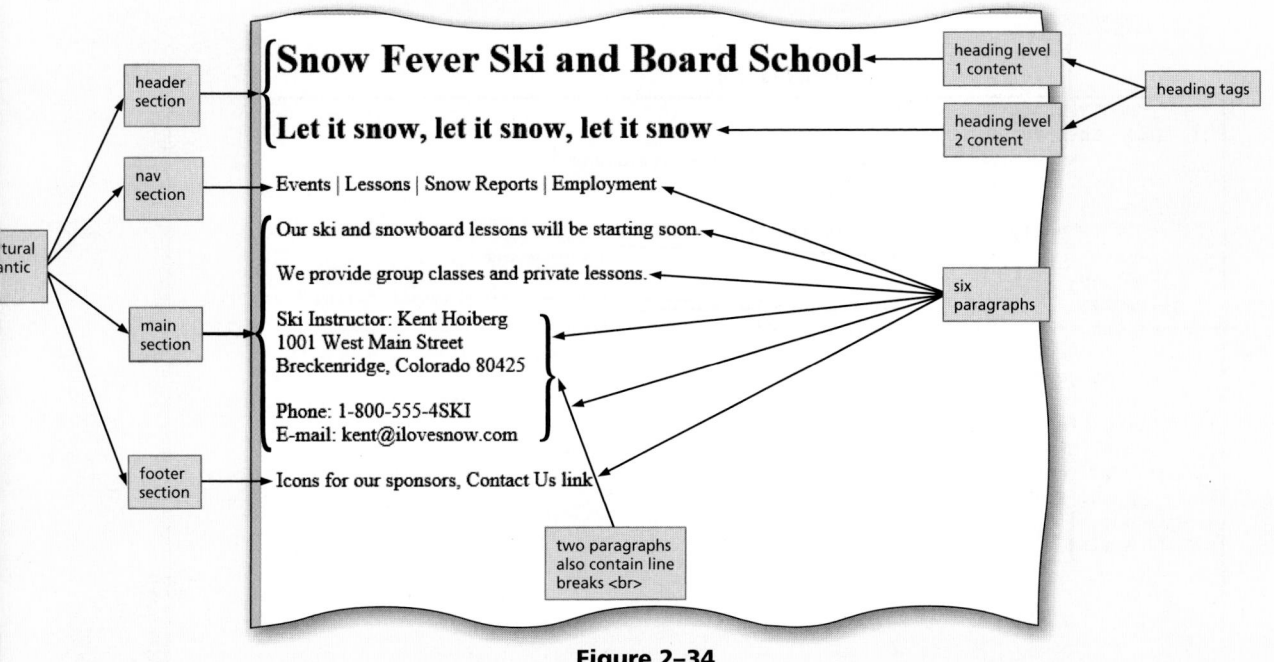

Figure 2–34

Continued >

Extend Your Knowledge *continued*

2. Save and review your work. Check the spelling of the content on the webpage.

3. Validate your webpage using the W3C validator at validator.w3.org and fix any errors that it identifies. Validation is complete when the validator returns the message "This document was successfully checked as HTML5!" in a green bar near the top of the webpage.

4. Submit the ski02.html file in a format specified by your instructor.

5. ✹ After reflecting on this exercise and using outside resources if needed, answer the following questions that further explore the appropriate use of the `div` element.

   a. What does the `div` element represent?

   b. What is the `div` element used for?

   c. Why do HTML5 webpages use fewer `div` tags than HTML4 pages?

   d. Why is the `div` element still used in HTML5?

   e. Why is the `id` attribute almost always used with the `div` element?

Analyze, Correct, Improve

Analyze a webpage, correct all errors, and improve it.

Correcting HTML Errors

Note to instructors and students: From this point forward, the exercises at the end of the chapter use <div id="main"> to identify the main content in the wireframe instead of <main> tag. Using <div id="main"> accommodates browsers that may not yet support the semantic <main> tag.

Instructions: Open your HTML editor and then open the analyze02.html file from the Data Files for Students. Ten HTML5 best practices are listed in the body section of this webpage, but the page contains many errors identified with callouts in Figure 2–35. You will use the W3C validator at validator.w3.org to find and correct the HTML errors on the webpage as instructed.

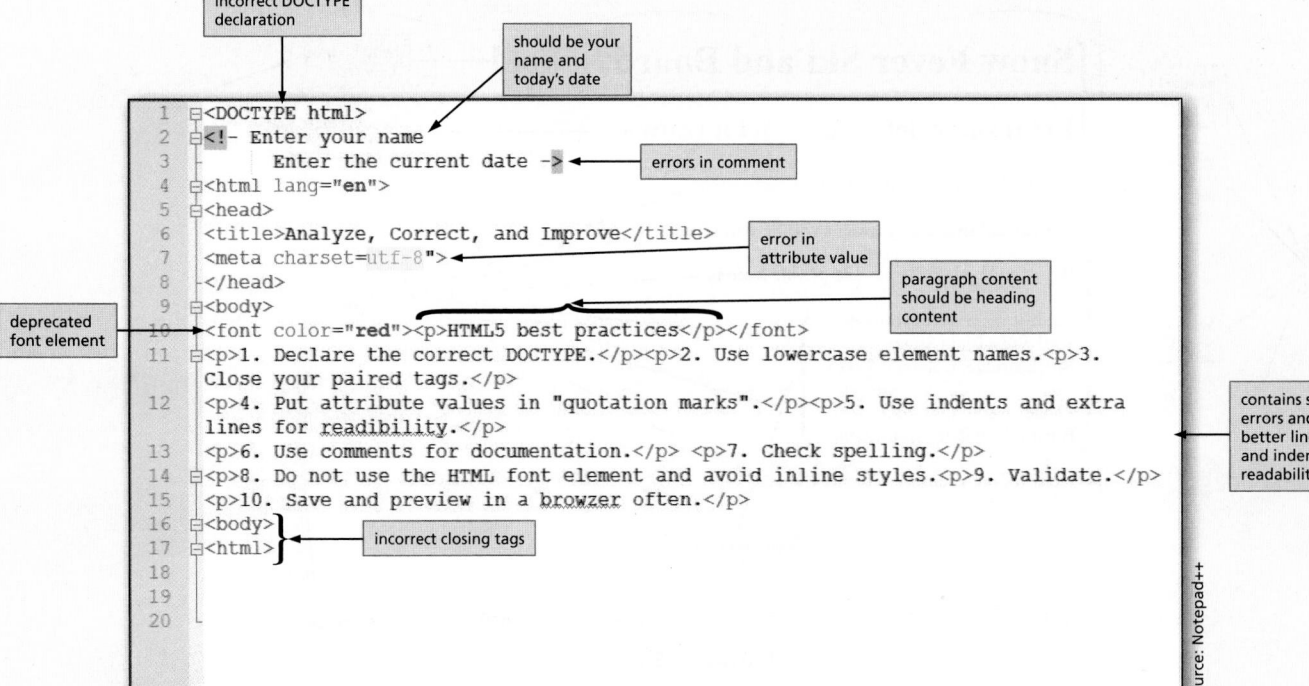

Figure 2–35

1. Correct

   a. Open the `analyze02.html` file in your HTML editor.

   b. Open a browser and go to the W3C validator at http://validator.w3.org.

   c. Using either the Validate by File Upload or Validate by Direct Input method, validate the analyze02.html file. (*Hint*: To use the Validate by Direct Input method, tap or click that tab and then copy and paste the code from analyze02.html directly into the 'Validate by direct input' box.)

The validator returns a message that it found several errors and warnings.

   d. Scroll down the validation webpage to the "Validation Output" section. The first two errors refer to Line 1, the DOCTYPE statement. Correct the DOCTYPE statement in your analyze02.html file. It should include a leading exclamation point character, as in `<!DOCTYPE html>`.

   e. Save and revalidate the updated page. The validator returns a message that it found several errors and warnings. Fixing the DOCTYPE error allowed the validator to successfully read other parts of the webpage where it found more errors.

   f. Scroll down the validation webpage to the "Validation Output" section. The first error identified refers to Line 2, the comment. Correct the comment statement in your analyze02 .html file. Both the opening and closing tags should include two dashes instead of one, as follows:

```
<!-- Enter your name

Enter the current date -->
```

   g. Save and revalidate analyze02.html. Scroll down the validation webpage to the "Validation Output" section. The first error identified refers to Line 7, the `meta` tag. Notice that the attribute value is not properly surrounded with quotation marks on each side. Correct the attribute and value to `charset="utf-8"`

   h. Save and revalidate analyze02.html. Scroll down the validation webpage to the "Validation Output" section and then read each of these errors. You will fix each of these errors in this pass.

      • Delete the `<font color="red">` and `</font>` tags. The <font> tag has been deprecated (removed) from the HTML5 standard. You will style your content with Cascading Style Sheets (CSS) in upcoming chapters.

      • On Lines 16 and 17, change the `<body>` and `<html>` tags into closing `</body>` and `</html>` tags.

   i. Save and revalidate analyze02.html. Your validation process is complete when you see the green message "This document was successfully checked as HTML5!"

2. Improve

   a. Although the webpage has been successfully validated, the HTML validator only checks for HTML issues: correct elements, attributes, and syntax. The validator does not check for readability such as white space and indents, whether tags are semantically correct, or the whether the content is spelled correctly. You will work on readability first. To make the webpage more readable in the HTML editor, press the ENTER key after every closing </p> tag to move each numbered item to its own line.

   b. Indent every line within the <head>…</head> and <body>…</body> sections to make them easier to read.

Continued >

STUDENT ASSIGNMENTS

Analyze, Correct, Improve *continued*

    c. Change the <p>...</p> tags that surround the HTML5 best practices title to <h1>...</h1> tags. The <h1> (heading level 1) tag is more meaningful (semantic) for this content than the <p> (paragraph) tag.

    d. Find and correct the two spelling errors. (*Hint*: The word *lowercase* and *inline* are spelled correctly in this context.)

    e. Replace the placeholder text in the comment with your own name and the current date.

3. Submit the analyze02.html file in a format specified by your instructor.

4. ✷ After reflecting on this exercise and using outside resources if needed, answer these questions.

    a. Identify three types of errors the W3C validator helps you find and correct.

    b. Identify three types of errors that the W3C validator will *not* help you find and correct.

    c. Identify three reasons it is a good practice to validate all webpages.

In the Lab

Labs 1 and 2, which increase in difficulty, require you to create webpages based on what you learned in the chapter; Lab 3 requires you to dive deeper into a topic covered in the chapter.

Lab 1: **Creating a Home Page for City Farmer**

Problem: You work for a local but rapidly growing gardening supply company called City Farmer that specializes in products that support food self-sufficiency. The company has identified a small number of extremely successful products that they want to market through a website and have hired you to get started. Create the webpage shown in Figure 2–36 that contains the textual content that City Farmer wants on their home page.

Instructions: Perform the following tasks:

    1. If you created the cityfarmer.html file in the Lab 1 exercise from Chapter 1, open the file and then save it with the name **cityfarmer02.html**. If you did not create the cityfarmer.html file, enter the required HTML tags as shown in Figure 2–36 and save the file with the name **cityfarmer02.html**.

    2. Make sure the <title>...</title> tags contain the text **City Farmer Home Page**.

    3. Delete the existing content in the body section, and add the content in the <header>, <nav>, <div id="main">, and <footer> sections as shown in Figure 2–36a.

    4. Indent the code and content within the **head** and **body** sections to make each section distinct and readable.

    5. Add or modify the comment after the opening <!DOCTYPE html> statement to contain your name and the current date.

    6. Validate your code and fix any errors.

    7. Check the spelling of the text so it matches the code in Figure 2–36a, which shows the file in Notepad++ (the appearance varies if you are using a different HTML editor).

    8. Save and open the page within a browser as shown in Figure 2–36b.

    9. Submit your assignment in the format specified by your instructor.

```
1    <!DOCTYPE html>
2    <!-- Student Name and current date -->
3  ⊟<html lang="en">
4  ⊟<head>
5        <title>City Farmer Home Page</title>
6        <meta charset="utf-8">
7   </head>
8  ⊟<body>
9  ⊟    <header>
10           <p>City Farmer</p> <!--Company Name-->
11           <p>...today's urban cowboy</p><!--Company tagline-->
12           <!--Add Company Logo here-->
13       </header>
14 ⊟     <nav>Products  
15           Order  
16           News  
17           Events  
18       </nav>
19 ⊟     <div id="main">
20 ⊟         <!-- Main content will include a monthly newsletter
21            with articles, photos, and tips for the urban farmer-->
22       </div> <!--end main-->
23 ⊟     <footer>
24           <p>&copy; Copyright 2015 <br> feedback@cityfarmer.com</p>
25       </footer>
26
27  </body>
28  </html>
```

a) cityfarmer02.html in HTML editor

b) cityfarmer02.html in browser

City Farmer

...today's urban cowboy

Products Order News Events

© Copyright 2015
feedback@cityfarmer.com

Source: Notepad++

Figure 2–36

10. ✳ What are the benefits of entering the wireframe HTML elements such as `header, nav,` `<div id="main">,` and `footer` before entering the textual content for the webpage?

Lab 2: Creating a Home Page for Cycle Out Cancer

Problem: You are part of a philanthropic group of motorcyclists who participate in community events and parades to distribute cancer awareness information. Your group is called Cycle Out Cancer and the director has asked you to help create a website for them. Create the webpage shown in Figure 2–37 that better defines the wireframe and content desired on the organization's home page. In later chapters, you'll replace the placeholders with actual text and images.

Instructions: Perform the following tasks:

1. If you created the cycle.html file in the Lab 2 exercise from Chapter 1, open the file and then save it with the name `cycle02.html`. If you did not create the cycle.html file, enter the required HTML tags as show in Figure 2–37a and save the file with the name `cycle02.html`. Be sure to modify the <main> tag as <div id="main">. Be sure to change the closing </main> tag to </div>. Given the </div> tag is not semantic, add the comment <!--end main--> after the closing </div> tag.

2. Make sure the <title>…</title> tags contain the text `Cycle Out Cancer Home Page`.

3. Modify the `body` element by adding the content in the <header>, <nav>, <div id="main">, and <footer> sections in Figure 2–37a, which shows the file in Notepad++ (the appearance varies if you are using a different HTML editor).

4. Indent the code and content within the `head` and `body` elements to make each section distinct and readable.

5. Add or modify the comment after the opening <!DOCTYPE html> statement to contain your name and the current date.

Continued >

In the Lab *continued*

6. Validate your code and fix any errors.

7. Check the spelling of the text so it matches the code shown in Figure 2–37a.

8. Save and open the page within a browser as shown in Figure 2–37b.

9. Submit your assignment in the format specified by your instructor.

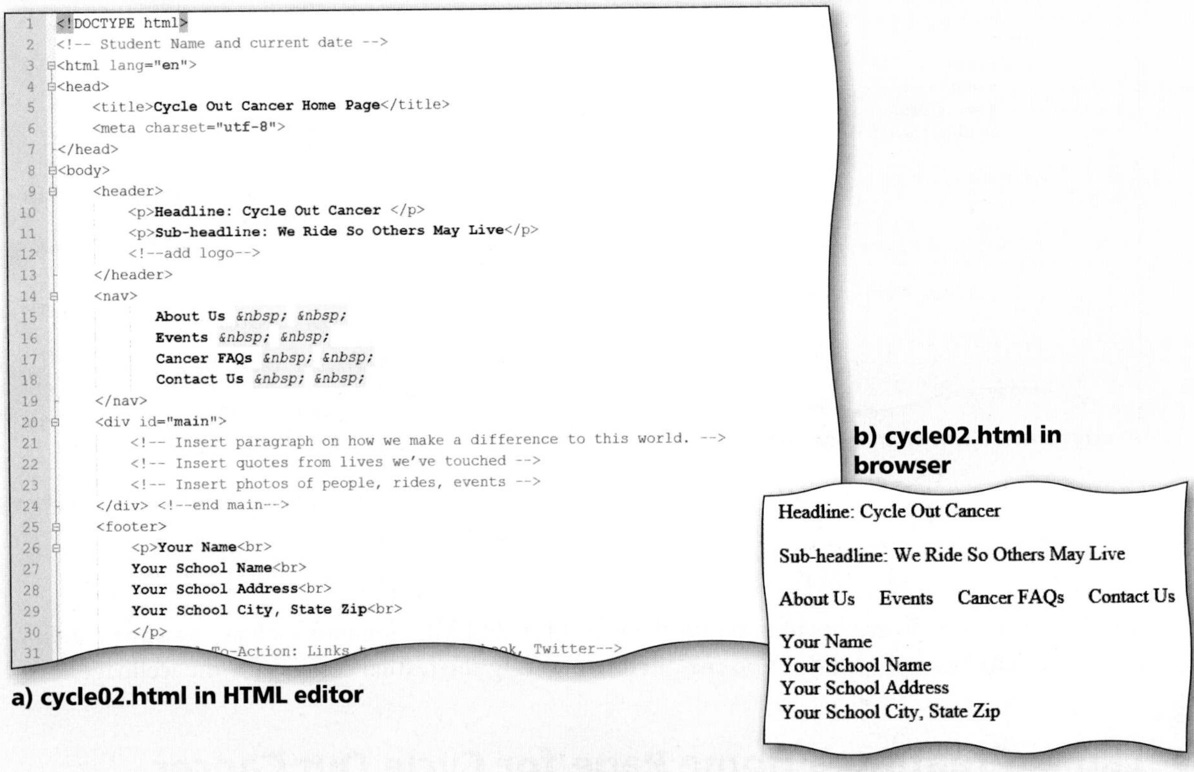

```
1   <!DOCTYPE html>
2   <!-- Student Name and current date -->
3   <html lang="en">
4   <head>
5       <title>Cycle Out Cancer Home Page</title>
6       <meta charset="utf-8">
7   </head>
8   <body>
9       <header>
10          <p>Headline: Cycle Out Cancer </p>
11          <p>Sub-headline: We Ride So Others May Live</p>
12          <!--add logo-->
13      </header>
14      <nav>
15          About Us    
16          Events    
17          Cancer FAQs    
18          Contact Us    
19      </nav>
20      <div id="main">
21          <!-- Insert paragraph on how we make a difference to this world. -->
22          <!-- Insert quotes from lives we've touched -->
23          <!-- Insert photos of people, rides, events -->
24      </div> <!--end main-->
25      <footer>
26          <p>Your Name<br>
27          Your School Name<br>
28          Your School Address<br>
29          Your School City, State Zip<br>
30          </p>
31              o-Action: Links         k, Twitter-->
```

a) cycle02.html in HTML editor

b) cycle02.html in browser

Headline: Cycle Out Cancer

Sub-headline: We Ride So Others May Live

About Us   Events   Cancer FAQs   Contact Us

Your Name
Your School Name
Your School Address
Your School City, State Zip

Source: Notepad++

Figure 2–37

10. ✱ It is easy to forget to check the spelling and grammar of your webpage content. But incorrectly spelled words as well as poor grammar can lead to negative impressions. What negative impressions might be created if you forget to check the spelling and grammar of the content on the webpages that you create or maintain?

Lab 3: Expand Your World
File and Folder Best Practices

Problem: Websites consist of many files such as webpages, images, and other files used to complete the website. In this chapter you were introduced to a folder organization that encouraged the use of five folders for a single website to keep the files well organized. In this exercise you'll expand your knowledge of file and folder management best practices.

Instructions:

1. Open the `filefolderbestpractices.docx` document from the Data Files for Students.

2. Using the information in this chapter as well as the web, complete the two tables by answering the questions posed in each. The first table, *File and Folder Organization*, asks questions about the types of files and the file name extensions of the files stored in the folders presented in Figure 2–4. The second table, *File and Folder Naming Conventions*, asks questions about best practices associated with file and folder names.

3. ✹ Identify three potential problems that could occur if you stored all of the files for an entire website in one folder. Identify three potential problems that could occur if you did not follow "best practice" file and folder naming conventions.

✹ Consider This: Your Turn

Apply your creative thinking and problem-solving skills to design and implement a solution.

1. Create the Home Page for Your Personal Portfolio Website

Personal

Part 1: In Chapter 1, you completed the personal portfolio website planning document to help think through the purpose, content, and organization of your personal portfolio website. In this exercise, you'll create the initial html semantic wireframe for your home page and add some content. Start by entering the basic required HTML tags in a new HTML document in your HTML editor. Include a title for the webpage that includes your name, such as Kris Lee Portfolio. Next, enter the four pairs of HTML tags to define the <header>, <nav>, <div id="main">, and <footer> sections according to your wireframe. Add a <!--end main> comment immediately after the closing </div> tag to better identify the end of the main content. Insert content in each section using the planning document you created in Chapter 1 as a guide. Customize the webpage with as much personal information for your own electronic portfolio as possible. Below the DOCTYPE declaration, insert a comment with your first and last names and the current date. Use other comments as placeholders for content that you will add in later chapters. Name the webpage `portfolio02.html`. Submit your assignment in the format specified by your instructor.

Part 2: ✹ Use your favorite search engine to find articles and images for electronic portfolios. What new ideas did you find that you want to incorporate into your own personal electronic portfolio? Include at least three links to sites that you like and your reasons for choosing those sites in your answer.

2. Create the Home Page for a Web Development and Consulting Business

Professional

Part 1: In Chapter 1, you completed the professional web consulting firm website planning document to help think through the purpose, content, and organization of your web consulting firm website. In this exercise, you'll create the initial html semantic wireframe for your home page and add some of the initial content. Start by entering the basic required HTML tags in a new HTML document in your HTML editor. Include an appropriate title for the webpage, such as the name of your business. Next, enter the four pairs of HTML tags to define the <header>, <nav>, <div id="main">, and <footer> sections according to your wireframe. Add a <!--end main> comment immediately after the closing </div> tag to better identify the end of the main content. Insert content in the header and nav sections using the planning document you created in Chapter 1 as a guide. Below the DOCTYPE declaration, insert a comment with your first and last names and the current date. Use other comments as placeholders for content that you will add in later chapters. Name the webpage `webdev02.html`. Submit your assignment in the format specified by your instructor.

Part 2: ✹ Your website will feature testimonials from satisfied customers. Contact a web development consulting firm in your area, introduce yourself as a student at your college, and ask to make an appointment to speak to a web developer in that firm. Once connected, explain that you are a student learning about web development, and ask the web developer if they could share a recent success story with you. Ask them to describe the project, the technologies and software they used to complete the project, and any other "keys to success." Substituting fictitious names, use this information to write an article on this success story to showcase it in your website.

Continued >

Consider This: Your Turn *continued*

3. Create the Home Page for the Dog Hall of Fame

Research and Collaboration

Part 1: In Chapter 1, you completed the dog hall of fame website planning document to craft the purpose, content, and organization of the website. In this exercise, each member of your team will create the initial html semantic wireframe for the home page and add some content. Start by entering the basic required HTML tags in a new HTML document in your HTML editor. Include an appropriate title for the webpage. Next, enter the four pairs of HTML tags to define the <header>, <nav>, <div id="main">, and <footer> sections according to your wireframe. Add a <!--end main> comment immediately after the closing </div> tag to better identify the end of the main content. Insert content in the header and nav sections using the planning document you created in Chapter 1 as a guide. Below the DOCTYPE declaration, insert a comment with your first and last names and the current date. Use other comments as placeholders for content that you will add in later chapters. Name the webpage `dogfame02.html`.

Part 2: ✺ Your team will require content in several areas. Assign one or more content areas to each team member to research. Ask each member to gather or create sample content to use in the website to represent the three different awards of Hero, Working, and Companion dog as described below.

- **Hero dog**: Find articles and pictures of dogs that have heroic stories. Hero dogs are ordinary dogs with extraordinary stories.

- **Working dog**: Find articles and pictures of dogs with astonishing stories in the "working dog" category. Examples include dogs who work to protect people, livestock, and property as well as dogs who hunt or track. Identify the common breeds of working dogs.

- **Companion dog**: Find articles and pictures of dogs that have amazing stories in the area of human companionship. Any dog can be a "companion" dog but examples often include dogs who provide an extraordinary benefit to someone who is suffering from health issues or other hardships.

Collect your research in a document in Word named `dogfame02.docx`. Submit your assignment in the format specified by your instructor.

3 | Enhancing a Website with Links and Images

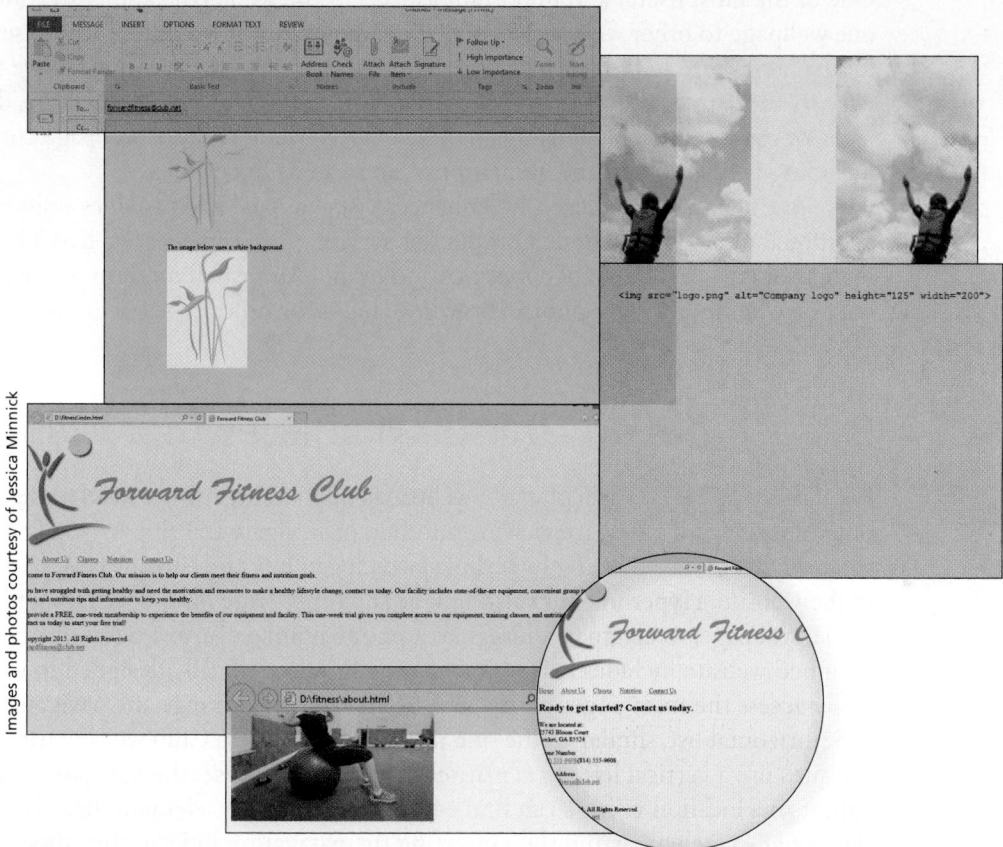

Images and photos courtesy of Jessica Minnick

Objectives

You will have mastered the material in this chapter when you can:

- Describe types of hyperlinks

- Create relative links, absolute links, email links, and telephone links

- Describe image file formats

- Describe the image tag and its attributes

- Add images to a website

- Explain div elements and attributes

- Use a div element to mark a page division

- Define the class attribute

- Describe and use HTML heading tags

- Describe the types of lists in an HTML document

- Create an unordered list and a description list

- Test and validate links on a webpage

3 | Enhancing a Website with Links and Images

Introduction

One of the most useful and important aspects of the web is the ability to connect (link) one webpage to other webpages — on the same server or on different web servers — located anywhere in the world. Using hyperlinks, a website visitor can move from one page to another, view a page on another website, start a new email message, download a file, or make a phone call from a mobile device. Many types of webpage content, including text, graphics, and animations, can serve as hyperlinks.

Adding images to a website enhances visual appeal and provides visitors with additional information about a product or service. Other images, such as a business logo, promote the company's presence and brand. Almost all modern webpages contain images, whether they are photos, drawings, logos, or other types of graphics.

Project — Add Links and Images to a Website

Because a website consists of many webpages of content, visitors need a way to open one webpage while they are viewing another, or navigate the site. As you know, visitors can navigate a website using hyperlinks, which can link the current page to other pages in the website. Hyperlinks can also link to any other page on the web, to a file other than a webpage, to an email address, to a phone number, or to a network server. A well-designed website includes a list of navigation links specifically designed to let visitors easily access the main pages on the site. Some websites arrange the navigation links in a horizontal list, similar to the one the Forward Fitness Club website uses. Other websites use a vertical list of navigation links. In either case, the navigation links should appear in a location visitors can find easily. Using a **nav** element directly below the **header** element and then inserting the navigation links in the **nav** element ensures that the links appear near the header, where visitors can access them easily. To create a link to a webpage, you insert code in an HTML document that references the webpage by its name and location. When a visitor taps or clicks the link, the browser retrieves the webpage identified in the code.

Most websites also use images to enhance the look and feel of their webpages. In fact, one reason the web is so popular is that its images create immediate visual appeal. However, recall that HTML files are simple text files. To display an image on a webpage, you insert code in an HTML document that references the name and location of the image file, similar to the way you create a hyperlink. When a visitor opens the webpage, the browser retrieves the image file identified in the code and displays it on the webpage.

In Chapter 2, you created a website template for the Forward Fitness Club. You then used the template to create the home page for the website. For this project, you edit the template to add hyperlinks to the text in the navigation area and add an image in the header area that displays the club's logo. You use the template to create two pages for the site: the About Us and Contact Us pages. Finally, you add content to the new pages, including headings, images, and links. Figure 3–1a shows the home page of the fitness site; Figure 3–1b shows the About Us page, which contains text and images; and Figure 3–1c shows the Contact Us page with the fitness club's contact information and contact links.

(a) Home page

(c) Contact Us page

(b) About Us page

Figure 3–1

Images courtesy of Jessica Minnick

Roadmap

In this chapter, you will learn how to create the webpages shown in Figure 3-1. The following roadmap identifies general activities you will perform as you progress through this chapter:

1. ADD HYPERLINKS to a template and to webpages.
2. ADD IMAGES to a template and to webpages.
3. ADD DIV ELEMENTS to a template.
4. ADD HEADINGS AND LISTS to webpages.
5. VIEW the WEBSITE IN a BROWSER AND TEST the webpage LINKS.
6. VALIDATE the new PAGES.

At the beginning of step instructions throughout the chapter, you will see an abbreviated form of this roadmap. The abbreviated roadmap uses colors to indicate chapter progress: gray means the chapter is beyond that activity; blue means the task being shown is covered in that activity; and black means that activity is yet to be covered. For example, the following abbreviated roadmap indicates the chapter would be showing a task in the 4 ADD HEADINGS & LISTS activity.

1 ADD HYPERLINKS | 2 ADD IMAGES | 3 ADD DIV ELEMENTS | 4 ADD HEADINGS & LISTS
5 VIEW WEBSITE IN BROWSER & TEST LINKS | 6 VALIDATE PAGES

Use the abbreviated roadmap as a progress guide while you read or step through the instructions in this chapter.

Adding Links to a Webpage

To allow a user to navigate a website and move from one page to another, web designers must add **hyperlinks**, or links, to a webpage. A **link** is text, an image, or other webpage content that visitors tap or click to instruct the browser to go to a location in a file or to request a file from a server. On the web, links are the primary way to navigate among webpages and websites. Links can reference webpages and other content, including graphics, sound, video, and program files; email addresses; and parts of the same webpage. Text links, also called hypertext links, are the most common type of hyperlink. For example, the text "About Us" in Figure 3–1 links to the About Us page in the Forward Fitness Club website.

When you code text as a hyperlink, it usually appears as underlined text in a color different from the rest of the webpage text. The default hyperlink color is blue. By default, the font color of link text changes to purple when a visitor taps or clicks the link. Most webpages also include image links. For example, the Forward Fitness Club logo in Figure 3–1 links to the home page. When a user taps or clicks the logo image, the browser displays the home page. A business logo often serves as an image link to the home page of a website. Although a hyperlinked image looks the same as other images on the page, some websites display a border around an image to indicate it is a link. As with hyperlink text, the image border is blue by default for unvisited image links and purple for image links visitors have selected.

BTW
Link Colors
You can change the link colors in popular browsers. For example, in Internet Explorer, tap or click the Tools button on the Command bar, tap or click Internet Options, General tab, and the Colors button under Appearance. You can then change colors by selecting a color from a color palette.

Anchor Element

You use an **anchor element** to create a hyperlink on a webpage. An anchor element begins with an <a> tag and ends with an </a> tag. Insert the text, image, or other webpage content you want to mark as a hyperlink between the starting and ending anchor tags. Include the **href** attribute (short for "hypertext reference") in the starting anchor tag to identify the webpage, email address, file, telephone number, or other content to access. Recall from Chapter 1 that when you use attributes in HTML code, you insert the attribute name followed by an equal sign and then insert the attribute value between quotation marks, as in *name="value"* where *name* is an attribute name such as href. The value of the `href` attribute is the content to link to, such as a file or a URL. Figure 3–2 shows an example of an anchor `(a)` element with an `href` attribute that links to a home page.

BTW
Anchor Element
An anchor element without an `href` attribute does not create a hyperlink. The element is called an anchor because you use it to anchor content to text or an object on a webpage.

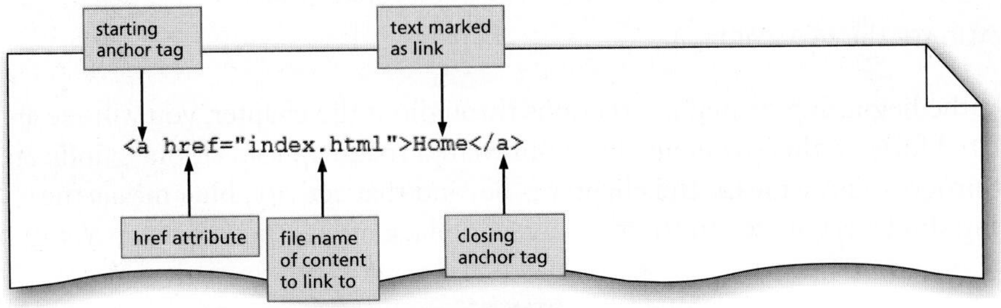

```
<a href="index.html">Home</a>
```

starting anchor tag

text marked as link

href attribute

file name of content to link to

closing anchor tag

Figure 3–2

Relative Links

Hyperlinks that link to other webpages within the same website are known as **relative links**. To create a relative link, use an anchor tag with an `href` attribute that designates the file name of the webpage or the path and the file name of the webpage. Figure 3–2 shows an example of a relative link to the home page named index.html.

Depending on the location of the page or file to be displayed, a relative link may include a file path. Recall that your root fitness folder contains four subfolders: css, images, media, and template. To reference a file in one of the subfolders, you must include the path to the subfolder along with the file name. For example, you would use the following code to create a link to the fitness template:

```
<a href="template/fitness.html">Fitness Template</a>
```

This code means the browser should create a link to the fitness.html file in the template folder using Fitness Template as the link text. To link to the template in this example, you must include the file path because the template file is not stored in the fitness root folder.

Absolute Links

Hyperlinks that link to other webpages outside of your website are known as **absolute links**. To create an absolute link, use an `anchor` element with an `href` attribute that designates a website URL. When assigning the attribute for the absolute link, begin with the http:// text, which references the HTTP protocol and indicates the webpage or other resource is located somewhere on the Internet. Next, include the website domain name such as www.cengage.com to link to that domain's home page. Figure 3–3 shows an example of an absolute link to the home page on the Cengage Learning website. This code means the browser should create a link to www.cengage .com using Cengage as the link text.

BTW
Link Text
When determining the text to use in a link, insert or use text that concisely indicates what appears when visitors tap or click the link. For example, text such as "tap or click here" invites the appropriate action but does not identify what the link is connected to.

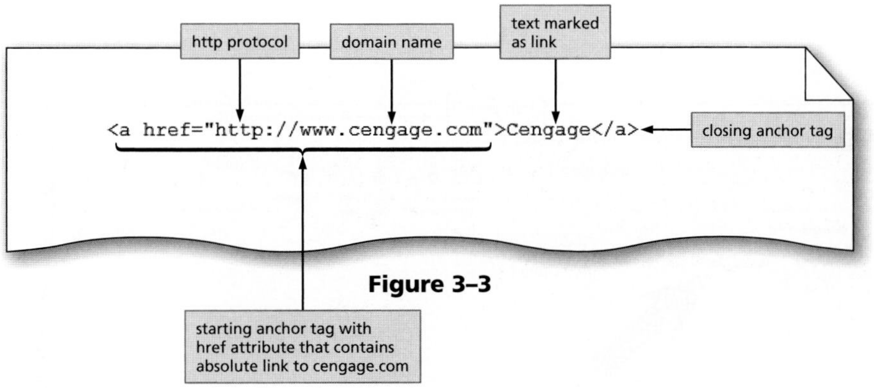

Figure 3–3

[http protocol] [domain name] [text marked as link]

```
<a href="http://www.cengage.com">Cengage</a>
```
[closing anchor tag]

starting anchor tag with href attribute that contains absolute link to cengage.com

Image Links

In addition to text, images can also link to another page within the site, another website, an email address, or a telephone number. To configure an image with a link, place the starting anchor tag before the image element and place the ending anchor tag after the image element. Figure 3–4 shows an example of an image with a relative link to the website's home page. This code means the browser should create a link to the index.html file for the website using the image file named image.png as the link object.

BTW
Nesting Elements
To follow proper syntax with nested elements, close each tag in the reverse order as you opened them.

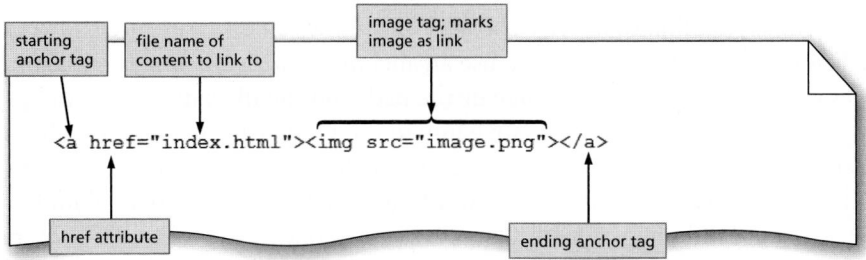

Figure 3–4

Email Links

Hyperlinks that link to an email address are called **email links**. Use **anchor** elements to link to an email address by including the **href** attribute followed by "mailto:" and then the email address. When a user taps or clicks an email link, their default email program runs and opens a new message with the designated email address in the To text box. Figure 3–5 shows an example of an email link. This code means the browser should create an email message addressed to forwardfitness@club.net when someone taps or clicks the "forwardfitness@club.net" link text. Figure 3–6 shows the result of a user tapping or clicking the email link shown in Figure 3–5.

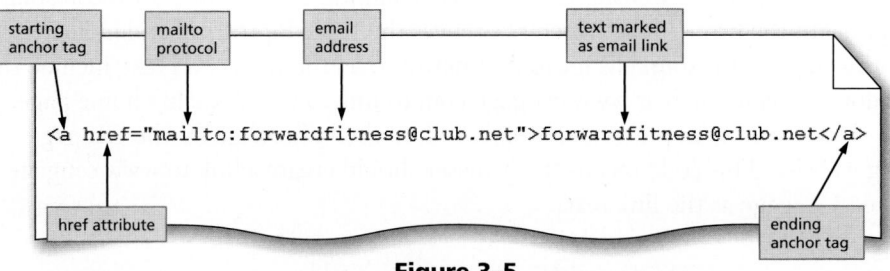

Figure 3–5

BTW
Email Links
You can assign more than one email address to a mailto: tag. Use the form *mailto:first@isp.com, second@isp.com* in the <a href=> tag. Some older browsers may not support this format.

Figure 3–6

Telephone Links

Hyperlinks that link to a telephone number are called **telephone links** and work primarily on smartphones. Use an **anchor** element to link to a telephone number by including the **href** attribute, followed by "tel:+1*number*" where +1 is the international dialing prefix (in this case, for the United States) and *number* is the phone number, including the area code. Including the international dialing prefix makes the link accurate in any location. When a user taps or clicks a telephone link from a mobile device, a dialog box is displayed, asking whether the user wants to call the phone number. Figure 3–7 shows an example of a telephone link. This code means the browser should dial the phone number 1-800-555-2356 when someone taps or clicks the "Call us today at 800-555-2356" link text.

BTW
Other Links
You also can create links to other locations on the Internet (that is, non-http) such as FTP sites and newsgroups. To link to an FTP site, type ftp:// URL rather than http:// URL. For a newsgroup, type news:newsgroup name, and for any particular article within the newsgroup, type news:article name as the entry.

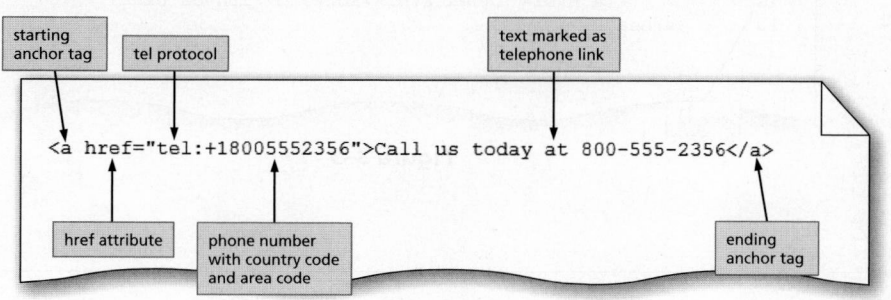

Figure 3–7

To Add Relative Links in a Website Template

1 ADD HYPERLINKS | 2 ADD IMAGES | 3 ADD DIV ELEMENTS | 4 ADD HEADINGS & LISTS
5 VIEW WEBSITE IN BROWSER & TEST LINKS | 6 VALIDATE PAGES

The **nav** section of the Forward Fitness Club website template and the home page currently contain text, but do not yet contain links to the pages in the website. Start by adding relative links to the navigation area of the website template to link to the home, About Us, Classes, Nutrition, and Contact Us pages. *Why? If you edit the template to include relative links, future pages created from the template will already have these links established.* The following steps add page links to a website template.

- Open your text editor to run the program.

- Tap or click File on the menu bar and then tap or click Open to display the Open dialog box.

- Navigate to your fitness folder and then double-tap or double-click the template folder to open it and display the fitness.html template file (Figure 3–8).

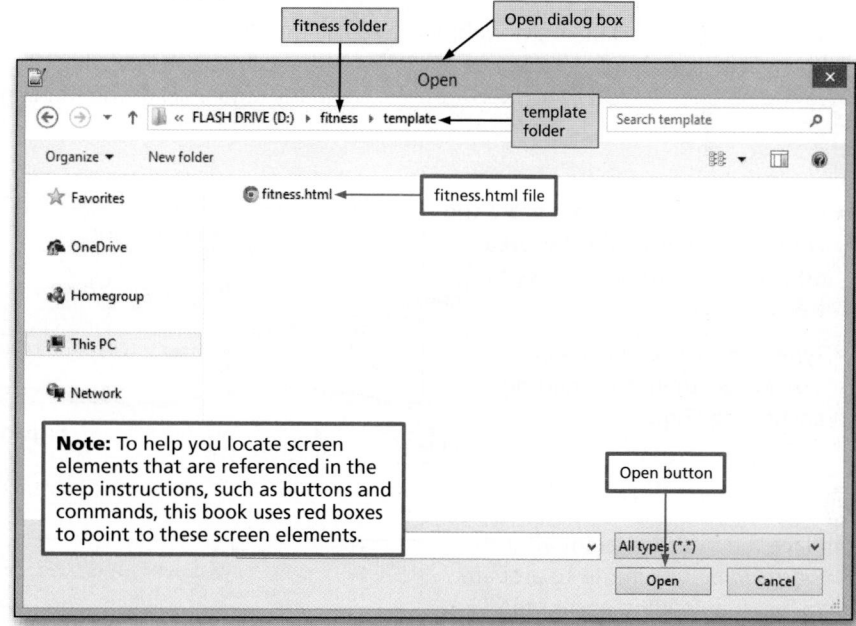

Figure 3–8

2

- Tap or click the fitness.html file and then tap or click the Open button to open the file in the text editor.

- Place the insertion point before the word *Forward* on Line 12 to prepare to insert a starting anchor tag.

- Type **<a href="index .html">** to insert a starting anchor tag (Figure 3–9).

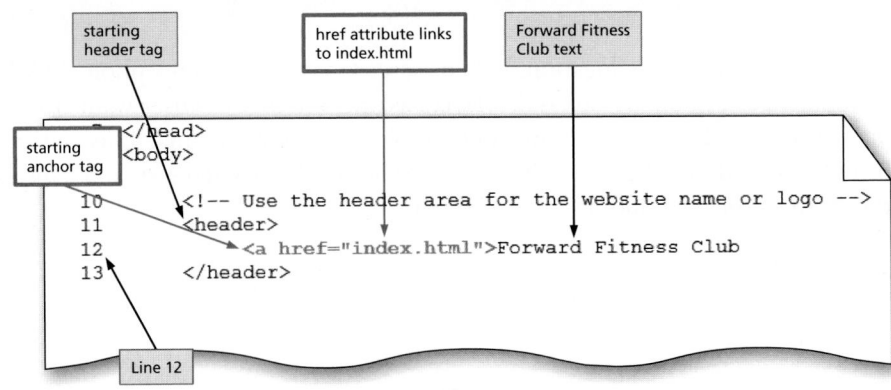

Figure 3–9

3

- Place the insertion point after the word *Club* on Line 12 to prepare to insert an ending anchor tag.

- Type **</a>** to insert an ending anchor tag (Figure 3–10).

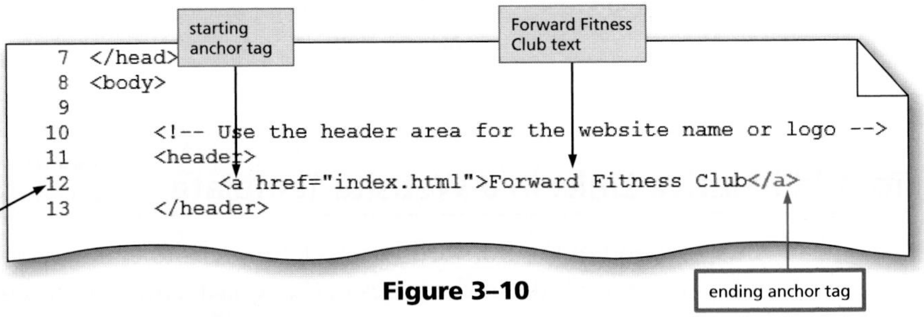

Q&A
Why is the ending tag </a> instead of </a href="index.html">?
An href attribute is defined only within the starting anchor tag. After you define an anchor with an attribute, you close the element with an </a> tag.

Why am I adding a link in the webpage header section?
You will soon replace the text in the header with a company logo, which should link to the home page. On many websites, the company logo links to the home page.

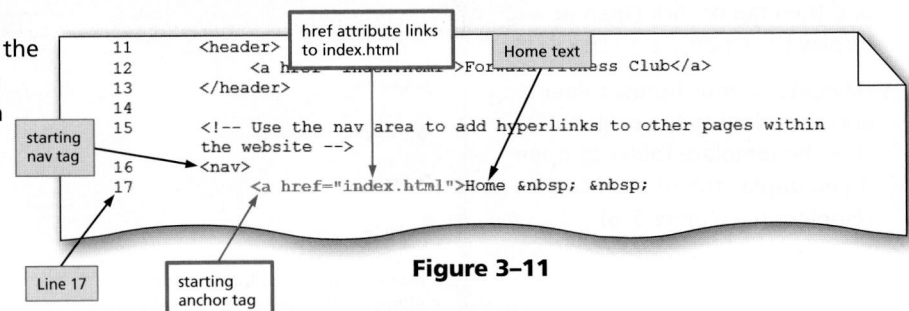

Figure 3–10

4

- Place the insertion point before the word *Home* within the nav area on Line 17 to prepare to insert a starting anchor tag.

- Type **<a href="index .html">** to insert a starting anchor tag (Figure 3–11).

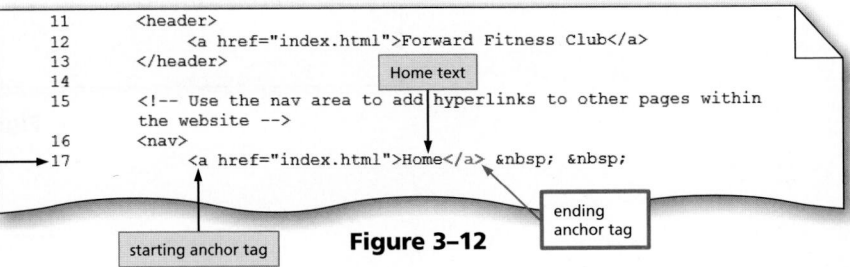

Figure 3–11

5

- Place the insertion point after the word *Home* on Line 17 to prepare to insert an ending anchor tag.

- Type **</a>** to insert an ending anchor tag (Figure 3–12).

Figure 3–12

6

- Place the insertion point before the word *About* on Line 18 to prepare to insert a starting anchor tag.

- Type `<a href="about .html">` to insert a starting anchor tag.

- Place the insertion point after the word *Us* on Line 18 to prepare to insert an ending anchor tag.

- Type `</a>` to insert an ending anchor tag (Figure 3–13).

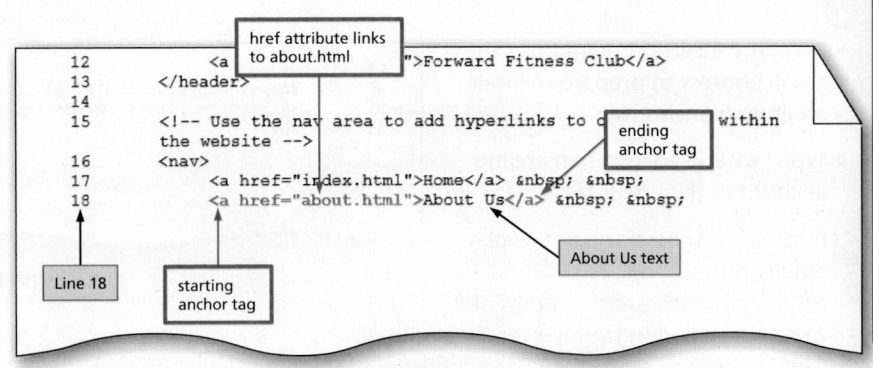

Figure 3–13

Q&A Why do I need to create a link to about.html when I have not yet created the about.html webpage?
You will use this template to create all future pages for this website. Creating the links now saves time coding for pages you create later.

7

- Using the same method as in Steps 2–5, insert anchor elements as shown in Table 3–1 to add hyperlinks to the remaining pages within the navigation area (Figure 3–14).

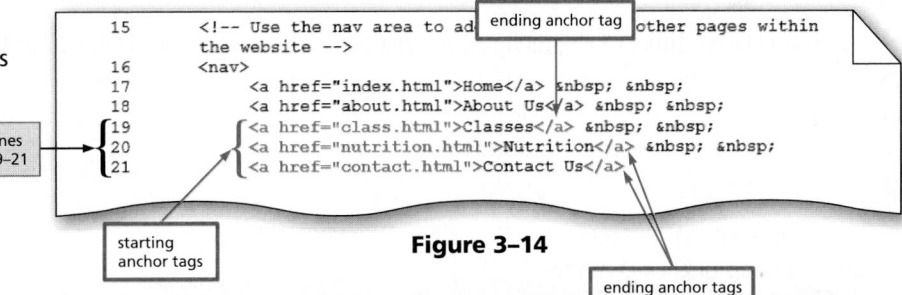

Figure 3–14

Table 3-1 Navigation Anchor Tags

Webpage Link	Anchor Tags
Classes	`<a href="class.html">Classes</a>`
Nutrition	`<a href="nutrition.html">Nutrition</a>`
Contact Us	`<a href="contact.html">Contact Us</a>`

To Add an Email Link in a Website Template

1 ADD HYPERLINKS | 2 ADD IMAGES | 3 ADD DIV ELEMENTS | 4 ADD HEADINGS & LISTS
5 VIEW WEBSITE IN BROWSER & TEST LINKS | 6 VALIDATE PAGES

Next, add an email link to the email address in the footer area of the template. *Why? Visitors can tap or click the link in the footer to quickly send an email message to the Forward Fitness Club.* The following steps insert an email link in a website template.

1

- Place your insertion point before forwardfitness@club.net on Line 31, located within the footer area, to prepare to insert an email anchor element.

- Type `<a href="mailto: forwardfitness@club.net">` to insert a starting anchor tag (Figure 3–15).

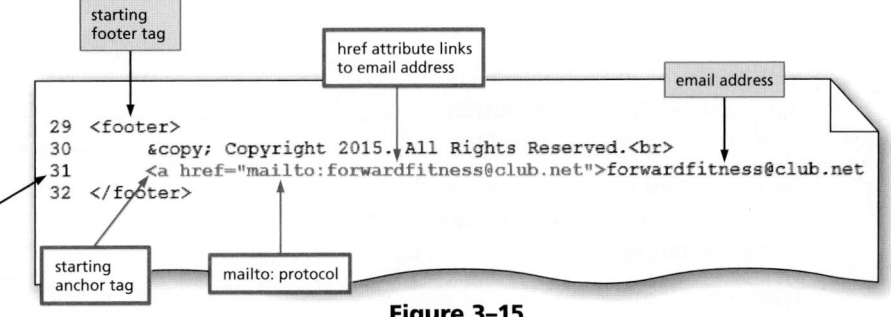

Figure 3–15

- Place the insertion point after the email address to prepare to insert an ending anchor tag.
  `Line 31`

- Type `</a>` to insert an ending anchor tag (Figure 3–16).

Q&A Is forwardfitness@club.net a valid email address?

No, forwardfitness@club.net is not a valid email address; however, tapping or clicking the email link still runs the default email application on your computer and creates a message addressed to forwardfitness@club.net. If you send a message to this email address, you will receive a delivery failure notice to advise you that the email submission failed.

```
29  <footer>
30      &copy; Copyright 2015. All Rights Reserved.<br>
31      <a href="mailto:forwardfitness@club.net">forwardfitness@club.net</a>
32  </footer>
```
`email address`
`starting anchor tag`
`ending anchor tag`

Figure 3–16

- Save your changes.

To Add Relative Links in the Home Page

1 ADD HYPERLINKS | 2 ADD IMAGES | 3 ADD DIV ELEMENTS | 4 ADD HEADINGS & LISTS
5 VIEW WEBSITE IN BROWSER & TEST LINKS | 6 VALIDATE PAGES

Add relative links to the navigation area of the home page to link to the home, About Us, Classes, Nutrition, and Contact Us pages. *Why? You have already created the home page, so it cannot benefit from the links you added to the template. The home page needs hyperlinks so visitors can navigate from the home page to other pages within the website.* The following steps add relative links to the home page.

- Tap or click File on the menu bar and then tap or click Open to display the Open dialog box.

- Navigate to your fitness folder to display the index.html file (Figure 3–17).

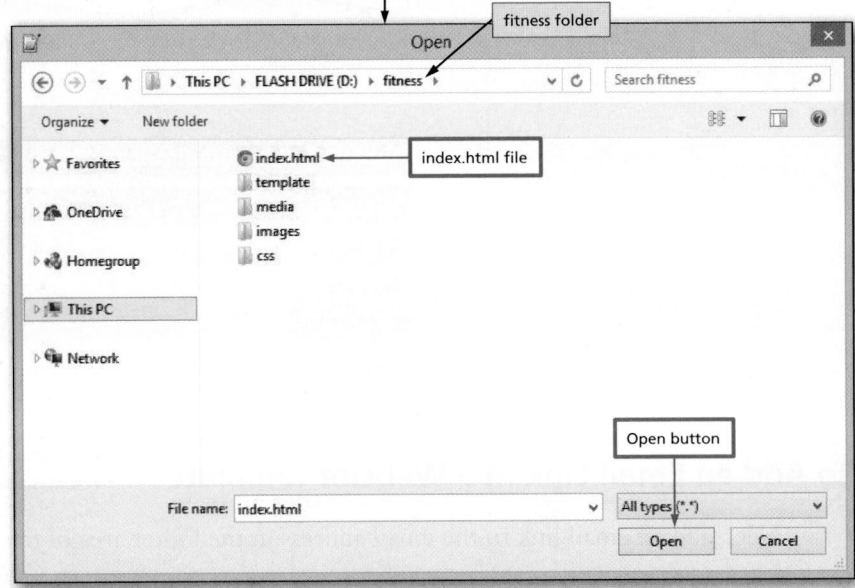

`Open dialog box`
`fitness folder`
`index.html file`
`Open button`

Figure 3–17

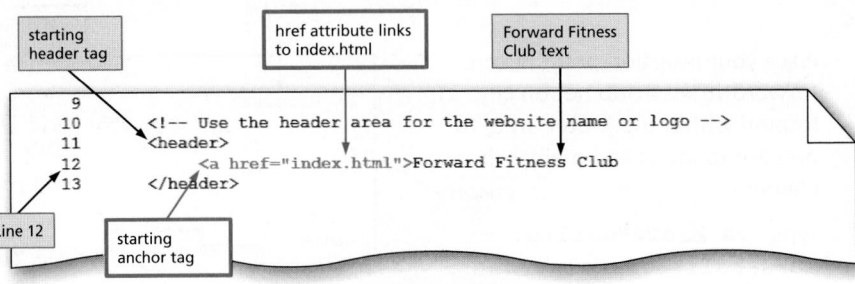

- Tap or click the index.html file and then tap or click the Open button to open the file in the text editor.

- Place the insertion point before the word *Forward* on Line 12 to prepare to insert a starting anchor tag.

- Type `<a href="index .html">` to insert a starting anchor tag (Figure 3–18).

```
 9
10      <!-- Use the header area for the website name or logo -->
11      <header>
12          <a href="index.html">Forward Fitness Club
13      </header>
```
`starting header tag`
`href attribute links to index.html`
`Forward Fitness Club text`
`Line 12`
`starting anchor tag`

Figure 3–18

3

- Place the insertion point after the word *Club* on Line 12 to prepare to insert an ending anchor tag.

- Type `</a>` to insert an ending anchor tag (Figure 3–19).

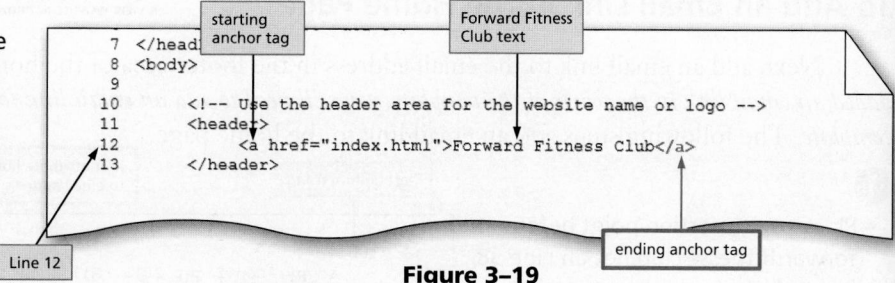

```
 7    </head
 8    <body>
 9
10        <!-- Use the header area for the website name or logo -->
11        <header>
12            <a href="index.html">Forward Fitness Club</a>
13        </header>
```

starting anchor tag

Forward Fitness Club text

Line 12

ending anchor tag

Figure 3–19

4

- Place the insertion point before the word *Home* within the nav area on Line 17 to prepare to insert a starting anchor tag.

- Type `<a href="index .html">` to insert a starting anchor tag (Figure 3–20).

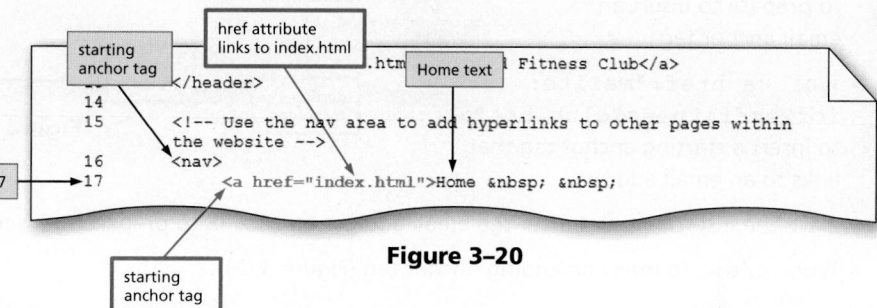

```
        .htm        Fitness Club</a>
    </header>
14
15        <!-- Use the nav area to add hyperlinks to other pages within
          the website -->
16        <nav>
17            <a href="index.html">Home    
```

starting anchor tag

href attribute links to index.html

Home text

Line 17

starting anchor tag

Figure 3–20

5

- Place the insertion point after the word *Home* on Line 17 to prepare to insert an ending anchor tag.

- Type `</a>` to insert an ending anchor tag (Figure 3–21).

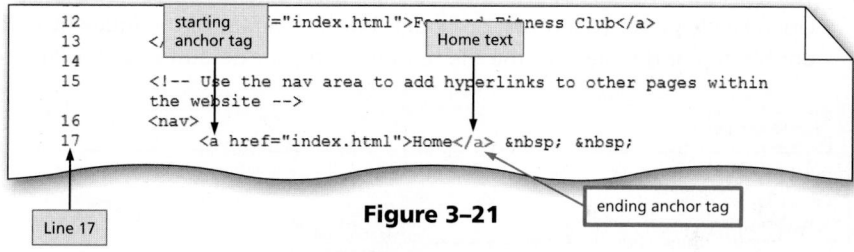

```
12                ="index.html">Forward Fitness Club</a>
13        </
14
15        <!-- Use the nav area to add hyperlinks to other pages within
          the website -->
16        <nav>
17            <a href="index.html">Home</a>    
```

starting anchor tag

Home text

Line 17

ending anchor tag

Figure 3–21

6

- Using the same method as in Steps 2–5, insert anchor elements as shown in Table 3–2 to add hyperlinks to the navigation area (Figure 3–22).

```
<!-- Use the nav area to add hyperlinks to other pages within the
website -->
<nav>
    <a href="index.html">Home</a>    
    <a href="about.html">About Us</a>    
    <a href="class.html">Classes</a>    
    <a href="nutrition.html">Nutrition</a>    
    <a href="contact.html">Contact Us</a>
```

ending anchor tags

starting anchor tags

ending anchor tags

Figure 3–22

Table 3-2 Navigation Anchor Tags

Webpage Link	Anchor Tags
About Us	`<a href="about.html">About Us</a>`
Classes	`<a href="class.html">Classes</a>`
Nutrition	`<a href="nutrition.html">Nutrition</a>`
Contact Us	`<a href="contact.html">Contact Us</a>`

To Add an Email Link in the Home Page

Next, add an email link to the email address in the footer area of the home page. *Why? Although you added an email link in the footer of the template, you still need to add an email link to the home page to match the website template.* The following steps add an email link to the home page.

● Place your insertion point before forwardfitness@club.net on Line 38, located within the footer area, to prepare to insert an email anchor tag.

● Type `<a href="mailto: forwardfitness@club.net">` to insert a starting anchor tag that links to an email address.

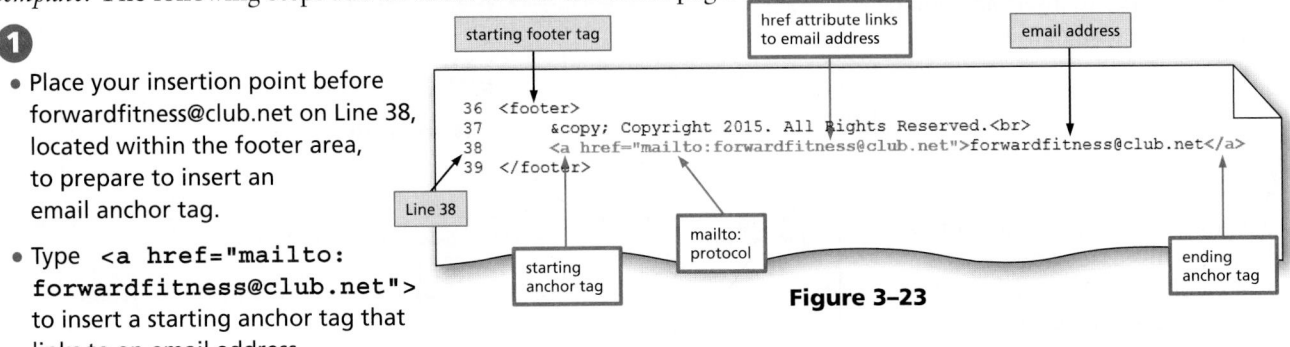

Figure 3–23

● Place the insertion point after the email address on Line 38 to prepare to insert an ending anchor tag.

● Type `</a>` to insert an ending anchor tag (Figure 3–23).

2

● Tap or click the Save button on the toolbar to save your changes.

● Open File Explorer (Windows) or Finder (Mac), navigate to the index.html file in the fitness folder, and then double-tap or double-click the file to open it in your default browser (Figure 3–24).

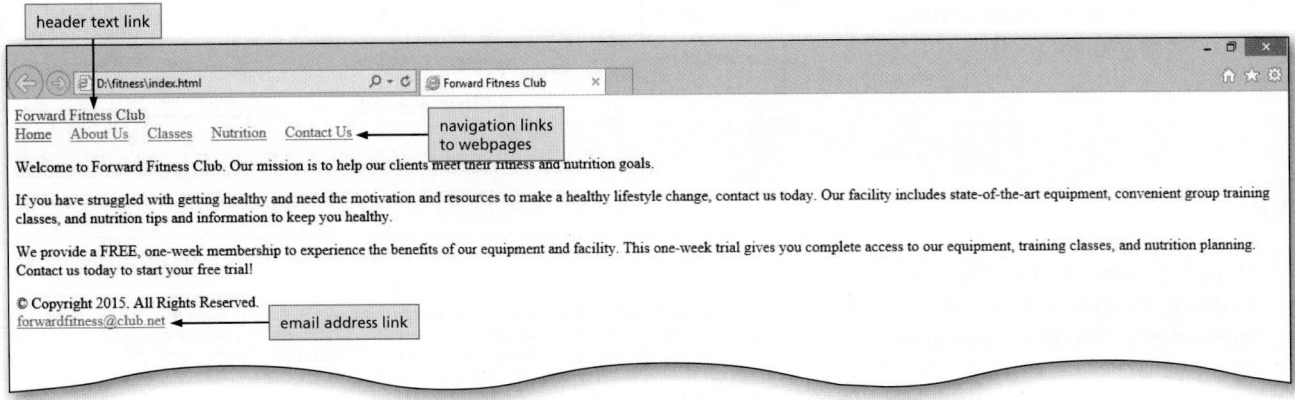

Figure 3–24

Experiment

● Tap or click the Home link and the email link, and then close the window for the new email message and close the browser.

BTW

Overusing Images

Be cautious about overusing images on a webpage. Using too many images may give your webpage a cluttered look or distract the visitor from the purpose of the webpage. An image should have a purpose, such as to convey content, visually organize a page, provide a hyperlink, or serve another function.

Adding Images to a Website

Images include photos, drawings, diagrams, charts, and other graphics that convey visual information. On a webpage, they help break up text and contribute to the design and aesthetics of a website. However, rather than merely decorate a webpage, images should support the purpose of the page or illustrate content. Images can also provide visual representations of a company's products and services. When determining what images to use within your website, choose those that relate directly to the content. Images that do not support the content can be distracting or confusing. For example, using images on a business website that do not pertain to the business may be perceived as unprofessional or may leave the user wondering what the business is actually selling. Figure 3–25 shows the website for Let's Move, an educational website created by the U.S. government to promote healthy eating. Note the use of the site's logo and photo to demonstrate a healthy lifestyle.

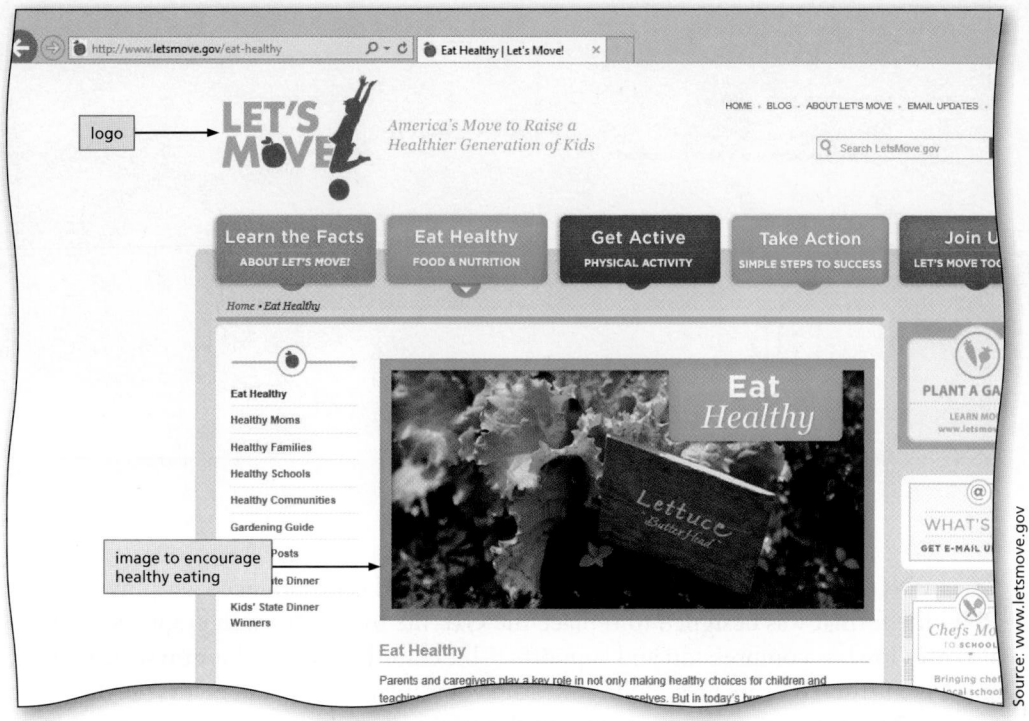

Figure 3–25

Image File Formats

When incorporating images into a website, web designers need to consider the file format, image dimensions, and file size. These factors affect the appearance of an image on a webpage and how long it takes the browser to display the image.

Image files are created in several formats; however, when adding images to a webpage, you must use image files in the GIF, PNG, JPG, or SVG format.

GIF stands for Graphics Interchange Format and is pronounced "jiff." GIF is the oldest web file format and supports transparency and frame animation. To create images that do not display a background color but have a transparent, or clear, background instead, you use a file format that supports transparency, such as GIF. Figure 3–26 shows an example of an image with and without transparency. GIF files can also be images that use frame animation, which is a series of drawings quickly displayed in a sequence to give the illusion of movement. To compress an image, or reduce its file size, the GIF format uses a technique called **lossless compression** that maintains the file's color information. GIF files are 8-bit images that can display up to 256 colors, making the file sizes relatively small. Because of the small color palette in GIF files, they are suitable for icons and line drawings, but not high-quality pictures or photos.

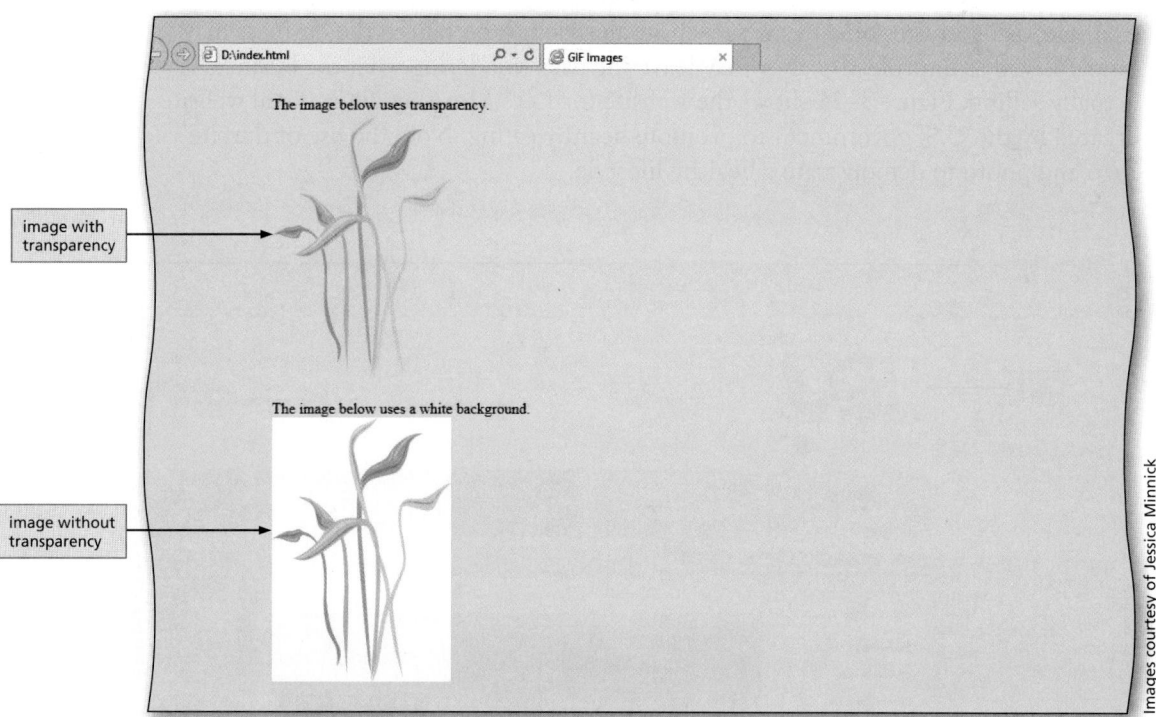

image with transparency

image without transparency

Images courtesy of Jessica Minnick

Figure 3–26

BTW
Animated GIF
To see an example of an animated GIF file, visit en.wikipedia.org/wiki/GIF.

PNG stands for Portable Network Graphics and is pronounced as "ping." The PNG file format was designed to replace the GIF file format for web graphics. PNG also uses lossless compression and supports 8-bit color images, 16-bit grayscale images, and 24-bit true-color images. PNG8 files are 8-bit images with 256 colors. PNG24 files are 24-bit images that can contain millions of colors. This is one advantage to using PNG compared to GIF: PNG24 can support over 16 million colors, whereas GIF supports only 256 colors. PNG also supports transparency, but not animation. In addition, PNG is not ideal for photographic images, as its lossless compression is not as efficient as that of the JPG format. Figure 3–27 shows an example of a website (usa.gov) that contains both GIF and PNG files.

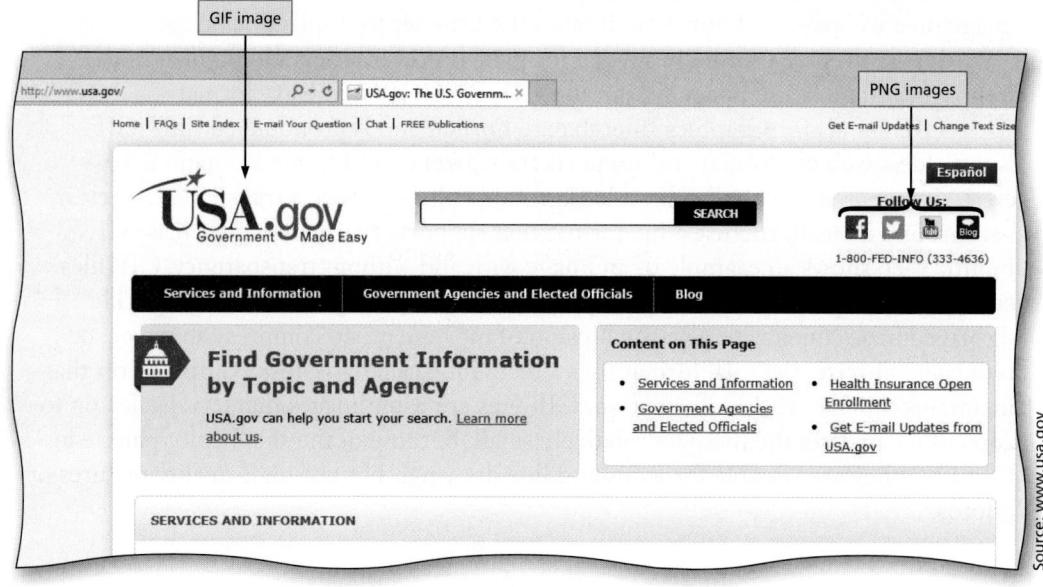

GIF image

PNG images

Source: www.usa.gov

Figure 3–27

JPG or **JPEG** stands for Joint Photographic Experts Group and is pronounced "jay-peg." This is the standard file format for a digital photo, such as one taken with a digital camera. The JPG format is a 24-bit image that supports 16.7 million colors, which is why it is used for digital photos and other pictures with a high level of detail or color complexity, such as shadows. JPG uses a **lossy compression** made exclusively for digital photos. To reduce file size, a lossy compression discards some of the color information in the image, which reduces its original quality. If you include a digital photo in your website, use a JPG or JPEG file format. Figure 3–28 shows a page from the National Park Service website that contains several JPG image files.

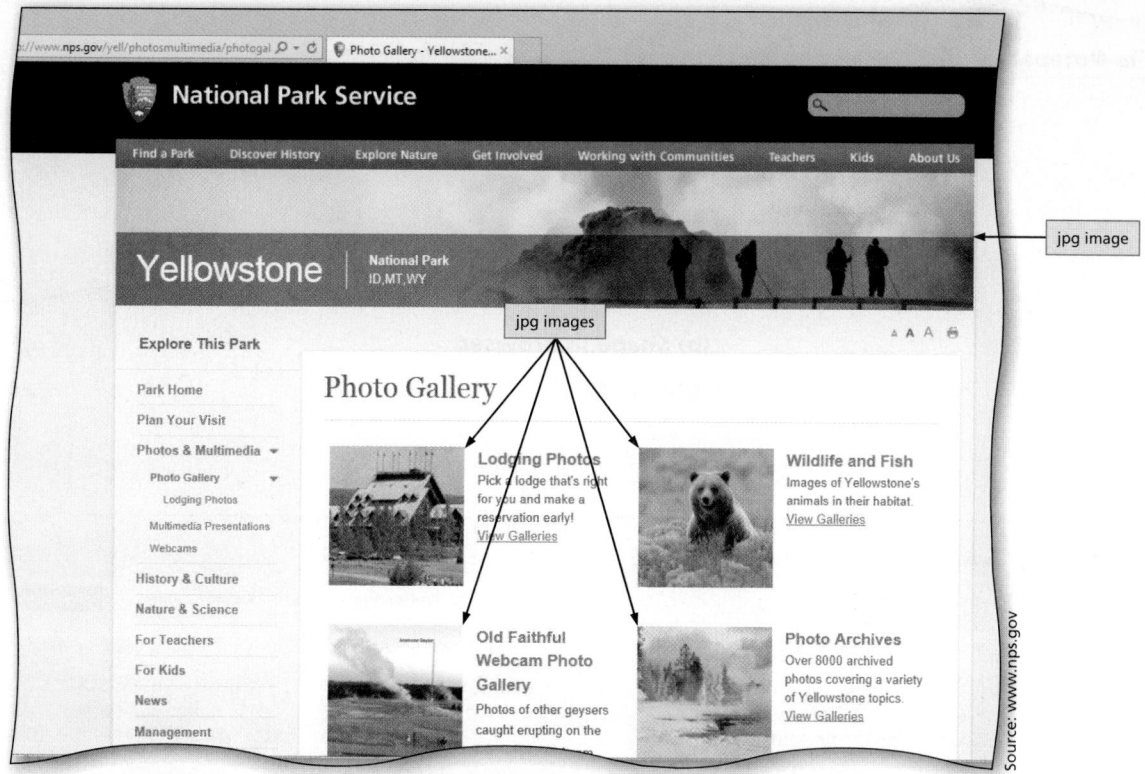

Figure 3–28

SVG stands for Scalable Vector Graphics, a format that uses markup language to create two-dimensional graphics, images, and animations. It is a royalty-free graphic format developed by the SVG working group at the W3C. The latest edition of SVG recommended by the W3C is version 1.1, second edition. Use SVG to create shapes such as circles, squares, rectangles, and lines. Only modern browsers can display SVG graphics, though no browser supports all SVG elements, so you must test for browser compatibility, which you can do at caniuse.com/svg. Currently, SVG is not a common image format on the web. Figure 3–29a shows an example of the SVG code required to create the circle shown on the webpage displayed in Figure 3–29b. An example of an SVG animation game is shown in Figure 3–30.

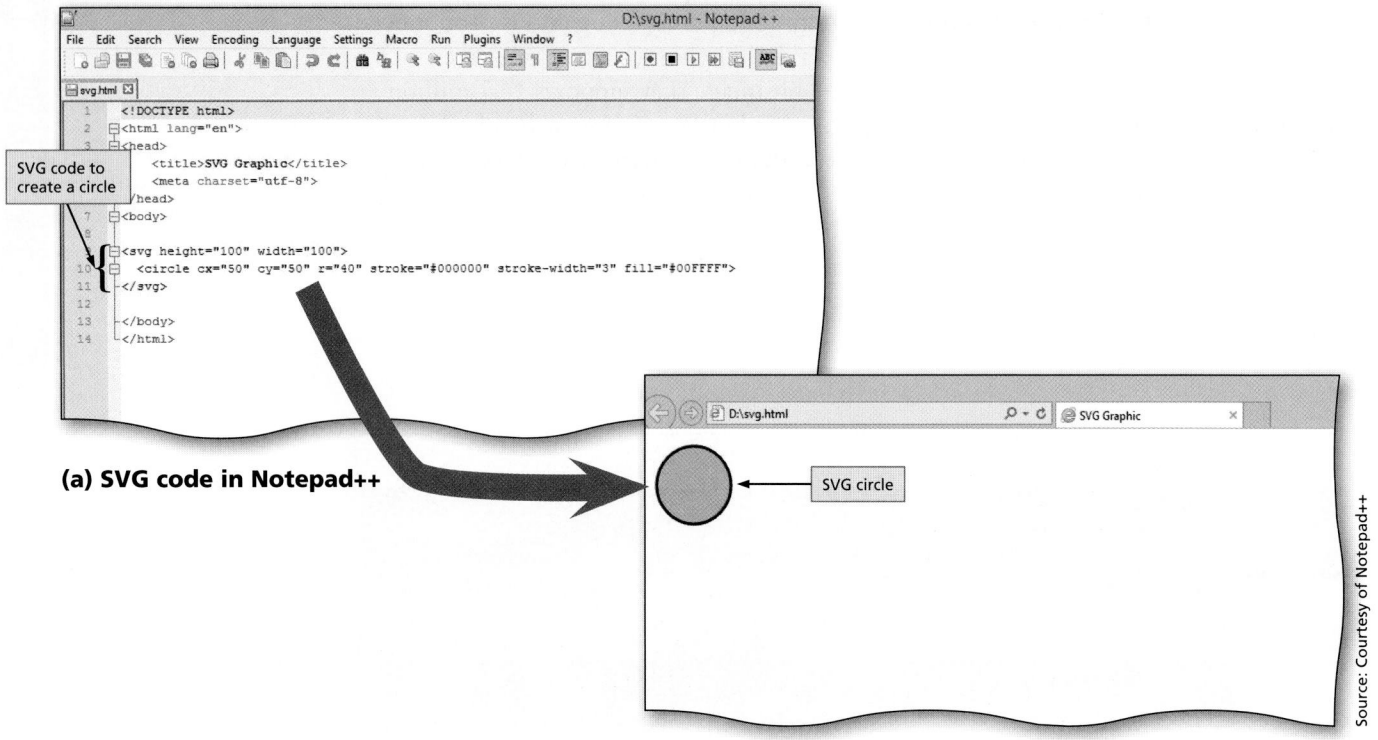

(a) SVG code in Notepad++

(b) Shape in browser

Figure 3–29

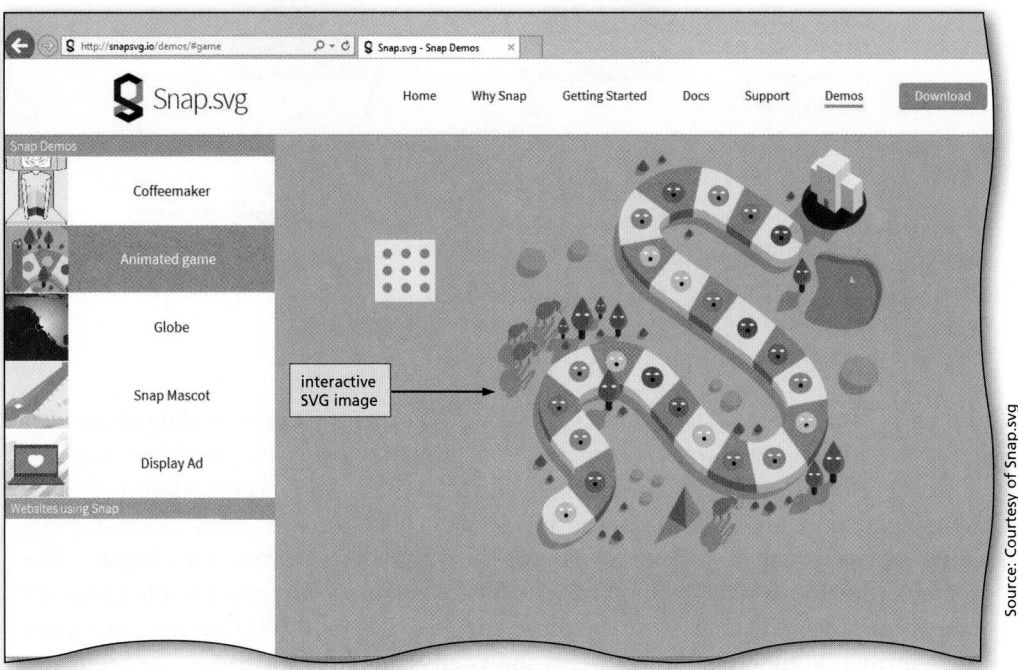

Figure 3–30

Table 3–3 summarizes the pros and cons of each image file format for the web.

Table 3-3 Choosing an Image File Format			
Format	**Pros**	**Cons**	**Use for**
GIF	Small file size; supports transparency and animation	Limited to 256 colors	Line drawings; replaced by PNG file format
PNG	Small file size; supports transparency and more than a million colors	Does not support animation	Images that are not digital photos
JPG	Supports more than a million colors	Larger file size	Digital photos
SVG	Flexible; scalable; no files needed because graphics are created with code	Not supported by older browsers and not all modern browsers support it 100 percent	Shapes, lines, text, and gradients

Image Dimensions and File Size

To display content, monitors and other screen devices use pixels. A **pixel**, a term coined from "picture element," is the smallest element of light or color on a device displaying images. Pixels are arranged in rows and columns to compose an image, but are usually so small that you cannot see them, making the image appear smooth and fluid. Webpage images can be measured in pixels. For example, an image may be 200 × 200 pixels, which means it has a height of 200 pixels and a width of 200 pixels.

Monitors and other screen devices have a default resolution, which determines the clarity of the content displayed on the screen. The higher the screen resolution, the sharper text and images appear. A common resolution for today's laptops is 1366 × 768 pixels. The resolution of a device's screen dictates the number of pixels that can appear in an image. The higher the resolution, the greater the number of pixels in the image, resulting in a sharp, clear image.

File size is the number of bytes a file contains, though the size of an image file is usually expressed as kilobytes (KB), thousands of bytes; megabytes (MB), millions of bytes; or gigabytes (GB), billions of bytes. The disadvantage of an image with a high resolution is that it also has a large file size. If a webpage contains an image, the file size of the image can determine how long it takes for the webpage to load in a browser. If a webpage contains several large image files, the page might be slow to load, especially on a mobile device. Today's users expect pages to load as soon as they tap or click a link. The key to reducing page load time is keeping the webpage file small. Though a webpage itself may load quickly, large images on the webpage can take longer to appear.

When you choose a file format for an image, file size is a major factor. For example, JPG files can be large files; a detailed digital photo contains much more data than a simple line drawing in a GIF format. If you are using images with large file sizes, use a photo or graphics editor, such as Adobe Photoshop, to **optimize** the graphic for web use. Optimizing an image reduces its file size and load time. To optimize an image file for web use, you can crop the image, modify its dimensions to make it smaller, adjust the quality, or convert the image file format. When preparing an image file for web use, keep in mind that reducing the file size can also decrease the quality of the image. To retain the original high-quality image, make a copy of the original file and optimize the copy. Figure 3–31 shows the same image at various levels of compression that reduced file size. As the figure shows, too much compression can degrade the quality of the image.

original image   reduced image quality   further reduced image quality

Source: Courtesy of Jessica Minnick

Figure 3–31

In Adobe Photoshop, you use the Save for Web dialog box to adjust the file format, file quality, and size of an image file to optimize the image for web use. The dialog box displays the same image at different quality settings along with the corresponding file size and load time. For example, Figure 3–32 shows the same image as in Figure 3–31, with the file size of 549 K for the original image. Changing the Quality setting to 100 reduces the file size to 142 K and estimates a load time of 7 seconds without a noticeable change in quality. Changing the Quality setting to 10 further reduces the file size to 13.26 K and the load time to 1 second, but also degrades the image quality.

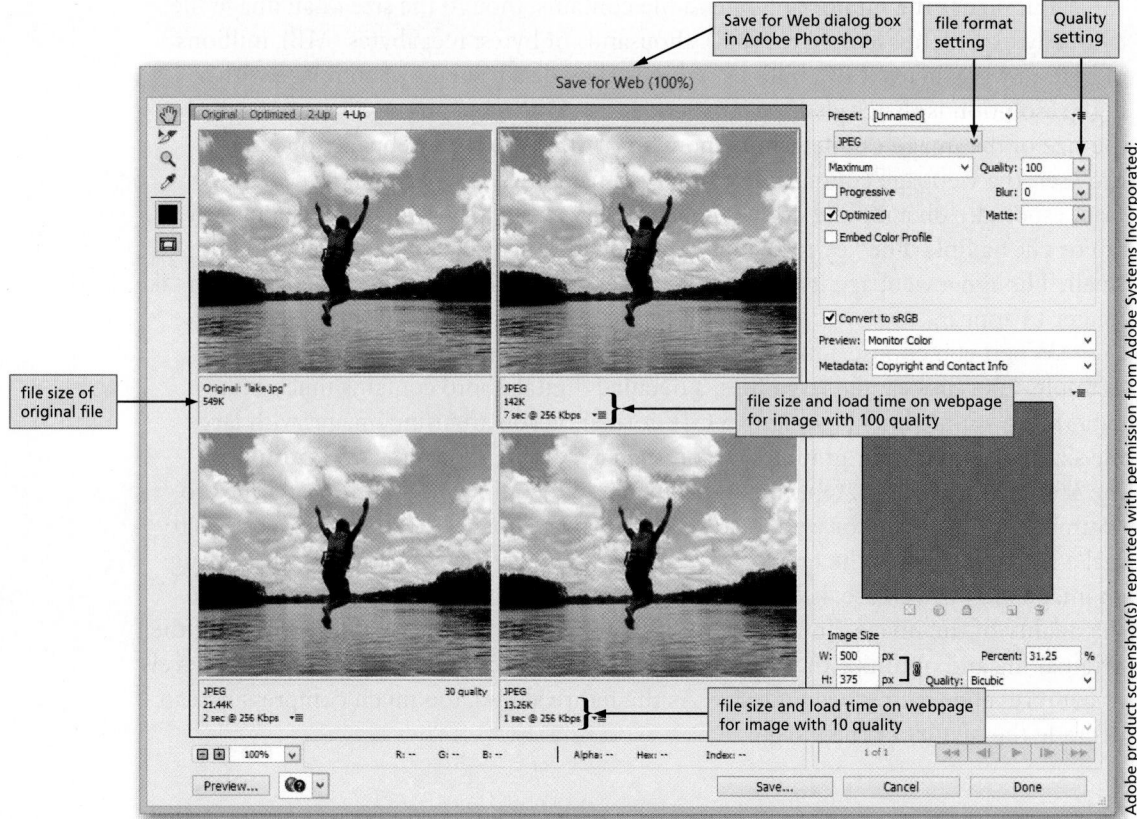

Save for Web dialog box in Adobe Photoshop   file format setting   Quality setting

file size of original file

file size and load time on webpage for image with 100 quality

file size and load time on webpage for image with 10 quality

Adobe product screenshot(s) reprinted with permission from Adobe Systems Incorporated; photo courtesy of Jessica Minnick

Figure 3–32

To Optimize an Image for Web Use with Adobe Photoshop

Before you use a digital photo on a webpage, you should optimize the photo for web use to reduce its file size. If you want to optimize an image using Photoshop, you would complete the following steps.

1. Open the digital photo in Adobe Photoshop.
2. Tap or click File on the application bar to display the File menu.
3. Tap or click Save for Web to display the Save for Web dialog box.
4. Tap or click the 4-up tab to display the different load times and file sizes of the image.
5. Select the JPEG file format setting, and then adjust the photo quality and the image size.
6. Tap or click the image you want to save, and then tap or click the Save button to save the image file.

Image Tag and Its Attributes

The **image tag**, <img>, is an empty HTML tag used to add an image to a webpage. As an empty tag, the image tag does not have an ending tag. It includes many attributes, such as the required file source attribute, **src**, which identifies the image file being inserted. An example of an image element with a source attribute is <img src="logo .png">. This code tells the browser to display the image file named logo.png. Table 3–4 shows a list of common attributes used with the image element.

Table 3-4 Image Element Attributes	
Attribute	**Function**
src	Identifies the file name of the image to display
alt	Specifies alternate text to display when an image is being loaded
	Especially useful for screen readers, which translate information on a computer screen into audio output
	Should briefly describe the purpose of the image in 50 characters or less
height	Defines the height of the image in pixels, which improves loading time
width	Defines the width of the image in pixels, which improves loading time

You should always use the **alt** attribute in an image tag to specify alternate text in case the image cannot be displayed in a browser. The alternate text briefly describes the image. Screen readers recite alternate text to address accessibility. An example of an image tag with **src** and **alt** attributes is <img src= "logo. png"alt ="Company logo">. This code means the browser should retrieve and display the image file named logo.png and provide "Company logo" as the alternate text. Figure 3–33 shows an example of alternative text displayed in a browser that is unable to display an image.

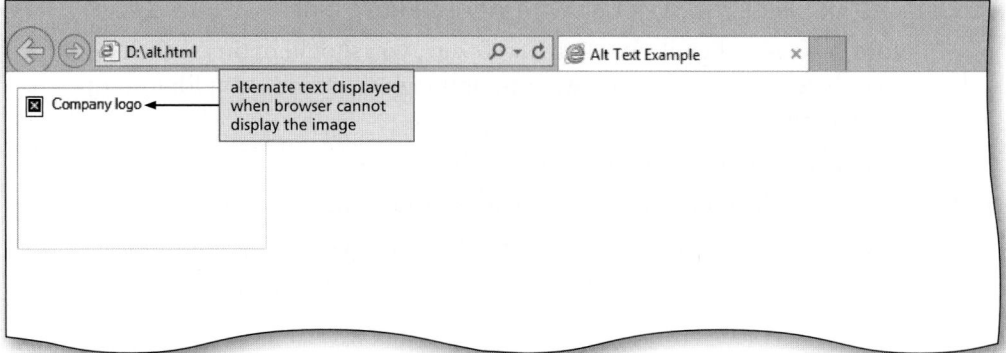

Figure 3–33

When you add an image to a webpage, you can also define the image's height and width. A browser uses these attributes to reserve the amount of space needed for the image. An example of an image tag with attributes is shown in Figure 3–34.

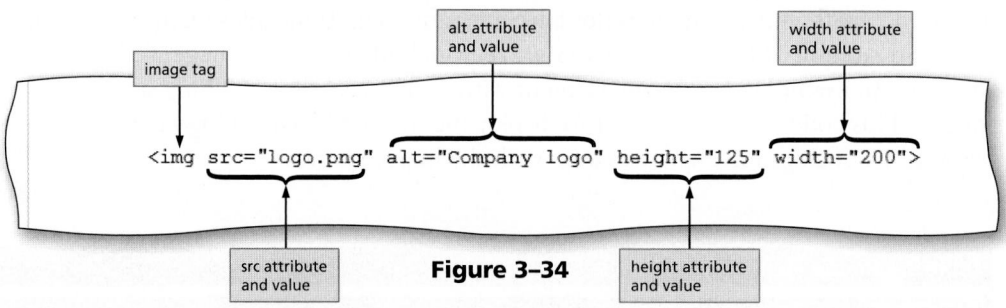

Figure 3–34

A browser interprets the code in Figure 3–34 as follows:

1. First, the browser reads the starting image tag, which indicates the browser should display an image on the webpage.
2. The src="logo.png" attribute and value identify the name of the image to display.
3. The alt="Company logo" attribute and value identify the alternate text to display if the browser cannot display the image.
4. The height="125" attribute and value reserve the height needed to display the image in a browser.
5. The width="200" attribute and value reserve the width needed to display the image in a browser, and the right angle bracket (>) closes the image element.

When specifying values for the **height** and **width** attributes of an image, use the actual dimensions of the image. For example, the code shown in Figure 3–34 is appropriate for an image with a height of 125 pixels and a width of 200 pixels. (You can find the dimensions of an image file by opening it in a graphics editor such as Photoshop or Paint or by displaying the file's properties using File Explorer or Finder.) If you make the dimensions larger than the actual image, you reduce the quality, which can result in a blurry or distorted image. Making the dimensions smaller than the actual image does not improve the browser's page load time because the image file size remains the same. If you need to use a smaller image, adjust its dimensions in a graphics editor first. Many graphics editors, including Photoshop, let you change the width and height of an image. Be sure to use an option such as "Constrain proportions" or "Maintain aspect ratio" to change each dimension in proportion to the other, which is called maintaining the aspect ratio. Otherwise, you are likely to distort the image. Figure 3–35 shows an example of an image displayed in a browser with its original dimensions and with larger dimensions. The bottom image uses dimensions larger than the file size and does not maintain the aspect ratio, which distorts the image.

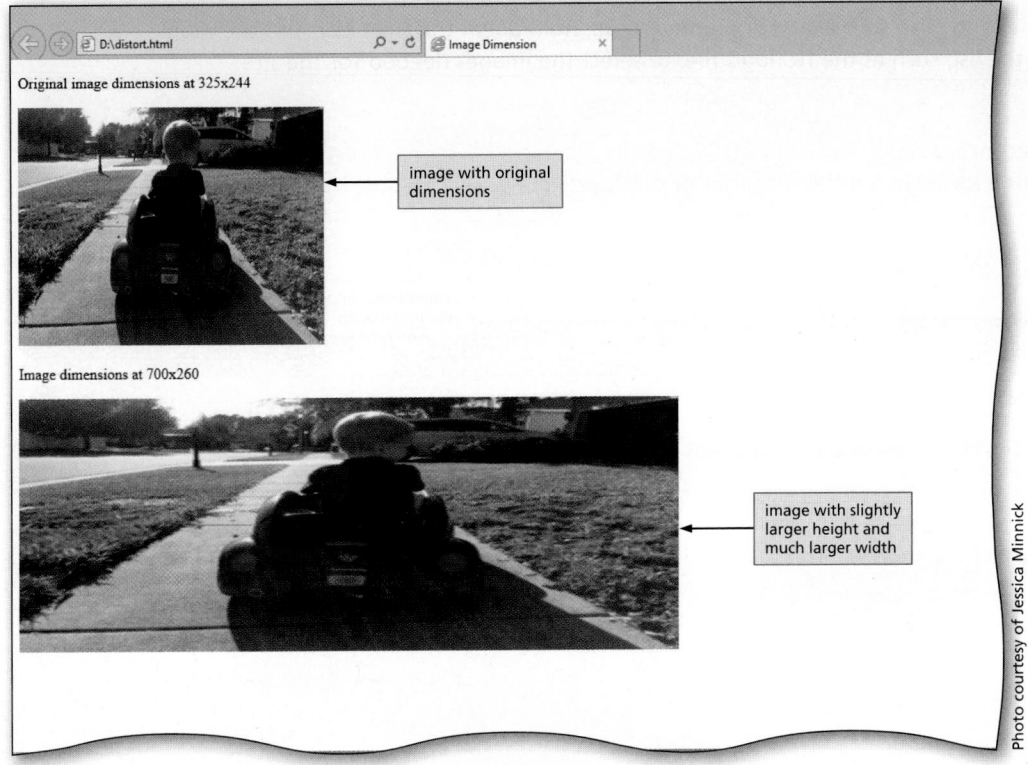

Photo courtesy of Jessica Minnick

Figure 3–35

Using the **height** and **width** attributes in an image element establishes a fixed size for the image, which can affect the webpage layout. A webpage can have a fixed layout or a fluid layout (also called a flexible or a responsive layout). A webpage with a fixed layout does not change when the browser window is resized or the page is displayed at varying resolutions. In a fixed layout, every element has a predefined height and width. However, as you progress further into this book and begin to design responsively for mobile, tablet, and desktop devices, you will learn how to create fluid layouts and images with CSS. Fluid images adjust their size for optimal display on a desktop, tablet, and mobile device.

To Copy Files into the Images Folder

Before you can add an image to a site, you need to acquire the images and store them in the folder designated for images on your website. *Why? You need to have image files and know where they are stored before you can add them to a webpage. In the following steps, you copy image files to your images folder.* The following steps copy four images files from the Data Files for Students to the images folder for the fitness site.

- If necessary, insert the drive containing the Data Files for Students into an available port.

- Use File Explorer (Windows) or Finder (Mac) to navigate to the storage location of the Data Files for Students.

- Double-tap or double-click the chapter03 folder, double-tap or double-click the fitness folder, and then double-tap or double-click the images folder to open the images folder and display the image files.

- Tap or click the first file in the list, such as the equipment1 file, hold down the SHIFT key, and then tap or click the last file in the list, such as the ffc_logo file, to select the images needed for the site (Figure 3–36).

Q&A Why is my file list different?
Your list of files might be sorted in a different order or displayed in a view different from the one shown in Figure 3–36.

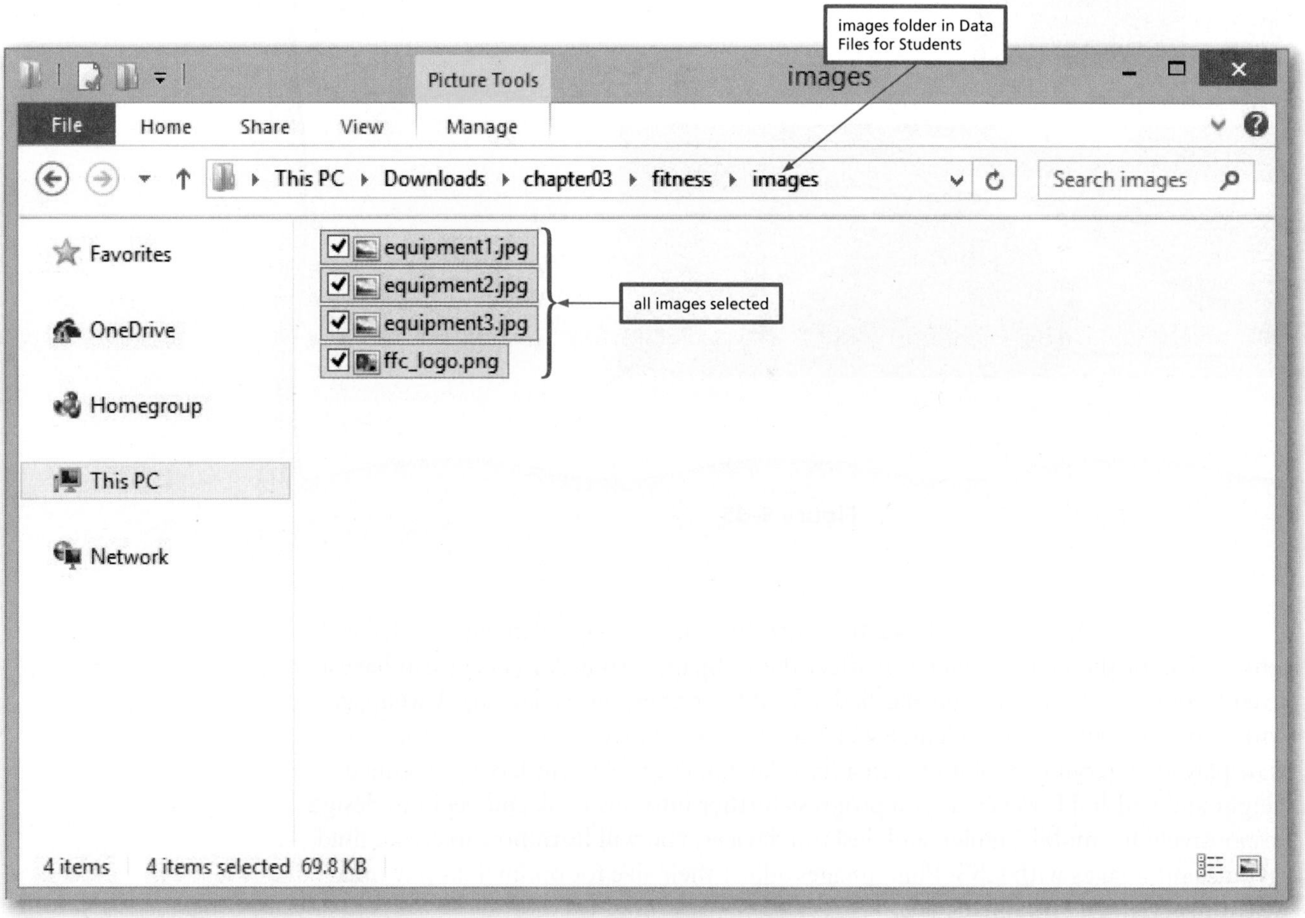

Figure 3–36

2

- Press and hold or right-click the selected files, tap or click Copy on the shortcut menu, and then navigate to the images folder in your fitness folder to prepare to copy the files to your images folder.

- Press and hold or right-click a blank area in the open window, and then tap or click Paste on the shortcut menu to copy the files into the images folder.

- Verify that the folder now contains four images (Figure 3–37).

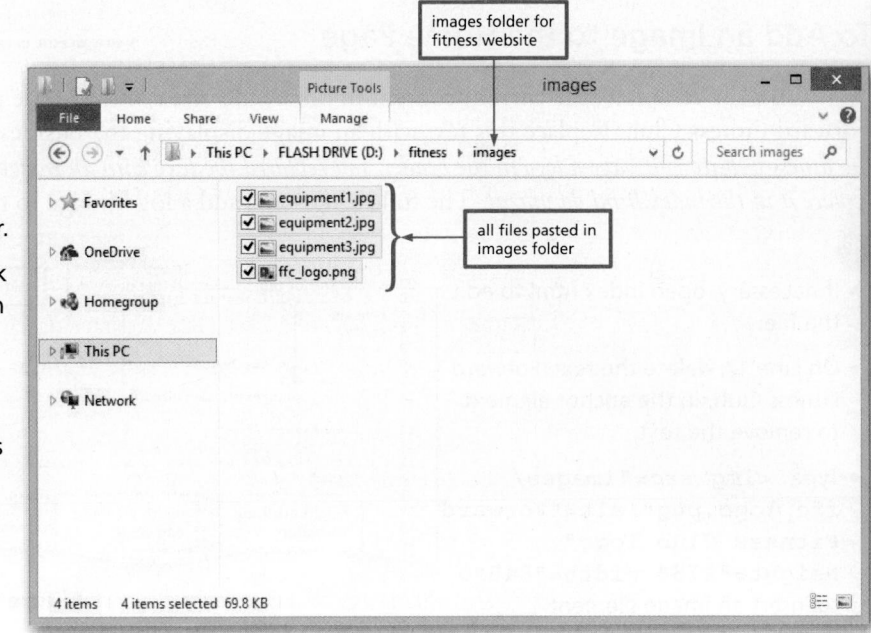

Figure 3–37

Other Ways

1 Select files, tap or click Copy button (Home tab | Clipboard group), navigate to destination folder, tap or click Paste button (Home tab | Clipboard group)

2 Select files, press CTRL+C, navigate to destination folder, press CTRL+V (Mac users: press COMMAND+C and COMMAND+V)

To Add an Image to a Website Template

1 ADD HYPERLINKS | 2 ADD IMAGES | 3 ADD DIV ELEMENTS | 4 ADD HEADINGS & LISTS
5 VIEW WEBSITE IN BROWSER & TEST LINKS | 6 VALIDATE PAGES

In the template, the current content in the header area is the name of the business, Forward Fitness Club. Replace this text with an image displaying the business logo. *Why? Most businesses use a logo on their webpages to promote their business and brand.* The following steps add a logo image to a website template.

1

- If necessary, open fitness.html to open the template file.

- On Line 12, delete the text, Forward Fitness Club, in the anchor element to remove the text.

- Type `<img src="images/ffc_logo.png" alt="Forward Fitness Club logo" height="275" width="845">` to insert an image element (Figure 3–38).

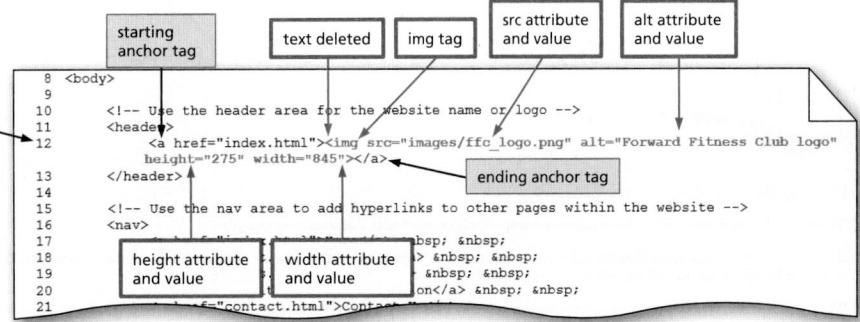

Figure 3–38

 Why do I need to type images/ before the name of the logo file?
All images, including the logo, are stored in the images folder, so you must include the folder name in the path to the logo file.

2

- Save your changes.

After I saved my changes, I viewed the template in my browser and the alternate text appears instead of the logo. Why?
You save the template file in the template folder, so the browser is looking for the ffc_logo.png file in an images subfolder of the template folder, which does not exist. When you create pages based on the template, you will store them in the fitness folder, which does contain the image folder, so this path will be correct for each webpage.

To Add an Image to the Home Page

Like the template, the current content in the header area of the home page is the name of the business, Forward Fitness Club. Replace this text with an image displaying the business logo. *Why? All of the pages in the fitness website will have a logo in the header. You replaced the text with an image in the template file, but still need to replace it in the index.html document.* The following steps add a logo image to the home page.

- If necessary, open index.html to edit the file.

- On Line 12, delete the text, Forward Fitness Club, in the anchor element to remove the text.

- Type `<img src="images/ffc_logo.png" alt="Forward Fitness Club logo" height="275" width="845">` to insert an image element (Figure 3–39).

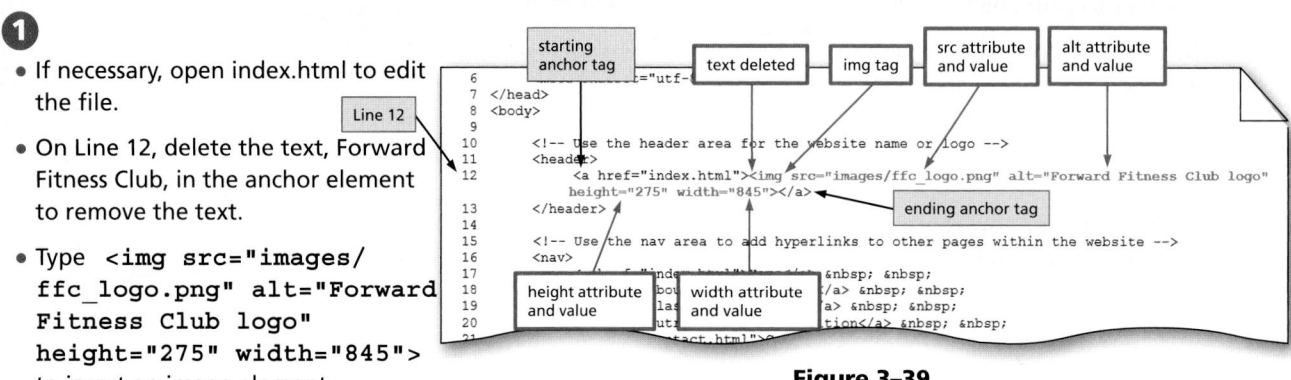

Figure 3–39

- Save your changes.

- Open File Explorer (Windows) or Finder (Mac), navigate to the index.html file, and then double-tap or double-click the file to open it in your default browser (Figure 3–40).

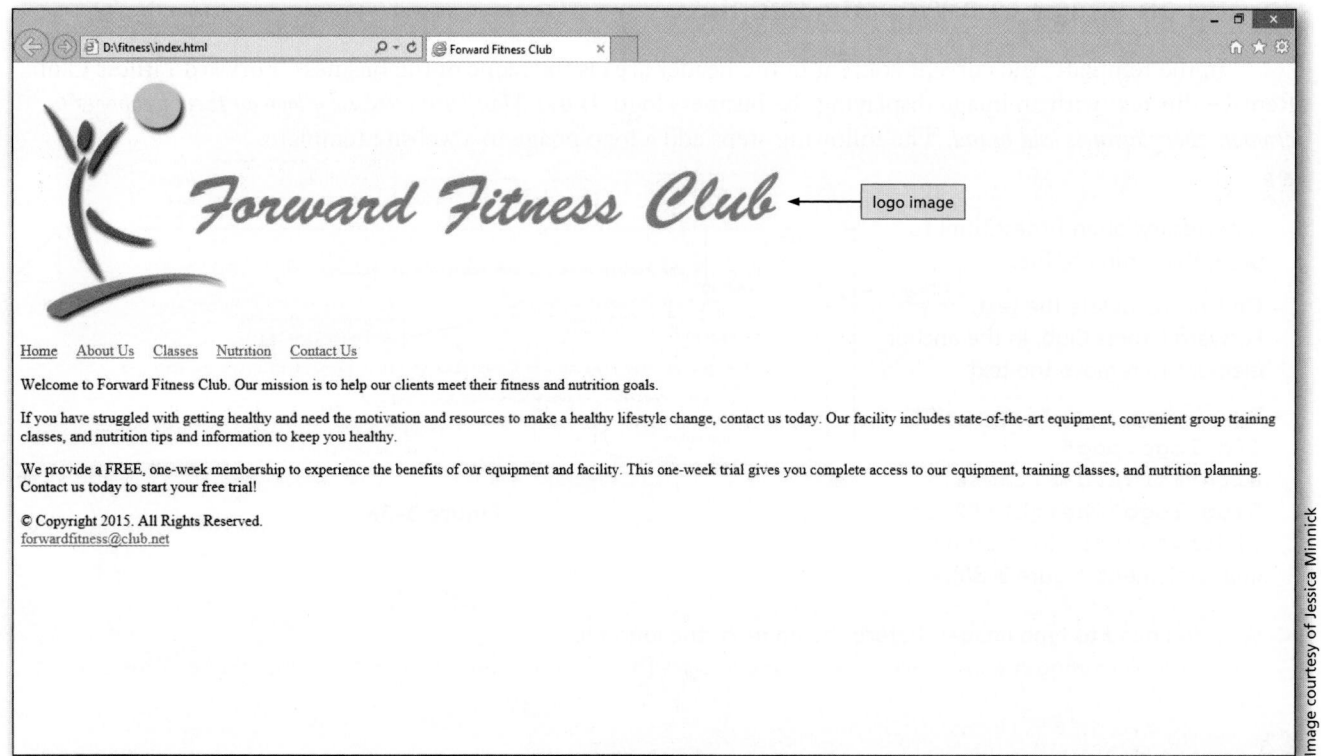

Figure 3–40

Image courtesy of Jessica Minnick

Break Point: If you want to take a break, this is a good place to do so. You can exit the text editor now. To resume at a later time, run your text editor, open the file called fitness.html, and continue following the steps from this location forward.

Exploring Div Elements

As you have learned, every webpage consists of several essential lines of HTML code used to display and support content in a browser. In addition, you use HTML5 tags to identify specific areas on a webpage, such as the header, navigation area, main content area, and the footer. These are just a few of the basic HTML tags used to display a webpage. You can use other types of HTML tags to organize and display content on a webpage.

Div Element

Use a **div element** to define an area or a division in a webpage. You insert `div` elements with the <div> and </div> tags. Prior to HTML5, `div` elements defined specific areas on a webpage, such as the header, navigation area, main content area, and footer. The HTML5 semantic elements replace the `div` elements for these areas because the new, more meaningful HTML5 elements better reflect their purpose. However, web designers still use the `div` element on their websites; it is not an obsolete element. One reason is that many well-established websites still have webpages that were created using `div` elements where more semantic HTML5 elements would now apply. Some people and organizations use older browsers that can read `div` elements but not HTML5 elements. More commonly, web designers use `div` elements to structure parts of a webpage to which an HTML5 element does not apply. For example, recall that the `main` element identifies the primary content for the page and that you can have only one `main` element on a webpage. You can also use `div` elements within the `main` element to further divide the primary content area into separate sections, such as the introduction, a long quotation, a list of "See Also" links, and a conclusion. Figure 3–41 shows a wireframe with four `div` elements inside the `main` element.

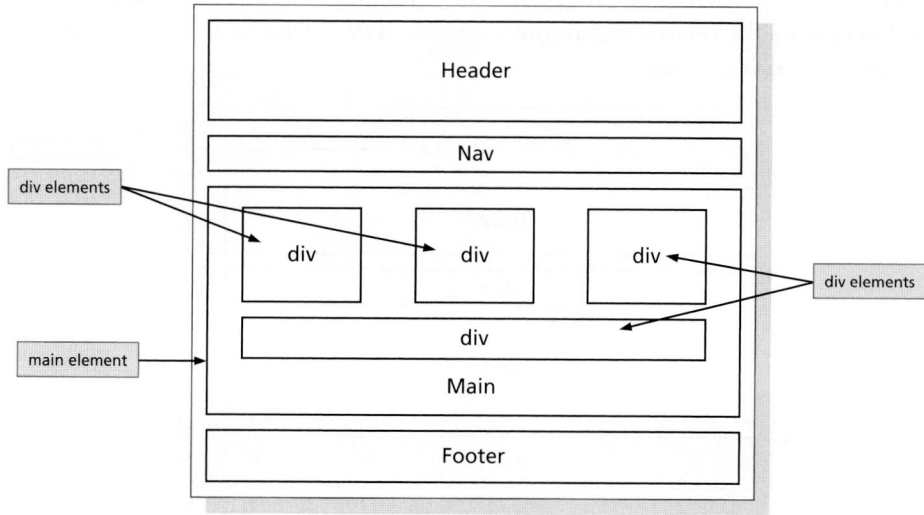

Figure 3–41

Div Attributes

Like other elements, `div` elements have attributes that provide more meaningful information about the element. One div attribute is **id**, which identifies a unique area on a webpage and distinguishes it from other page divisions. For example, <div id="menu"> is a starting div tag with an `id` attribute that has a value of `menu`. You might use this element to identify a menu of options on the webpage. The `id` attribute value must be unique — no other `div` element on the webpage can have an `id` attribute value of `menu`. Figure 3–42 shows an example of `div` elements used in lieu of HTML5 semantic elements. Because each `div` element has a different `id` attribute value, browsers interpret the content in those elements as belonging to different areas of the webpage.

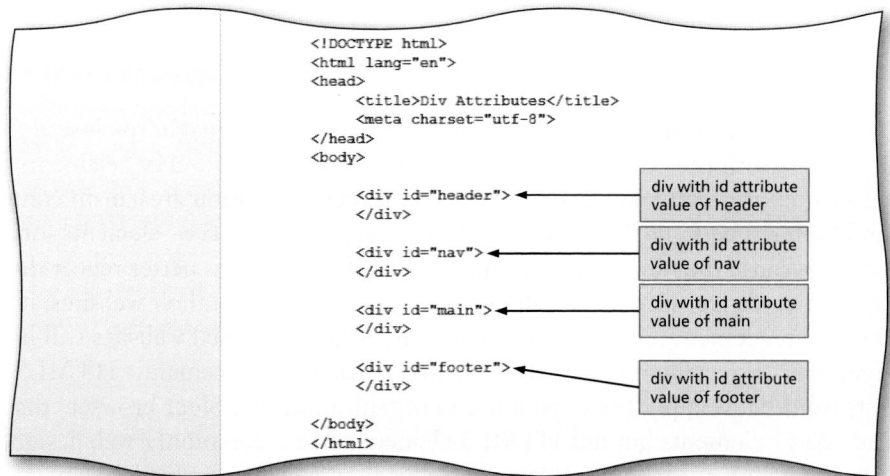

Figure 3–42

To gain flexibility in formatting the webpages on the Forward Fitness Club website, you can add a `div` element to the wireframe and template of the website. The purpose of the new `div` element is to contain all of the other webpage elements, including **header, nav, main,** and **footer**. Containing these HTML5 elements within a single `div` element prepares the template and future pages for CSS styles, such as one that centers the webpage in a browser window. Figure 3–43 shows the revised wireframe with the `div` element and `id` attribute value defined as `container`.

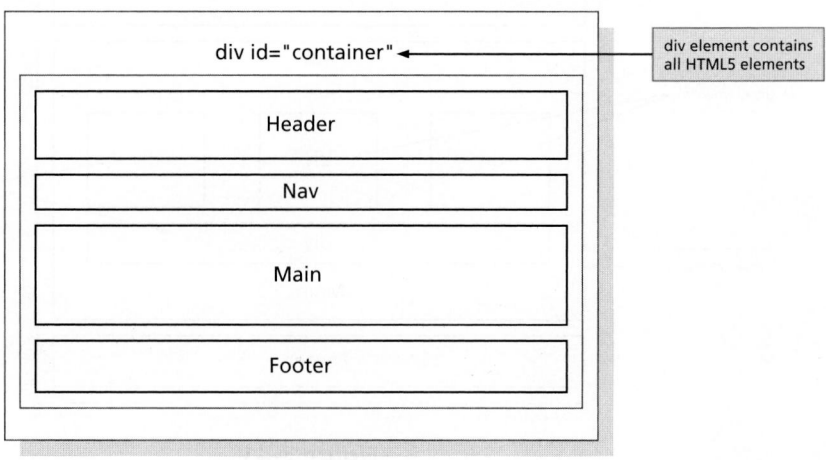

Figure 3–43

Why is "container" the value of the id attribute?
Because this div element will contain all of the webpage elements, it is commonly referred to as the container or the wrapper because it contains or wraps around all of the webpage elements, similar to how a fence wraps around a physical piece of property to contain things on the property.

To Add a Div Element to a Website Template

1 ADD HYPERLINKS | 2 ADD IMAGES | 3 ADD DIV ELEMENTS | 4 ADD HEADINGS & LISTS
5 VIEW WEBSITE IN BROWSER & TEST LINKS | 6 VALIDATE PAGES

Apply the changes from the Forward Fitness website wireframe to the template. Add a **div** element with an **id** attribute and an attribute value of **container** to contain all of the HTML5 webpage elements in the fitness template, including **header, nav, main,** and **footer.** *Why? Because the template will be used to create future pages for the website, edit the template so that all pages use the same layout.* The following steps add a **div** element with an **id** attribute value of **container** to the website template.

1

- If necessary, open the fitness.html template file to prepare to insert a div element.

- Place the insertion point after the starting <body> tag and then press the ENTER key two times to create a new Line 10.

- Press the TAB key to indent the line.

- Type **<div id="container">** to insert a div element with an id attribute and value (Figure 3–44).

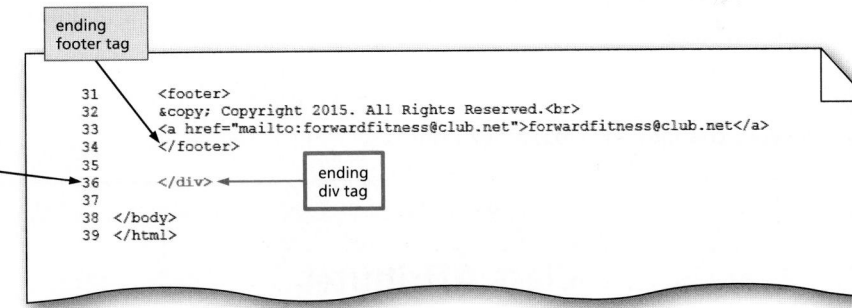

```
starting          div element with id
body tag          attribute and value

 8  <body>
 9
10       <div id="container">
11
12       <!-- Use the header area for the website name or logo -->
13       <header>
14            <a href="index.html"><img src="images/ffc_logo.png" alt="Forward Fitness Club logo"
                  height="275" width="845"></a>
15       </header>
    Line 10
```

Figure 3–44

2

- Place the insertion point after the ending </footer> tag and press the ENTER key two times to create a new Line 36.

- If necessary, press the TAB key to increase the indent.

- Type **</div>** to close the div element (Figure 3–45).

```
ending
footer tag

31       <footer>
32       &copy; Copyright 2015. All Rights Reserved.<br>
33       <a href="mailto:forwardfitness@club.net">forwardfitness@club.net</a>
34       </footer>
35
Line 36  36       </div>           ending
37                                div tag
38  </body>
39  </html>
```

Figure 3–45

 Q&A Why is the ending div tag </div> instead of </div id="container">?
A div attribute is defined only within the starting div tag. After a div is defined with an attribute, you close it with a </div> tag.

3

- Save your changes.

To Add a Div Element to the Home Page

You must also edit the home page of the website by adding a **div** element with an **id** attribute and value of **container** to make it consistent with the website template. *Why? All of the pages within the website should use the same general template layout.* The following steps add a **div** element with an **id** attribute and value to the home page.

- If necessary, open the index.html file to prepare to insert a div element.

- Place the insertion point after the starting <body> tag and then press the ENTER key two times to create a new Line 10.

- Press the TAB key to increase the indent.

- Type **<div id="container">** to insert a div element with an id attribute and value (Figure 3–46).

Figure 3–46

- Place the insertion point after the ending </footer> tag and then press the ENTER key two times to create a new Line 43.

- If necessary, press the TAB key to increase the indent.

- Type **</div>** to close the div element (Figure 3–47).

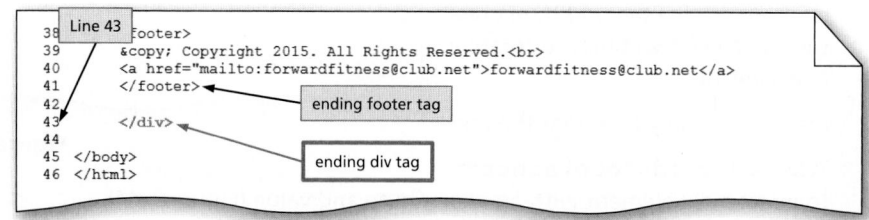

Figure 3–47

- Save your changes and close index.html.

Class Attributes

The **class** attribute is also commonly used in HTML. Unlike the **id** attribute, a **class** attribute name can be applied to more than one **div** or other HTML element on a webpage. Classes provide another level of control over the styling or formatting of specific elements on a webpage. For example, rather than having all paragraphs of text appear with the same formatting, you might want to format the first paragraph after a heading to be different from other paragraphs of text. You can define the first paragraph after a heading with a class attribute and name, such as <p class="first">. This makes it easier to format every paragraph after a heading the same way. In another example, <img class="product"> is an image tag with a **class** attribute that has a value of **product**. You might use this element to collect all product photos in a single category and then format those images to have a border or to position them in a specific area on a webpage. Figure 3–48 shows an example of a **class** attribute used within an image tag.

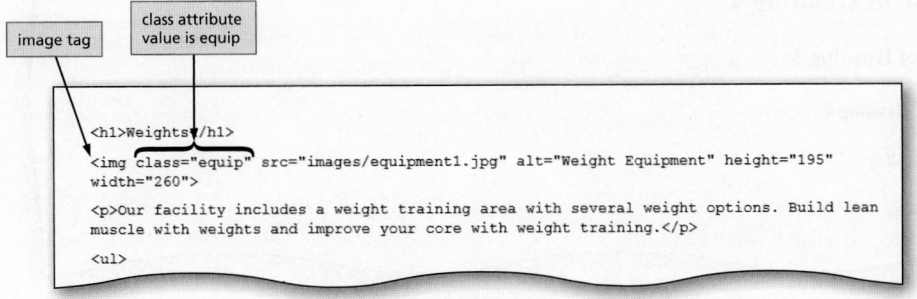

Figure 3–48

To mark an element as belonging to a class, add the class attribute and name to the element. In Figure 3–48, **equip** is the name of the class. Any word can be used as a class name, as long as it does not contain spaces. In general, however, you should use descriptive names that illustrate the purpose of a class (for example, **beginning, legallanguage,** or **copyrighttext**), rather than names that describe the appearance of the class (for example, **bluetext, largeritalic,** or **boldsmallarial**). Using names that describe the purpose of the class makes the code more flexible and easier to read. In Chapter 4, you will apply styles to classes to format more than one element at a time.

Adding Headings and Lists

Some HTML elements are designed to group information on a webpage. For example, the **p** element groups text into a paragraph and the **div** element groups elements into an area or section. Two other grouping elements are heading elements and lists. Headings indicate that a new topic is starting and typically identify or summarize the topic. Lists group related items together in a sequence or collection.

Heading Elements

You use **heading elements** to provide a title or heading before a paragraph of text or section of a page. On a webpage, headings appear in a larger font size than normal text, making it easy for users to quickly scan the page and identify its sections. Heading levels run from 1 (the most important) to 6 (the least important). Heading level 1 is designed to mark major headings, while heading levels 2–6 are for subheadings. The start tag for heading level 1 is <h1> and the end tag is </h1>. The start tag for heading level 2 is <h2> and the end tag is </h2>, and so on. Figure 3–49 displays the default formatting for heading levels 1 through 6. In the upcoming steps, you insert headings in the About Us and Contact Us pages for the fitness website.

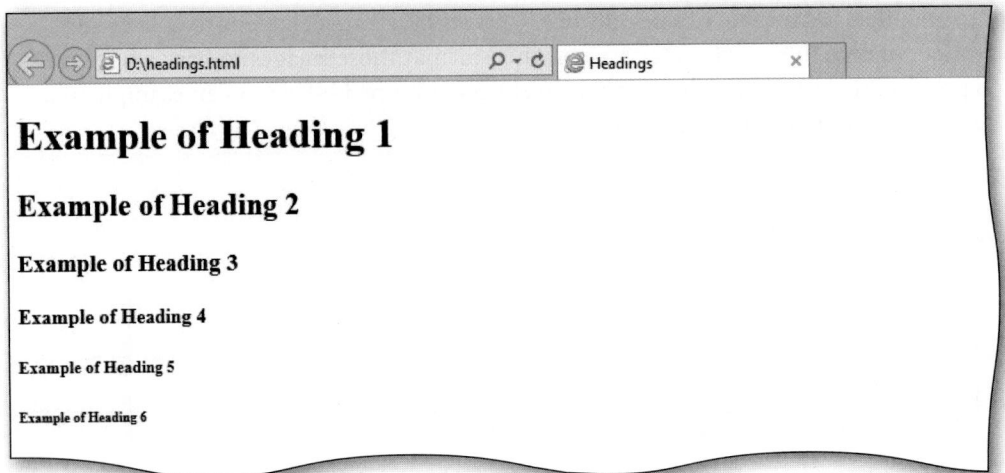

Figure 3–49

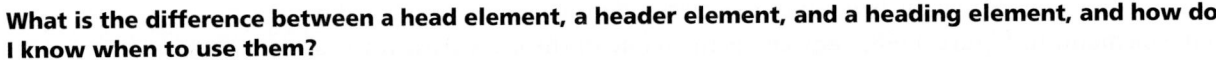

CONSIDER THIS

What is the difference between a head element, a header element, and a heading element, and how do I know when to use them?

Recall from Chapter 1 that the *head element* is a required element for an HTML webpage and belongs near the top of the page. A head element is defined by <head> and </head> tags and contains information about the webpage, such as the webpage title and the defined character set, not website content. A *header element* is a set of HTML5 tags (<header> and </header>) that define the header area of a webpage and generally come after the starting <body> tag. Header elements contain webpage content, such as a business name or logo. A *heading element*, h1, h2, h3, h4, h5, or h6, defines a heading in a webpage and is generally placed above other webpage content. Heading elements also contain webpage content. A heading element can appear in a header element, a main element, or other HTML elements. A heading level 1 element is defined by <h1> and </h1> tags.

Lists

Lists structure text into an itemized format. An **unordered list**, also called a bulleted list, displays a small graphic called a bullet before each item of information. In an unordered list, the bulleted items can appear in any sequence. To mark an unordered list, insert the <ul> tag at the start of the list and the </ul> tag at the end of the list. Mark each item in an unordered list with a set of list item tags (<li> and </li>). The following code creates a bulleted list of two items:

```
<ul>
  <li>First item</li>
  <li>Second item</li>
</ul>
```

An **ordered list**, also called a numbered list, displays information in a series using numbers or letters. An ordered list works well to organize items where sequence matters, such as in a series of steps. To mark an ordered list, insert the <ol> and </ol> tags at the start and end of the list. As with unordered lists, you mark each item in an ordered list with a set of <li> and </li> tags. The following code creates a numbered list of two items:

```
<ol>
  <li>First item</li>
  <li>Second item</li>
</ol>
```

Figure 3–50 shows a webpage with an unordered and an ordered list.

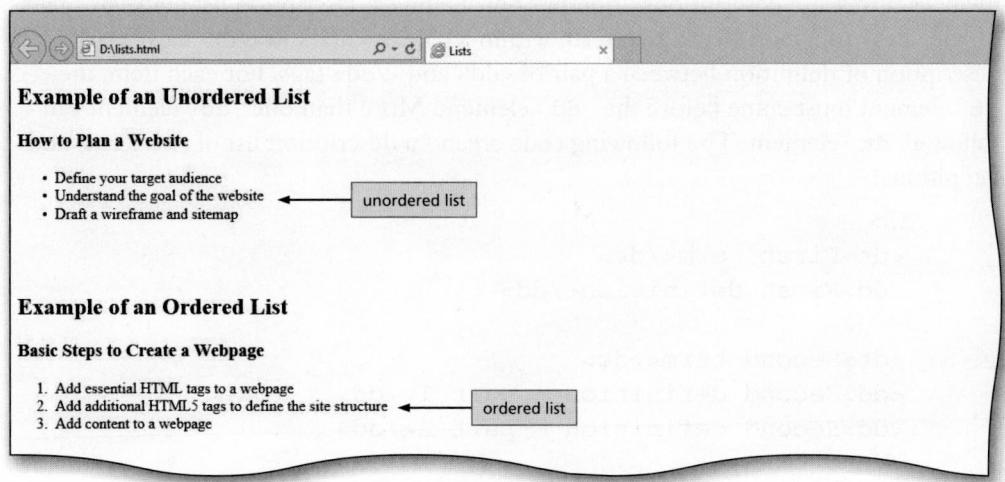

Figure 3–50

Unordered and ordered lists have optional bullet and number types. An unordered list can use one of three bullet options: disc, square, or circle. If no type is identified, the browser displays the default type, a disc. You can also specify an image to use as a bullet. An ordered list can use numbers, letters, or Roman numerals. The default option is to use Arabic numbers, such as 1, 2, and 3. Table 3–5 shows the different values and examples of unordered and ordered list options. Although you can use the `style` attribute to specify the style of bullets and numbers, the recommended method for changing bullet list and number styles is with CSS, which is covered in Chapter 4.

Table 3-5 List Type Attributes	
Unordered Lists	
Value	**Example**
disc (default)	●
square	■
circle	o
Ordered Lists	
1	1. 2. 3.
A	A. B. C.
a	a. b. c.
I	I. II. III.
i	i. ii. iii.

A **description list** contains terms and descriptions. Use a description list to create a glossary or to list questions and answers, for example. A description list includes terms and descriptions or definitions. Define a description list between a pair of <dl> and </dl> tags. Mark each term within a pair of <dt> and </dt> tags. Mark each description or definition between a pair of <dd> and </dd> tags. For each item, the `dt` element must come before the `dd` element. More than one `dd` element can follow a `dt` element. The following code creates a description list of two terms and definitions:

```
<dl>
  <dt>First term</dt>
  <dd>First definition</dd>

  <dt>Second term</dt>
  <dd>Second definition - part 1</dd>
  <dd>Second definition - part 2</dd>
</dl>
```

Figure 3–51 shows an example of a description list.

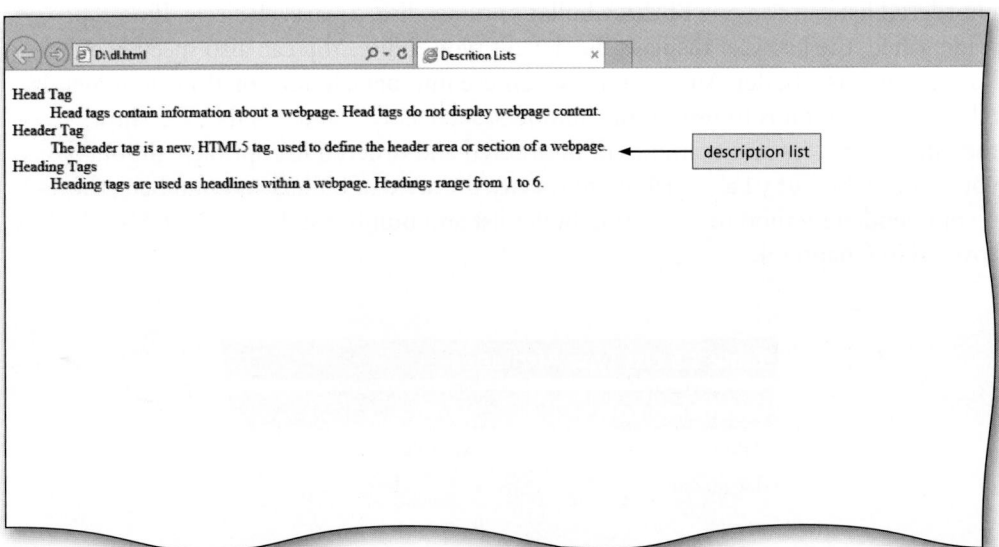

Figure 3–51

To Create the About Us Webpage and Add a Heading and Image

1 ADD HYPERLINKS | 2 ADD IMAGES | 3 ADD DIV ELEMENTS | 4 ADD HEADING ELEMENTS & LISTS
5 VIEW WEBSITE IN BROWSER & TEST LINKS | 6 VALIDATE PAGES

The About Us page provides additional information about the Forward Fitness Club, including pictures of its facility. It also includes headings to identify the topics on the page. Use the website template to create the About Us page. *Why? The website template already contains the basic HTML code for the website. Using the template saves time coding.* The following steps create the About Us page for the fitness website using the website template.

- If necessary, reopen the fitness .html template file to create a new webpage using the template file.
- Tap or click File on the menu bar and then tap or click Save As to display the Save As dialog box.
- If necessary, navigate up one level to access the fitness folder.
- Type **about** in the File name text box to name the file (Figure 3–52).

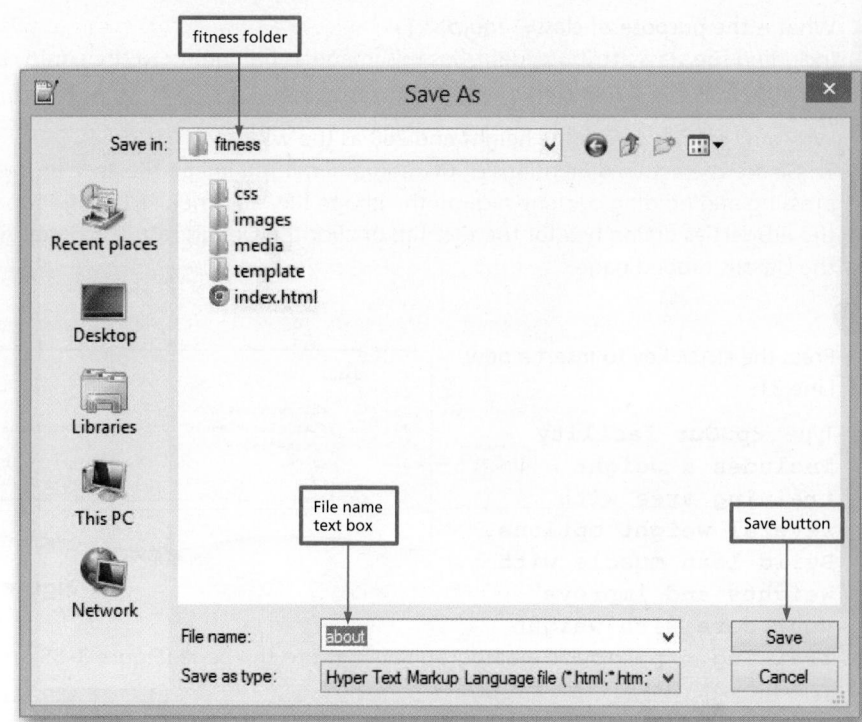

Figure 3–52

- Tap or click the Save button to save the file in the fitness folder.
- Place your insertion point after the starting <main> tag on Line 27 and then press the ENTER key twice to insert new Lines 28 and 29.
- On Line 29, press the TAB key and then type **<h1>Weights</h1>** to add heading 1 tags and content to the page (Figure 3–53).

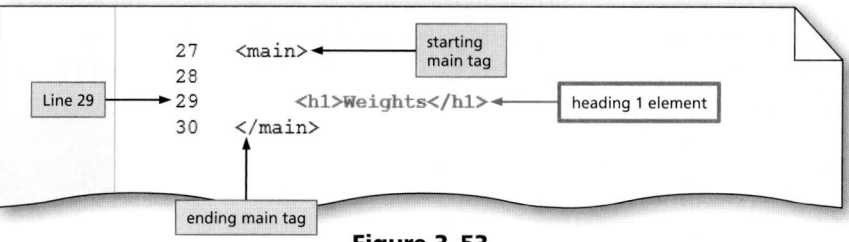

Figure 3–53

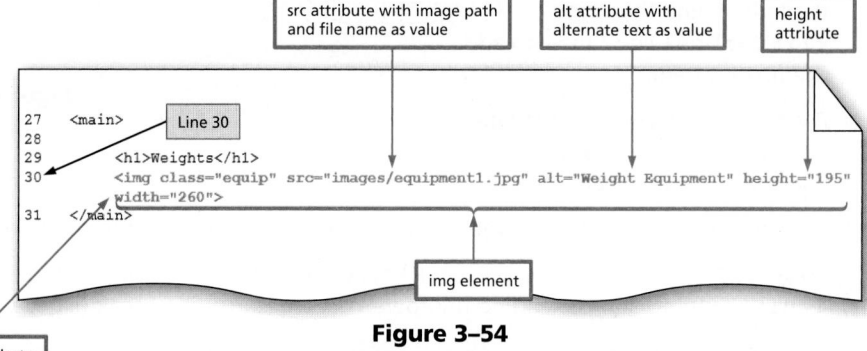

- Press the ENTER key to insert a new Line 30.
- Type **<img class="equip" src="images/equipment1 .jpg" alt="Weight Equipment" height="195" width="260">** to add an image element to the page (Figure 3–54).

Figure 3–54

What is the purpose of class="equip"?

Including the class attribute identifies this image as belonging to the equip class. In Chapter 4, you will format all the images in the equip class in the same way.

Why am I setting 195 as the height and 260 as the width?

These are the actual dimensions of the equipment1.jpg image file. In Windows, you can verify the dimensions by pressing and holding or right-clicking the image file, and then selecting Properties on the shortcut menu to display the Properties dialog box for the file. Tap or click the Details tab. The dimensions are listed in the Image section of the Details tabbed page.

4

- Press the ENTER key to insert a new Line 31.

- Type `<p>Our facility includes a weight training area with several weight options. Build lean muscle with weights and improve your core with weight training.</p>` to add a paragraph element to the page (Figure 3–55).

```
27    <main>
28
29        <h1>Weights</h1>
30        <img class="equip" src="images/equipment1.jpg" alt="Weight Equipment" height="195"
          width="260">
31        <p>Our facility includes a weight training area with several weight options. Build lean
          muscle with weights and improve your core with weight training.</p>
32    </main>
```

Line 31 → 31

paragraph element

Figure 3–55

To Add Unordered Lists to the About Us Webpage

1 ADD HYPERLINKS | 2 ADD IMAGES | 3 ADD DIV ELEMENTS | **4 ADD HEADING ELEMENTS & LISTS**
5 VIEW WEBSITE IN BROWSER & TEST LINKS | 6 VALIDATE PAGES

The About Us page should list the types of equipment the Forward Fitness Club provides to its members. You can include these items using unordered lists. *Why? The types of equipment can appear in any order in the lists, so the items are appropriate for unordered lists.* The following steps add headings and unordered lists to the About Us page.

1

- With the insertion point at the end of Line 31, press the ENTER key to insert a new Line 32.

- Type `<ul>` to insert a starting unordered list tag.

- Press the ENTER key, increase the indent, and then type `<li>Dumbbells</li>` to add the first list item.

- Press the ENTER key and then type `<li>Kettle bells</li>` to add the second list item.

- Press the ENTER key and then type `<li>Barbells</li>` to add the third list item.

- Press the ENTER key, press the SHIFT+TAB keys to decrease the indent, and then type `</ul><br>` to add the ending unordered list tag and a line break (Figure 3–56).

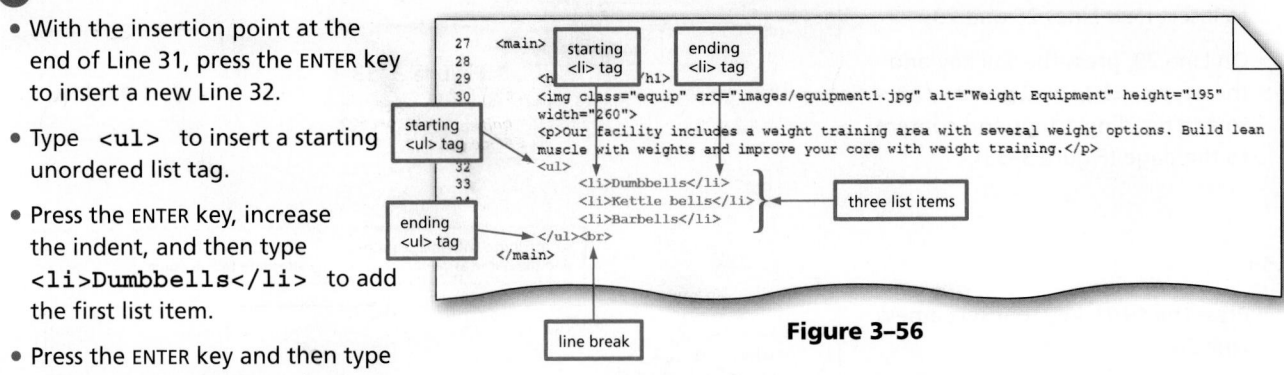

starting `<li>` tag   ending `<li>` tag

starting `<ul>` tag

ending `<ul>` tag

line break

three list items

```
27    <main>
28
29        <h1>Weights</h1>
30        <img class="equip" src="images/equipment1.jpg" alt="Weight Equipment" height="195"
          width="260">
31        <p>Our facility includes a weight training area with several weight options. Build lean
          muscle with weights and improve your core with weight training.</p>
32        <ul>
33            <li>Dumbbells</li>
34            <li>Kettle bells</li>
              <li>Barbells</li>
          </ul><br>
      </main>
```

Figure 3–56

2

- Press the ENTER key two times to insert new Lines 37 and 38.

- Type the code shown in Table 3–6 to insert additional elements for headings, images, and unordered lists (Figure 3–57).

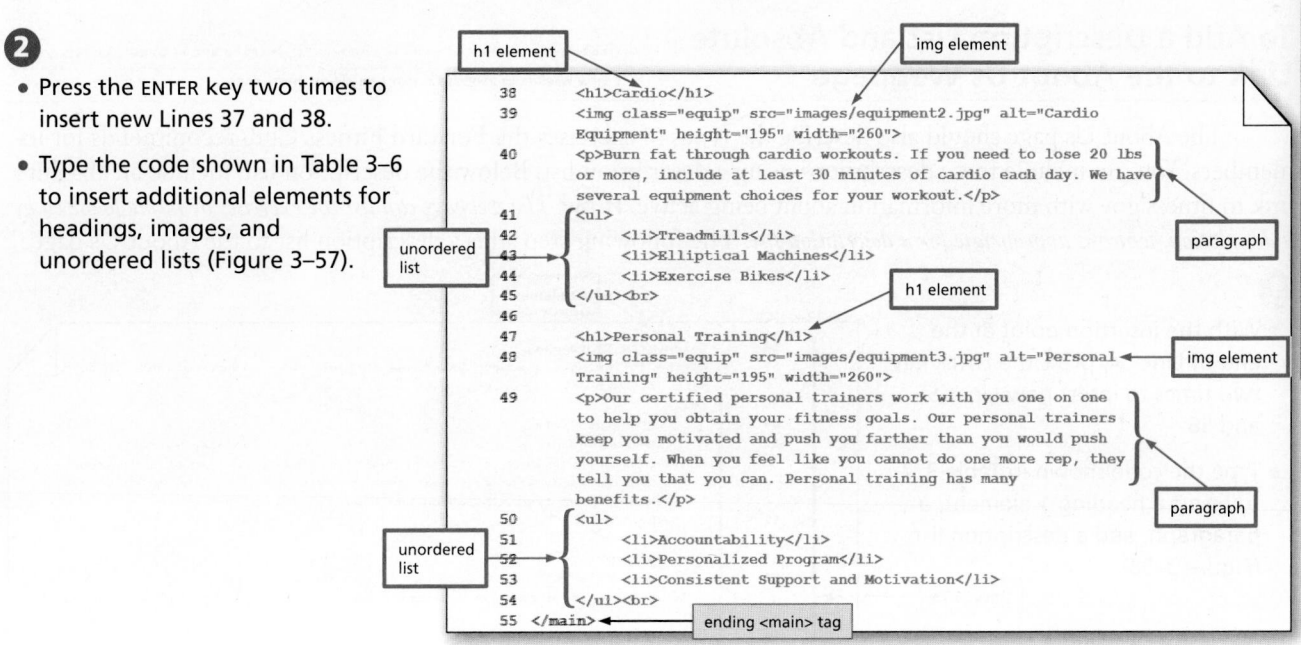

Figure 3–57

Table 3-6 About Us Code for Lines 38–54

Line Number	Code to Insert
38	<h1>Cardio</h1>
39	<img class="equip" src="images/equipment2.jpg" alt="Cardio Equipment" height="195" width="260">
40	<p>Burn fat through cardio workouts. If you need to lose 20 lbs or more, include at least 30 minutes of cardio each day. We have several equipment choices for your workout.</p>
41	<ul>
42	<li>Treadmills</li>
43	<li>Elliptical Machines</li>
44	<li>Exercise Bikes</li>
45	</ul>
46	
47	<h1>Personal Training</h1>
48	<img class="equip" src="images/equipment3.jpg" alt="Personal Training" height="195" width="260">
49	<p>Our certified personal trainers work with you one on one to help you obtain your fitness goals. Our personal trainers keep you motivated and push you farther than you would push yourself. When you feel like you cannot do one more rep, they tell you that you can. Personal training has many benefits.</p>
50	<ul>
51	<li>Accountability</li>
52	<li>Personalized Program</li>
53	<li>Consistent Support and Motivation</li>
54	</ul>

To Add a Description List and Absolute Link to the About Us Webpage

The About Us page should also describe the types of exercises the Forward Fitness Club recommends for its members. You can include these descriptions using a description list. Below the description list, include an absolute link to fitness.gov with more information about being active. *Why? The webpage can list the exercises by name followed by a description, which is appropriate for a description list.* The following step adds a description list to the About Us page.

1

- With the insertion point at the end of Line 54, press the ENTER key two times to insert new Lines 55 and 56.
- Type the code shown in Table 3–7 to insert a heading 1 element, a paragraph, and a description list (Figure 3–58).

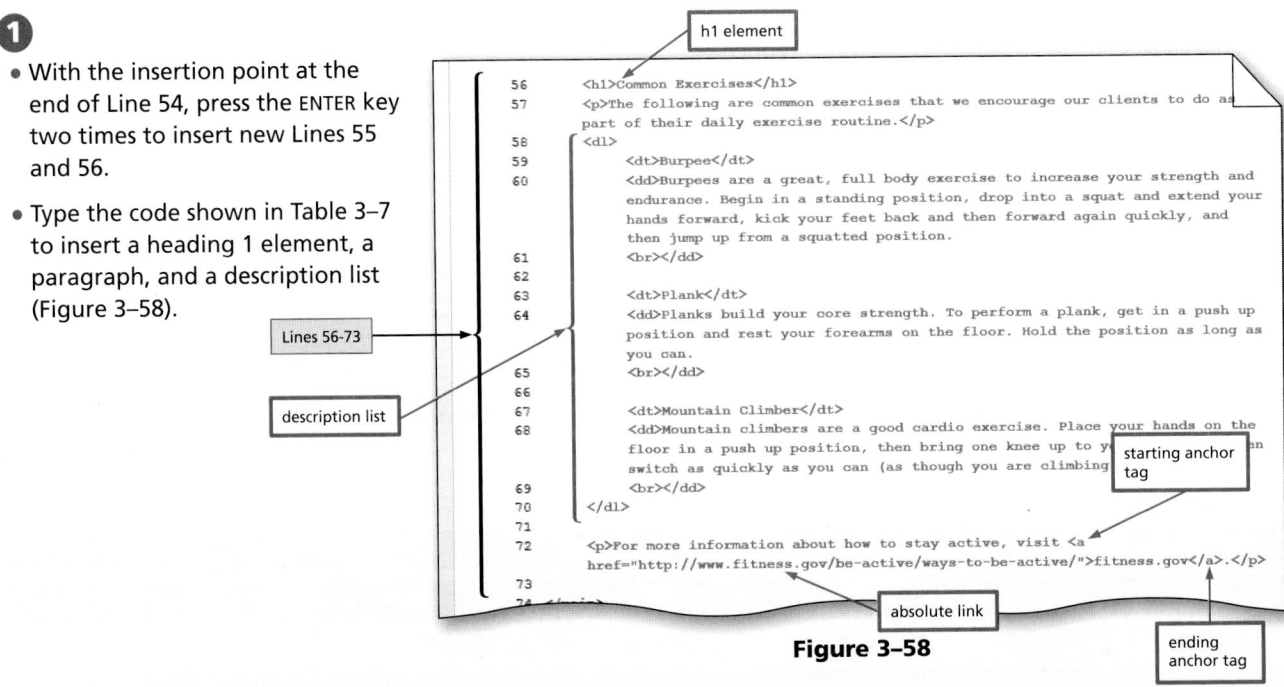

Figure 3–58

Line Number	Code to Insert
Table 3-7 About Us Code for Lines 56–73	
56	\<h1\>Common Exercises\</h1\>
57	\<p\>The following are common exercises that we encourage our clients to do as part of their daily exercise routine.\</p\>
58	\<dl\>
59	\<dt\>Burpee\</dt\>
60	\<dd\>Burpees are a great, full body exercise to increase your strength and endurance. Begin in a standing position, drop into a squat and extend your hands forward, kick your feet back and then forward again quickly, and then jump up from a squatted position.
61	\<br\>\</dd\>
62	
63	\<dt\>Plank\</dt\>
64	\<dd\>Planks build your core strength. To perform a plank, get in a push up position and rest your forearms on the floor. Hold the position as long as you can.
65	\<br\>\</dd\>
66	
67	\<dt\>Mountain Climber\</dt\>
68	\<dd\>Mountain climbers are a good cardio exercise. Place your hands on the floor in a push up position, then bring one knee up to your chest and then switch as quickly as you can (as though you are climbing a mountain).
69	\<br\>\</dd\>
70	\</dl\>
71	
72	\<p\>For more information about how to stay active, visit \<a href="http://www.fitness.gov/be-active/ways-to-be-active/"\>fitness.gov\</a\>.\</p\>
73	

To Save the About Us Webpage and View It in a Browser

The About Us page is finished for now. The following steps save the webpage and view it in your default browser.

1 Check the spelling in your document to find misspelled words and correct them as necessary.

2 Save and close the about.html file.

3 Using File Explorer (Windows) or Finder (Mac), navigate to the about.html file, and then open the file to display it in your default browser (Figure 3–59).

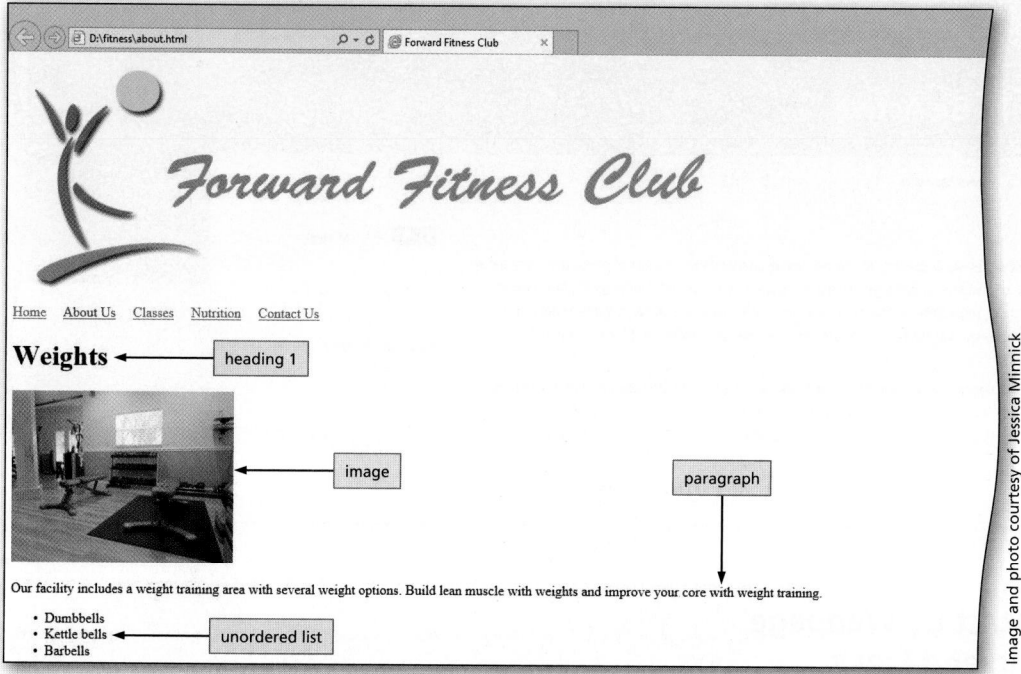

Image and photo courtesy of Jessica Minnick

Figure 3–59

4 Scroll down the page and display the description list (Figure 3–60).

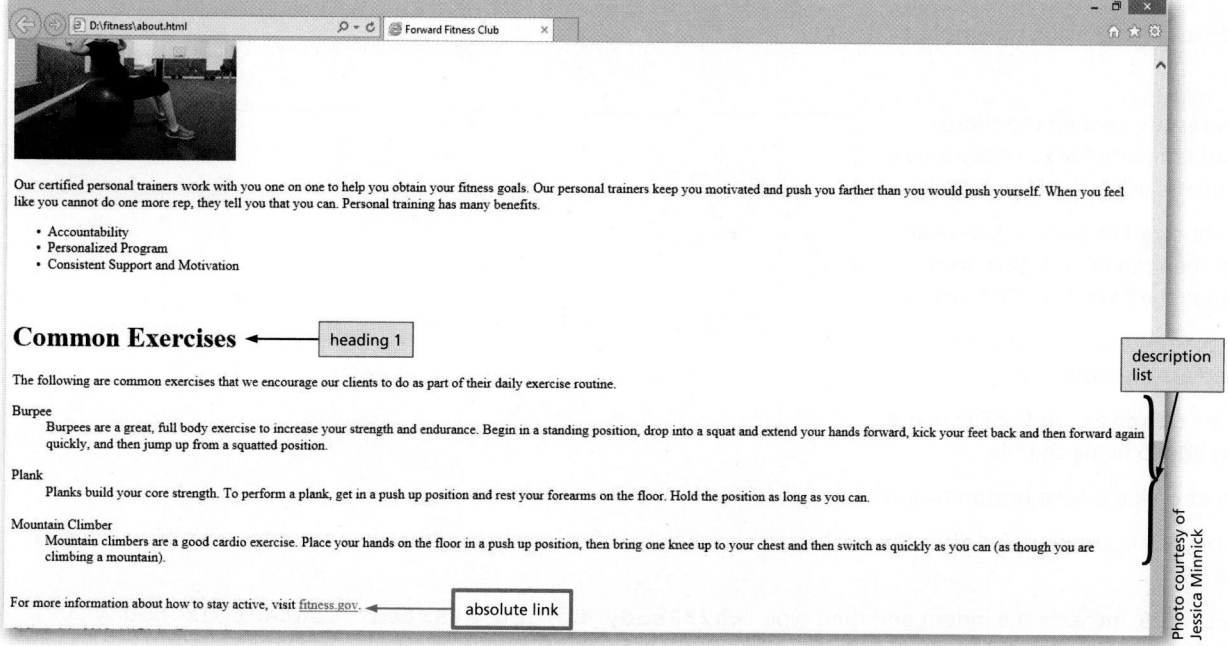

Photo courtesy of Jessica Minnick

Figure 3–60

⑤ Tap or click the fitness.gov link to open the fitness.gov website (Figure 3–61).

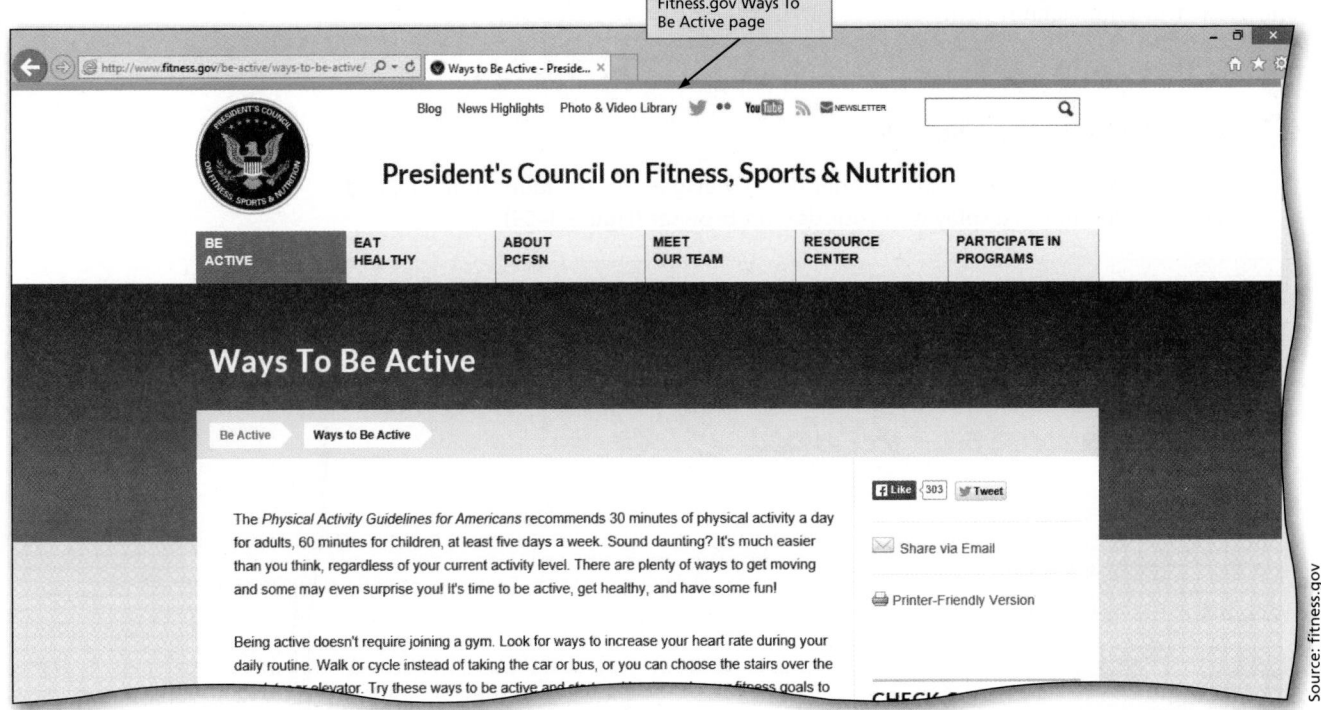

Figure 3–61

To Create the Contact Us Webpage and Add a Heading and Links

1 ADD HYPERLINKS | 2 ADD IMAGES | 3 ADD DIV ELEMENTS | 4 ADD HEADING ELEMENTS & LISTS
5 VIEW WEBSITE IN BROWSER & TEST LINKS | 6 VALIDATE PAGES

The Contact Us page provides an address, a phone number, and an email address for the Forward Fitness Club. Insert a heading to identify the new information, and then add the phone number and email address to the webpage as link text. *Why? If you mark the text as links, visitors can select the links to make a phone call or send an email message directly to the Forward Fitness Club.* The following steps create the Contact Us page for the fitness website using the website template.

- If necessary, reopen the fitness .html template file to create a new webpage using the template file.

- Tap or click File on the menu bar and then tap or click Save As to display the Save As dialog box.

- If necessary, navigate up one level to access the fitness folder.

- Type **contact** in the File name text box to name the file.

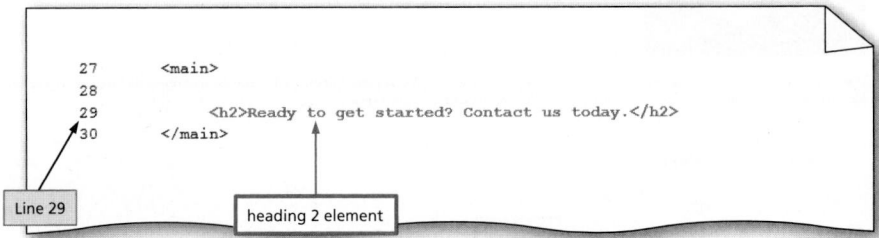

Figure 3–62

- Tap or click the Save button to save the contact file in the fitness folder.

- Place your insertion point after the starting <main> tag and then press the ENTER key twice to insert new Lines 28 and 29.

- On Line 29, increase the indent and then type **<h2>Ready to get started? Contact us today. </h2>** to add a heading 2 element to the page (Figure 3–62).

2

- Press the ENTER key to insert a new Line 30.

- Type the code shown in Table 3–8 to add paragraphs and link text, indenting each line beginning on Line 30 and continuing through Line 40 (Figure 3–63).

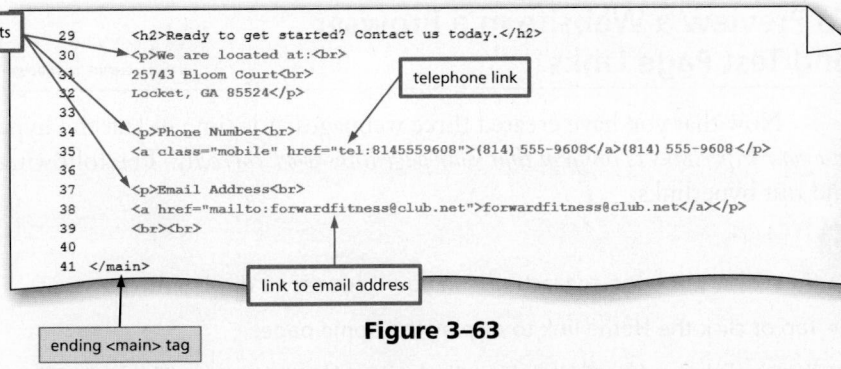

```
29      <h2>Ready to get started? Contact us today.</h2>
30      <p>We are located at:<br>
31      25743 Bloom Court<br>
32      Locket, GA 85524</p>
33
34      <p>Phone Number<br>
35      <a class="mobile" href="tel:8145559608">(814) 555-9608</a>(814) 555-9608</p>
36
37      <p>Email Address<br>
38      <a href="mailto:forwardfitness@club.net">forwardfitness@club.net</a></p>
39      <br><br>
40
41  </main>
```

paragraph elements

telephone link

link to email address

ending <main> tag

Figure 3–63

Q&A

Why is the phone number shown twice?

The first phone number is for mobile display and will allow a mobile device user to tap and call the business. The other phone number is for a desktop and tablet display. You will hide the mobile display for desktop and tablet in a later chapter so that only one number is displayed.

Table 3-8 Contact Us Code for Lines 30–40

Line Number	Code to Add
30	<p>We are located at:
31	25743 Bloom Court
32	Locket, GA 85524</p>
33	
34	<p>Phone Number
35	<a class="mobile" href="tel:8145559608">(814) 555-9608</a>(814) 555-9608</p>
36	
37	<p>Email Address
38	<a href="mailto:forwardfitness@club.net">forwardfitness@club.net</a></p>
39	
40	

To Save the Contact Us Webpage and View It in a Browser

The Contact Us page is finished for now. The following steps save the webpage and view it in your default browser.

1 Check the spelling in your document to find misspelled words and correct them as necessary.

2 Save and close the contact.html file.

3 In File Explorer (Windows) or Finder (Mac), navigate to the contact.html file, and then open the file in your default browser (Figure 3–64).

Q&A

Why does the telephone number appear twice on the page?

One telephone number contains a link and the other does not. The telephone number with the link will be used for mobile display. You will format this link in a later chapter so it is not displayed on a desktop view, leaving the telephone number without the link.

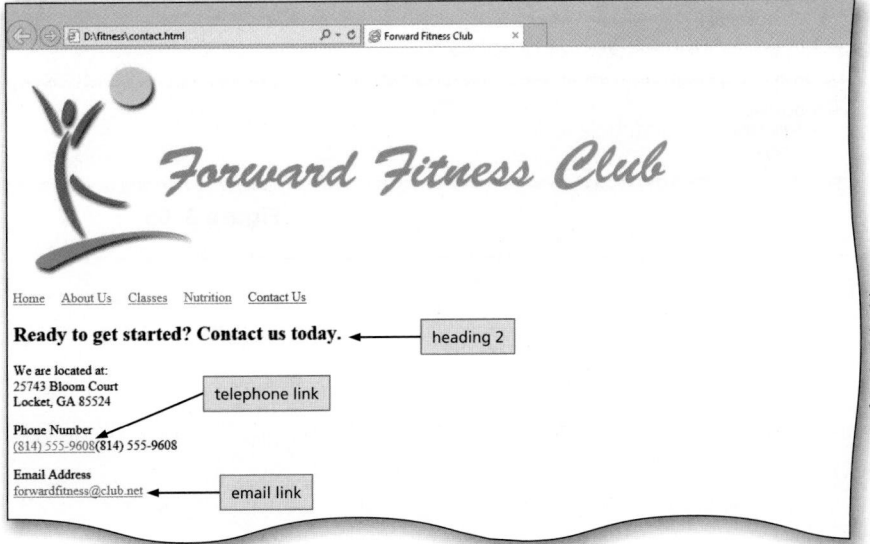

heading 2

telephone link

email link

Figure 3–64

Image courtesy of Jessica Minnick

To Preview a Website in a Browser and Test Page Links

Now that you have created three webpages, it is time to test the hyperlinks in a browser. *Why? You need to test your hyperlinks to confirm that your page links work correctly.* The following step displays a webpage in a browser and test hyperlinks.

- If necessary, reopen contact.html in your browser to display the page.

- Tap or click the Home link to display the home page.

- Tap or click the About Us link to display the About Us page (Figure 3–65).

Q&A Why do I receive an error message when I tap or click the classes and nutrition links?

You have not yet created these pages, but specified their file names in the href attribute. The browser looks for the file specified in the href attribute and displays an error message when it cannot find the file.

Figure 3–65

Image courtesy of Jessica Minnick

To Validate the About Us and Contact Us Pages

Every time you create a new webpage, run it through the W3C validator to check the document for errors and correct them. The following steps validate an HTML document.

1 Open your browser and type `http://validator .w3.org/` in the address bar to display the W3C validator page.

2 Tap or click the Validate by File Upload tab to display the Validate by File Upload tab information, and then upload the about.html file to the W3C validator.

3 Tap or click the Check button to send the document through the validator and display the validation results page (Figure 3–66).

4 If necessary, correct any errors, save your changes, and run through the validator again to revalidate the page.

5 Perform Steps 1–4 to validate the contact.html page and correct any errors.

6 Close the browser, and then close the HTML text editor.

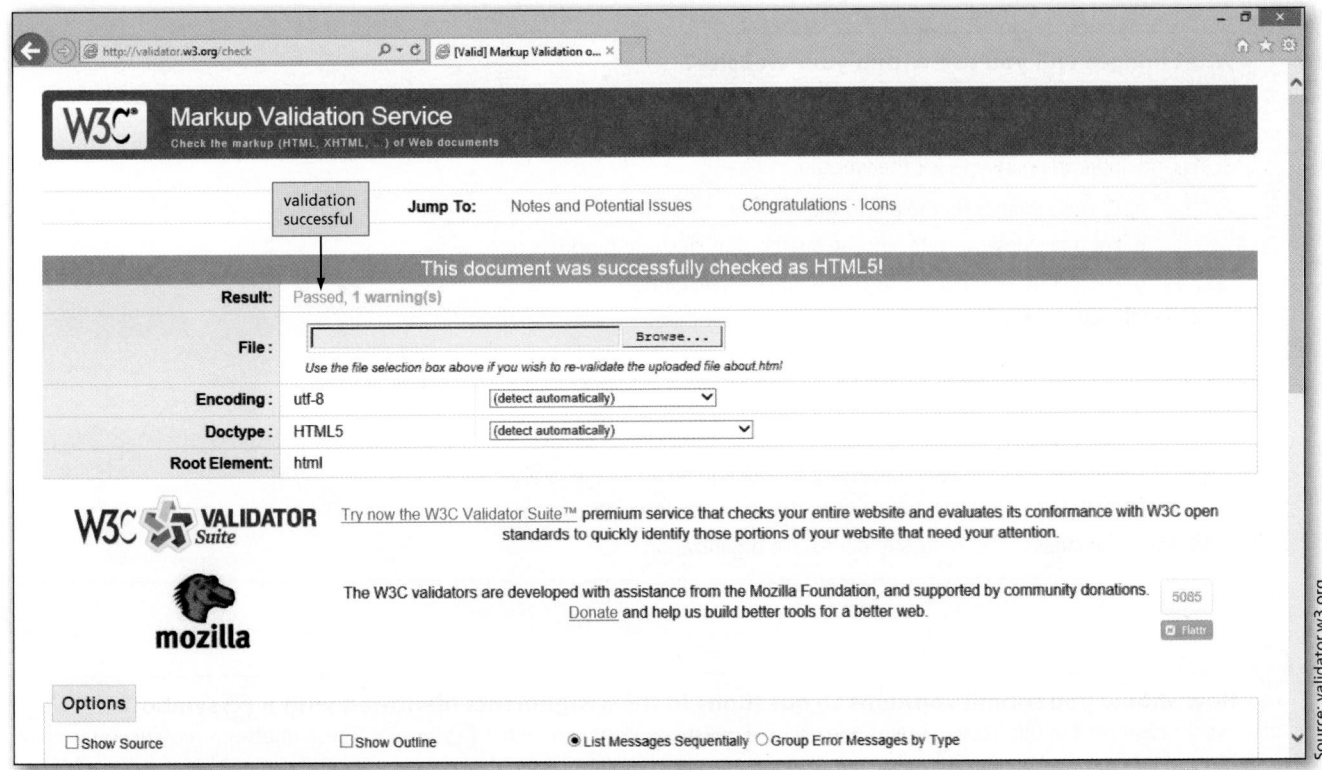

Figure 3–66

Source: validator.w3.org

Chapter Summary

In this chapter, you have learned how to create many types of hyperlinks. You also inserted new HTML elements, including div elements, image elements, headings, and lists. The items listed below include all the new concepts and skills you have learned in this chapter, with the tasks grouped by activity.

Adding Links to a Webpage
Add Relative Links to a Webpage (HTML 114)
Add an Email Link to a Webpage
(HTML 89, HTML 92)
Add Absolute Links to a Webpage (HTML 87)
Add Image Links to a Webpage (HTML 88)
Add Telephone Links to a Webpage (HTML 88)

Adding Images to a Website
Copy Files into the Images Folder (HTML 104)
Add an Image to a Webpage (HTML 105,
HTML 106)

Exploring Div Elements
Add a Div Element to a Webpage (HTML 109)

Adding Headings and Lists
Create the About Us Webpage and Add a Heading
(HTML 114)
Add Unordered Lists to the About Us Webpage
(HTML 116)
Add a Description List to the About Us Webpage
(HTML 118)
Test Page Links (HTML 122)

CONSIDER THIS

What images will you use within your website?
Use these guidelines as you complete the assignments in this chapter and as you create your own webpages outside of this class.

1. Find appropriate images for the website.

   a. Choose images that relate to the website.

   b. For a business website, choose images that illustrate products or services.

   c. Use a logo or other identifying graphic on all pages.

2. Use the correct file format.

   a. Use PNG, GIF, JPG, or SVG images.

   b. Convert all other image files to an appropriate format suitable for web use.

3. Optimize images for web use.

   a. Reduce file size, when necessary, before adding an image to a website.

   b. Use photo-editing software to optimize images for web use.

4. Save all images in the images folder for file organization.

CONSIDER THIS

How should you submit solutions to questions in the assignments identified with a symbol?
Every assignment in this book contains one or more questions identified with a symbol. These questions require you to think beyond the assigned presentation. Present your solutions to the questions in the format required by your instructor. Possible formats may include one or more of these options: create a document that contains the answer; present your answer to the class; discuss your answer in a group; record the answer as audio or video using a webcam, smartphone, or portable media player; or post answers on a blog, wiki, or website.

Apply Your Knowledge

Reinforce the skills and apply the concepts you learned in this chapter.

Creating a Page with Links, Images, Lists, and Headings

Instructions: In this exercise, you will use your HTML editor to enter the needed tags and content to create a template for the pages for a new website as well as the home page for the Durango Jewelry and Gem Shop. The completed home page is shown in Figure 3–67. It contains the content as well as the HTML5 tags required to insert an image, headings, links, lists, and paragraphs of information for this page. You will also use professional web development best practices to indent, space, validate, and check the spelling of your work.

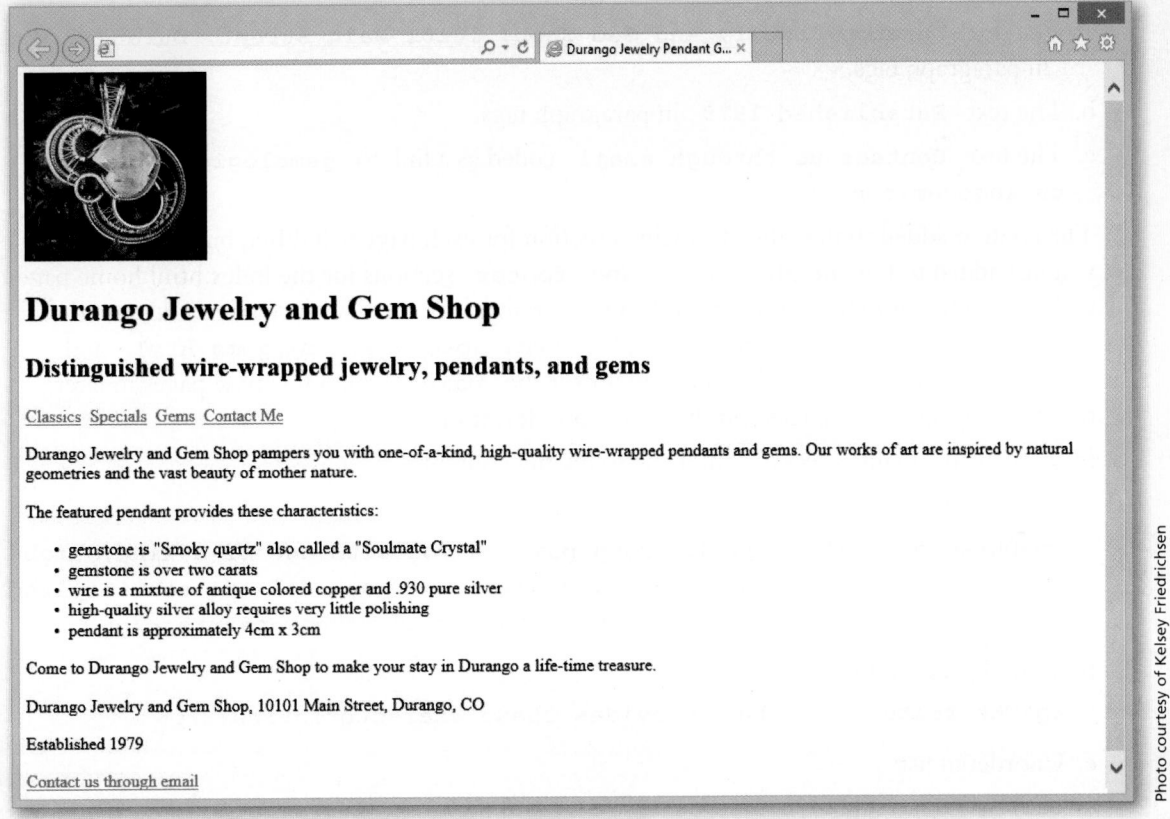

Figure 3–67

Photo courtesy of Kelsey Friedrichsen

Perform the following tasks:

1. Open your HTML editor and then open the apply03.html file from the Data Files for Students. Use the File Save As feature to save the webpage in the chapter03\apply folder with the name `index.html` to create the home page.

2. Modify the comment at the top of the page to include your name and today's date.

3. Enter `Durango Jewelry Pendant Gem` in the <title> tags. Recall that content in the title tags appears in the tab at the top of the browser and is also used by search engines.

4. In the `header` section, enter the following content, each on its own line in the HTML editor.

   a. An image element coded as follows:

   ```
   <img src="wirewrap01.jpg" alt="smoky quartz pendant" width="171"
   height="171">
   ```

Continued >

Apply Your Knowledge *continued*

b. The text `Durango Jewelry and Gem Shop` in \<h1\> tags to insert the name of the store.

c. The text `Distinguished wire-wrapped jewelry, pendants, and gems` in \<h2\> tags to serve as the tagline.

5. In the `nav` section, enter the following links, each on its own line in the HTML editor.

```
<a href="classics.html">Classics</a> 

<a href="specials.html">Specials</a> 

<a href="gems.html">Gems</a> 

<a href="contact.html">Contact Me</a> 
```

6. In the `footer` section, enter the following content, each on its own line in the HTML editor.

a. The text `Durango Jewelry and Gem Shop, 10101 Main Street, Durango, CO` in paragraph tags.

b. The text `Established 1979` in paragraph tags.

c. The text `Contact us through email` coded as a link to `gemologist@durangogem.com`

7. The content added to the \<div id="main"\> section for each page will differ, but the content you just added to the `header, nav,` and `footer` sections for the index.html home page will be the same for all pages in the website. Therefore, use the Save As feature to create the four other pages for this website: `classics.html, specials.html, gems.html,` and `contact.html`. You will fill in the content for the `main` section for these pages in later tutorials, so close these pages and then reopen index.html.

8. In the \<div id="main"\> section, enter the following content.

a. First paragraph:

```
<p>Durango Jewelry and Gem Shop pampers you with one-of-a-kind, high-
quality wire wrapped pendants and gems. Our works of art are inspired
by natural geometries and the vast beauty of mother nature.</p>
```

b. Second paragraph:

```
<p>The featured pendant provides these characteristics:</p>
```

c. Unordered list:

```
<ul>
  <li>gemstone is "Smoky quartz" also called a "Soulmate Crystal"</li>
  <li>gemstone is over two carats</li>
  <li>wire is a mixture of antique colored copper and .930 pure
silver</li>
  <li>high-quality silver alloy requires very little polishing</li>
  <li>pendant is approximately 4cm x 3cm</li>
</ul>
```

d. Final paragraph:

```
<p>Come to Durango Jewelry and Gem Shop to make your stay in Durango
a life-time treasure.</p>
```

9. Review and check the spelling of your textual content.

10. Validate your webpage using the W3C validator found at validator.w3.org and fix any errors that are identified. Validation is complete when the validator returns the message *"This document was successfully checked as HTML5!"* in a green bar near the top of the webpage.

11. Submit the `index.html` file in a format specified by your instructor.

12. ✳ In this exercise, you were instructed to use the <div id="main"> tag instead of the HTML5 <main> tag to mark up the main content in the body of the webpage. Because browsers are constantly changing and improving, it's important to make sure that the audience you are trying to reach supports the HTML5 elements and attributes you are using on your website. Find two websites that address the issue of HTML5 browser compatibility. Paste those links and a screenshot of the webpage into a document. (*Hint:* To take a screenshot of the webpage, press the PrtSc or Print Screen key on your keyboard, tap or click your document, and then tap or click the Paste button.)

Use your research to answer these questions:

a. When is the div element used within a webpage written with HTML5 tags?

b. What are the HTML5 semantic tags?

c. What is the primary advantage and the primary disadvantage of using the <main> tag versus <div id="main">?

Extend Your Knowledge

Extend the skills you learned in this chapter and experiment with new skills. You may need to use additional resources to complete the assignment.

Inserting Links

Instructions: In this exercise, you will use your HTML editor to enter the needed tags and content to create several different types of links. The completed page is shown in Figure 3–68. The starting file contains comments to note the location of links you will add to the page. You will also use professional web development best practices to indent, space, validate, and check the spelling of your work.

Perform the following tasks:

1. Open the `ski03.html` file from the Data Files for Students and then modify the comment at the top of the page to include your name and today's date.

2. After the <!--Insert an image with a link--> comment, insert an <img> tag as follows:

```
<img src="ski.jpg" alt="happy skiers" height="343" width="514">
```

3. Make the image a link to `http://www.breckenridge.com`

4. Make each word in the <nav> section a link to another page on the website. Put each link on its own line for readability as follows:

```
<a href="events.html">Events</a> |
<a href="lessons.html">Lessons</a> |
<a href="snowreports.html">Snow Reports</a> |
<a href="employment.html">Employment</a>
```

5. In the <div id="content"> section, make the phone number, 1-800-555-4SKI, a telephone link to that number. (*Hint:* The letters SKI translate to the numbers 754 on a phone keypad.)

6. Make the text "Write to Kent" an email link to `kent@ilovesnow.com`

7. In the `footer`, make the text "snow.com" a link to `http://www.snow.com`

8. To make it easier for users to navigate the home page, add two links in the footer section that will quickly take the user back to the top and main areas of the webpage.

Continued >

STUDENT ASSIGNMENTS

Extend Your Knowledge continued

Snow Fever Ski and Board School

Let it snow, let it snow, let it snow

Events | Lessons | Snow Reports | Employment

Children's Lessons

Children's full-day lessons meet from 10 am through 3:30 pm and include lift access, rentals (ski or snowboard), and lunch. All children (ages 4-12) are welcome regardless of ability or prior experience. Our expert ski and snowboard instructors provide special care and attention to teach children the correct way to ski and ride, from the basics of carving turns to safety instruction to advanced lessons and multi-week programs. We focus on having fun in a safe and responsible way!

Terrain Park Lessons

Our terrain park lessons meet from 12:30 pm to 4 pm at the base of the Powder Keg Terrain Park and include lift access, rentals (ski or snowboard), and an afternoon snack. We start with the basics and progress through all skill levels. Learn how to ride the rails, half pipe, and jumps. Must be 13 years old. Our proven techniques will teach you how to maneuver through any terrain park in a fun and safe way!

Adult Lessons

Adult full-day lessons from 9 am through 3 pm include lift access, rentals (ski or snowboard), and lunch. Adults are divided by ability and experience. We have expert instructors for all levels!

Cost

All of our lessons are $100/day. If you prepay for three full days, you will receive a free season pass to keep practicing your skiing or snowboarding skills for the rest of the season!

Registration

Call or email our Ski School Manager: Kent Hoiberg
1001 West Main Street
Breckenridge, Colorado 80425

Phone: 1-800-555-4SKI
E-mail: Write to Kent

Our Sponsor: snow.com

Lessons   Top   Rental Agreement

© gorillaimages/Shutterstock.com

Figure 3–68

In the `footer` section, make Lessons link to the id="content" location on same page. When a link goes to a location on the same page, the `href` attribute value starts with a # (pound sign or hash tag) followed by the `id` value of the target location as follows:

```
<a href="#content">Lessons</a>
```

9. In the `footer,` make Top link to the top of the page. Because the location for this link is not yet identified, you need to insert an appropriate attribute value pair to the opening <header> tag as follows to mark this location: `<header id="top">`

With the location identified, go back to the `footer` and mark up the Top text with a link as follows: `<a href="#top">Top</a>`

Navigational links at the bottom of the webpage are especially useful to those who are viewing the page on a small device because they help minimize excessive scrolling.

10. In the `footer` section, make Rental Agreement link to a document named legal.pdf as follows: `<a href="legal.pdf">Rental Agreement</a>`

11. Save and view your work in a browser. Tap or click each of the 11 links you inserted starting with the image link to make sure they work as desired. Note that the links in the `nav` section currently point to pages you have not created yet. Also, depending on the device you are using to check your work, the telephone and email links may not work.

12. Check the spelling of the content on the page.

13. Validate your webpage using the W3C validator found at validator.w3.org and fix any errors that are identified. Validation is complete when the validator returns the message *"This document was successfully checked as HTML5!"* in a green bar near the top of the webpage.

14. Submit the `ski03.html` file in a format specified by your instructor.

15. ✳ The html validator at http://validator.w3.org allows you to validate a webpage by entering a URL, uploading a file, or directly inputting the code into the validation window. Which method(s) does the link checker at http://validator.w3.org/checklink use? (*Hint:* A URL is created by software on the web server when you publish a webpage. See your instructor to determine if a web server is available for student use at your school.)

Analyze, Correct, Improve

Analyze a webpage, correct all errors, and improve it.

Correcting Image, Link, Heading, and List Errors

Instructions: Open your HTML editor and then open the resources03.html file from the Data Files for Students. Eight HTML5 resource URLs are listed in the body section of this webpage, but the addresses are not configured as links. Refer to Figure 3–69 to create an unordered list of HTML5 resources using these URLs. You will also use professional web development best practices to indent, space, validate, and check the spelling of your work.

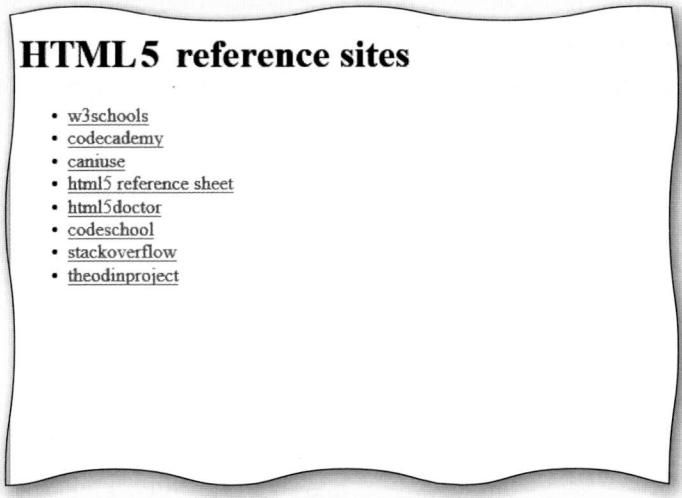

HTML5 reference sites

- w3schools
- codecademy
- caniuse
- html5 reference sheet
- html5doctor
- codeschool
- stackoverflow
- theodinproject

Figure 3–69

Continued >

Analyze, Correct, Improve *continued*

1. Correct

a. With the resources03.html file open in your HTML editor, modify the comment at the top of the page to include your name and today's date.

b. Enter **HTML5 resources** in the <title> tags.

c. Several URLs are listed in the <div id="main"> section of this webpage. Each is a reference to an HTML5 resource. Convert each URL to a link by using the URL as the value for the **href** attribute value and adding text for the link as shown in Figure 3–69.

d. Save the page, and then view it in a browser. Notice that all of the links are positioned on the same line.

e. Tap or click each of the eight links to test them.

2. Improve

a. The **anchor** element is an *inline* element, meaning that the content within the opening and closing <a> tags are displayed in the same line rather than on a new line. Most other paired elements such as all of the heading tags, **h1** through **h6, p, div, ul, ol, dl,** and **li** are *block* elements, meaning that the content within the opening and closing tags creates its own block by starting on a new line. Because this list of links would look better if each item were on its own line, mark up the links as an unordered list. Insert the opening **<ul>** tag on a new line after the <h1> content and before the first link. Add the closing **</ul>** tag after the last link and just before the closing </div> tag.

b. Indent and surround each link with an opening and closing list item tag **<li>** and **</li>** For example, the opening <ul> tag and first link would be coded as:
```
<ul>
  <li><a href="http://www.w3schools.com/">w3schools</a></li>
```
(*Hint:* Note that tags must be *nested properly*. For example, content marked by <li><a> tags must be closed as </a></li>. Improperly nested tags will cause validation errors.)

c. Save the page and view it in a browser. Because the <li> tags are block elements, each link creates its own block by starting on a new line.

d. Check the spelling of the content on the page.

e. Validate your webpage using the W3C validator found at validator.w3.org and fix any errors that are identified.

4. ✳ After reviewing the webpages documented by each of these links, provide a brief description of each website.

In the Lab

Labs 1 and 2, which increase in difficulty, require you to create webpages based on what you learned in the chapter; Lab 3 requires you to dive deeper into a topic covered in the chapter.

Lab 1: Marking Up Content and Links for City Farmer

Problem: You work for a local but rapidly growing gardening supply company called City Farmer that specializes in products that support food self-sufficiency. The company has hired you to add content in the form of images, headings, paragraphs, and lists to the home page. You will also identify several links. Create the webpage shown in Figure 3–70 that contains the textual content that City Farmer wants on their home page.

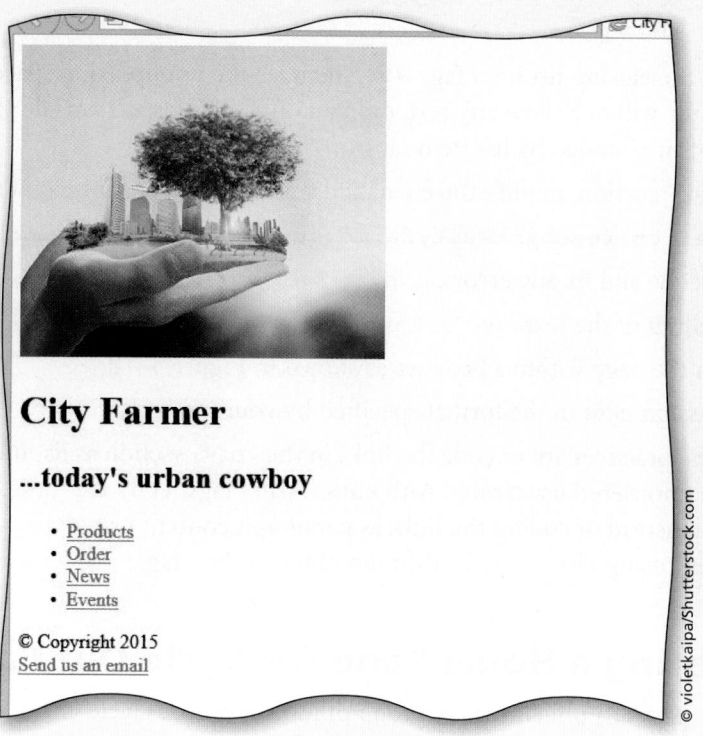

Figure 3–70

Instructions: Perform the following tasks:

1. Open the `cityfarmer03.html` file in your HTML editor and then modify the comment at the top of the page to include your name and today's date. Make sure the <title>…</title> tags contain the text `City Farmer Home Page.`

2. Delete the first comment in the header section and add an `img` element to insert the cityfarmer.jpg file as follows:

```
<img src="cityfarmer.jpg" alt="City Farmer logo" width="303"
height="252">
```

3. Change the <p>…</p> tags that mark up "City Farmer" in the `header` section to <h1>…</h1> tags.

4. Change the <p>…</p> tags that mark up "…today's urban cowboy" in the `header` section to <h2>…</h2> tags.

5. Modify the content in the `nav` section to create an unordered list of links to each of the future pages of the website as follows:

```
<ul>
     <li><a href="products.html">Products</a> </li>
     <li><a href="order.html">Order</a> </li>
     <li><a href="news.html">News</a> </li>
     <li><a href="events.html">Events</a> </li>
</ul>
```

(*Hint:* Note that the ending anchor tag, </a>, is positioned immediately after the word that becomes the link such as Products or Order. The ending anchor tag, </a>, does not include the nonbreaking space, ` `. This results in a clean link such as <u>Products</u> or <u>Order</u> instead of a link that adds a space on the end such as <u>Products </u>or <u>Order </u>.

Continued >

In the Lab continued

Also note that the closing list item tag, </li>, includes the nonbreaking space ` `. The HTML validator will not allow any text, even a nonbreaking space, inside an unordered list <ul> that is not surrounded by list item <li>....</li> tags.)

6. In the `footer` section, modify the email address to be a hyperlink as follows:

    `<a href="mailto:feedback@cityfarmer.com">Send us an email</a>`

7. Validate your code and fix any errors.

8. Check the spelling of the text.

9. Save and open the page within a browser as shown in Figure 3–70.

10. Submit your assignment in the format specified by your instructor.

11. ✳ Current best practices are to code the links in the <nav> section as list items using <li>...</li> tags within an unordered list created with <ul>...</ul> tags. Why are these best practices recommended instead of coding the links as paragraph content using <p>...</p> tags or as heading content using <h1>...</h1> through <h6>...</h6> tags?

Lab 2: Creating a Home Page for Cycle Out Cancer

Problem: You are part of a philanthropic group of motorcyclists, Cycle Out Cancer, who participate in community events and parades to distribute cancer awareness information. Create the webpage shown in Figure 3–71 that marks up the content on the organization's home page.

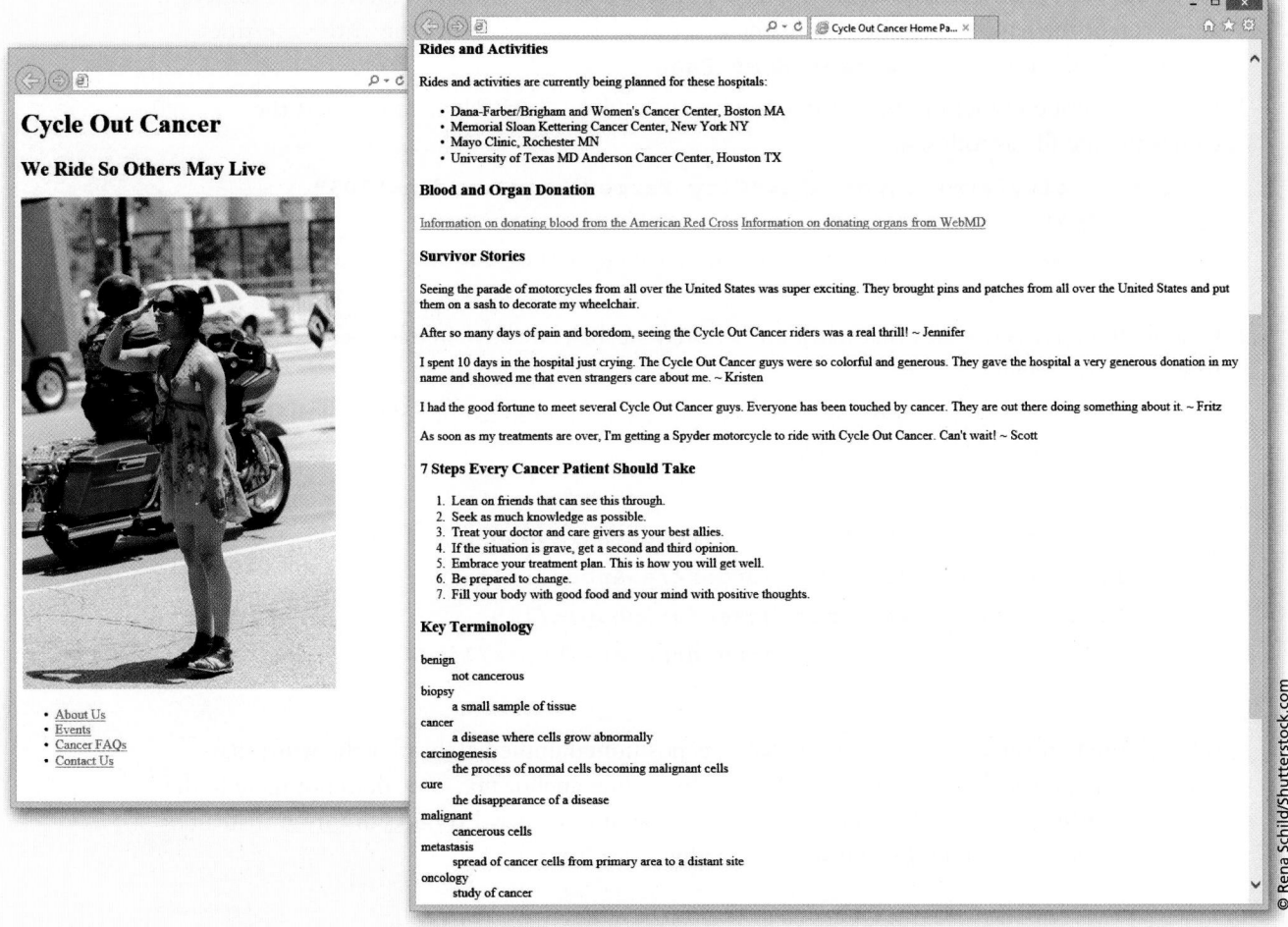

Figure 3–71

© Rena Schild/Shutterstock.com

Instructions: Perform the following tasks:

1. Open the `cycle03.html` in your HTML editor and then modify the comment at the top of the page to include your name and today's date. Make sure the <title>…</title> tags contain the text `Cycle Out Cancer Home Page`.

2. Change the <p>…</p> tags that mark up "Cycle Out Cancer" in the **header** section to <h1>…</h1> tags.

3. Change the <p>…</p> tags that mark up "We Ride So Others May Live" in the **header** section to <h2>…</h2> tags.

4. Delete the <!-- add photo--> comment in the **header** section and add an **img** tag with the following attributes and values:

   ```
   src="cycle.jpg"
   alt="Woman saluting riders"
   width="385"
   height="578"
   ```

5. Modify the content in the nav section to create links to each of the future pages of the website with the href attribute values as follows:

   ```
   <a href="about.html">About Us</a>
   <a href="events.html">Events</a>
   <a href="faq.html">Cancer FAQs</a>
   <a href="contact.html">Contact Us</a>
   ```

6. Modify the list of links in the **nav** section to be indented list items using <li>…</li> tags within an unordered list created with <ul>…</ul> tags. The two nonbreaking space codes ` ` should be positioned after the closing </a> tag but before the closing </li> tag for each item.

7. In the <div id="main"> section, mark up the following headings with <h3>…</h3> tags:

   Rides and Activities
   Blood and Organ Donation
   Survivor Stories
   7 Steps Every Cancer Patient Should Take
   Key Terminology

8. Below the "Rides and Activities" heading in the <div id="main"> section, mark up the first line ("Rides and activities are…") with <p>…</p> tags. Mark up the list of four hospitals as an unordered list.

9. Below the "Blood and Organ Donation" heading in the <div id="main"> section, use the first URL as the **href** attribute value to create a link with the text `Information on donating blood from the American Red Cross`.

   Use the second URL as the **href** attribute value to create a link with the text `Information on donating organs from WebMD`.

10. Below the "Survivor Stories" heading in the <div id="main"> section, mark up the four testimonials using <p>…</p> tags. (*Hint:* Each paragraph ends with the name of a person.)

11. Below the "7 Steps Every Cancer Patient Should Take" heading in the <div id="main"> section, delete numbers 1 through 7, and then mark up and indent the seven steps as list items using <li>…</li> tags within an ordered list created with <ol>…</ol> tags.

12. Below the "Key Terminology" heading in the <div id="main"> section, mark up the entire section as a description list using <dl>…</dl> tags. Mark up each term as a definition term with <dt>…</dt> tags and each definition with <dd>…</dd> tags.

Continued >

In the Lab *continued*

13. Validate your code and fix any errors.

14. Check the spelling of the text.

15. Save and open the page within a browser as shown in Figure 3–71.

16. Submit your assignment in the format specified by your instructor.

17. ✺ It's easy to confuse head, header, and heading HTML elements. Describe the purpose for each.

Lab 3: Expand Your World
HTML Terminology and Syntax

Problem: Every programming language has its own body of terminology needed to describe the components and capabilities of the language. In addition, every programming language has unique syntax, or rules, by which the code must be authored. In this exercise, you will create a large HTML description list to mark up some of the key terms and definitions for html. The final webpage is shown in Figure 3–72.

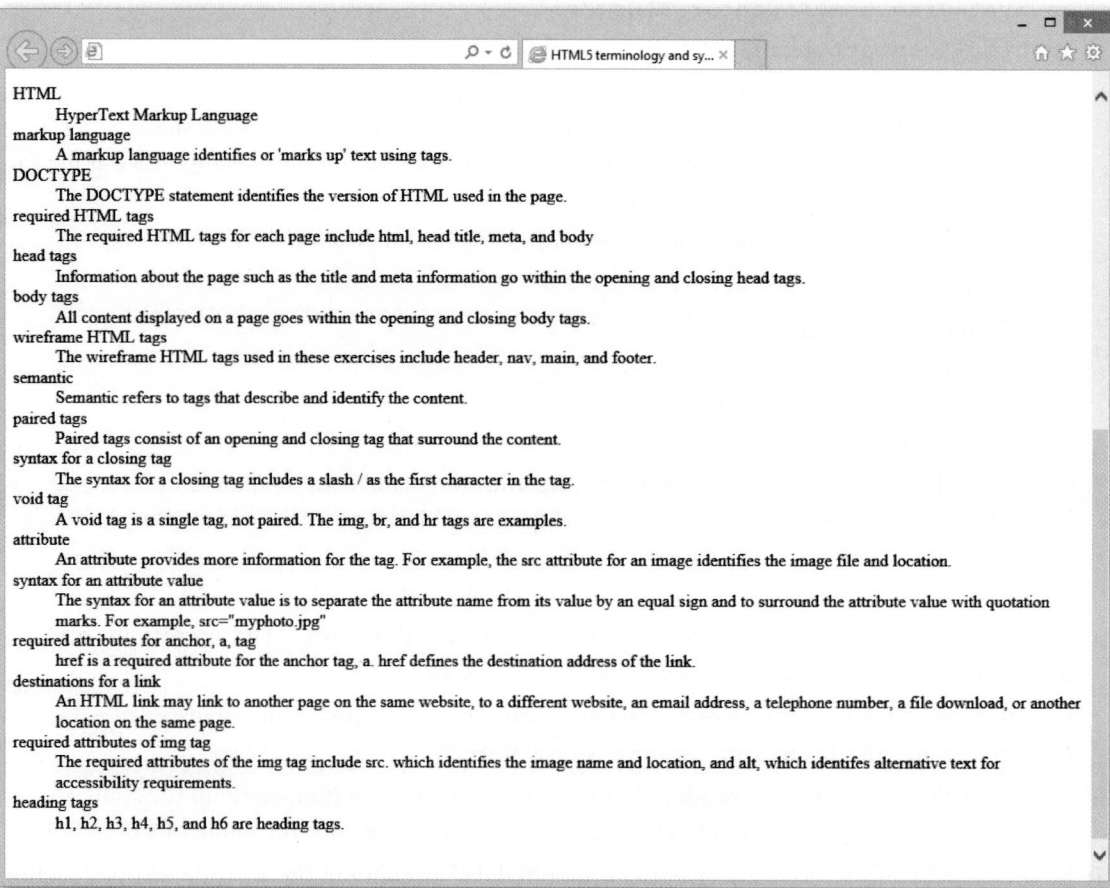

Figure 3–72

Instructions:

1. Open `terminology03.html` in your HTML editor and then modify the comment at the top of the page to include your name and today's date. Enter `HTML5 terminology and syntax` within the <title> tags.

2. Using the information in this chapter as well as the web, mark up the entire content in the <div id="terminology"> section as a description list using <dl>…</dl> tags. Mark up each term as a term using <dt>…</dt> tags.

3. After each term, research and enter a definition for that term using <dd>…</dd> tags. Indent the definition under the term it defines as shown in Figure 3–72.

4. Validate your code and fix any errors.

5. Check the spelling of the text.

6. Save and open the page within a browser as shown in Figure 3–72.

7. Submit your assignment in the format specified by your instructor.

8. ✳ Identify three problems that might occur for a web developer if the terminology and syntax discussed in this exercise are not understood.

Consider This: Your Turn

Apply your creative thinking and problem-solving skills to design and implement a solution.

1. Create the Home Page for Your Personal Portfolio Website

Personal

Part 1: In Chapter 2, you completed a wireframe and site map for your personal portfolio website in the `portfolio.html` webpage. In this exercise, you will update that page with content and HTML tags. Include the following updates:

1. Add an `img` tag as the first line in the `header` section with a professional picture of yourself. Be sure to include appropriate values for the `alt, width,` and `height` attributes. (*Hint:* To determine the actual width and height measurements of any image, open it in an image-editing program such as Paint or Photoshop. Information about the file's width and height measurements is usually presented in the status bar of the program. If your image is larger than 500 × 500 pixels, use the image-editing program to resize the image to make it as small and efficient for the web as possible. As you resize the image, be careful to maintain the current width/height ratio so that you do not skew or distort the image.)

2. In the `nav` section, create an unordered list of links to future pages that link to `education.html, experience.html, samples.html,` and `contact.html`.

3. To make sure the webpage will render successfully in all browsers, identify the main section using the <div id="main"> and </div> tags versus <main> and </main>, and include three <h2> headings in that section that mark up the headings of `Strengths, Technologies,` and `Other`.

4. Include paragraph content listing *your* strengths, technologies, and other applicable business skills below each <h2> heading.

5. Add an email hyperlink and a telephone hyperlink to the email and telephone content in the `header` section.

6. Validate and correct your webpage, spell check the content, and submit your assignment in the format specified by your instructor.

Part 2: ✳ Use your favorite search engine to find articles on search engine optimization (SEO). Identify three tips that you can add to your webpage to improve its SEO performance.

Continued >

Consider This: Your Turn *continued*

2. Create the Home Page for a Web Development and Consulting Business

Professional

Part 1: In Chapter 2, you completed a wireframe and site map for the web development firm website in the `webdev.html` webpage. In this exercise, you will update that page with content and HTML tags. Submit your assignment in the format specified by your instructor.

Validate and correct your webpage, spell check the content, and submit your assignment in the format specified by your instructor.

1. Save the webdev.html page as `index.html` because it will serve as your home page for this site.

2. Add an `img` tag as the first line in the `header` section using the company logo stored in the Data Files for Students as webdevpros.jpg with the following attribute values:

```
alt="WebDevPros logo"
height="260"
width="389"
```

3. In the `nav` section, create an unordered list of links to future pages that link to `index .html`, `services.html`, `testimonials.html`, `aboutus.html`, and `contactus.html`.

4. To make sure the webpage will render successfully in all browsers, identify the main section using the <div id="main"> and </div> tags versus <main> and </main>.

5. Save the page and then save it with the name `services.html`.

6. In the services.html page, create content in the <div id="main"> section using this text within <p>...</p> tags:

```
WebDevPros offers a full stack of web development services
from front-end webpage design and development through back-end
e-commerce solutions. Our development principles consider these web
development strategies:
```

7. In the services.html page, below the paragraph in the <div id="main"> section, create a description list of five principles of web development that start with these three terms. Code the phrases as data terms using <dt>...</dt> tags and their definitions using <dd>...</dd> tags.

Term: `Separation of presentation, content, and behavior where prudent`
Definition: `Striving to use html to describe the structure of content, external css style sheets to style and position the content, and external JavaScript files to create interactions between the webpage and the user.`

Term: `Responsive Web Design`
Definition: `Building websites to provide an optimal viewing experience across a wide range of devices.`

Term: `Progressive Enhancement`
Definition: `Designing websites using a layered approach that provides basic content and functionality to all users while providing enhanced functionality to those using advanced technology.`

(Add two more terms and definitions that relate to web development.)

Part 2: ✸ In Chapter 2, you contacted a web development consulting firm to interview them about a successful project to showcase as content on your home page. Open the index.html page and save it as `testimonials.html`. Delete the existing content in the <div id="main"> section. Using information from your interview, create a three- or four-sentence testimonial from a satisfied customer and enter it within paragraph tags within the <div id="main"> section. The testimonial will be fictitious, but strive to make it professional and realistic.

Validate and correct your webpages, spell check the content, and check the links between the index.html, testimonial.html, and services.html pages. Submit your assignment in the format specified by your instructor.

3. Create the Home Page for the Dog Hall of Fame

Research and Collaboration

Part 1: In Chapter 2, you completed a wireframe and site map for the Dog Hall of Fame website in the `dogfame.html` webpage. In this exercise, you'll update that page with content and HTML tags. Submit your assignment in the format specified by your instructor.

1. Save the dogfame.html page as `index.html` because it will serve as your home page for this site.

2. Add the banner.jpg image as the first line of content in the <header> section with the following attribute values:

```
alt="banner logo for Dog Hall of Fame"
height="300"
width="720"
```

3. Create an unordered list of links to future pages that link to `index.html`, `winners.html`, and `nominations.html` in the `nav` section.

4. In Chapter 2, your team collected content, images, and stories to add to the Dog Hall of Fame website in these three areas: Hero dog, Working dog, and Companion dog. Add that content to the <div id="main"> section of the index.html page using heading, paragraph, and list tags as appropriate. Four dog images are provided in the Data Files for Students if needed for this project.

5. Validate and correct your webpage, spell check the content, and check the links between the index.html page and the services.html page. Submit your assignment in the format specified by your instructor.

Part 2: ✺ Anytime you gather information or images from the web, copyright laws and academic fair use policies and ethics come into play. Work with your instructor to identify and apply the fair use and copyright policies that apply to the content you gather on the Internet as applied to the exercises for this class.

4 Applying CSS Styles to Webpages

Source: CSSZenGarden.com

Objectives

You will have mastered the material in this chapter when you can:

- Explain the importance of separating design from content
- Describe Cascading Style Sheets (CSS)
- Define inline, embedded, and external styles and their order of precedence
- Describe a CSS rule and its syntax
- Explain the difference between a selector, property, and value
- Create styles that use text and color properties
- Explain the difference between inline and block content

- Describe the CSS box model and how to apply margins, padding, and borders
- Create an external style sheet and link it to an HTML page
- Create styles that use padding, border, and margin properties
- Float an image
- Create styles that use list properties
- Add comments to an external style sheet
- Validate a CSS file

4 | Applying CSS Styles to Webpages

Introduction

Creating a well-designed website that captures your audience's attention is vital in attracting and obtaining new customers. To do so, a web developer can use formatting such as font styles, font colors, white space, and background colors or images to increase the visual appeal of the webpages. Websites developed with HTML5 alone can be functional, but they lack this important element of visual appeal. To improve the appearance of a website by including color, formatting text, and adding margins, borders, and shadows, for example, you need to apply styles created with **Cascading Style Sheets (CSS)**, a language you use to describe the formatting of a document written in a markup language such as HTML5. While HTML provides the structural foundation of a webpage, you use CSS styles to determine the formatting for a webpage. By defining CSS styles in a style sheet separate from the HTML code, you can format a webpage in an unlimited number of ways, such as changing the background color of the webpage, increasing the size of text or bolding it, applying margins to a section, and adding borders to elements.

Project — Format Webpages with CSS

In previous chapters, you created a website template and three webpages for the Forward Fitness Club website. You also added content and links to the home page, the About Us page, and the Contact Us page. However, these pages lack formatting to enhance their appearance.

In Chapter 2, you created a website plan to guide the design and development of the Forward Fitness Club website. The plan provides information about the desired typography and colors to enhance the business brand and logo. The plan includes a wireframe, which specifies passive white space between HTML elements. To add these design elements according to your plan, you create and apply CSS styles in an external style sheet, a separate file that contains the styles for the website.

The project in this chapter enhances a website with CSS. You apply styles to the HTML5 elements on each page to give the site a certain look and feel. After creating a style sheet, you link it to all of the pages in the website, including the template. As you add styles to the style sheet, they immediately format the attached webpages when you open or refresh the pages in a browser. Figure 4–1 shows the home page after it has been enhanced by CSS.

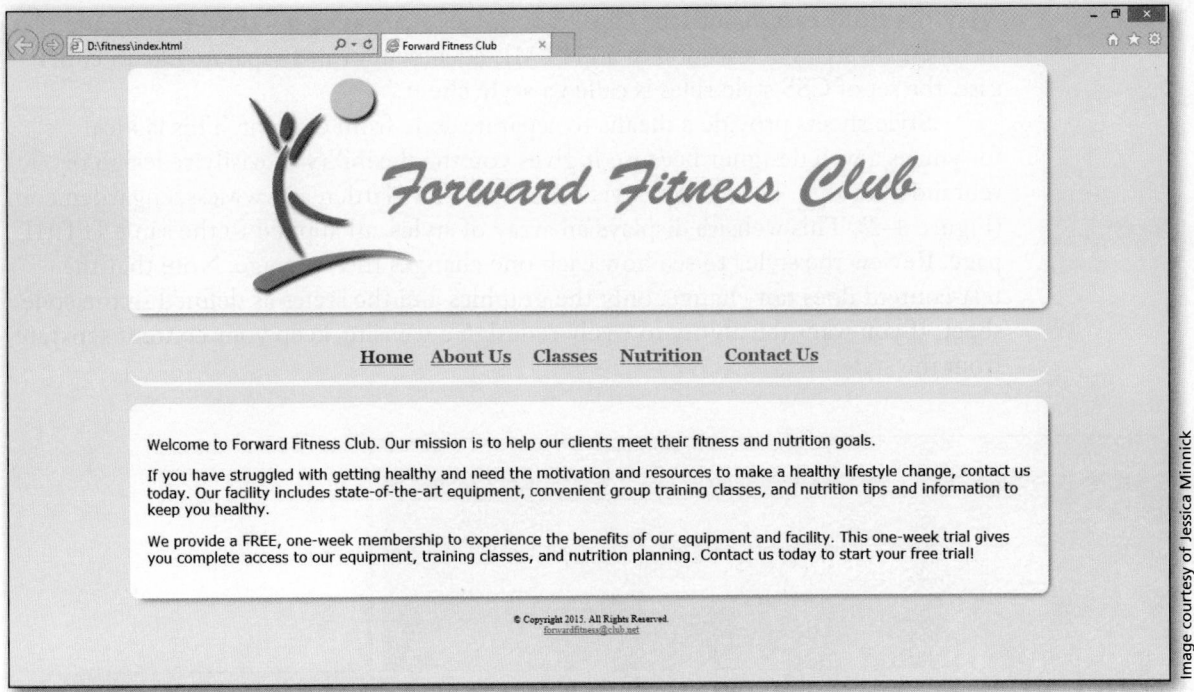

Image courtesy of Jessica Minnick

Figure 4–1

Roadmap

In this chapter, you will learn how to create the webpage shown in Figure 4–1. The following roadmap identifies general activities you will perform as you progress through this chapter:

1. CREATE a CSS FILE.

2. LINK HTML PAGES TO a CSS FILE.

3. CREATE STYLE RULES.

4. ADD COMMENTS to the CSS file.

5. VALIDATE the CSS FILE.

At the beginning of step instructions throughout the chapter, you will see an abbreviated form of this roadmap. The abbreviated roadmap uses colors to indicate chapter progress: gray means the chapter is beyond that activity; blue means the task being shown is covered in that activity; and black means that activity is yet to be covered. For example, the following abbreviated roadmap indicates the chapter would be showing a task in the 4 ADD COMMENTS activity.

1 CREATE CSS FILE | 2 LINK PAGES TO CSS FILE | 3 CREATE STYLE RULES

4 ADD COMMENTS | 5 VALIDATE CSS FILE

Use the abbreviated roadmap as a progress guide while you read or step through the instructions in this chapter.

Using Cascading Style Sheets

Although HTML allows web developers to make changes to the structure and content of a webpage, HTML is limited in its ability to define the appearance of one or more webpages. Instead, you use CSS styles to position and format elements on a webpage.

A **style** is a rule that defines the appearance of an element on a webpage. You can include CSS styles in a section of an HTML document or in a separate file. In either case, the set of CSS style rules is called a **style sheet**.

Style sheets provide a means to separate style from content. This is ideal for you as a web designer because it gives you the flexibility to easily redesign or rebrand a website. For example, visit the CSS Zen Garden at www.csszengarden.com (Figure 4–2). This website displays an array of styles, all applied to the same HTML page. Review the styles to see how each one changes the webpage. Note that the text content does not change, only the graphics and the styles as defined in the style sheet. If you want the ability to easily redesign a website, keep your content separate from the style.

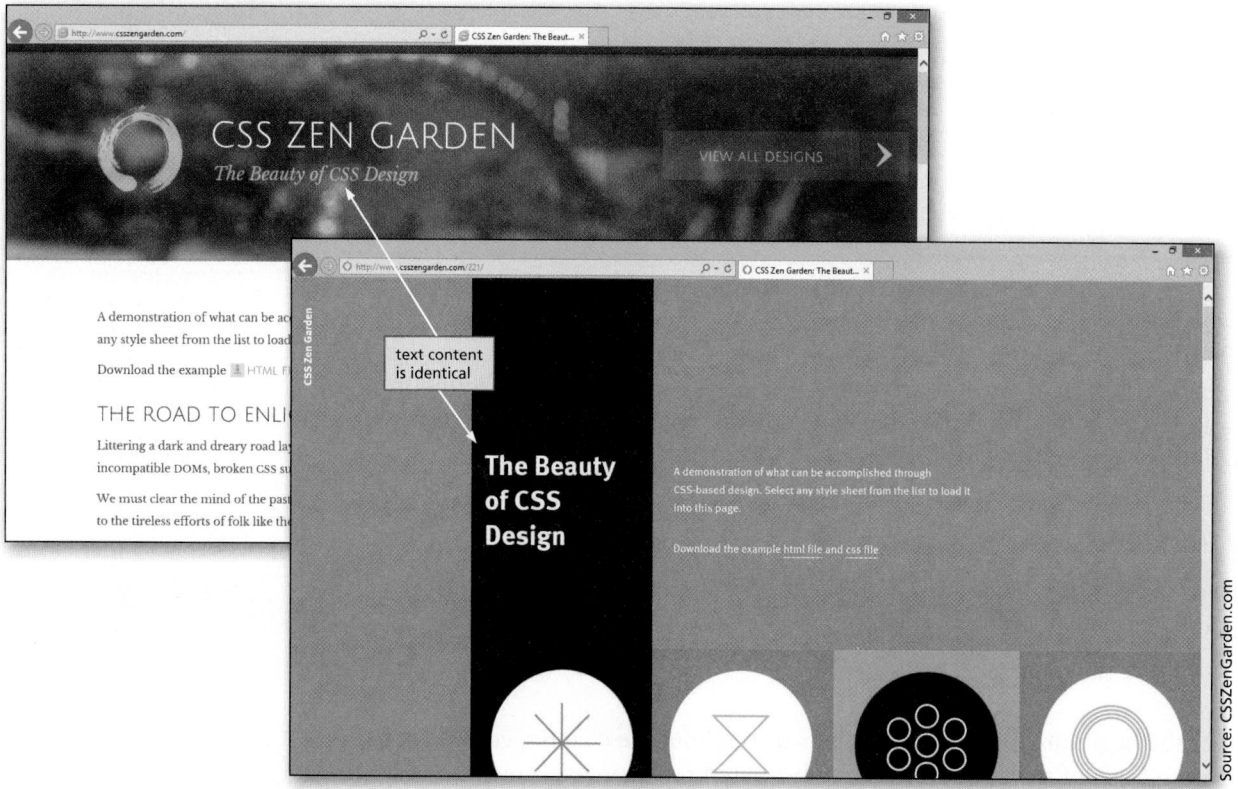

Figure 4–2

Separating content from style is even more important when you are maintaining a large website. You can define styles in a single CSS style sheet file, and then attach the single file to several webpages to apply the styles to all the attached pages. If you decide to use a different background color on all the webpages in the site, for example, you can make one change to the CSS style sheet to automatically update every page. Not only does this save a lot of time, it also means less maintenance for you or another web developer. If the site contained styles in the HTML code, locating those styles and removing them could be a time-consuming process.

CSS was developed by the W3C and is still evolving. The first version of CSS, CSS 1, was released in 1996. This version of CSS included styles for text, color, alignment, borders, padding, and margins. The second version of CSS, CSS 2, was released two years later in 1998 and included new styles to control the positioning of elements. The latest version of CSS is CSS3, which adds many new style features, including shadows, rounded borders, and enhanced text effects. CSS3 is currently still in working draft status at the W3C, which means W3C members, the public, and other technical organizations are reviewing it and might change its details. For a full list of CSS3 styles, visit w3.org. To work with an excellent tutorial for HTML5 elements and CSS3 properties, visit w3schools.com.

Modern browsers support CSS 1 and 2 and many of the new CSS3 features. However, browsers may vary in how they apply CSS styles, so be sure to test and view your site in all the major browsers. Visit www.quirksmode.org to learn which browsers support each CSS style.

The W3C developed CSS as the primary way to format webpages, so you should not use HTML tags to style page content. Tags, such as the <font> tag, have been deemed as obsolete by W3C and should not be used.

Inline Styles

CSS supports inline, embedded (or internal), and external styles. With an **inline style**, you add a style to the start tag for an element, such as a heading or paragraph, using the **style attribute**. The style changes the content marked up by a specific pair of tags, but does not affect other content in the document. Because inline styles take precedence over other types of styles and affect the style for individual pieces of content, they are helpful when you need to format only one section of a webpage in a unique way. However, inline styles defeat the purpose and advantages of separating style from content, so they should be used sparingly. An example of an inline style is shown in Figure 4–3. The style rule applies only to the content in this `h1` element, the "Special Note" text. In the starting <h1> tag, you begin writing an inline style using the `style` attribute. The inline style shown in Figure 4–3 defines the font color of the "Special Note" text as navy blue.

BTW

Deprecated and Unsupported Elements

A **deprecated** element or attribute is one that is outdated. Deprecated elements may become obsolete in the future, though most browsers continue to support deprecated elements for backward compatibility. In addition, many tags and attributes are not supported by HTML5, as noted in Appendix A. You can also visit w3c.org to find a list of deprecated HTML tags.

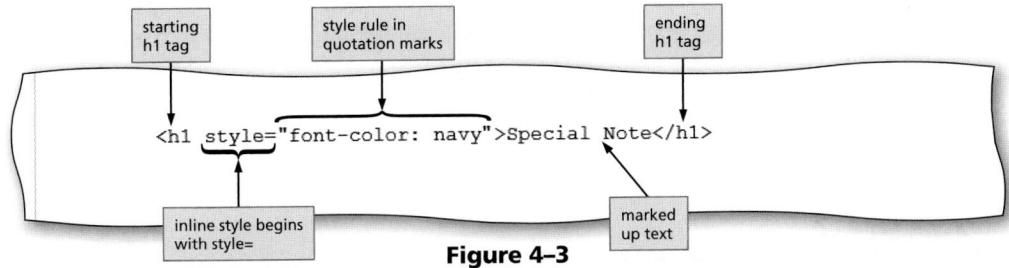

Figure 4–3

Embedded Style Sheets

An **embedded style sheet**, also called an **internal style sheet**, includes the style sheet within the opening <head> and closing </head> tags of the HTML document. Use an embedded style sheet when you want to create styles for a single webpage that are different from the rest of the website. An embedded style sheet takes precedence over an external style sheet. An example of an embedded style sheet is shown in Figure 4–4. In embedded style sheets, you place the style rules between the opening <style> and closing </style> tags. The style rule shown in Figure 4–4 sets the background color for the body section to green for the current webpage only.

Figure 4–4

External Style Sheets

An **external style sheet**, also called a **linked style sheet**, is a CSS file that contains all of the styles you want to apply to more than one page in the website. An external style sheet is a text file with the **.css** file extension. To apply an external style sheet, you link it (or attach it) to a webpage using a link tag in the head section of the webpage. External style sheets give you the most flexibility to quickly change webpage formats because the styles in an external style sheet are applied to every page linked to that style sheet. Changing the look of an entire website is sometimes called **reskinning** the website. You will create an external style sheet for the Forward Fitness Club's website to enhance the styles of the **body,** the **div id="container",** **header, nav, main,** and **footer** sections, lists, and classes. An example of a style rule for an external style sheet is shown in Figure 4–5. Like the style rule shown in Figure 4–4, this one sets the background color for the body section to green. Note that external style sheets do not contain any HTML tags.

Figure 4–5

Style Sheet Precedence

Style sheets are said to "cascade" because each type of style has a specified level of precedence (or priority) in relationship to the others. For example, suppose you create an inline style to change the text color of an **h1** heading to red. In the **head** section of a webpage, you also create a style in an embedded style sheet to change **h1** headings to blue, and in an external style sheet, you create a style to change **h1** headings to green. What color would **h1** headings be in the webpage with the inline style? They would be red because the style closest to the content takes precedence. In other words, inline styles beat embedded styles, and embedded styles beat external styles.

CSS properties can be inherited from a parent element. This principle is called **inheritance**. For example, paragraphs and headings inherit the font and color rules for the body selector. If a selector has more than one CSS rule, **specificity** determines which CSS rule to apply. The more specific selector is applied. For example, if the value of the background-color property for the body selector is green but the one for p is blue, the p elements will have a blue background because the p selector is more specific than the body selector.

The best practice is to apply inline styles when you want to control the style of content within one pair of HTML tags, an embedded style sheet when you want to change the style of one page, and external or linked style sheets for the styles that apply to many or all pages in the website.

Web designers use external style sheets for most of their styles for many reasons. First, they can create or modify all of the styles in one style sheet file and then link the file to all of the HTML documents. This provides consistency throughout the website and lessens the need for coding beyond the single style sheet. Second, when an HTML document is linked to a CSS file, the page can load in a browser quickly. Third, if web designers need to change the appearance of a particular HTML element, they can do so in one file. The browser applies the change to all of the linked pages, reducing errors and redundancies.

CSS Basics

To write an inline CSS style, you use a style attribute within the HTML element, as shown in Figure 4–3. To write a CSS style, or rule, for an embedded or external style sheet, you write a statement that follows the CSS syntax. Each CSS rule consists of a selector and a declaration. See Figure 4–6.

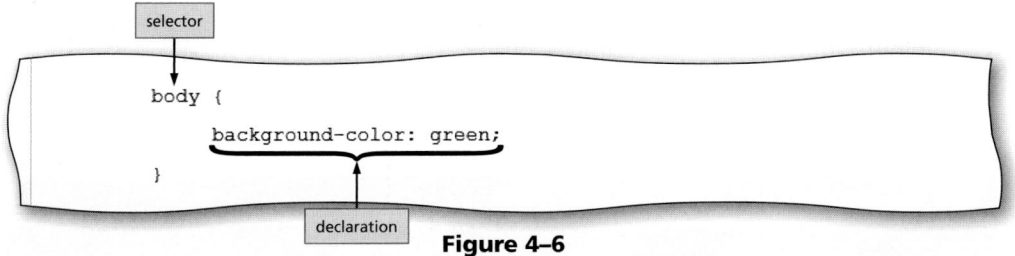

Figure 4–6

The **selector** is the part of the statement that identifies what to style. Any HTML5 element such as body, header, nav, main, or footer may be a selector. For example, if you want to format the content in the `body` section of a webpage, use `body` as the selector in the style statement. A selector may also be the value of an id or class attribute. For example, if you want to format the content in the `div id="container"` section, use `#container` as the selector. (You will learn about including a # sign with selectors shortly.)

The **declaration** defines the exact formatting of the style. A declaration consists of a property and a value, separated by a colon and followed by a semicolon (;). The **property** identifies the style quality or characteristic to apply, such as color (text color), background-color, text-indent, border-width, or font-style. A declaration includes at least one property to apply to the selected element.

For each property, the declaration includes a related **value** that identifies the particular property value to apply, such as green for color or 150% for font-size. You can use only certain values with each property based on the styles that property can define. The font-color property, for example, can accept navy as a value, but cannot

BTW

Style Rule Syntax
The correct syntax for styles is to use all lowercase letters for the property name without any spaces. The same is true for values: use all lowercase characters and no spaces.

BTW
CSS Syntax Color Coding in Notepad++
Notepad++ and other text editors use color coding to help you write style rules using the correct syntax. For example, when a declaration is written with correct syntax, the value is displayed in black and the property is displayed in a contrasting color by default.

accept 150% because that is not a valid value for the color property. See Appendix B for a list of properties and valid values.

Figure 4–7 shows the correct syntax for the style rule shown in Figure 4–4 and Figure 4–5. To create a style for an embedded or external style sheet, you first identify the selector, followed by a space and an opening brace. Next, you specify the property, followed by a colon, and then provide a value for the property, followed by a semicolon. Close the rule with a closing brace.

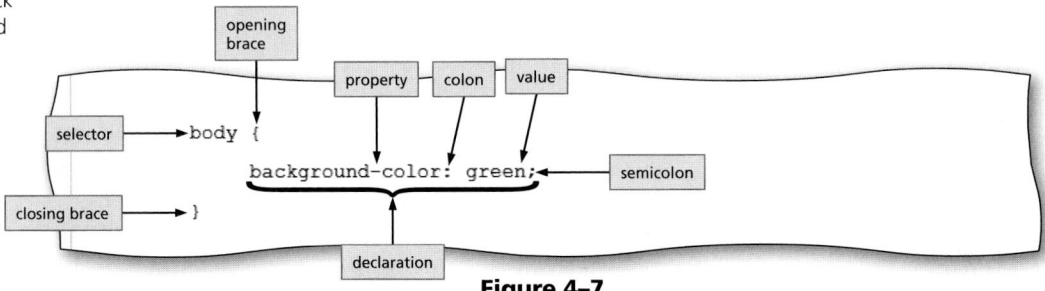

Figure 4–7

What is the difference between HTML attributes and CSS properties?

You use attributes in HTML elements to define more information for an element. Enter an attribute in an element's start tag as a name="value" pair. For example, in an **img** element, you include an attribute such as **src="logo.png"** to specify the source of the image. In this example, "src" is the attribute name and "logo.png" is the value. In a similar way, a CSS style defines the formatting for one or more elements. A style rule includes a selector and a declaration that consists of a property: value; pair. For example, **h1 {color: blue;}** formats **h1** elements using blue text. Enter a declaration for a selector in a style sheet.

CSS Text Properties

You can use CSS styles to format webpage text in a variety of ways. For example, use the font-family property to define a specific font. Use the font-size property to define a specific font size.

Table 4–1 lists common text properties and values.

Table 4–1 Common Text Properties and Values		
Property	**Description**	**Common Values**
font-family	Specific and general font names	font-family: Cambria, "Times New Roman", serif; font-family: Verdana, Arial, sans-serif; font-family: Georgia, "Times New Roman", serif;
font-size	Absolute or relative size of a font	font-size: 1.5em; font-size: 50%; font-size: x-large; font-size: 14pt;
font-weight	Weight of a font	font-weight: bold; font-weight: bolder; font-weight: lighter;
font-style	Style of a font	font-style: normal; font-style: italic; font-style: oblique;
text-align	Alignment of text	text-align: center; text-align: right; text-align: justify;
color	Color of text	color: red; color: blue; color: green;

Notice that the font-family property may include multiple values. In fact, you should provide more than one value for this property in case the browser does not support the primary font. The additional values are called **fallback values**. If the browser does not support the primary font, it displays the second font family indicated and if the browser does not support the second font family value, the browser uses the next font family. Commas separate each value. The desired value is listed first and the value of serif or sans-serif is listed last. For example, the declaration `font-family: Cambria, "Times New Roman", serif;` means that the browser should use the Cambria font; if the browser cannot use Cambria, it should use Times New Roman, which is listed in quotation marks because the font family name contains more than one word. Finally, if the browser does not support Cambria or Times New Roman, it should use its default serif font.

BTW
Font Names
The W3C recommends quoting font family names that contain spaces, digits, or punctuation characters other than hyphens.

Why would a browser not support certain fonts?

Fonts are installed on a computer, so a computer must have the font installed before a browser can display it. For a list of common web fonts, visit www.w3schools.com/cssref/css_websafe_fonts.asp.

CONSIDER THIS

CSS measures font size using many measurement units, including pixels, points, and ems, and by keyword or percentage. Table 4–2 lists units for measuring font size.

Table 4–2 Font Size Measurement Units

Unit	Definition	Example	Comments
em	Relative to the default font size of the element	font-size: 1.25em;	Recommended by W3C; sizes are relative to the browser's default font size
%	Relative to the default font size of the element	font-size: 50%;	Recommended by W3C; sizes are relative to the browser's default font size
px	Number of pixels	font-size: 25px;	Depends on screen resolution
pt	Number of points	font-size: 12pt;	Use for printing webpages
keyword	Relative to a limited range of sizes	font-size: xx-small;	Sizes are relative to the browser's default font size, but size options are limited

The em is a relative measurement unit that the W3C recommends for values of the font-size property. The size of an em is relative to the current font size of the element. For example, 1.25em means 1.25 times the size of the current font. If a browser displays paragraphs using 16-point text by default, a font-size property value of 1em is 16 points and 1.25em is 20 points.

Percentage measurements work in a similar way. A font-size property value of 2em and of 200% appear the same when displayed in a browser. Note that no spaces appear in the font-size property value, so 1.25em and 50% are correct, but 1.25 em is not correct.

CSS Colors

One way to help capture a webpage visitor's attention is to use color as a webpage background or for text, borders, or links. HTML uses color names or codes to designate color values. When using a color name, you specify a word such as aqua or black as a value. Following are 16 basic color names. For more color names, visit www.w3schools.com/htmL/html_colornames.asp.

aqua	navy
black	olive
blue	purple
fuchsia	red
gray	silver
green	teal
lime	white
maroon	yellow

Color codes are more commonly used in web design. You can use two types of color codes with CSS: hexadecimal and RGB.

Hexadecimal values consist of a six-digit number code that corresponds to **RGB (Red, Green, Blue)** color values. When noting color values in CSS, include a number sign (#) before the code. Hexadecimal is a combination of the base-16 numbering system, which includes letters A through F. An example of a hexadecimal color value is 0000FF, which is blue. The first two digits (00) indicate the red value, which is none in this case. The next two digits (00) indicate the green value, which is also none in this case. The last two digits (FF) indicate the blue value. Because FF is the highest two-digit hexadecimal number, 0000FF specifies a pure blue.

RGB notation is used to display colors on a screen, though not in print. RGB blends red, green, and blue color channels to create a color. (A **channel** contains the number of red, green, or blue pixels necessary to create a specified color.) Each color channel is expressed as a number, 0 through 255. For example, the color blue is expressed as rgb(0,0,255). The first number represents the red color channel. The zero represents no pixels from a color channel; in the example, color channels red and green contribute no pixels to the color. The last channel represents the blue color channel; the number 255 represents the truest form of the color channel, in this case, blue. Hexadecimal 0000FF and rgb(0,0,255) are two ways of expressing the same color, pure blue.

Table 4–3 shows a common list of colors, with the corresponding hexadecimal and RGB color codes.

BTW
Colors
For more information about webpage colors, see Appendix C, which includes a list of websites that can help you determine the name, hexadecimal number, and RGB value for colors.

BTW
Quick Color Picker
W3 Schools provides a quick color picker reference at www.w3schools.com/tags/ref_colorpicker.asp. Here, you can select a color, view various shades of the color, and find the hexadecimal color value.

Table 4–3 Color Values

Color	Hexadecimal	RGB
Black	#000000	rgb(0,0,0)
White	#FFFFFF	rgb(255,255,255)
Red	#FF0000	rgb(255,0,0)
Green	#008000	rgb(0,128,0)
Blue	#0000FF	rgb(0,0,255)
Yellow	#FFFF00	rgb(255,255,0)
Orange	#FFA500	rgb(255,165,0)
Gray	#808080	rgb(128,128,128)

To use a color in a style rule declaration, use the color value as the property value. For example, to style a background color as gray, you use the background-color property with a value of #808080, as shown in the following example:

```
background-color: #808080;
```

Understanding Inline Elements and Block Elements

When you format webpages with CSS, you set rules that describe how the HTML elements should appear in a browser. As you create rules for the elements, review the structure of the HTML document because it plays a part in how a browser displays the element on a webpage.

HTML elements are positioned on the webpage as a block or as inline content. A **block element** appears as a block because it starts and ends with a new line, such as the main element or a paragraph element. Block elements can contain content, other block elements, and inline elements. **Inline elements** are displayed without line breaks so they flow within the same line. Inline content always appears within block elements. Examples of inline elements are the span tag (<span>) and the anchor tag (<a>). You use the span element to group inline elements. To format one or more words in a paragraph, for example, include an inline style in the opening span tag that groups the words, as in the following example, which formats only "Warning" in red text.

```
<span style="color: red;">"Warning"</span>
```

An `img` element is also an inline element because it flows in the same line, although it has natural height and width properties unlike other inline elements. Figure 4–8 shows an example of an inline element in a block element.

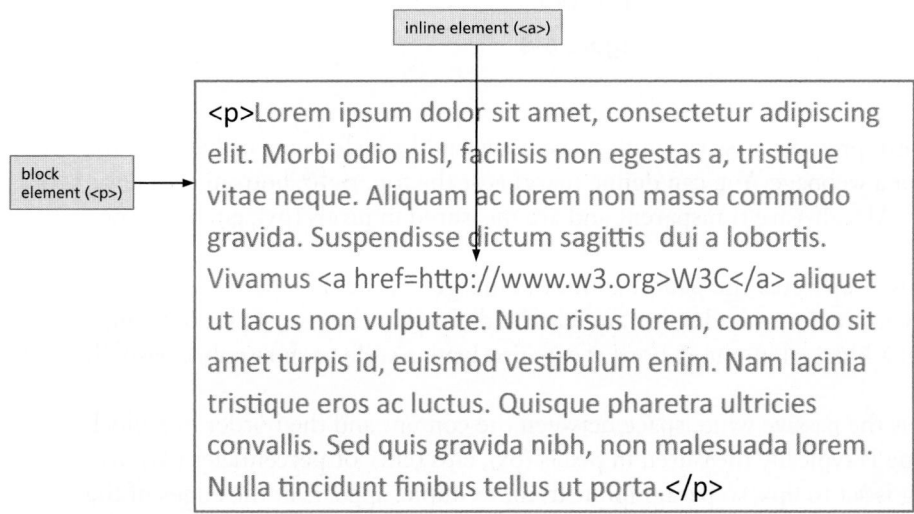

Figure 4–8

Header, nav, main, and footer are all examples of block elements. When you apply CSS styles to these block elements in the website you created for the Forward Fitness Club, you must consider their hierarchical structure to produce the visual effect you intend. Styles applied to elements below or above another element can affect their placement on a webpage. For example, as a block element, the `header` element normally starts on a new line and spans the width of the webpage. A new line also appears after the `header` element. If you want the `nav` element to appear to the right of the header, apply styles to both the `header` element and the `nav` element to accomplish this effect.

CSS Box Model

Each block element such as a header, nav, main, and footer element has a top, right, bottom, and left side. In other words, the element is displayed in a browser as a box with content. The **CSS box model** describes these boxes of content on a webpage. Each content box can have margins, borders, and padding, as shown in Figure 4–9. You refer to the sides of a box in clockwise order: top, right, bottom, and left.

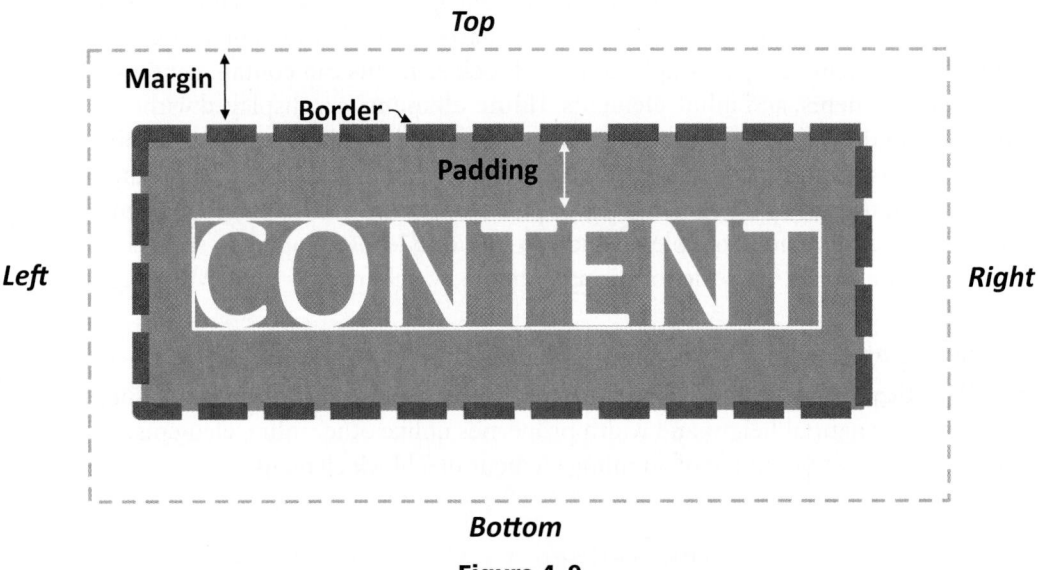

Figure 4–9

The **margin** provides passive white space between block elements or between the top or bottom of a webpage. You can define margins at the top, right, bottom, and left of a block element. Margins are transparent and are measured in pixels (px), ems (em), or percentages (%).

The **border** separates the padding and the margin of the block element. A border can vary in thickness and color and can be defined at the top, right, bottom, and left sides of a block element. A border can also have a style such as solid, dashed, or dotted.

Padding is the passive white space between the content and the border of a block element. Padding is typically measured in pixels (px), ems (em), or percentages (%). By default, padding is set to 0px, so paragraph text, for example, appears at the edges of the block element. You can increase the padding to improve legibility. The box model shown in Figure 4–9 includes more than the default amount of padding. The background color for the padding and content is always the same.

Using CSS, you can set the margin, border, or padding properties for all four sides of a block element using a single declaration. For example, the following declaration sets the top, right, bottom, and left margins of a block element to 2em:

```
margin: 2em;
```

You can use a similar shorthand notation to set the style, width, and color for all four sides of a block element's border. The property values can appear in any order. The following declaration sets the top, right, bottom, and left borders of a block element to a solid line using a width of 1 pixel and a color of black:

```
border: solid 1px #000000;
```

Writing the declaration using shorthand notation is helpful when all four sides of the block element use the same property values. If you want to use different property values on one or more sides of the block element, include a declaration for each side of the block element. For example, you can use the following declarations to set the padding for each side of a block element:

```
padding-top: 5px;

padding-right: 15px;

padding-bottom: 12px;

padding-left: 10px;
```

You can set even more specific property options for the border, such as border-top-width and border-right-color. For example, the following declaration sets only the left border of the block element to a width of 2 pixels:

```
border-left-width: 2px;
```

Table 4–4 lists common CSS box model properties used to style block elements.

Table 4–4 Common CSS Box Model Properties

Property	Description	Examples
margin	Sets the amount of space around the block element (top, right, bottom, left)	margin: 20px; margin-top: 2em; margin-bottom: 150%;
padding	Sets the amount of space between content and the border of its block element	padding: 10px; padding-left: 1.5em; padding-right: 125%;
border	Sets the format of the block element's border	border: solid 1px #000000;
border-style	Designates the style of a border	border-top-style: solid; border-top-style: dotted;
border-width	Designates the width of a border	border-top-width: 1px; border-bottom-width: thick;
border-color	Designates the border color	border-top-color: #000000; border-bottom-color: gray;
border-radius	Rounds the corners of a block element's border	border-radius: 10px;
box-shadow	Adds a shadow to a block element's border	box-shadow: 8px 8px 8px #000000;

To have a border appear around the content in a block element, you must specify a border style in a CSS statement. You can include the style value with the border property or use the border-style property with an assigned value.

The border-radius and box-shadow properties are new to CSS3. As with the other border properties, you can list more than one value to set the top, right, bottom, and left radius values for the border. For the box-shadow property, you must specify the horizontal and vertical offset measurements. In addition, you can set the distance of the shadow's blur, the size of the shadow, and its color. The default color is black.

BTW
CSS Box Properties
Appendix B contains a comprehensive list of the CSS box properties and their acceptable values.

Creating an External Style Sheet

To create styles that apply to more than one webpage in a website, use an external style sheet. Recall that an external style sheet is a text file that contains the style rules (selectors and declarations) you want to apply to more than one page in the website.

Using an external style sheet involves two steps. First, use a text editor to create and save a document with a .css extension. In the CSS document, create style rules for elements such as body, header, nav, main, and footer to improve the visual appeal of the website. Use styles to add color and borders, apply text properties, align items, and increase white space for padding and margins. Next, link the CSS file to the webpages that should be formatted using the styles defined in the external style sheet.

Selectors

Recall that a style rule begins with a selector, which specifies the element to style. A selector can be an HTML element name, an id attribute value, or a class attribute value. If the selector is an HTML element, you use the element name for the selector. Figure 4–10 shows how a selector in a CSS file selects the content to be styled for an HTML element, an id attribute, and a class attribute for HTML elements in an HTML file.

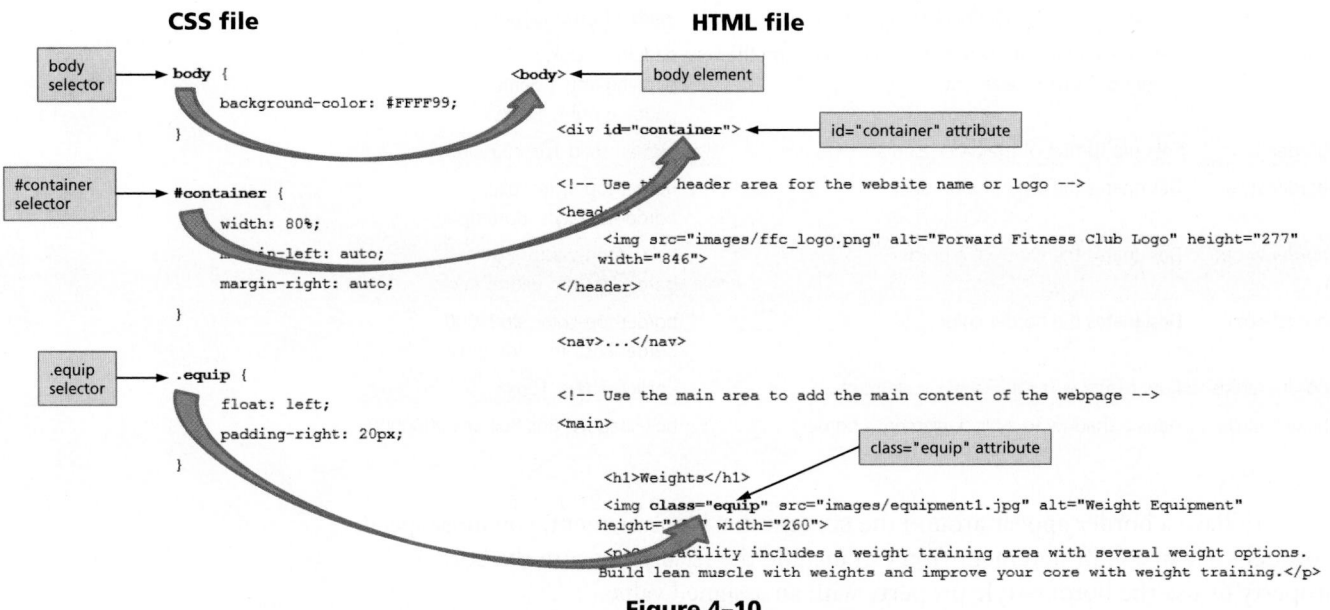

Figure 4–10

For example, to style the header element, use **header** as the name of the selector. To define the style of all p elements so they display white text on a black background, use the following style rule:

```
p {
    color: white;
    background-color: black;
}
```

If you want to apply styles to some p elements but not others, for example, you can create an id or a class selector. An **id selector** uses the id attribute value of an HTML element to select a single element. To create an id selector, you begin the style rule with a number sign (#) followed by the id attribute value. For example, to style the `div id="container"` element, use `#container` as the selector. The following style rule applies a solid 2-pixel border to only the `div id="container"` element:

```
#container {

  border: solid 2px;

}
```

Use a **class selector** to select elements that include a certain class attribute. To create a class selector, you begin the style rule with a period (.) followed by the class attribute value. For example, to style class="mobile", use `.mobile` as the selector. The following style rule sets the font size to 10 points for all elements that use mobile as their class attribute value:

```
.mobile {

  font-size: 10pt;

}
```

If you want to create a style that applies to more than one element, you can list more than one selector in the style rule. For example, the following style rule sets the same font family property and values for the `header, nav,` and `footer` elements:

```
header, nav, footer {

  font-family: Calibri, Arial, sans-serif;

}
```

If you want to create a style that applies to an element contained within another element, you list the elements in the order they appear to create the selector in the style rule. This type of selector is called a **descendant selector**. For example, the following style rule sets the list-style property to none for list items in an unordered list included in the navigation area:

```
nav ul li {

  list-style: none;

}
```

To Create a CSS File and a Style Rule for the Body Element

1 CREATE CSS FILE | **2 LINK PAGES TO CSS FILE** | **3 CREATE STYLE RULES**
4 ADD COMMENTS | **5 VALIDATE CSS FILE**

To apply styles to the Forward Fitness Club website, you can create them in an external style sheet. *Why?* *The styles defined in the external style sheet will apply to all the webpages in the website.* To create a CSS file, you use your preferred text editor to create a file and save it as a CSS document. Next, include one or more style rules that apply to all the webpages linked to the CSS document. The first style rule you add sets the background color of the webpages. This rule uses "body" as the selector and the background-color property in the declaration. Because the `body` element contains all of the content displayed on a webpage, using "body" as the selector sets the background color of the entire webpage. The following steps create a CSS file and a style rule.

1

- Open your text editor, tap or click File on the menu bar, and then tap or click New if you need to open a new blank document.

- Tap or click File on the menu bar and then tap or click Save As to display the Save As dialog box.

- Navigate to your fitness folder and then double-tap or double-click the css folder to open it.

- In the File name box, type **styles** to name the file.

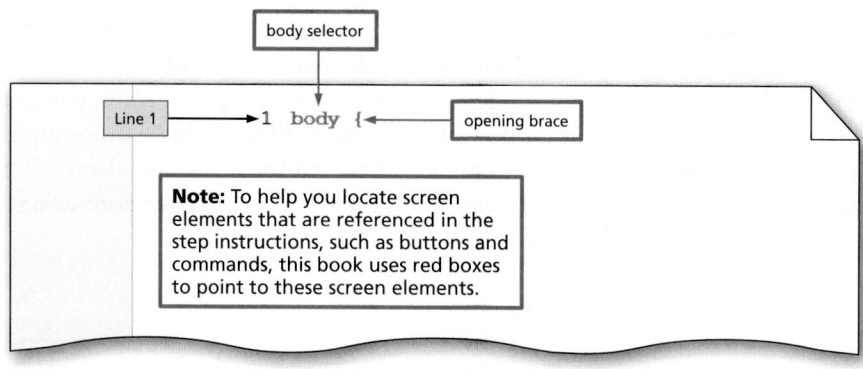

Figure 4–11

Q&A | Is "styles" the required file name for the CSS file?
No. You can give a CSS file any meaningful name, but a common name for an external style sheet is styles.css. An external style sheet must end with a .css extension.

- Tap or click the Save as type button, and then tap or click Cascading Style Sheets or CSS to select the file format.

- Tap or click the Save button to save the file in the css folder.

- On Line 1 of the text editor, type **body** { to begin a new style rule for the body element (Figure 4–11).

Q&A | Why should I use "body" as the selector?
Using "body" as the selector means the style rule applies to all of the body elements in the webpages linked to the style sheet. In this case, you are creating a style rule that sets the background color for the entire webpage because the body element contains all of the content displayed on a webpage.

2

- Press the ENTER key to add Line 2, press the TAB key to indent the new line, and then type **background-color: #FFFF99;** to add a declaration that sets the background color.

- Press the ENTER key to add Line 3, press the SHIFT+TAB keys to decrease the indent, and then type **}** to add a closing brace (Figure 4–12).

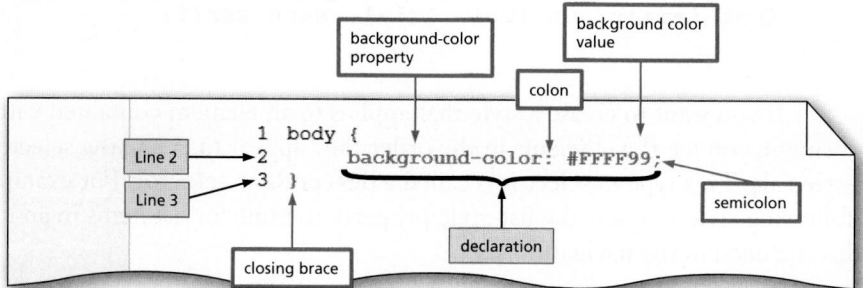

Figure 4–12

Q&A | What color does FFFF99 represent?
The color specified by FFFF99 is a light yellow.

3

- Save your changes.

Linking an HTML Document to a CSS File

After creating a CSS file, link it to all the webpages that will use its styles. Otherwise, the browser will not find and apply the styles in the external style sheet. Insert a **link** element on the HTML page within the <head> and </head> tags, which is the section of an HTML document that provides information to browsers and search engines but is not displayed on the webpage itself.

The **link** element uses two attributes, **rel** and **href**. The **rel** attribute uses the **stylesheet** value to indicate that the document is linked to a style sheet. The **href** attribute value specifies the file path or file name of the CSS file. Following is an example of a link to a style sheet named styles.css and stored in the css folder:

```
<link rel="stylesheet" href="css/styles.css">
```

The **type="text/css"** attribute and value is also commonly used within a **link** element to reference a CSS file. However, with HTML5, the **type** attribute is not necessary. The W3C says that the use of the **type** attribute within the **link** element is "purely advisory."

To Link HTML Pages to the CSS File

1 CREATE CSS FILE | 2 LINK PAGES TO CSS FILE | 3 CREATE STYLE RULES
| 4 ADD COMMENTS | 5 VALIDATE CSS FILE

To link the styles.css file to an HTML page, you include a link to the style sheet within the **head** section of the document. Next, view the changes to the webpage in a browser. *Why? To apply the CSS style rules to a webpage, you must link the webpage to the CSS file. To view the applied styles, open the home page in a browser.* If you link the website template to the style sheet file, any new pages created from the template will already be linked to the style sheet. The following steps link the home, about, contact, and template HTML documents to the external style sheet file and then view one page in a browser.

- Open index.html in your text editor to prepare to link the page to the CSS file.

- Place the insertion point after the beginning <head> tag on Line 4 and press the ENTER key to create a new Line 5.

- Press the TAB key to indent the line and then type **<link rel="stylesheet" href="css/styles.css">** to create a link to the style sheet file (Figure 4–13).

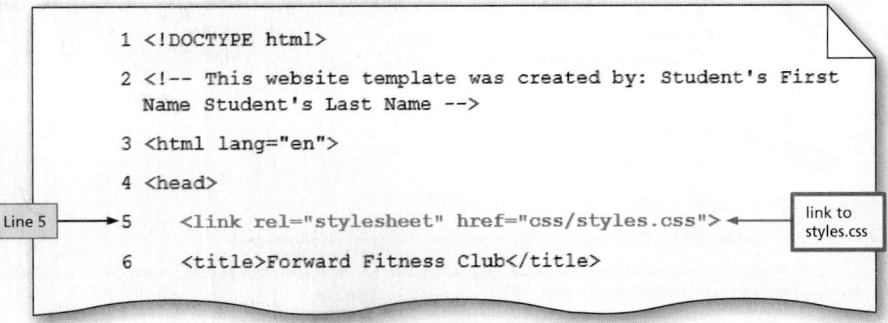

```
1  <!DOCTYPE html>
2  <!-- This website template was created by: Student's First
      Name Student's Last Name -->
3  <html lang="en">
4  <head>
5      <link rel="stylesheet" href="css/styles.css">        ← link to
                                                                styles.css
6      <title>Forward Fitness Club</title>
```
Line 5 →

Figure 4–13

Q&A Why do I need to include css/ before the name of the file?

The styles.css file is located within the css folder. Because the file is not stored in the same folder as the index.html document, you must include the folder name as well as the file name in the **href** attribute value.

- Save the index.html page to preserve your changes.

- Open about.html in your text editor to prepare to link the page to the CSS file.

- Place the insertion point after the beginning <head> tag on Line 4 and press the ENTER key to create a new Line 5.

- Press the TAB key to indent the line and then type `<link rel="stylesheet" href="css/styles.css">` to create a link to the style sheet file.

- Save your changes and close the file.

- Open contact.html in your text editor, place the insertion point after the beginning <head> tag on Line 4, and then press the ENTER key to create a new Line 5.

- Press the TAB key and then type `<link rel="stylesheet" href="css/styles.css">` to create a link to the style sheet file.

- Save your changes and close the file.

- Open fitness.html, located in the template folder, place the insertion point after the beginning <head> tag on Line 4, and then press the ENTER key to create a new Line 5.

- Press the TAB key and then type `<link rel="stylesheet" href="css/styles.css">` to create a link to the style sheet file.

- Save your changes and close the file.

- View the home page in your default browser to view the page with the linked style sheet (Figure 4–14).

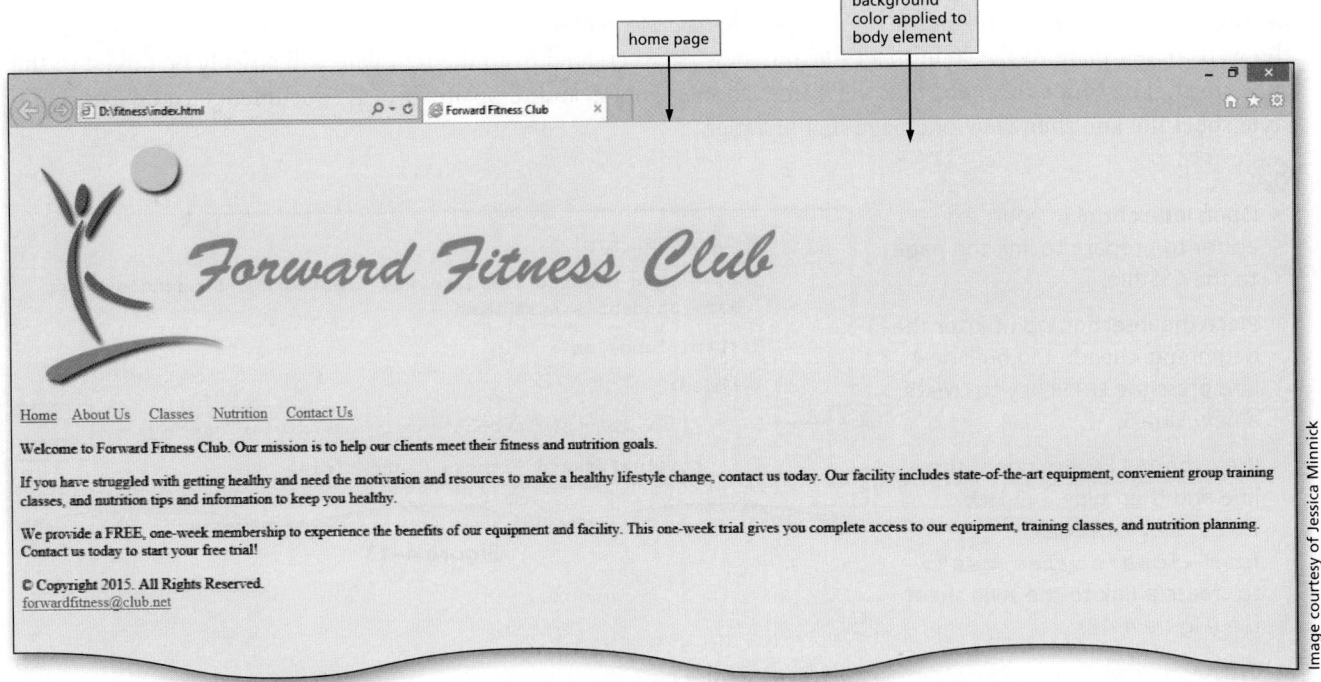

Figure 4–14

Image courtesy of Jessica Minnick

CONSIDER THIS

How can I confirm that my styles have been correctly applied to a webpage?

After creating a CSS file, link it to one of your webpages. Include a complete style rule or add a declaration to a selector, save your changes, and then view the webpage in a browser to view the effects of the new or modified style. If the style is not applied as you intended, return to your CSS file to check for syntax errors, confirm that you saved the CSS file, and check for value errors. It is much easier to find mistakes when you code and test each new style or declaration.

Aligning Webpage Content

One way to align webpage content is to use the text-align property, which applies to block elements. Use the text-align property to set the horizontal alignment for the lines of text in an element. The text-align property can use one of four values: left (the default), center, right, or justify. Use the justify value to align text on the left and right margins by adding white space to the lines of text. Use the center value to center content within an element. For example, the following rule centers an `h1` element:

```
h1 {
  text-align: center;
}
```

Another way to center webpage content is to use the margin property. To center all of the elements so that the page appears centered within a browser window, you create styles to set the left and right margins to auto. You also set the width property to a percentage to specify how much of the page to use for content. For example, if you set the width to 80%, you leave 20 percent of the page for margins. Using "auto" as the property value means that the left and right margins split the available 20 percent equally, leaving 10 percent of the page for the left margin and 10 percent of the page for the right margin. The following declaration specifies the width of the `div id="container"` section as 80 percent of the page and sets the left and right margins to "auto," centering all of the content in that section:

```
container {
  width: 80%;
  margin-left: auto;
  margin-right: auto;
}
```

To Center Content

1 CREATE CSS FILE | 2 LINK PAGES TO CSS FILE | **3 CREATE STYLE RULES**
4 ADD COMMENTS | 5 VALIDATE CSS FILE

Now that you have created a style for the `body` element, return to your CSS file to create style rules for the `div id="container"` section. Recall that this section contains all of the other structural areas of the webpage, including the `header, nav, main,` and `footer` elements. Currently, these elements are not centered on the page when displayed in a browser. To center all of these elements using a single style rule, you set the left and right margins to `auto` for the `div id="container"` element. In addition, set the width to 80% so that the elements do not span 100 percent of the browser window. Because "container" is an id value, use `#container` as the selector. The following steps center the contents of an element using margin and width properties.

- In the text editor, return to the styles.css file.

- Place the insertion point after the closing brace on Line 3 and press the ENTER key twice to insert new Lines 4 and 5.

- On Line 5, type `#container { to add the container selector and an opening brace (Figure 4–15).

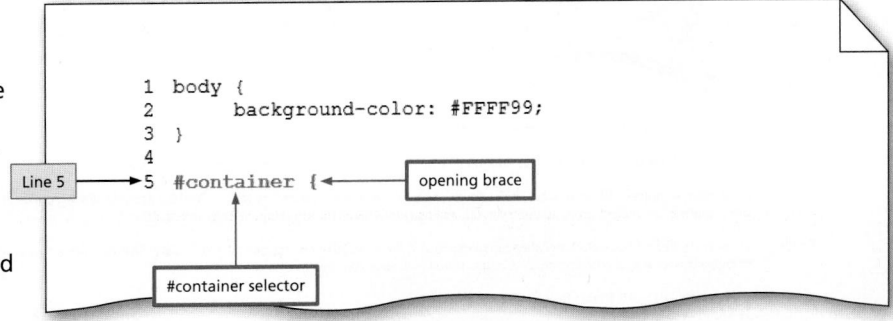

```
1  body {
2       background-color: #FFFF99;
3  }
4
5  #container {
```

Line 5 → 5 #container {   ← opening brace

#container selector

Figure 4–15

Q&A Why is Line 4 blank?
Reading and reviewing several lines of code can be hard on the eyes. For improved readability, insert blank lines between each style rule.

2

- Press the ENTER key to add Line 6, press the TAB key to indent the line, and then type **width: 80%;** to add a declaration that sets the width of the element.

- Press the ENTER key to add Line 7 and then type **margin-left: auto;** to add a declaration that sets the left margin.

- Press the ENTER key to add Line 8 and then type **margin-right: auto;** to add a declaration that sets the right margin.

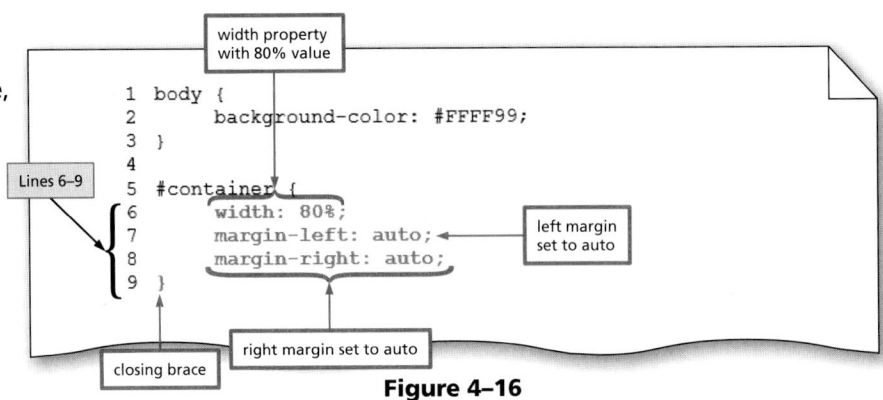

Figure 4–16

- Press the ENTER key to add Line 9, press the SHIFT+TAB keys to decrease the indent, and then type } to close the declarations for the #container selector (Figure 4–16).

Q&A

Why do I need to set the width to 80%?
Currently, the elements on the webpage will span the entire width of the browser window. Setting the width to 80% restricts the width of all the elements in the container to 80 percent of the width of the browser window.

Why am I using the value "auto" for the left and right margins?
Setting the left and right margins of a div element that contains all of the elements of a webpage, such as the container div, centers all of the elements on the page.

Do I have to enter each property and value on a separate line?
No. However, listing each property and value on separate lines enhances the readability of the style sheet. A style rule with many declarations is difficult to read unless the declarations are listed on separate lines. Readability helps to find and correct syntax errors.

3

- Save your changes.

- View the home page in a browser to see the applied styles (Figure 4–17).

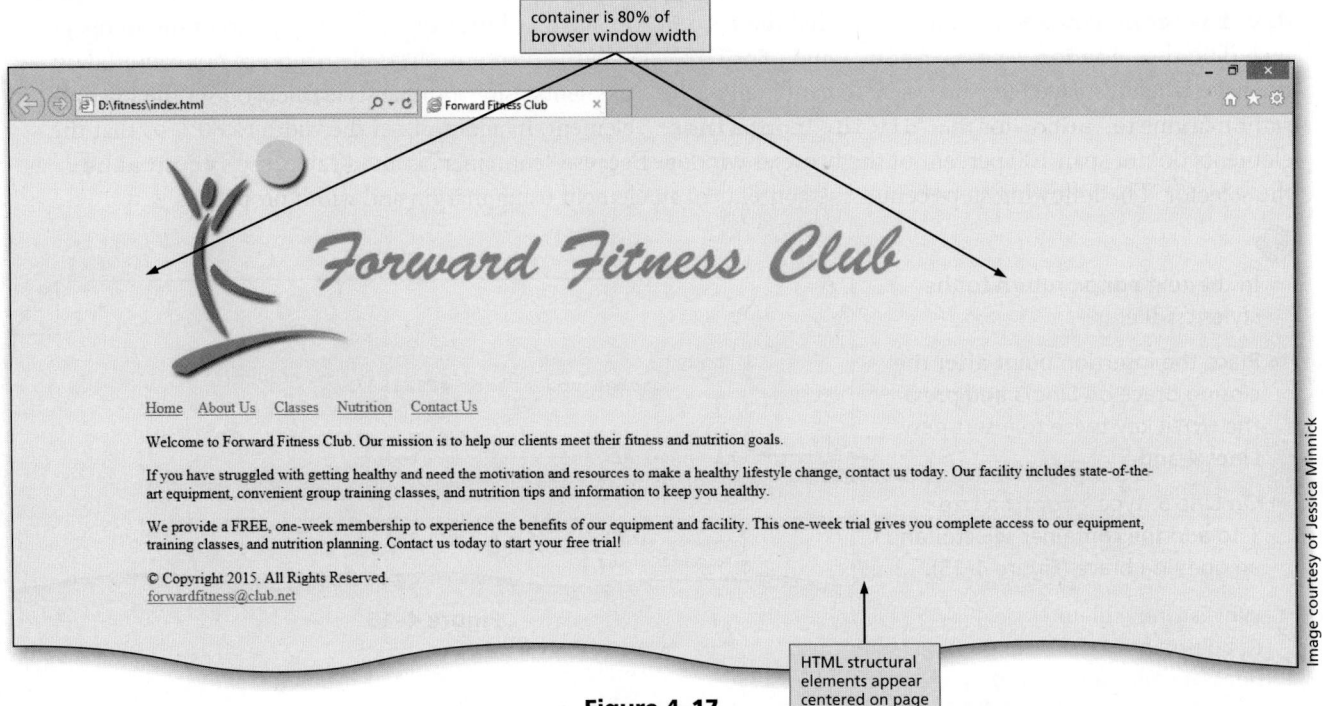

Figure 4–17

Creating Style Rules for Structural Elements

The next formatting task is to create style rules for the HTML5 structural elements used in the Forward Fitness Center website. Because the header section appears at the top of the webpage, it needs formatting that makes the header contents stand out and attract visitors to the page. To achieve this effect, you can use CSS text properties and box model properties to adjust the margins, add a border and background color, and center the contents of the header section.

The nav section should also be prominent and easy to find on the webpage, so you should format it differently from the other structural elements. Because the nav section contains only text, use CSS text properties to determine the text's appearance. Use CSS box model properties to specify the padding, margins, and borders of the `nav` element.

Unlike the other structural sections, the main section should be formatted using the display property. Internet Explorer versions 9 through 11 treat the `main` element as an inline element rather than a block element. To apply text and box model properties to the main section and have them appear as you intend in Internet Explorer, use the **display property**, which determines how the browser displays an element. Including the display property with a value of "block" in the declaration list of the main selector means that all browsers will display the main section as a block element.

Finally, create a style rule that formats the footer section by defining the font size, text alignment, and top margin of the `footer` element.

BTW

CSS Style Rule Order
Although the styles in a style sheet are not required to follow a specific order, most designers list the styles in the same general order that they will be used on a webpage. In other words, styles that apply to the body, outer container, and sections of the wireframe are typically listed first. Styles that apply to more specific areas of content such as headings, lists, and links are generally listed next.

To Create a Style Rule for the Header Element

1 CREATE CSS FILE | 2 LINK PAGES TO CSS FILE | **3 CREATE STYLE RULES**
4 ADD COMMENTS | 5 VALIDATE CSS FILE

Next, you will create a style rule for the header, which is located at the top of the HTML page and currently contains the Forward Fitness Center logo. The rule will use "header" as the selector and list a few declarations to format the `header` element. To separate the header from the rest of the webpage, add declarations to apply top and bottom margins and a background color. To create a more distinctive design for the header element, apply a rounded border and a shadow. Finally, to improve the appearance of the logo within the header, use the text-align property to center the `header` element's contents. The following steps create a style rule for the `header` element.

1

- Place the insertion point after the closing brace on Line 9 and press the ENTER key twice to insert new Lines 10 and 11.

- On Line 11, type **header {** to add the header selector and an opening brace (Figure 4–18).

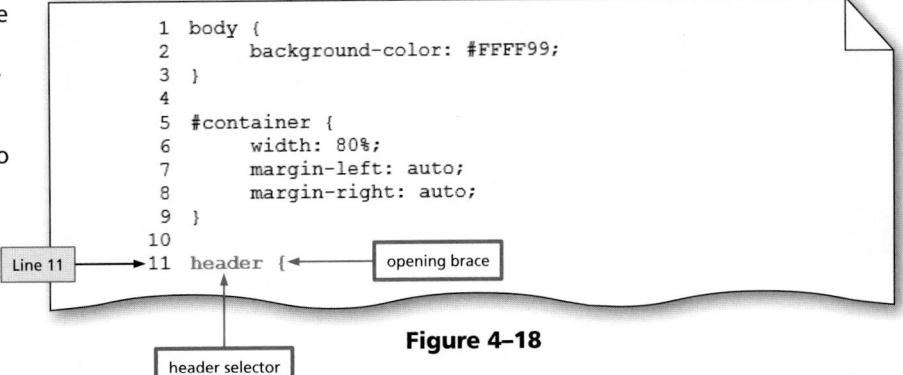

```
1  body {
2      background-color: #FFFF99;
3  }
4
5  #container {
6      width: 80%;
7      margin-left: auto;
8      margin-right: auto;
9  }
10
11 header {
```

Line 11

opening brace

header selector

Figure 4–18

2

- Press the ENTER key to add Line 12, press the TAB key to indent the line, and then type **margin-top: 10px;** to add a declaration that sets the top margin.

- Press the ENTER key to add Line 13 and then type **margin-bottom: 20px;** to add a declaration that sets the bottom margin.

- Press the ENTER key to add Line 14 and then type **background-color: #FFFFFF;** to add a declaration that sets the background color to white.

- Press the ENTER key to add Line 15 and then type **border-radius: 10px;** to add a declaration that defines a rounded border around the element.

- Press the ENTER key to add Line 16 and then type **box-shadow: 12px 12px 12px #404040;** to add a declaration that defines a shadow.

- Press the ENTER key to add Line 17 and then type **text-align: center;** to add a declaration for text alignment.

- Press the ENTER key to add Line 18, press the SHIFT+TAB keys to decrease the indent, and then type **}** to close the declarations for the header selector (Figure 4–19).

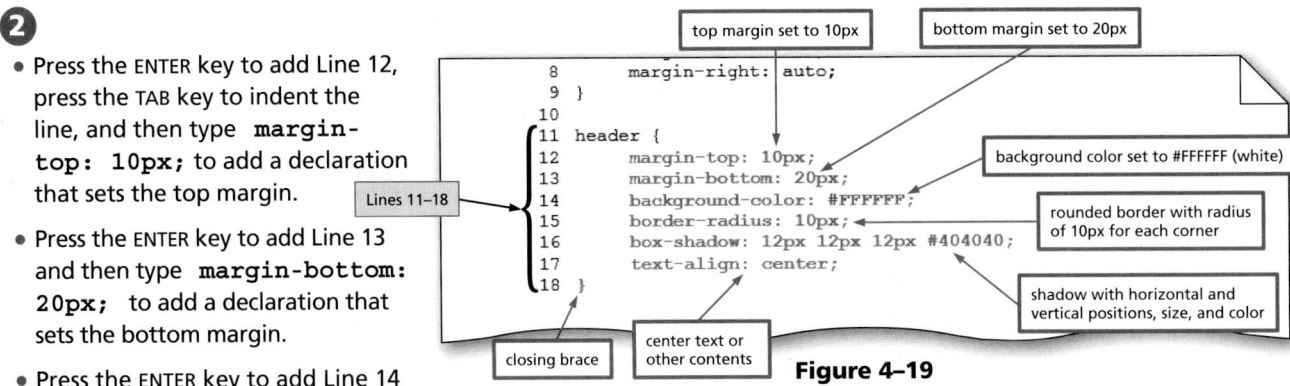

```
 8          margin-right: auto;
 9  }
10
11  header {
12          margin-top: 10px;
13          margin-bottom: 20px;
14          background-color: #FFFFFF;
15          border-radius: 10px;
16          box-shadow: 12px 12px 12px #404040;
17          text-align: center;
18  }
```

Lines 11–18

top margin set to 10px

bottom margin set to 20px

background color set to #FFFFFF (white)

rounded border with radius of 10px for each corner

shadow with horizontal and vertical positions, size, and color

center text or other contents

closing brace

Figure 4–19

Q&A What do the four values for the box-shadow property mean?

The first value (12px) sets the horizontal position of the shadow in relation to the element. The second value (12px) sets the vertical position of the shadow. The third value (12px) sets the distance of the blur in the shadow, and the fourth value (#404040) sets the color to a dark gray.

The header element does not contain any text. Why do I need to add a text-align property with a value of center for the header?

The text-align property is applied to the header's contents, including image tags such as the one used to display the Forward Fitness Center logo.

3

- Save your changes.
- View the home page in a browser to see the applied styles (Figure 4–20).

Q&A When I display the home page, the shadow looks different from the one in the figure. Why is that?

Browsers vary in how they interpret the box-shadow property and display shadows. If your CSS code matches the code shown in Figure 4–19, you are entering the style rule correctly.

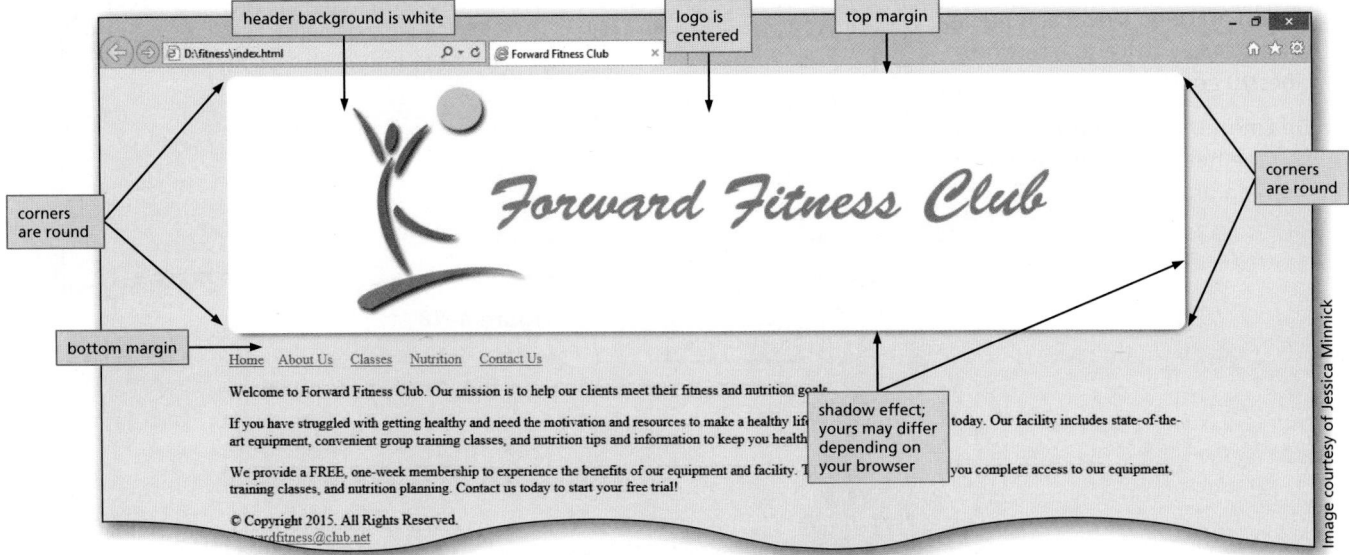

header background is white

logo is centered

top margin

corners are round

corners are round

bottom margin

shadow effect; yours may differ depending on your browser

Image courtesy of Jessica Minnick

Figure 4–20

To Create a Style Rule for the Nav Element

Next, you will create a style rule for the nav element. The **nav** area is located below the header on the webpage and currently contains links to all pages in the website. As with the header style rule, the one for the **nav** element will include "nav" as the selector and many declarations to format the element's contents. First, you add declarations to format the text, including font-family, font-size, font-weight, and text-align properties and values. You also add declarations to specify the padding, margins, and rounded borders for the nav element. *Why? Applying these properties and values sets the nav element apart from other elements on the webpage.* The following steps create a style rule for the nav element.

1

- Place the insertion point after the closing brace on Line 18 and press the ENTER key twice to insert new Lines 19 and 20.

- On Line 20, type **nav {** to add the nav selector and an opening brace.

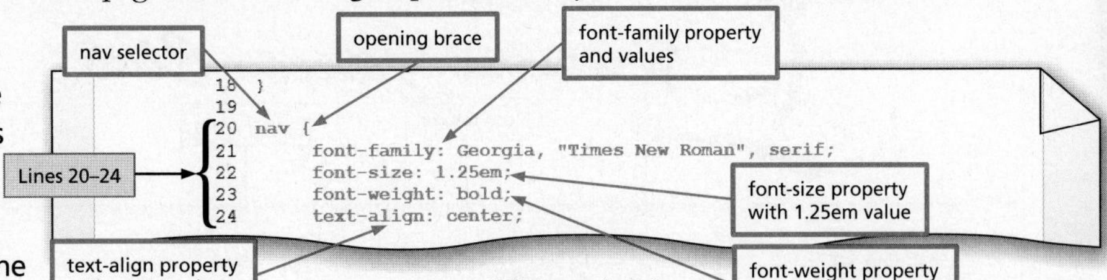

Figure 4–21

- Press the ENTER key to add Line 21, press the TAB key to indent the line, and then type **font-family: Georgia, "Times New Roman", serif;** to add a declaration that specifies a font family with a range of alternative values.

- Press the ENTER key to add Line 22 and then type **font-size: 1.25em;** to add a declaration that sets the font size.

- Press the ENTER key to add Line 23 and then type **font-weight: bold;** to add a declaration that sets the font weight.

- Press the ENTER key to add Line 24 and then type **text-align: center;** to add a declaration for text alignment (Figure 4–21).

Q&A Why do I need to include three values for the font-family property?
If the browser cannot display the first font, it will use the next specified font. If the browser cannot display the second font, it will use a serif font installed on the user's computer.

What does the 1.25em value mean for the font-size property?
Setting the font-size property to 1.25em means the font size of the nav section is 1.25 times larger than the default font size of the browser. If the default size is 16 points, for example, the font size in the nav section is 20 points.

2

- Press the ENTER key to add Line 25 and then type **padding: 15px;** to add a declaration for padding.

- Press the ENTER key to add Line 26 and then type **margin-top: 10px;** to add a declaration that sets the top margin.

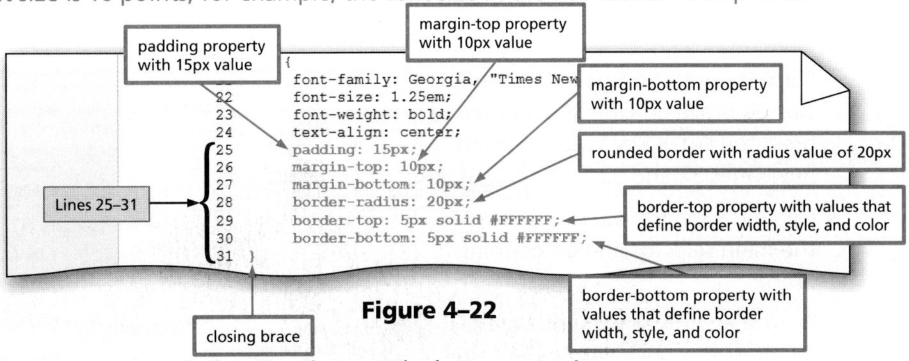

- Press the ENTER key to add Line 27 and then type **margin-bottom: 10px;** to add a declaration that sets the bottom margin.

Figure 4–22

- Press the ENTER key to add Line 28 and then type **border-radius: 20px;** to add a declaration that defines a rounded border around the element.

- Press the ENTER key to add Line 29 and then type **border-top: 5px solid #FFFFFF;** to add a declaration that formats the top border of the element.

- Press the ENTER key to add Line 30 and then type **border-bottom: 5px solid #FFFFFF;** to add a declaration that formats the bottom border of the element.

- Press the ENTER key to add Line 31, press the SHIFT+TAB keys to decrease the indent, and then type **}** to close the declarations for the nav selector (Figure 4–22).

Q&A Should I apply padding to the top, right, bottom, and left sides of the nav element?
When you use the padding property, the padding value is applied to all sides. If you need to apply padding only to the bottom, for example, use the padding-bottom property.

- Save your changes.

- View the home page in a browser to see the applied styles (Figure 4–23).

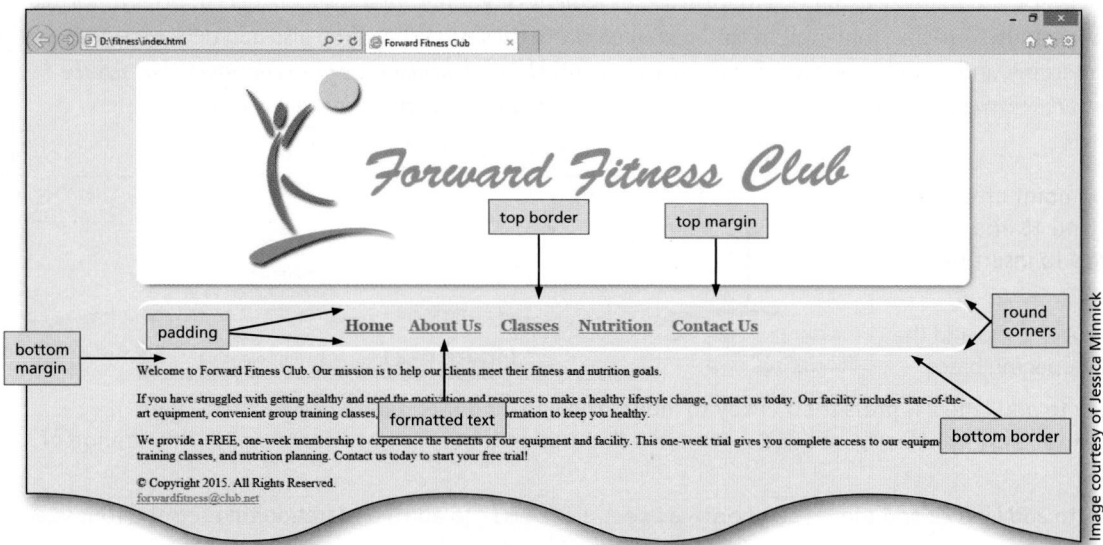

Figure 4–23

To Create a Style Rule for the Main Element

1 CREATE CSS FILE | 2 LINK PAGES TO CSS FILE | **3 CREATE STYLE RULES**
4 ADD COMMENTS | 5 VALIDATE CSS FILE

The main area is located below the **nav** element and contains the primary content of the webpage. The first declaration to add to the style rule for the **main** element sets the display property to "block." **Why?** *At the time of this writing, Internet Explorer versions 9 through 11 treat the semantic HTML5* **main** *element as an inline element, not a block element. Using the display property with a value of "block" ensures the main element will be displayed consistently as a block.* Next, add text and box model properties to specify the font family, font size, padding, margins, and rounded borders. The following steps create a style rule for the **main** element.

- Place the insertion point after the closing brace on Line 31 and then press the ENTER key twice to insert new Lines 32 and 33.

- On Line 33, type **main {** to add the main selector and an opening brace.

- Press the ENTER key to add Line 34, press the TAB key to indent the line, and then type **display: block;** to add a declaration for the display property.

```
28        border-radius: 20px;
29        border-top: 5px solid #FFFFFF;
30        border-bottom: 5px solid #FFFFFF;
31  }
32
33  main {
34        display: block;
35        font-family: Verdana, Arial, sans-serif;
36        font-size: 1em;
37        margin-top: 20px;
38        margin-bottom: 10px;
```

Figure 4–24

- Press the ENTER key to add Line 35 and then type **font-family: Verdana, Arial, sans-serif;** to add a declaration that specifies a font family with a range of alternate values.

- Press the ENTER key to add Line 36 and then type **font-size: 1em;** to add a declaration that sets the font size.

- Press the ENTER key to add Line 37 and then type **margin-top: 20px;** to add a declaration that sets the top margin.

- Press the ENTER key to add Line 38 and then type **margin-bottom: 10px;** to add a declaration that sets the bottom margin (Figure 4–24).

Q&A

Why do I need to include the display property with a value of "block"?

The main element is an HTML5 block element, but is not fully supported by Internet Explorer 9 through 11. You must add this declaration so that Internet Explorer will correctly display the main element as a block element in the webpage.

Why do I need to set the font-size property to 1em?

When you set the font size to 1em, the browser uses its default font size.

2

- Press the ENTER key to add Line 39 and then type **padding: 20px;** to add a declaration that sets the padding.

- Press the ENTER key to add Line 40 and then type **border-radius: 10px;** to add a declaration that defines a rounded border around the element.

- Press the ENTER key to add Line 41 and then type **background-color: #FFFFFF;** to add a declaration that sets the background color of the element.

- Press the ENTER key to add Line 42 and then type **box-shadow: 12px 12px 12px #404040;** to add a declaration that defines a shadow.

- Press the ENTER key to add Line 43, press the SHIFT+TAB keys to decrease the indent, and then type } to close the declarations for the main selector (Figure 4–25).

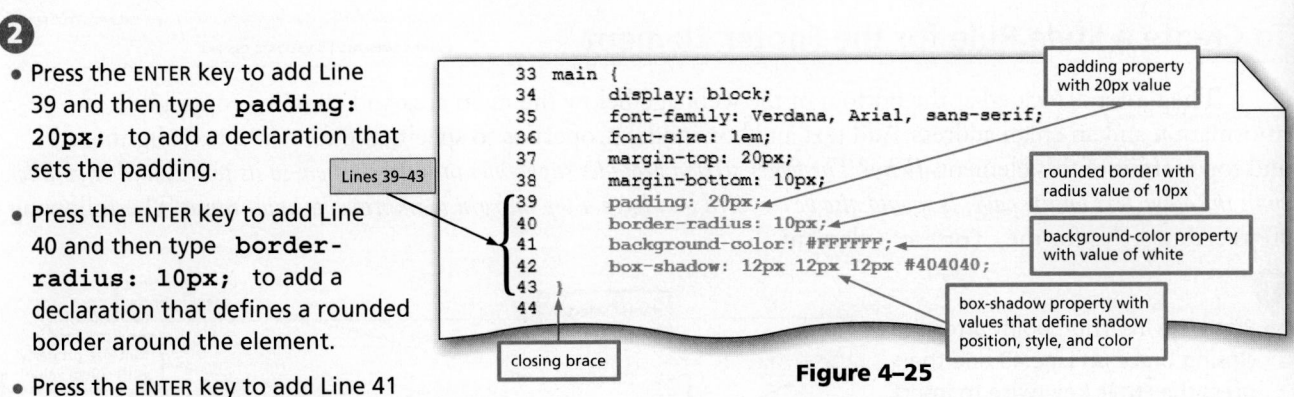

Lines 39–43

```
33  main {
34      display: block;
35      font-family: Verdana, Arial, sans-serif;
36      font-size: 1em;
37      margin-top: 20px;
38      margin-bottom: 10px;
39      padding: 20px;
40      border-radius: 10px;
41      background-color: #FFFFFF;
42      box-shadow: 12px 12px 12px #404040;
43  }
44
```

padding property with 20px value

rounded border with radius value of 10px

background-color property with value of white

box-shadow property with values that define shadow position, style, and color

closing brace

Figure 4–25

3

- Save your changes.

- View the home page in a browser to see the applied styles (Figure 4–26).

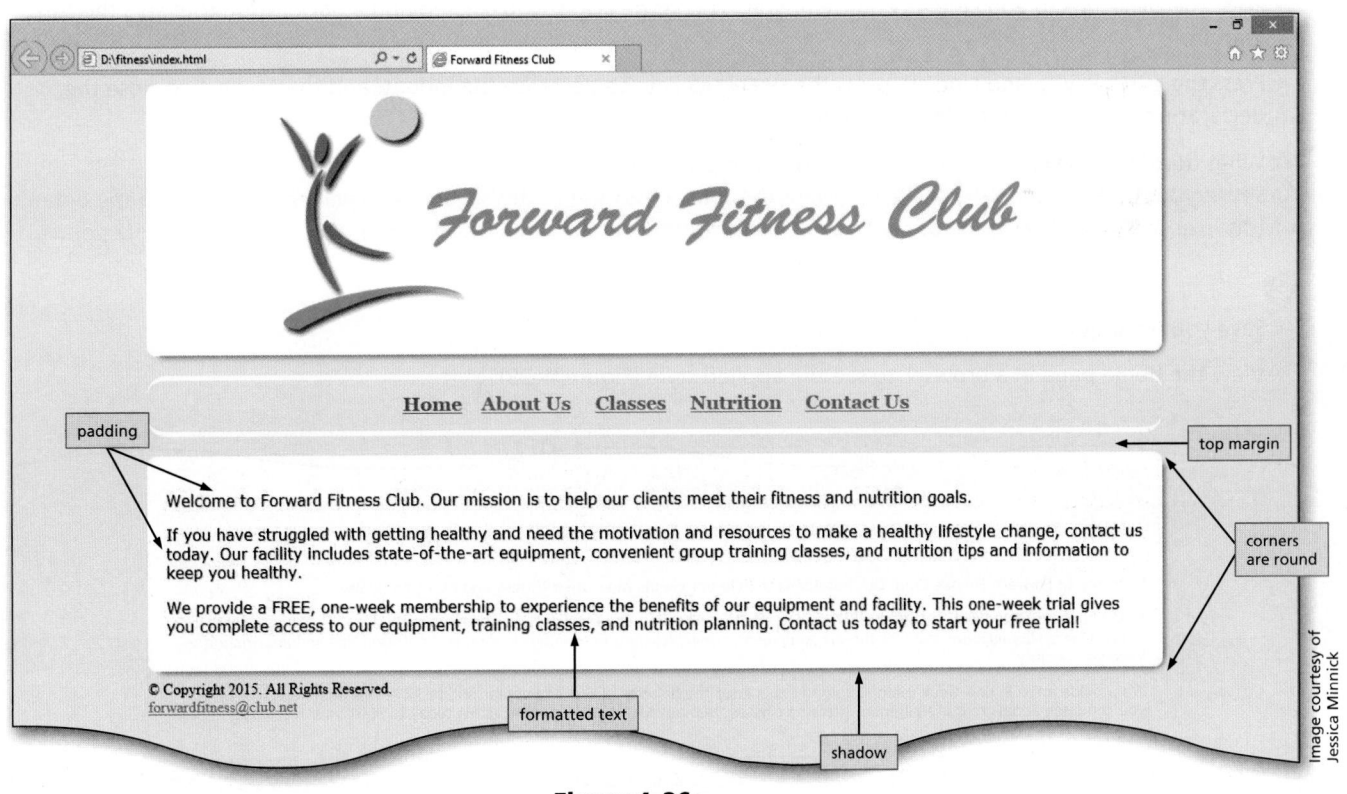

Figure 4–26

Image courtesy of Jessica Minnick

To Create a Style Rule for the Footer Element

The footer is located at the bottom of the webpage below the main area and contains copyright information and an email address. Add text and box model properties to specify the font size, text alignment, and top margin of this element. ***Why?*** *The footer section provides supplemental information, so its text should be smaller than the other text on the page. It should also be centered and have a top margin to improve its appearance.* The following steps create styles for the **footer** element.

- Place the insertion point after the closing brace on Line 43 and then press the ENTER key twice to insert new Lines 44 and 45.

- On Line 45, type **footer { to add the footer selector and an opening brace.

- Press the ENTER key to add Line 46, press the TAB key to indent the line, and then type **font-size: .70em;** to add a declaration that sets the font size.

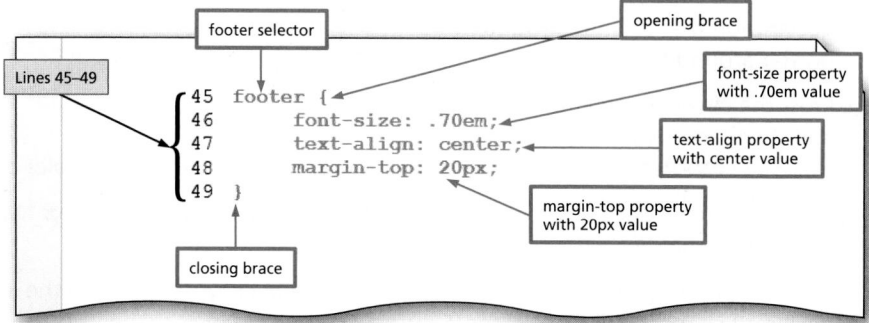

Figure 4–27

- Press the ENTER key to add Line 47 and then type **text-align: center;** to add a declaration for text alignment.

- Press the ENTER key to add Line 48 and then type **margin-top: 20px;** to add a declaration that sets the top margin.

- Press the ENTER key to add Line 49, press the SHIFT+TAB keys to decrease the indent, and then type } to close the declarations for the footer selector (Figure 4–27).

Q&A | What does the .70em value mean for the font-size property?
Setting the font-size property to .70em means the font size of the footer section is 70 percent smaller than the default font size of the browser. If the default size is 16 points, for example, the font size in the footer section is 11.2 points.

- Save your changes.

- View the home page in a browser to see the applied style (Figure 4–28).

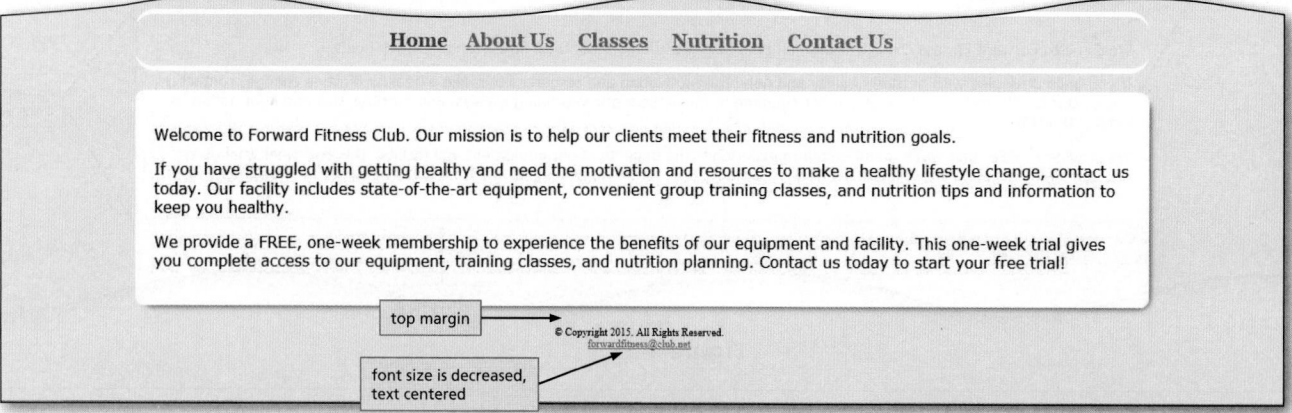

Figure 4–28

Break Point: If you want to take a break, this is a good place to do so. You can exit the text editor now. To resume at a later time, run your text editor, open the file called styles.css, and continue following the steps from this location forward.

Creating Style Rules for Classes

In Chapter 3, you added a class attribute to the `img` elements specifying the images displayed on the About Us page. For example, you added the following `img` element after the Weights heading on the About Us page:

```
<img class="equip" src="images/equipment1.jpg" alt="Weight
Equipment" height="195" width="260">
```

This element displays the equipment1.jpg image. The first attribute and value, `class="equip"`, assigns this element to the equip class. The `img` elements that display the equipment2.jpg and equipment3.jpg images also include the `class="equip"` attribute and value to assign them to the equip class. Including the `class="equip"` attribute and value in each `img` element means you can format all the elements assigned to the equip class with a single style rule. For example, the following style rule adds 20 pixels of padding to the right side of elements in the `equip` class:

```
.equip {
 padding-right: 20px;
}
```

To indicate you are using a class name as a selector, include a period (.) before the class name, similar to the way you include a number sign (#) with an id selector. The effect of this style rule is to add 20 pixels of padding to the right of the three images on the About Us page. However, the three images do not actually need the additional padding as they are currently positioned (Figure 4–29).

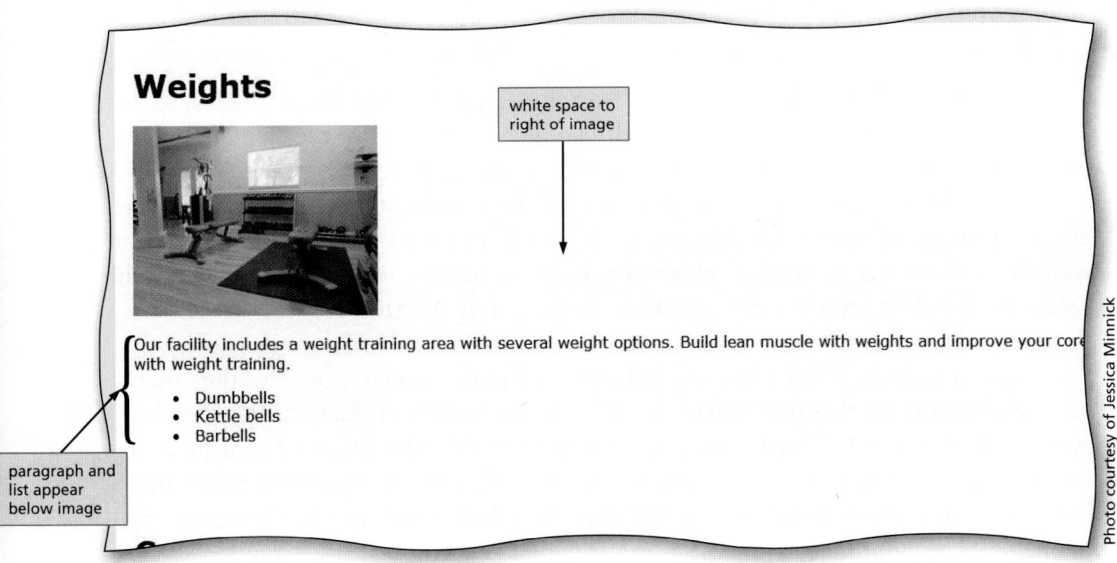

Figure 4–29

The About Us page would look more professional if the paragraph and list currently displayed below each image were displayed to the right of each image instead. To achieve this effect, you use the **float property**, which lets you position an element to the right or left of other elements. The valid values for the float property are `right` and `left,` indicating where to display (or float) the element. Figure 4–30 shows the image floating to the left of the text on the About Us page.

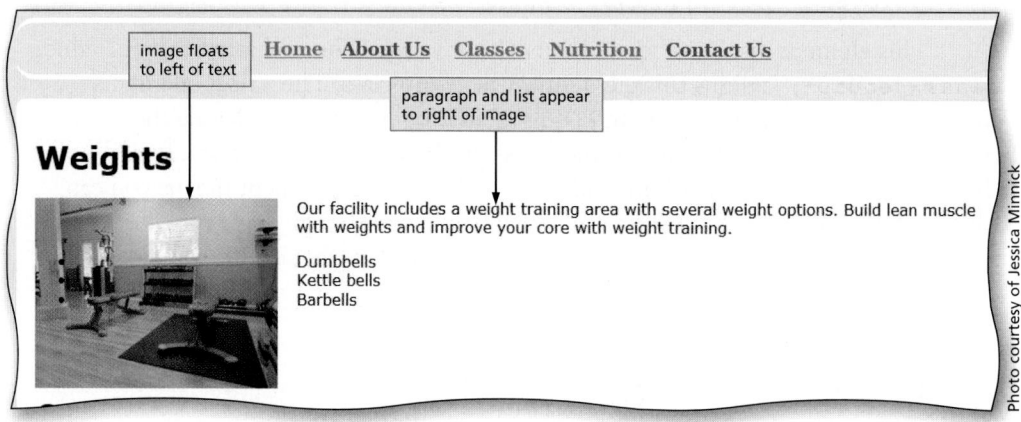

Figure 4–30

To have all three images on the About Us page float to the left of the text, add a `float: left;` declaration to the style rule for the equip class as follows:

```
.equip {
 float: left;
 padding-right: 20px;
}
```

Now the style rule floats all elements in the equip class (the three images) to the left of other elements and adds 20 pixels of padding to the right of the elements in the equip class. The padding creates white space between the images and the text.

If you float an image to the right or left of elements containing text content, the effect is to wrap the text around the image. If you do not want text, such as headings, to wrap around the image, use the **clear property** to remove the float effect. The valid values for the clear property are `right, left,` and `both`. To clear an element that is floating left, use the `clear: left;` declaration. Likewise, to clear an element that is floating right, use the `clear: right;` declaration. Use the `both` value if elements are floating on both the right and left sides of the text. Add the clear property to the style rule that affects the element you do not want to wrap around the floating element. For example, if you want all `h1` elements to appear on a new line below an image, create a style rule using h1 as the selector and use the clear property in one of its declarations.

To Create a Style Rule for the equip Class

1 CREATE CSS FILE | 2 LINK PAGES TO CSS FILE | 3 CREATE STYLE RULES
4 ADD COMMENTS | 5 VALIDATE CSS FILE

The images on the About Us page should appear on the left and the text should appear on the right side of each image. To accomplish this task, you use the float property to float the images left and then apply padding to the right side of the images to provide white space between each image and the text on the page. Add declarations including the float and padding properties to a style rule that uses the .equip class selector. *Why? Using the .equip class selector will apply the style rule to all elements in the equip class.* The following steps create a style rule for the equip class.

- Place the insertion point after the closing brace on Line 48 and then press the ENTER key twice to insert new Lines 50 and 51.

- On Line 51, type `.equip {` to add the .equip selector and an opening brace.

- Press the ENTER key to add Line 52, press the TAB key to indent the line, and then type `float: left;` to add a declaration that floats elements in the specified class.

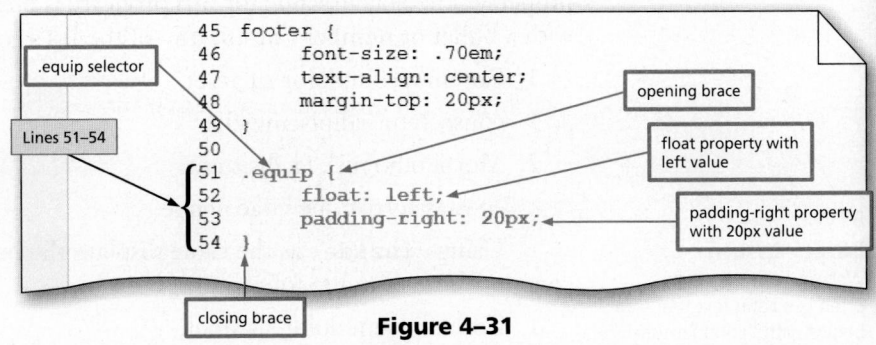

Figure 4–31

- Press the ENTER key to add Line 53 and then type `padding-right: 20px;` to add a declaration for padding.

- Press the ENTER key to add Line 54, press the SHIFT+TAB keys to decrease the indent, and then type `}` to close the declarations for the .equip selector (Figure 4–31).

Q&A

Why does the .equip selector start with a period?
To style a class, you insert a period before the class name to specify the selector in the CSS file.

How will the `float: left;` declaration change the About Us webpage?
This declaration places images on the left side of the webpage, allowing the text after each image to wrap around the image on the right.

How do you stop content from floating so that it starts on its own line?
To stop floating an element, use the clear property. For example, apply the following declaration to the content that you want to start on its own line, or clear the float: `clear: left;` (clear left float), `clear: right;` (clear right float), or `clear: both;` (clear left and right float).

Using CSS List Properties

To control the appearance of numbered and bulleted lists, you use the CSS **list-style properties**. By default, lists marked with the <ul> and </ul> tags display a solid bullet before each list item. Lists marked with the <ol> and </ol> tags display Arabic numerals (1, 2, 3, and so on) before the list items. You use the list-style-type property to specify a different type of bullet or a different numbering style to use in a list. For example, the following style rule defines a filled square bullet for an unordered list:

```
ul {
  list-style-type: square;
}
```

The following style rule defines lowercase Roman numerals for an ordered list:

```
ol {
  list-style-type: lower-roman;
}
```

If you want to display an image instead of a bullet, use the list-style-image property. To indicate the file name of the image file, begin the value with "url" followed by the file name or path in parentheses. For example, the following style rule defines the image in the arrow.png file as the bullet for unordered lists:

```
ul {
  list-style-image: url(arrow.png);
}
```

To specify the position of the bullet or number in a list, use the list-style-position property. The default value for this property is outside, which displays the list item with a bullet or number `outside` of the list's content block as in the following text:

1. Lorem ipsum dolor sit amet,
   consectetur adipiscing elit.
2. Morbi odio nisl, facilisis non
   egestas a, tristique vitae neque.

Using `inside` as the value displays the bullet or number inside the list's content block, as in the following text:

1. Lorem ipsum dolor sit amet,
   consectetur adipiscing elit.
2. Morbi odio nisl, facilisis non
   egestas a, tristique vitae neque.

For example, in the bulleted lists on the About Us page, the bullets appear outside the content block for each list by default. After floating the images on the About Us page, the images overlap the bullets in the lists, as shown in Figure 4–30 on page 166. To fix this problem, create a style rule for the lists and use inside as the value for the list-style-position property to display the bullets.

BTW

Lorem Ipsum
Web and print designers often use Latin text that begins with "Lorem ipsum" as filler text when they want to focus on design or formatting rather than content.

BTW

List Properties
Appendix B provides a full description of the list properties and their valid values.

To Create Styles for List Elements

1 CREATE CSS FILE | 2 LINK PAGES TO CSS FILE | 3 CREATE STYLE RULES
4 ADD COMMENTS | 5 VALIDATE CSS FILE

Next, you style the bulleted lists and the description list that appear on the About Us page. The HTML elements in this case are the unordered list (`ul` element) and the description list (`dt` and `dd` elements). First, apply a large bottom margin to the unordered list to separate subsequent text from the list. Next, set the position of the bullets so they appear inside the list's content block. *Why? The current position of the bullets is outside, the default, where they are hidden by the floating images. Setting the position to inside makes the bullets visible.* To format the definition list at the bottom of the About Us page, create a style rule that bolds the terms (the `dt` element) and another rule that adds padding below each definition (the `dd` element). The following steps create styles for the `ul, dt,` and `dd` elements.

- Place the insertion point after the closing brace on Line 54 and then press the ENTER key twice to insert new Lines 55 and 56.

- On Line 56, type `ul {` to add the ul selector and an opening brace.

- Press the ENTER key to add Line 57, press the TAB key to indent the line, and then type **margin-bottom: 50px;** to add a declaration that sets the bottom margin.

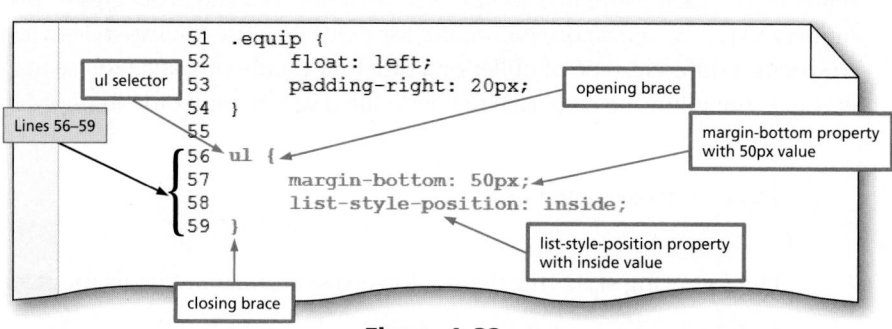

Figure 4–32

- Press the ENTER key to add Line 58 and then type **list-style-position: inside;** to add a declaration to define the position of list items.

- Press the ENTER key to add Line 59, press the SHIFT+TAB keys to decrease the indent, and then type } to close the declarations for the ul selector (Figure 4–32).

Q&A What is the purpose of the `list-style-position: inside;` declaration?
Including this declaration in the style for the unordered list displays the bullets for the list items. Otherwise, the bullets are not displayed because they are hidden by the images.

2

- Place the insertion point after the closing brace on Line 59 and then press the ENTER key twice to insert new Lines 60 and 61.

- On Line 61, type **dt {** to add the dt selector and an opening brace.

- Press the ENTER key to add Line 62, press the TAB key to indent the line, and then type **font-weight: bold;** to add a declaration that sets the font weight.

- Press the ENTER key to add Line 63, press the SHIFT+TAB keys to decrease the indent, and then type } to close the declaration for the dt selector (Figure 4–33).

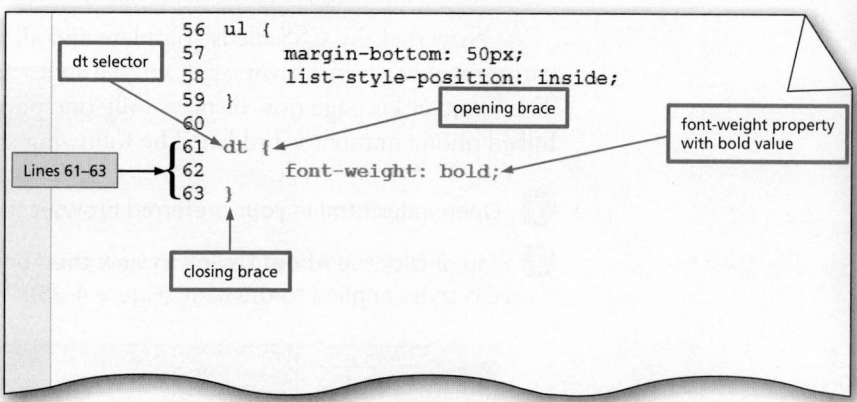

Figure 4–33

3

- Place the insertion point after the closing brace on Line 63 and then press the ENTER key twice to insert new Lines 64 and 65.

- On Line 65, type **dd {** to add the dd selector and an opening brace.

- Press the ENTER key to add Line 66, press the TAB key to indent the line, and then type **padding-bottom: 20px;** to add a declaration that sets the bottom padding.

- Press the ENTER key to add Line 67, press the SHIFT+TAB keys to decrease the indent, and then type } to close the declaration for the dd selector (Figure 4–34).

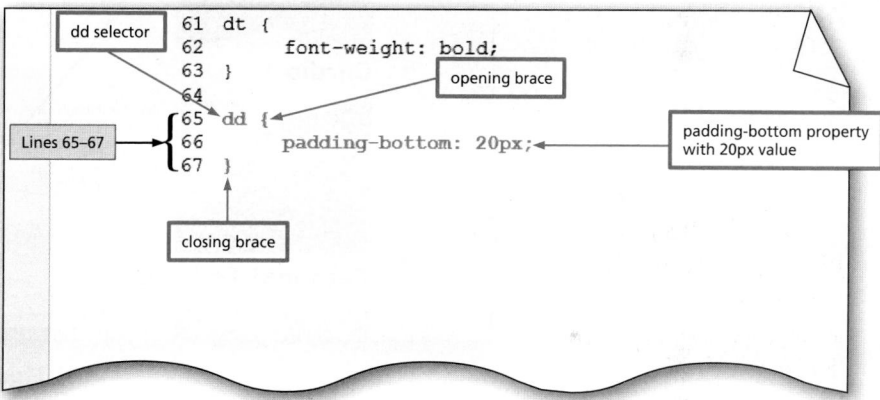

Figure 4–34

To View the Website in a Browser

Now that the CSS file is complete and all pages are linked to the file, view the current webpages in a browser to see the styles applied across all of the HTML pages. The Contact Us page now displays only one phone number, not two, because the linked phone number is hidden. The following steps view a website in a browser.

1 Open index.html in your preferred browser to display the page.

2 Tap or click the About Us link to view the About Us page and scroll down to see the CSS styles applied to the page (Figure 4–35).

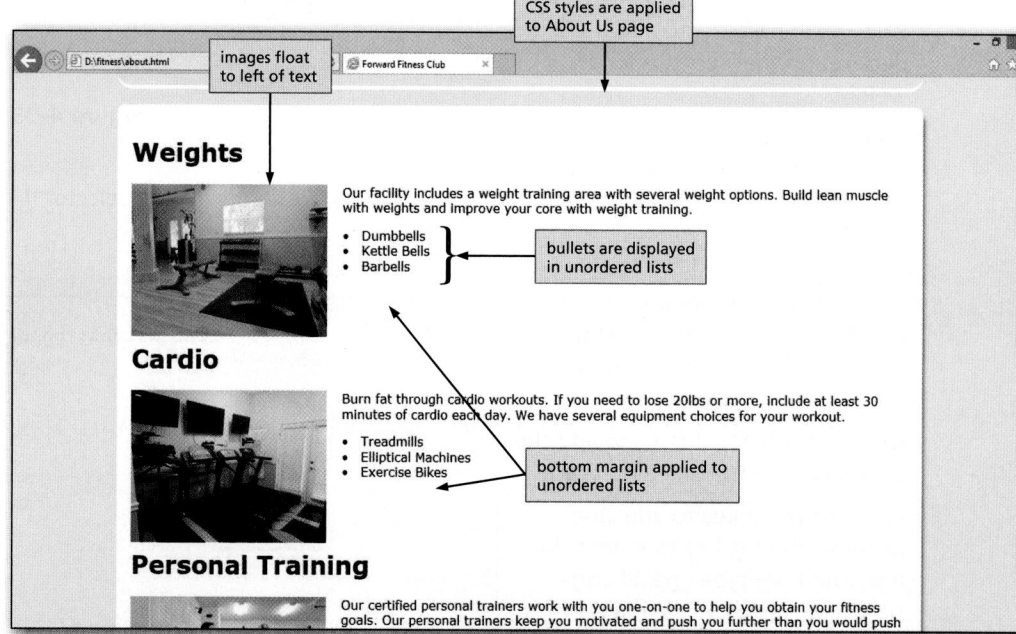

Figure 4–35

3 Tap or click the Contact Us link to view the Contact Us page and see the CSS styles applied to the page (Figure 4–36).

Figure 4–36

4 Close your browser.

Adding Comments to CSS Files

As you create a CSS file, include comments about each rule to identify its purpose. Comments can provide additional information about the area where the styles are applied or other helpful explanations, such as what the styles do. Add a comment above a selector using the following syntax:

```
/* Place your comment here */
```

CSS comment syntax specifies a forward slash at the beginning and at the end of the comment. After the first forward slash, insert an asterisk (*) followed by the comment text. For example, the comment text might identify the group of styles or the author of the style sheet. Close the comment by adding another asterisk, followed by a forward slash.

BTW

CSS Comments in Notepad++
When you correctly add comments to a CSS file using Notepad++, the comments appear in green.

To Add Comments to a CSS File

1 CREATE CSS FILE | 2 LINK PAGES TO CSS FILE | 3 CREATE STYLE RULES
4 ADD COMMENTS | **5 VALIDATE CSS FILE**

When you create a CSS file, including comments provides additional information about each style rule. You can also use a comment to identify that you are the author of the webpage. *Why? When you or another web designer are editing a CSS file, comments provide insight on the purpose of the style or its declarations.* The following steps add comments to a CSS file.

1

- Place the insertion point before the body selector on Line 1, and then press the ENTER key twice to place the body selector on Line 3.

- On Line 1 type /* Style sheet created by: Student's First Name Student's Last Name, Today's Date */ to add a comment at the beginning of the document that identifies the author (Figure 4–37).

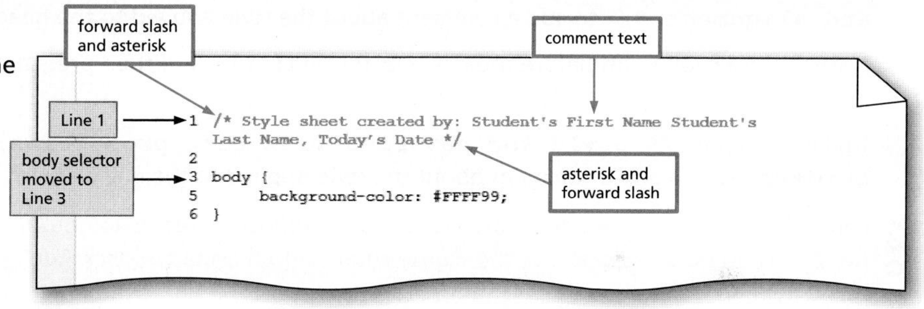

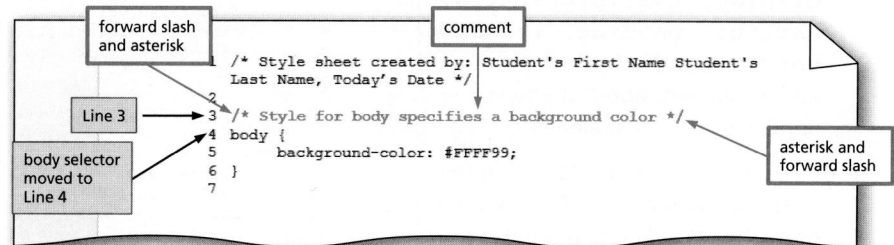

```
1 /* Style sheet created by: Student's First Name Student's
  Last Name, Today's Date */
2
3 body {
5       background-color: #FFFF99;
6 }
```

forward slash and asterisk · comment text · Line 1 · body selector moved to Line 3 · asterisk and forward slash

Figure 4–37

Q&A Are comments required in a CSS file?

No. Comments are optional, but using comments in a CSS file is a best practice to document the author and date of the last update. Comments also help to organize categories of styles in the style sheet.

2

- Place the insertion point before the body selector on Line 3, and then press the ENTER key to place the body selector on Line 4.

- On Line 3 type /* Style for body specifies a background color */ to add a comment providing information about the style applied to the body element (Figure 4–38).

```
1 /* Style sheet created by: Student's First Name Student's
  Last Name, Today's Date */
2
3 /* Style for body specifies a background color */
4 body {
5       background-color: #FFFF99;
6 }
7
```

forward slash and asterisk · comment · Line 3 · body selector moved to Line 4 · asterisk and forward slash

Figure 4–38

- Place the insertion point before the #container selector on Line 8, and then press the ENTER key to place the #container selector on Line 9.

- On Line 8 type `/* Style for container centers the page and sets the element width */` to add a comment about the style applied to the <div id="container"> element.

- Place the insertion point before the header selector on Line 15, and then press the ENTER key to place the header selector on Line 16.

- On Line 15 type `/* Style for header specifies top and bottom margins, background color, rounded border, shadow, and alignment */` to add a comment about the style applied to the header element.

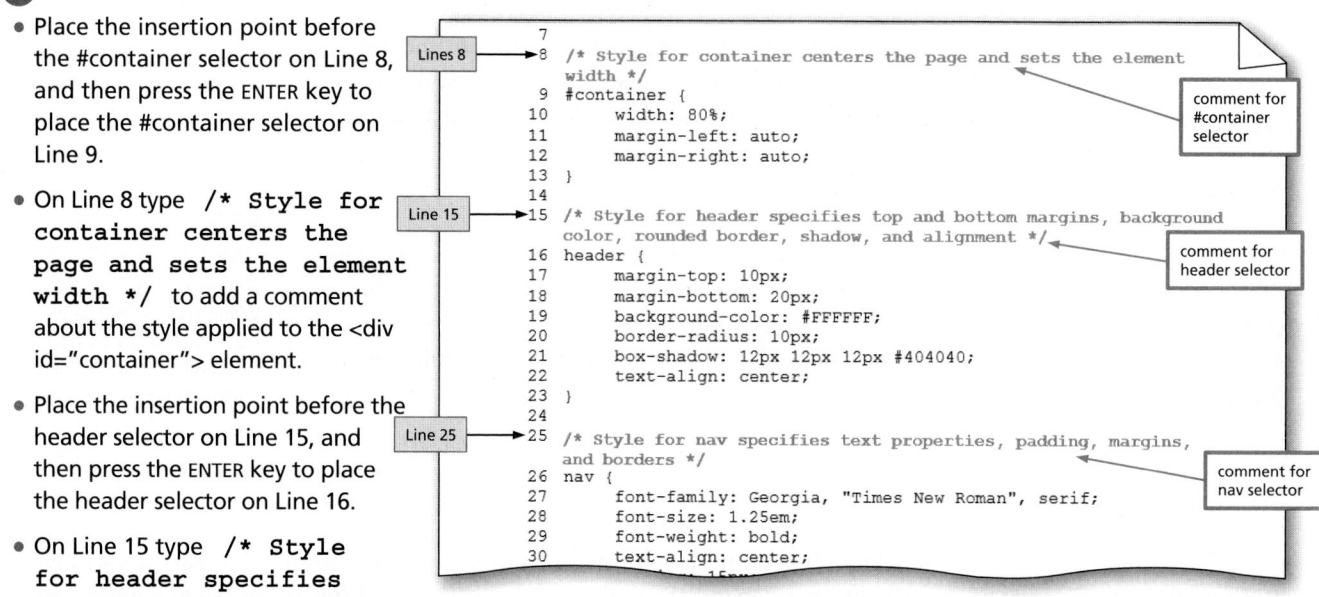

Figure 4–39

- Place the insertion point before the nav selector on Line 25, and then press the ENTER key to place the nav selector on Line 26.

- On Line 25 type `/* Style for nav specifies text properties, padding, margins, and borders */` to add a comment about the style applied to the nav element (Figure 4–39).

Q&A I am using Notepad++ and the word *centers* is underlined in red. Is something wrong?
No. Press and hold or right-click the word *centers*, and then tap or click Add "centers" to Dictionary to add the correctly spelled word to the program's dictionary.

4

- Place the insertion point before the main selector on Line 39, and then press the ENTER key to place the main selector on Line 40.

- On Line 39 type `/* Style for main specifies a block display, text properties, margins, padding, rounded border, and shadow */` to add a comment about the style applied to the main element.

- Place the insertion point before the footer selector on Line 52, and then press the ENTER key to place the footer selector on Line 53.

- On Line 52 type `/* Style for footer specifies font size, text alignment, and top margin */` to add a comment about the style applied to the footer element (Figure 4–40).

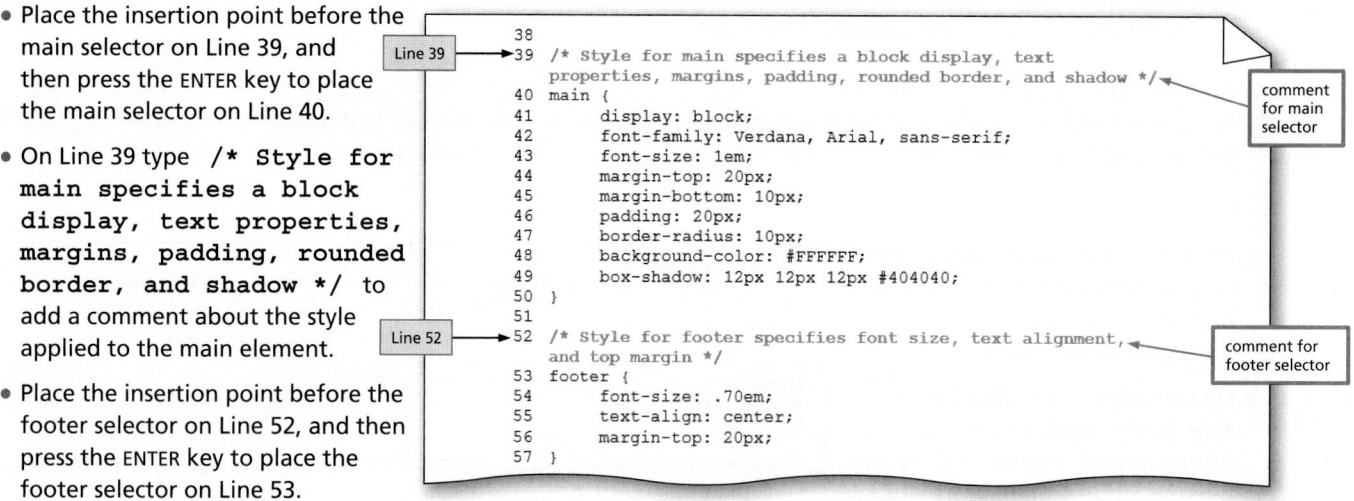

Figure 4–40

- Save your changes.

Validating CSS Files

Once you have created a CSS file, you validate it to verify the validity of the CSS code, similar to how you validate an HTML document to make sure it uses proper HTML syntax. When you validate a CSS document, you confirm that all of the code is correct and follows the established rules for CSS. You can use many online validation services to assure that your CSS code follows standards. Validation should always be a part of your web development testing. The validation service used in this book is the W3C Markup Validation Service (jigsaw.w3.org/css-validator/). You start by uploading your CSS file to the validator, which means you copy the file from your computer to the website. The validator reviews each line of code and locates any errors.

If validation detects an error in your CSS code, a warning such as "Sorry! We found the following error(s)!" appears in the header bar. The results also indicate the number of errors and detailed comments regarding each error.

To Validate the CSS File

1 CREATE CSS FILE | 2 LINK PAGES TO CSS FILE | 3 CREATE STYLE RULES
4 ADD COMMENTS | 5 VALIDATE CSS FILE

After making changes to a CSS file, run the file through W3C's validator to check the document for errors. *Why? If the document has any errors, validating gives you a chance to identify and correct them.* The following steps validate a CSS file.

- Open your browser and type **http://jigsaw.w3.org/css-validator/** in the address bar to display the W3C CSS Validation Service page.
- Tap or click the By file upload tab to display the Validate by file upload information.
- Tap or click the Browse button to display the Choose File to Upload dialog box.
- Navigate to your css folder to find the styles.css file (Figure 4–41).

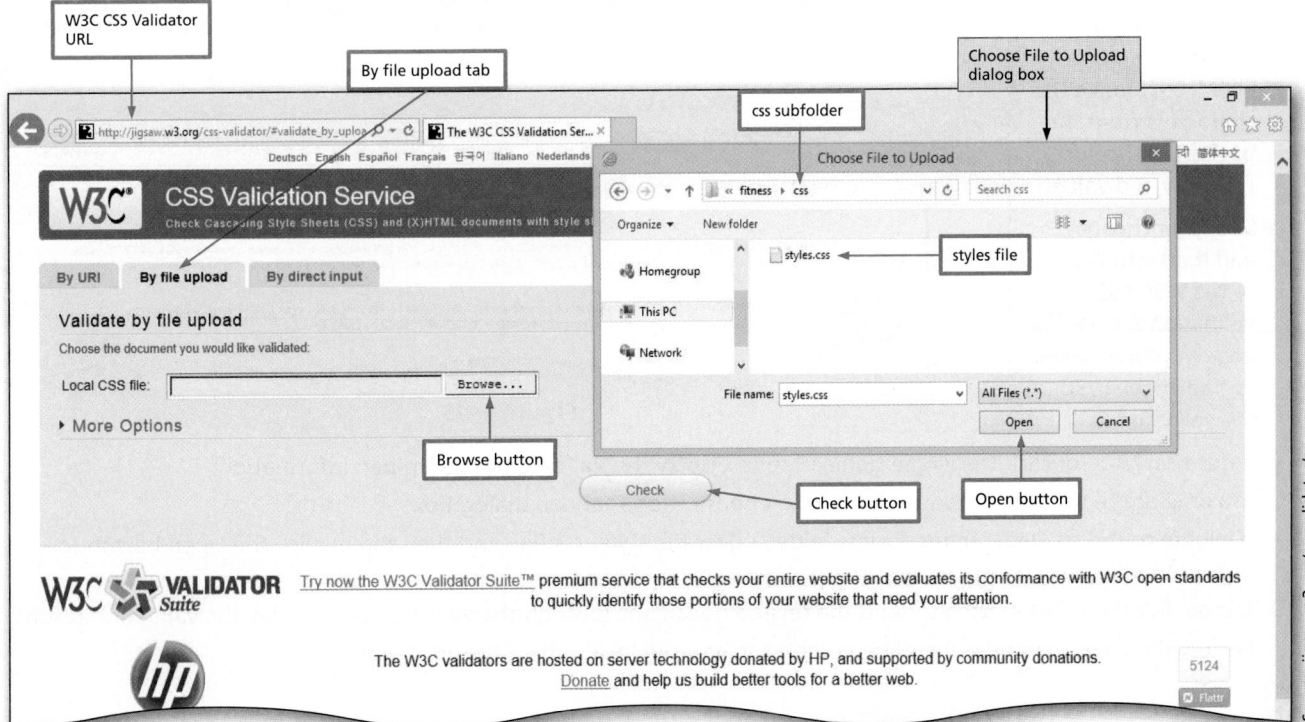

Figure 4–41

Source: jigsaw.w3.org/css-validator/

- Tap or click the styles.css document to select it.

- Tap or click the Open button to upload the selected file to the W3C CSS validator.

- Tap or click the Check button to send the document through the validator and display the validation results page (Figure 4–42).

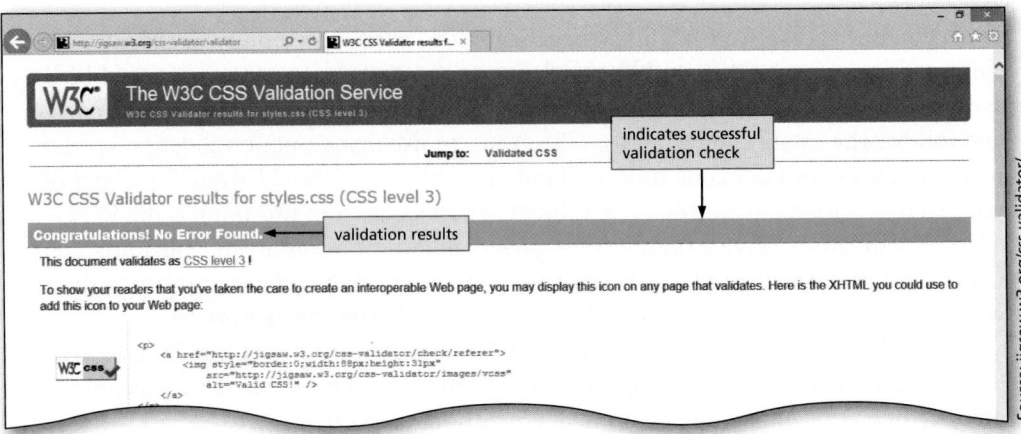

Figure 4–42

Q&A My results show errors. How do I correct them?

Scroll down the page to display the Notes and Potential Issues section. Review the errors listed below the validation output. Any line number that contains an error is shown in this section.

To Validate a CSS File with Errors

1 CREATE CSS FILE | 2 LINK PAGES TO CSS FILE | 3 CREATE STYLE RULES
4 ADD COMMENTS | **5 VALIDATE CSS FILE**

If you created the CSS file correctly, you should not receive any errors, but you can look at what the validator provides when you upload a style sheet file with errors. *Why? When errors are detected in a CSS file, the validator provides information about the location of each error so you can identify and correct them.* The following steps insert an error in the styles CSS file and then validate the document with the W3C CSS validator.

- Return to the styles .css document in your text editor and delete the colon and semicolon on Line 5 to remove the characters from the background-color property and value.

- Save your changes, and then return to the W3C CSS Validation Service page in your browser to display the W3C CSS validator.

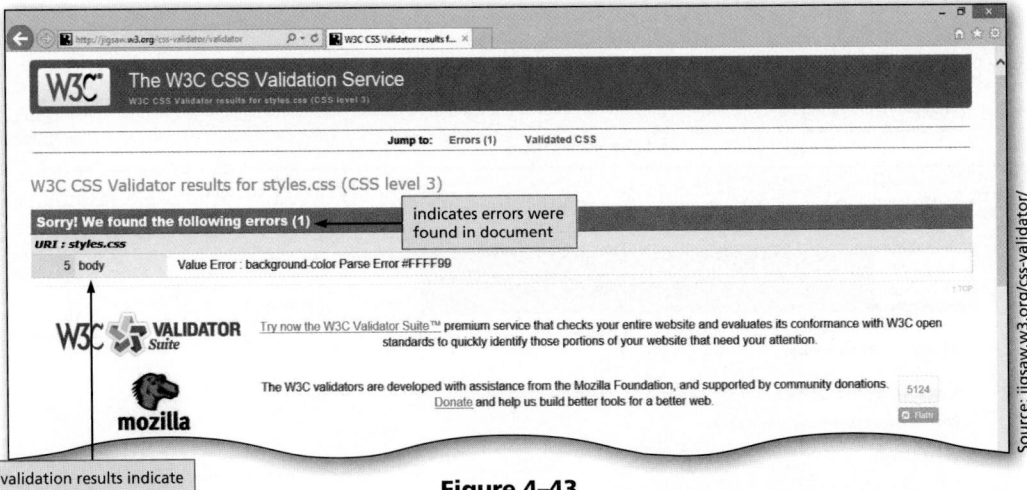

Figure 4–43

- If necessary, tap or click the By file upload tab to display the Validate by File Upload information.

- Tap or click the Browse button to display the Choose File to Upload dialog box.

- Navigate to the css folder in the fitness folder, select the styles.css file, and then tap or click the Open button to upload the file.

- Tap or click the Check button to send the revised document through the validator and display the validation results.

- Review the errors and note their line numbers so you can locate them (Figure 4–43).

- Return to your text editor and type **:** after the background-color property and type **;** after the #FFFF99 value on Line 5 to correct the errors.

- Save your changes and validate the document again to confirm it does not contain any errors.

Chapter Summary

In this chapter, you learned how to create a CSS file with rules to style HTML elements on a webpage. You linked the CSS file to all of the webpages for the fitness website. The items listed below include all the new concepts and skills you have learned in this chapter, with the tasks grouped by activity.

Using Cascading Style Sheets
Inline, Embedded, and External Style Sheets (HTML 143)
CSS Basics (HTML 145)
CSS Text Properties (HTML 146)
CSS Colors (HTML 147)

Understanding Inline Elements and Block Elements
CSS Box Model (HTML 150)

Creating an External Style Sheet
Create a CSS File (HTML 153)
Create a Style Rule for the Body Element (HTML 153)

Linking an HTML Document to a CSS File
Link HTML Pages to the CSS File (HTML 155)

Aligning Webpage Content
Center Content (HTML 157)

Creating Style Rules for Structural Elements
Create Style Rules for the Header, Nav, Main, and Footer Elements (HTML 159–HTML 164)

Creating Style Rules for Classes
Create a Style Rule for the equip Class (HTML 166)

Using CSS List Properties
Create a Style Rule for List Elements (HTML 168)

Adding Comments to CSS Files
Add Comments to a CSS File (HTML 171)

Validating CSS Files
Validate the CSS File (HTML 173)

What decisions will you need to make when creating your next CSS file?
Use these guidelines as you complete the assignments in this chapter and create your own websites outside of this class.

1. Determine properties for your HTML elements (such as header, nav, main, and footer).

   a. Set webpage width and centering characteristics.

   b. Decide on any necessary text properties to use for font face, size, and style.

   c. Set text and background colors.

   d. Decide if you need borders, and then set the style, size, and color of the border.

   e. Float any content that needs to appear on the same line.

   f. Determine the amount of margins and padding to use.

2. Link the CSS file to your HTML pages and website template.

   a. Add comments to your CSS file, noting the declarations for each selector.

   b. Validate your CSS file to confirm that it does not contain any errors.

   c. View your website in a browser to see the applied styles throughout the development process.

   d. Determine any changes that need to be made and revalidate.

3. Depending on the structure of your website, determine if you should create additional CSS files to accommodate multiple wireframes or different media such as mobile or print. Styling for multiple devices will be covered in later chapters.

How should you submit solutions to questions in the assignments identified with a ✻ symbol? Every assignment in this book contains one or more questions identified with a ✻ symbol. These questions require you to think beyond the assigned presentation. Present your solutions to the questions in the format required by your instructor. Possible formats may include one or more of these options: create a document that contains the answer; present your answer to the class; discuss your answer in a group; record the answer as audio or video using a webcam, smartphone, or portable media player; or post answers on a blog, wiki, or website.

CONSIDER THIS

Apply Your Knowledge

Reinforce the skills and apply the concepts you learned in this chapter.

Styling a Webpage

Instructions: In this exercise, you will use your text editor to create external, embedded, and inline styles for the Durango Jewelry and Gem Shop home page. You will style the sections of the semantic wireframe (`header, nav, main,` and `footer`) and a `div` element that surrounds all of the content to center the content on the page. You will also float an image to the left so that some of the content can fill the empty space to the right of the image. Finally, you will clear the float and add margins and borders to give your page a professional touch. The completed home page is shown in Figure 4–44. You will also use professional web development practices to indent, space, comment, and validate your code.

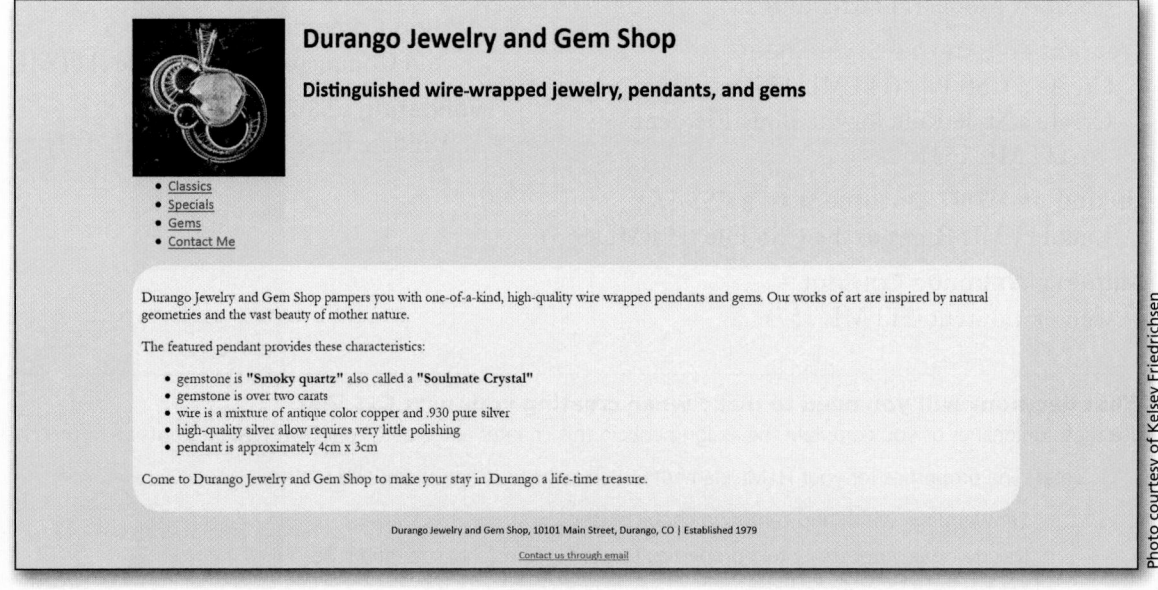

Figure 4–44

Perform the following tasks:

1. Open your text editor, and then open the apply04.html file from the Data Files for Students. Use the File Save As feature to save the webpage in the chapter04\apply folder with the name **index04.html** to create the home page.

2. Modify the comment at the top of the index.html page to include your name and today's date.

3. Start a new file in your text editor, and save it in the chapter04\apply folder with the name **styles04.css** to create a style sheet.

4. Enter a CSS comment as the first line of the external style sheet with *your* name and today's date. Recall that CSS comments are entered within **/*** and ***/** characters.

5. Style the **body** element with a uniform black text color and light-green background color:

```
body { color: #000000;
  background-color: #D9F1C1;
}
```

Photo courtesy of Kelsey Friedrichsen

6. In the `head` section of the index04.html file, enter an element to connect the page to the external style sheet:

```
<link rel="stylesheet" href="styles04.css">
```

Save your changes. Open or refresh index04.html in a browser to make sure that the style sheet is correctly connected to the HTML file.

7. Your next task is to center the content on the webpage. To do this, add <div> tags to surround the content in the wireframe, and then apply a style to center the content within the <div> tags as follows:

   a. In index04.html, insert the `<div id="outerwrapper">` opening tag just after the opening <body> tag.

   b. In index04.html, insert the `</div> <!--close the outerwrapper-->` closing tag and comment just before the closing </body> tag.

   c. In styles04.css, insert the following declarations to constrain the outerwrapper to 80% of the width of the screen and to center the content within the outerwrapper:

```
#outerwrapper { width: 80%;
  margin: 0 auto 0 auto;
  }
```

   d. Save your changes to both files, and then open or refresh index04.html in a browser to make sure that the content is centered within 80% of the browser window.

8. Apply common sans-serif fonts to the `header, nav,` and `footer` sections, and common serif fonts to the `div id="main"` section by adding the following style to the external stylesheet:

```
header, nav, footer { font-family: Calibri, Arial, sans-serif;
  }
#main { font-family: Garamond, "Times New Roman", serif;
  }
```

   (*Hint*: After each step, save index04.html and styles04.css and then refresh index04.html in the browser to make sure that each style is applied successfully.)

9. Style the text in the `footer` section to be 0.75em and centered by adding the following styles to the external stylesheet:

```
footer { font-size: 0.75em;
  text-align: center;
  }
```

10. Style the content within the `div id="main"` section to have a lighter background and 10px of padding on all four sides by adding the following declarations to the existing #main selector:

```
background-color: #F0F9E6;
padding: 10px;
```

11. Float the image to the left with the following style so that the existing `h1` and `h2` content moves to the right of the image:

```
img { float: left;
  }
```

12. Clear the float for the nav section with the following style:

```
nav { clear: both;
    }
```

13. Add a margin to the left of the `h1` and `h2` content in the `nav` section to insert white space between the headings and the image. Given you want to apply the same rule to two specific headings (but not other `h1` and `h2` content on the website), you will first give the tags the same class attribute value and then apply the style to that class as follows:

a. In index04.html, insert `class="addrightmargin"` to the opening <img> tag in the `header` section.

b. In styles04.css, insert the following style to increase the size of the right margin for content tagged with class="addrightmargin"

```
.addrightmargin { margin-right: 2%;
    }
```

14. In index04.html, insert an embedded style sheet just below the link tag in the `head` section to apply a rounded border to the `div id="main"` section:

```
<style>
    #main { border-radius: 2em; }
</style>
```

15. In index04.html, insert <span> and </span> tags around "Smoky quartz" and "Soulmate Crystal" in the first list item in the unordered list in the `div id="main"` section. Use the `style` attribute to give each opening <span> tag an inline style that bolds the font of the content within the <span> tags as follows:

```
<span style="font-weight:bold;">"Smoky quartz"</span>
<span style="font-weight:bold;">"Soulmate Crystal"</span>
```

16. Validate your HTML document using the W3C validator at validator.w3.org and fix any errors that are identified. Validation is complete when the validator returns the message "*This document was successfully checked as HTML5!*" in a green bar near the top of the webpage.

17. Add indents, spaces, and extra lines to your external style sheet to make it as professional and easy to read as possible. Employ these conventions:

- Put the selector and opening brace on the first line. Alternatively, put the selector, opening brace, and first declaration on the first line.
- Add second and subsequent declarations on their own lines.
- Make sure that each property is separated from its value with a colon (:)
- Make sure that there are no spaces in values such as 10px or 20%.
- Make sure that each declaration ends with a semicolon (;)
- For each set of styles, position the closing brace on its own line
- Add a blank line before each new selector line.

18. Validate your CSS file using the W3C validator at http://jigsaw.w3.org/css-validator/ and fix any errors that are identified. Validation is complete with the validator returns the message "*Congratulations! No Error Found.*"

19. Submit the index04.html and styles04.css files in a format specified by your instructor. Your instructor may also ask you to submit the wirewrap01.jpg file used with index04.html.

20. ✷ In this exercise you applied linked, embedded, and inline styles to style a home page. Use your experiences and research the web to answer these questions:

a. In step 7, you entered a comment <!--close the outerwrapper--> after the closing </div> tag. Why is a comment especially useful after a closing </div> tag?

b. What is the primary advantage of using an external versus embedded style sheet for the majority of your website styles?

c. In step 15, two <span> tags were given the same inline style. Why would you use inline styles versus embedded or external styles?

Extend Your Knowledge

Extend the skills you learned in this chapter and experiment with new skills. You may need to use additional resources to complete the assignment.

Styling Paragraphs, Headings, Lists, and Images

Instructions: In this exercise, you will use your text editor to create an external style sheet to extend your knowledge of CSS as applied to the home page for Snow Fever Ski and Board School. You will apply new styles to headings, lists, and links. You will use CSS to format an unordered list within the <nav> tags as a horizontal navigation bar. You will also add comments to an existing style sheet. The completed webpage is shown in Figure 4–45. You will also use professional web development practices to indent, space, and validate your code.

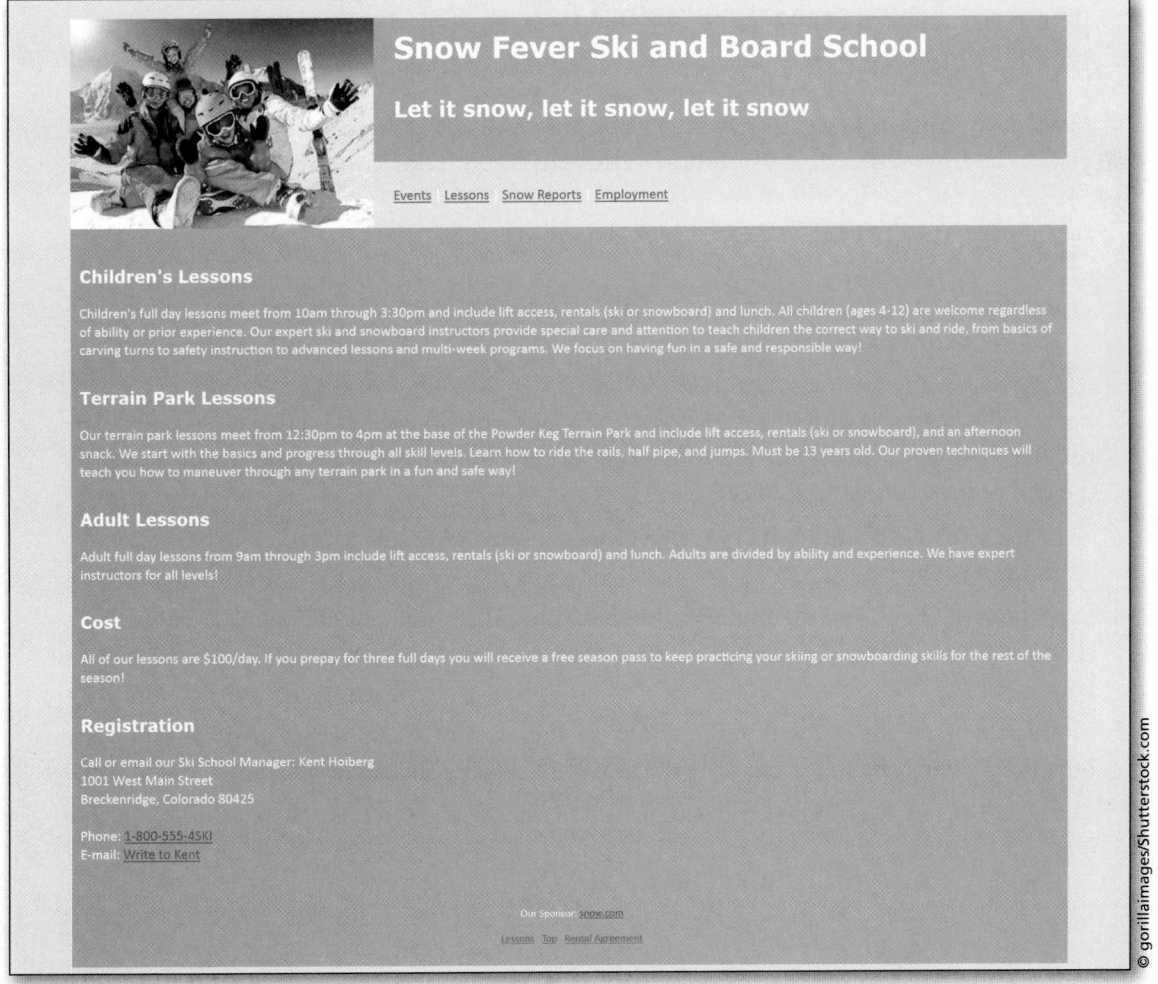

Figure 4–45

Perform the following tasks:

1. Open the `ski04.html` file from the Data Files for Students in your text editor and then modify the comment at the top of the page to include your name and today's date.

2. In the `head` section of the ski04.html file, enter a link tag to connect the page to the external style sheet:

```
<link rel="stylesheet" href="skistyles04.css">
```

   Save ski04.html and then preview it in a browser to make sure that the style sheet is correctly connected to the HTML file.

3. Open the `skistyles04.css` file from the Data Files for Students in your text editor and then modify the comment in the first line to include your name and today's date.

4. Document the existing style sheet before enhancing it. In the skistyles04.css file, add comments to the end of each declaration to document the existing styles as follows:

```
body { color: #FFFFFF; /*set text color to white*/
 background-color: #C9E4FF; /*set background color to light blue*/
 font-family: Calibri, sans-serif; /*set font to Calibri, or the
 generic sans-serif font*/
 }
#outer-wrapper { width: 90%; /*set width of id="outer-wrapper" to 90%*/
 margin: 0 auto 0 auto; /*center content within id="outer-wrapper"*/
 }
header, nav, #content, footer { background-color: #4CA6FF; /*set
 background color to bright blue*/
 padding: 10px; /*add 10px of padding on all four sides of the
 wireframe containers*/
}
footer { font-size: 0.75em; /*reduce the font size in the footer*/
 text-align: center; /*center the text in the footer*/
 }
img { float: left; /*float the image to the left*/
 }
.rightmargin { margin-right: 2%; /*add 2% right margin to
 class="rightmargin"*/
 }
```

5. Format the headings with <h1>, <h2>, or <h3> tags with a Verdana font face and a little padding between the content and top border of the block by adding the following styles to the end of the external style sheet:

```
h1, h2, h3 { font-family: Verdana, sans-serif;
 padding-top: 1%;}
```

6. Save the style sheet, and then refresh the ski04.html file in the browser to observe the changes. Refresh the webpage in a browser after each new style you apply to double check your work.

7. Modify the `li` content within the `nav` section so that the unordered list appears without bullets by adding the following style to the end of the external style sheet:

```
li { list-style-type: none; }
```

8. Modify the `li` content within the `nav` section so that the items appear on the same line instead of as new blocks of content by inserting the following declaration for the `li` selector. (*Hint*: Make sure you insert the declaration before the } closing brace.)

`display: inline;`

9. Save the stylesheet and refresh the ski04.html file in the browser to observe the changes.

10. Modify the `nav` section to have a light-blue background by inserting the following style at the end of the external style sheet:

`nav { background-color: #C9E4FF; }`

11. Make sure that the heading that starts with "Children's Lessons" does not float to the right of the image by clearing the float at that element. In the ski04.html file, add the following attribute/value pair to the opening <h3> tag that marks the Children's Lessons heading:

`class="clearfloat"`

12. In the skistyles04.css external style sheet, add a style to the end of the style sheet to clear the float for content marked class="clearfloat" as follows:

`.clearfloat { clear: both; }`

13. Add padding to the `header` section that contains the image, headings, and nav by styling the `header` section separately from the rest of the wireframe elements as follows:

   a. Delete `header` in the `header, nav, #content, footer` selector.

   b. Immediately below the `nav, #content, footer` selector, create a style for the `header` section to apply the desired background color and to change the padding on the `header` section to 0 top, 2% right, 2% bottom, and 0 left.

   ```
   header { background-color: #4CA6FF;
     padding: 0 2% 2% 0; }
   ```

14. Add tabs, spaces, and extra lines to your external style sheet to make it easy to read.

15. Add comments at the end of the new styles to document their application.

16. Validate your CSS file using the W3C validator at http://jigsaw.w3.org/css-validator/ and fix any errors that are identified. Validation is complete when the validator returns the message *"Congratulations! No Error Found."*

17. Validate your HTML webpage using the W3C validator at validator.w3.org and fix any errors that are identified. Validation is complete when the validator returns the message *"This document was successfully checked as HTML5!"* in a green bar near the top of the webpage.

18. Submit the `ski04.html` and `skistyles04.css` files in a format specified by your instructor. Your instructor may also ask you to submit the ski.jpg and legal.pdf files that are referenced by the webpage.

19. ✹ In step 10 you modified the rules for the header as follows:

   ```
   nav, #content, footer { background-color: #4CA6FF;
     padding: 10px;
     }
   header { background-color: #4CA6FF;
     padding: 0 2% 2% 0; }
   ```

   Given that the same background-color rule is found in two areas, rewrite these rules so that the background-color property is referenced only once. (*Hint*: You will need to create three selectors to do this.) What is the benefit of listing the same declaration only once?

STUDENT ASSIGNMENTS

Analyze, Correct, Improve

Analyze an external style sheet, correct all errors, and improve it.

Correcting CSS Errors

Instructions: Open your text editor and then open the cssbest04.html and cssbeststyles04.css files from the Data Files for Students. Several CSS "best practices" are listed on this webpage, but there are errors in both the HTML and CSS files that you will need to find and correct. Use Figure 4–46 as a guide to correct these files. You will also use professional web development best practices to comment, indent, space, and validate your work.

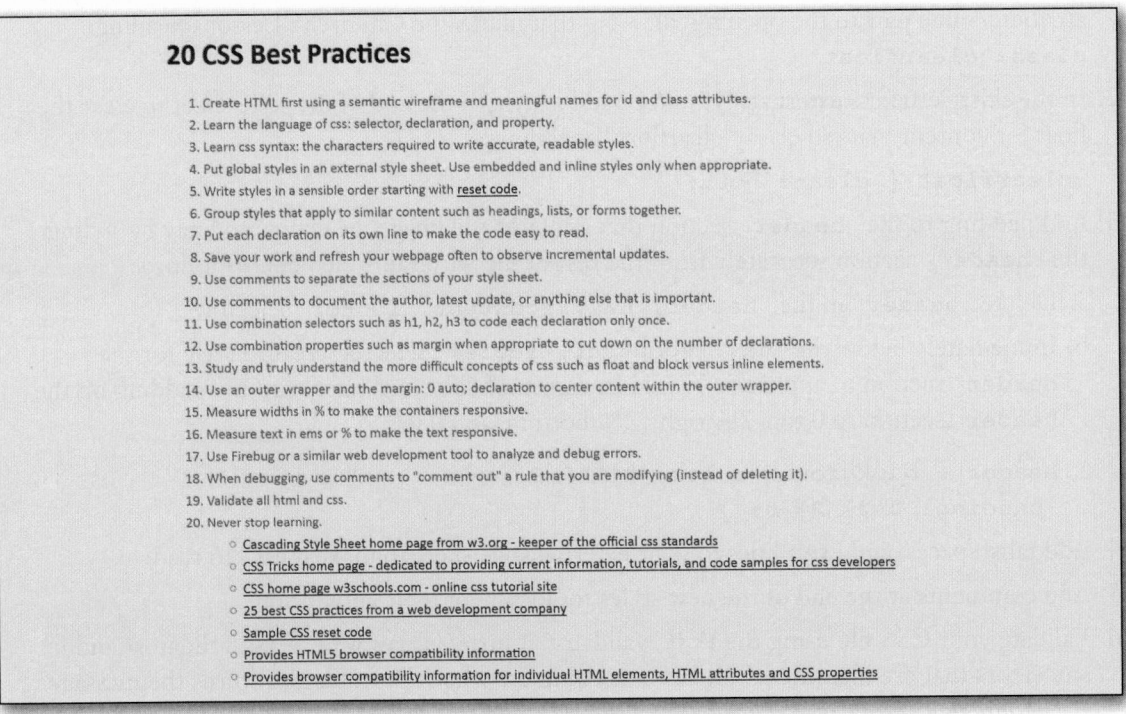

20 CSS Best Practices

1. Create HTML first using a semantic wireframe and meaningful names for id and class attributes.
2. Learn the language of css: selector, declaration, and property.
3. Learn css syntax: the characters required to write accurate, readable styles.
4. Put global styles in an external style sheet. Use embedded and inline styles only when appropriate.
5. Write styles in a sensible order starting with reset code.
6. Group styles that apply to similar content such as headings, lists, or forms together.
7. Put each declaration on its own line to make the code easy to read.
8. Save your work and refresh your webpage often to observe incremental updates.
9. Use comments to separate the sections of your style sheet.
10. Use comments to document the author, latest update, or anything else that is important.
11. Use combination selectors such as h1, h2, h3 to code each declaration only once.
12. Use combination properties such as margin when appropriate to cut down on the number of declarations.
13. Study and truly understand the more difficult concepts of css such as float and block versus inline elements.
14. Use an outer wrapper and the margin: 0 auto; declaration to center content within the outer wrapper.
15. Measure widths in % to make the containers responsive.
16. Measure text in ems or % to make the text responsive.
17. Use Firebug or a similar web development tool to analyze and debug errors.
18. When debugging, use comments to "comment out" a rule that you are modifying (instead of deleting it).
19. Validate all html and css.
20. Never stop learning.
    - Cascading Style Sheet home page from w3.org - keeper of the official css standards
    - CSS Tricks home page - dedicated to providing current information, tutorials, and code samples for css developers
    - CSS home page w3schools.com - online css tutorial site
    - 25 best CSS practices from a web development company
    - Sample CSS reset code
    - Provides HTML5 browser compatibility information
    - Provides browser compatibility information for individual HTML elements, HTML attributes and CSS properties

Figure 4–46

1. Correct

a. Open the `cssbest04.html` file in your editor and then modify the comment at the top of the document to include your name and today's date.

b. Open the `cssbeststyles04.css` file in your editor and then modify and correct the comment at the top of the style sheet to include your name and today's date. Correct the problem with the h1 style.

c. Enter a tag in the <head> section of the cssbest04.html file just below the <meta> tag to connect the webpage to the external style sheet.

```
<link rel="stylesheet" href="cssbeststyles04.css">
```

Open the webpage in a browser to make sure it is properly connected to the style sheet.

d. The current colors of the webpage are not a pleasing combination. Furthermore, the content goes "wall-to-wall" in your browser, meaning it spans the width of the browser window with no left or right margin. To fix this, add a `div` element to surround the content, and then resize and center it with CSS by completing the following:

- In the cssbest04.html document, after the opening <body> tag, add a `<div id="main">` tag.
- Just before the closing </body> tag, add a `</div><!--close main-->` tag and comment.

- In the cssbeststyles04.css file, add the following style between the body and h1 selectors to constrain the content within the <div id="main"> and </div> tags to 70% of the width of the screen and to center it.

```
#main { width: 70%;
 margin: 0 auto 0 auto;
 }
```

e. Save both files, then preview the webpage in a browser to observe the changes. Next, you will work on the colors. Go to **www.coolors.co** or any color scheme generation site and pick three complimentary colors for the body text, body background, and `h1` text. Apply the colors in your style sheet. The color declarations used in Figure 4–46 are:

```
color: #895D88; (for the body selector)
background-color: #F8F991; (for the body selector)
color: #3D315B; (for the h1 selector)
```

f. To improve the spacing between the list items, add the following rule to the end of your style sheet to add a half a line of space between list items:

```
li { line-height: 150%; }
```

2. Improve

a. Use http://validator.w3.org to validate your cssbest04.html page. The page flags an error at Line 34. In your cssbest04.html page, notice that the "Never stop learning" list item contains an unordered list starting on Line 34. Often, the validator flags the line after the actual error occurs. In this case, the closing </li> tag on Line 33 is in the wrong position. Move the </li> tag to below the closing </ul> tag on Line 42. In other words, the "Never stop learning" list item includes not only those three words, but the entire unordered list of links as well.

b. Save and revalidate the cssbest04.html page. Fix any errors and revalidate until you get the message "*This document was successfully checked as HTML5!*" A first step in creating clean CSS code is to validate your HTML code.

c. Use http://jigsaw.w3.org/css-validator/ to validate your CSS code. Unless you've already fixed it, you should see an error on Line 12 because the final brace } was not included for the h1 selector. Add that character and revalidate your CSS code. Fix any errors and revalidate until you get the message "*Congratulations! No Error Found.*"

3. ✻ After reviewing the 20 "best practices," comment on which of these practices you would like to understand better and why.

After reviewing the links in the "Never stop learning" list item, comment on which of these sites you would like to explore further and why.

In the Labs

Labs 1 and 2, which increase in difficulty, require you to create webpages based on what you learned in the chapter; Lab 3 requires you to dive deeper into a topic covered in the chapter.

Lab 1: **Creating an External Style Sheet for City Farmer**

Problem: You work for a local but rapidly growing gardening supply company called City Farmer that specializes in products that support food self-sufficiency. The company has hired you to help create the home page. The content for the home page is in place, but it needs to be styled. Style the webpage shown in Figure 4–47 with an external style sheet.

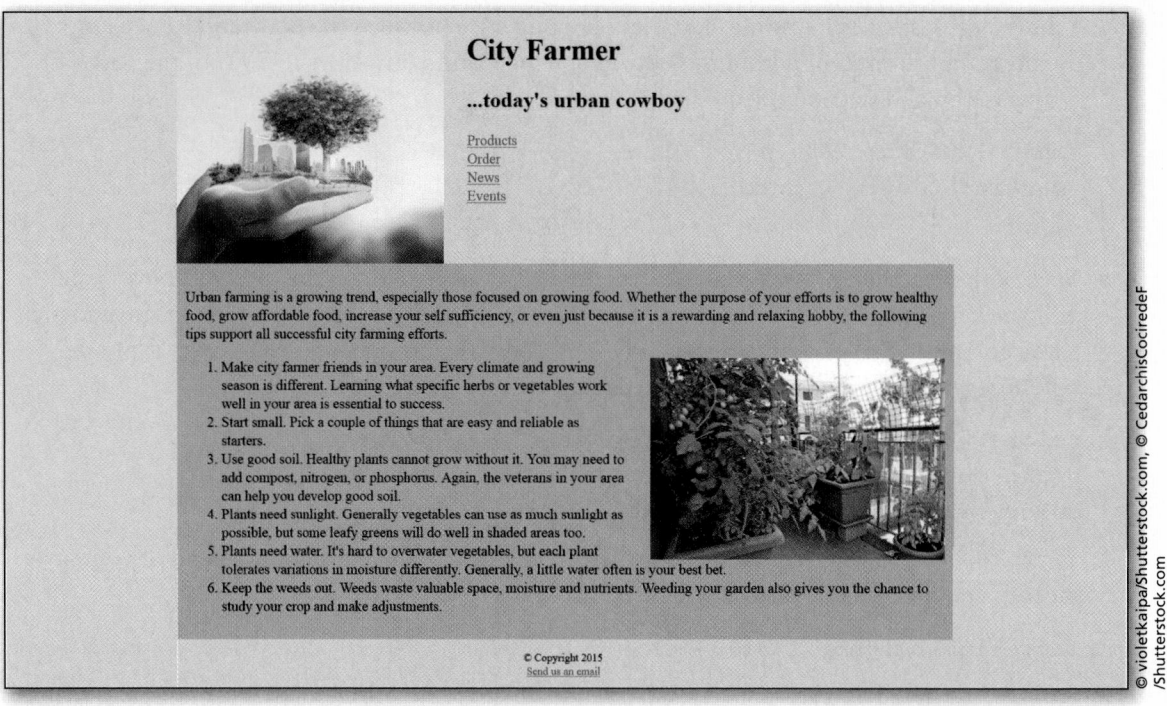

Figure 4–47

© violetkaipa/Shutterstock.com, © CedarchisCocíredeF /Shutterstock.com

Instructions: Perform the following tasks:

1. Open `cityfarmer04.html` in your HTML editor from the Data Files for Students and then modify the comment at the top of the page to include your name and today's date. Make sure the <title>...</title> tags contain the text `City Farmer Home Page`.

2. Start a new file in your text editor, and save it in the lab1\styles folder with the name `farmerstyles04.css`

3. Enter a CSS comment as the first line of the external style sheet with *your* name and today's date. Recall that CSS comments are entered within `/*` and `*/` characters.

4. Enter a style to apply a uniform black text color, a uniform serif font, and light-blue background color to the body:

```
body { color: #000000;
 background-color: #B8D1EB;
 font-family: "Times New Roman", serif;
 }
```

5. In the `head` section of the cityfarmer04.html file, enter an element to connect the page to the external style sheet:

```
<link rel="stylesheet" href="styles/farmerstyles04.css">
```

Save your changes, and then open or refresh cityfarmer04.html in a browser to make sure that the style sheet is correctly connected to the HTML file. Note that in this exercise, the style sheet is saved in the styles folder, so that path needs to be included in the `href` value.

6. Center the content by adding <div> and </div> tags to surround the content in the wireframe, and then applying styles to center the content within the <div> and </div> tags as follows:

   a. In cityfarmer04.html, insert the `<div id="outerwrapper">` opening tag just after the opening <body> tag.

   b. In cityfarmer04.html, insert the `</div> <!-- close the outerwrapper-->` closing tag and comment just before the closing </body> tag. Save your changes to cityfarmer04.html.

c. In farmerstyles04.css, insert the following style to constrain the outerwrapper to 70% of the width of the screen and to center the content within the outerwrapper:

```
#outerwrapper { width: 70%;
 margin: 0 auto 0 auto;
 }
```

Save your changes to farmerstyles04.css, and then open or refresh cityfarmer04.html in a browser to make sure that the content is centered within 70% of the browser window.

7. Style the text in the footer section to have a font size of 0.75em and appear centered by adding the following styles to the external stylesheet:

```
footer { font-size: 0.75em;
 text-align: center;
 }
```

(*Hint*: Save and refresh the cityfarmer04.html file in your browser after every step to observe and study the impact of each style.)

8. Style the content within the `div id="main"` section to have a light-brown background and 10px of padding on the top by adding the following style:

```
#main { background-color: #C5A98B;
 padding: 10px;
 }
```

9. Float the image in the header to the left with the following style so that the <h1>, <h2>, and <nav> content moves to the right of the image:

```
img { float: left;
 }
```

10. Remove the bullets from the list items in the `nav` section by adding the following style:

```
ul { list-style-type: none;
 }
```

11. Push the content away from the image by adding a right margin to the img selector with the following declaration:

```
margin-right: 3%;
```

12. Clear the float so that the content for the `div id="main"` section starts on its own line by adding a second style rule with a #main selector:

```
#main { clear: both;
 }
```

13. You decide to float the second image right instead of left. Right now, your float rule is written using the img selector so all img content is affected. To change the float value for the second image, complete the following:

a. Add a `class="floatleft"` attribute value pair to the first <img> tag (the logo) in the cityfarmer04.html file. (*Hint*: The order of attribute value pairs in the opening html tag do not affect how the code works in the browser, but typically the most important attributes are listed first so the class="floatleft" attribute would often be listed second or third.)

b. Add a `class="floatright"` attribute value pair to the second <img> tag (tomatoes in pots) in the cityfarmer04.html file.

c. In the farmerstyles04.css file, change the img selector to `.floatleft`

STUDENT ASSIGNMENTS

d. Just below the .floatleft style in the CSS file, add the following style to float the second image to the right:

```
.floatright { float: right;
margin-left: 3%;
}
```

Save both files and then refresh cityfarmer04.html in your browser.

14. To make sure the footer also starts on its own line, modify the selector for the rule that clears all float to include both the #main and footer areas as follows:

```
#main, footer { clear: both;
}
```

15. Validate your HTML code and fix any errors.

16. Validate your CSS code and fix any errors.

17. Save and open the cityfarmer04.html page within a browser as shown in Figure 4–47.

18. Submit your assignment in the format specified by your instructor.

19. ✳ In step 13, you inserted class="floatleft" and class="floatright" attributes in your HTML page instead of id="floatleft" and id="floatright". Why?

Lab 2: **Creating an External Style Sheet for Cycle Out Cancer**

Problem: You are part of a philanthropic group of motorcyclists, Cycle Out Cancer, who participate in community events and parades to distribute cancer awareness information. You have created content for the first four webpages of their website and updated the links in the `nav` section for each page. In this exercise you will create an external style sheet and link it to the four pages as shown in Figures 4–48 through 4–51.

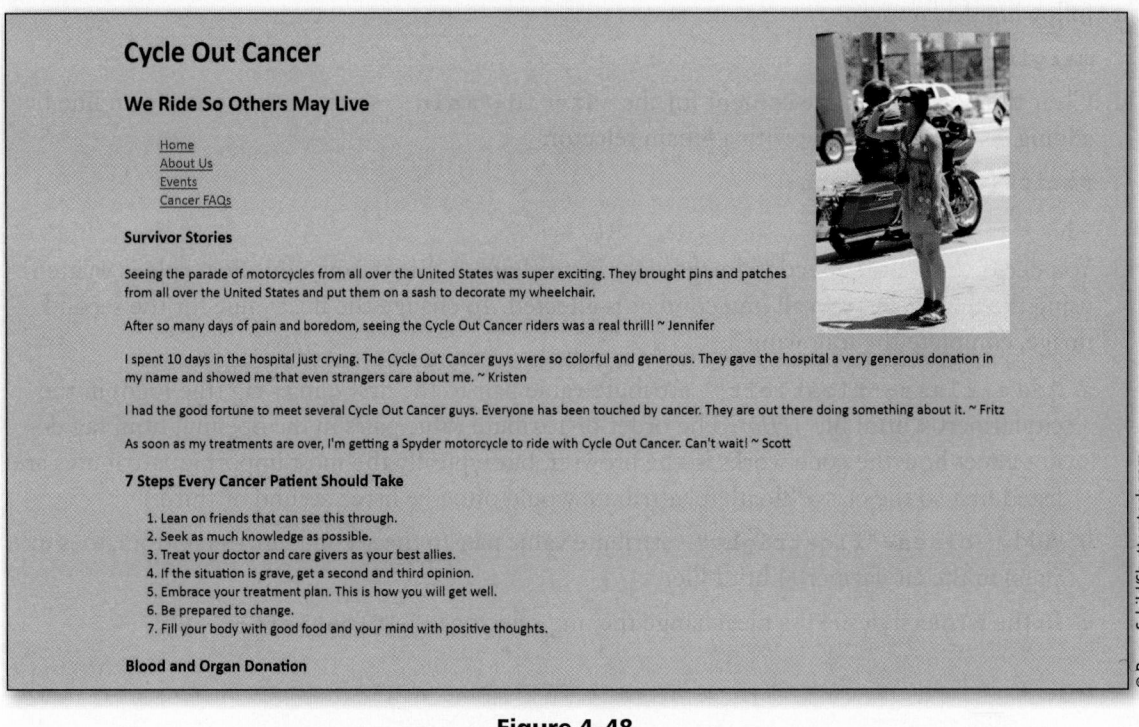

Figure 4–48

Cycle Out Cancer

We Ride So Others May Live

Home
About Us
Events
Cancer FAQs

About Us

Cycle Out Cancer is a volunteer organization that promotes cancer awareness. Cycle Out Cancer was founded by a group of three motorcycle enthusiasts from Kansas City who each found their lives interrupted by something else they unfortunately shared in common: cancer. Each made a vow to the other to fight their different forms of cancer to the best of their ability and some day, "ride again."

After a three years and countless medical procedures, their dream came true in May of 2000 when the threesome made their way from Kansas City to Branson, Missouri. At every stop in the short journey the three friends shared their amazing stories of how they fought their cancers. Over time, more and more people have joined their rides. Now Cycle Out Cancer is one of the largest all-volunteer motorcycle clubs in the midwest.

Anyone who is a motorcycle enthusiast is welcome to join. Many say that the best part of the ride are the inspiring stories shared by the members at the finish line.

Contact Cycle Out Cancer

© Jim Pruitt/Shutterstock.com

Figure 4–49

Cycle Out Cancer

We Ride So Others May Live

Home
About Us
Events
Cancer FAQs

Monthly Rides

First Friday of the Month - May - June - July - Aug - September

The first Friday of these months we honor past members who have had cancer but are no longer with us. Our route may include a lunch at their favorite watering hole, a visit to their surviving spouse, or a visit to the cemetary to decorate their grave. Contact Cycle Out Cancer for more information on commemorative rides in your area.

Rider Safety

All riders must adhere to basic safety rules while on our rides:

1. Gear up: Wear an approved helmet and protective clothing appropriate for the weather.
2. Maintain the big stuff: Check your tires, breaks, fluids, electronics, and frame before each ride.
3. Check the little stuff: Make sure your lights, blinkers, mirrors, and stands all work correctly.
4. Obey all traffic laws, lights, and signs.
5. Drive defensively and respectfully even when others do not.

Rides and Activities

Rides and activities are currently being planned for these hospitals in the coming year:

Contact Cycle Out Cancer for up-to-date schedules.

- Dana-Farber/Brigham and Women's Cancer Center, Boston MA
- Memorial Sloan Kettering Cancer Center, New York NY
- Mayo Clinic, Rochester MN
- University of Texas MD Anderson Cancer Center, Houston TX

Contact Cycle Out Cancer

© Rena Schild/Shutterstock.com

Figure 4–50

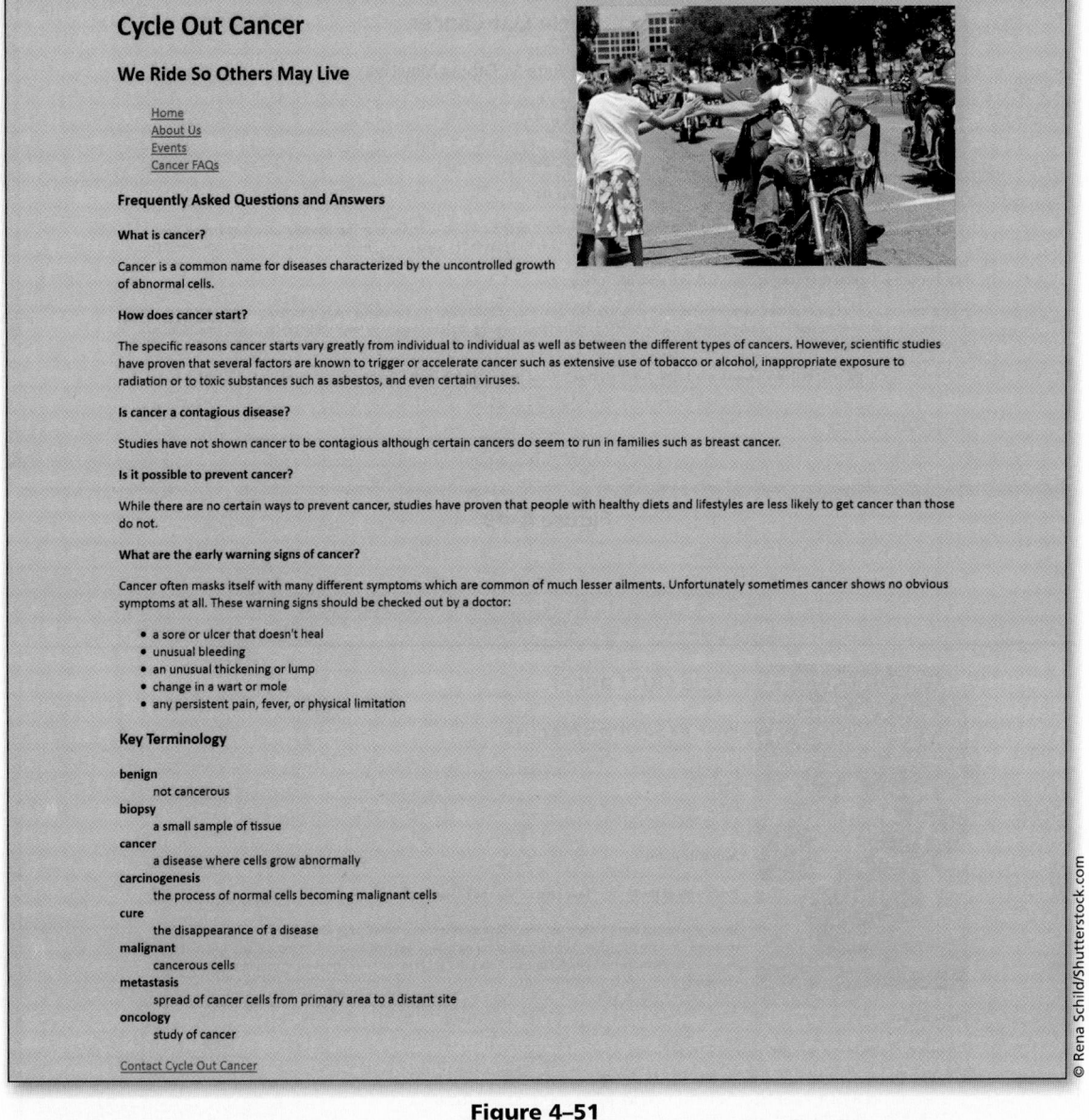

© Rena Schild/Shutterstock.com

Figure 4–51

Instructions: Perform the following tasks:

1. Open the `cyclehome04.html`, `cycleabout04.html`, `cycleevents04.html`, and `cyclefaq04.html` files in your HTML editor from the Data Files for Students and then modify the comment at the top of each page to include your name and today's date.

2. Start a new file in your text editor, and save it in the lab2\styles folder with the name `cyclestyles04.css`

3. Enter a CSS comment as the first line of the external style sheet with *your* name and today's date.

4. Enter the styles to apply a uniform black text color, Calibri and sans-serif font, and an orange (#FF9900) background color to the body.

5. In the `head` section of each of the four cycle HTML documents, enter an element to connect the page to the external style sheet.

   Save and then open or refresh each page in a browser to make sure that the stylesheet is correctly connected to the HTML files. Note that in this exercise, the style sheet is saved in the styles folder, so that path needs to be included in the `href` value.

6. Center the content by adding <div> and </div> tags to surround the content in the wireframe, and then apply styles to center the content within the <div> and </div> tags as follows:

 a. In each HTML page, insert the `<div id="wrapper">` opening tag just after the opening <body> tag.

 b. In each HTML page, insert the `</div> <!--close the wrapper-->` closing tag and comment just before the closing </body> tag.

 c. In cyclestyles04.css, add the styles to constrain the wrapper to 80% of the width of the window and to center the content within the wrapper.

 Save all files and then open or refresh the pages in a browser to make sure that the content is centered within 80% of the browser window. (*Hint*: Note that a `nav` section to link to each of the four pages follows the image on each page.)

9. On the cyclehome04.html and cyclefaq04.html pages, you want to float the image in the header to the right. On the cycleevents04.html and cycleabout04.html pages, you want to float the image in the header to the left. Complete these tasks as follows:

 a. Create styles in your style sheet with a selector that addresses the class names of floatleft and floatright. (*Hint*: A `class="floatleft"` attribute and value in the HTML document is referenced by a `.floatleft` selector in the CSS file.)

 b. Add two declarations to both the selectors. The first will float the content either left or right. The second will add a 2% margin to the inside edge of the content. For example, the declarations for the .floatleft selector would be:

```
.floatleft { float: left;
margin-right: 2%;
}
```

 Complete the declarations for the .floatright selector to make the image float right and add a 2% margin to the left side.

 c. Add `class="floatleft"` to the opening `img` tag in the cycleevents04.html and cycleabout04.html pages.

 d. Add `class="floatright"` to the opening `img` tag in the cyclehome04.html and cyclefaq04.html pages.

 e. Save all files and refresh them in your browser.

11. Remove the bullets from the list items only in the nav section by adding the following style:

```
nav ul { list-style-type: none;
 }
```

(*Hint*: In this example, you are using a descendant selector. Only the `ul` content within the `nav` content will be affected.) Save and refresh files and review them in your browser to make sure that only the bullets for the `ul` content within the `nav` section were removed.)

12. Create one more class named `boldtext` for the questions on the cyclefaq04.html page as follows so that you can style the questions in bold:

 a. Add `class="boldtext"` to the opening <p> tag for the five questions immediately below the <h3>Frequently Asked Questions and Answers </h3> heading in the cyclefaq04.html file.

 b. Add a style in the cyclestyles04.css file to apply bold to the content that is identified by the boldtext class as follows:

```
.boldtext { font-weight: bold; }
```

13. You also decide to bold the `dt` (definition term) content on the cyclefaq04.html page. Given you already have a declaration to apply bold, change the selector to include both the content identified by the boldtext class as well as the content marked up by the `dt` tag as follows:

```
.boldtext, dt { font-weight: bold; }
```

14. Validate your four HTML pages and fix any errors.

15. Validate your CSS code and fix any errors.

16. Save and open the pages within a browser as shown in Figures 4–48, 4–49, 4–50, and 4–51.

17. Submit your assignment in the format specified by your instructor.

18. ☀ Compare the selector of `nav ul` (step 11) to the selector of `.boldtext, dt` (step 13). One contains a comma and one does not. What is the significance of the comma? (*Hint:* Search for information on CSS grouping selectors and descendant selectors.)

Lab 3: Expand Your World
Styling Inline versus Block Content

Problem: CSS has its own terminology, syntax, and concepts such as the box model, float, and inline versus block content, all of which is critical to your ability to successfully apply styles and position content on your webpages. In this exercise you will create an external style sheet to experiment with styles as they relate to inline and block content. The webpages that you are styling summarize CSS terminology, syntax, and tips. The final, styled webpages are shown in Figures 4–52, 4–53, 4–54, and 4–55.

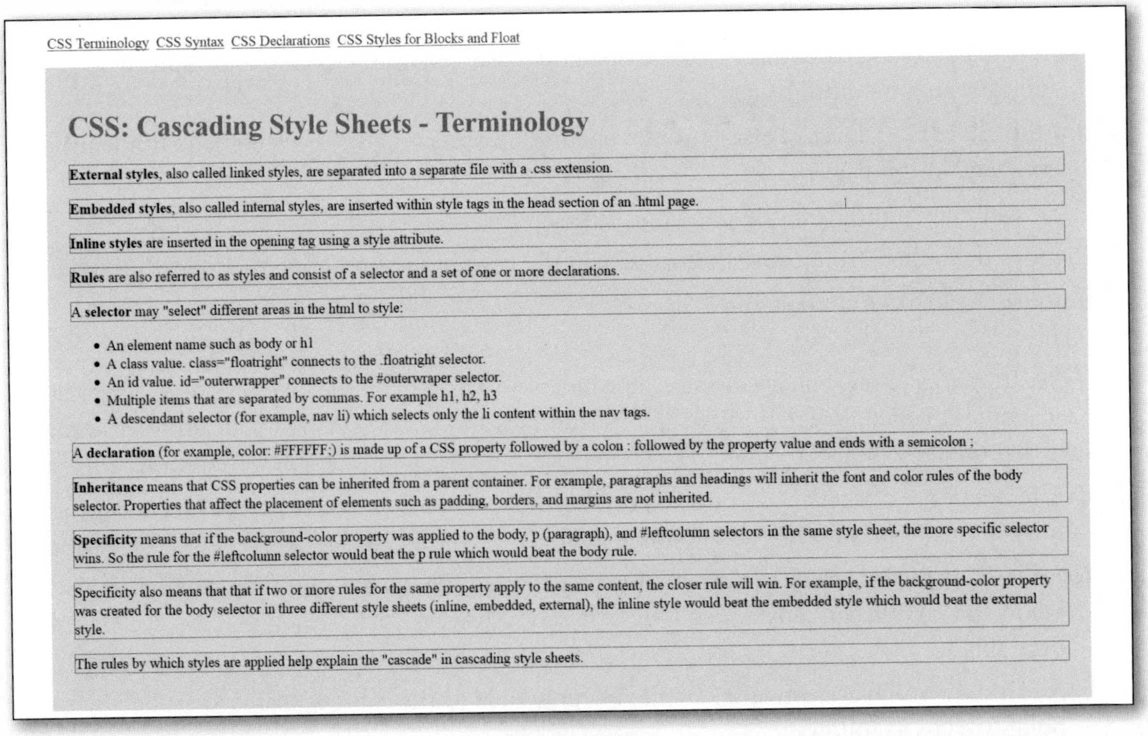

CSS Terminology CSS Syntax CSS Declarations CSS Styles for Blocks and Float

CSS: Cascading Style Sheets - Terminology

External styles, also called linked styles, are separated into a separate file with a .css extension.

Embedded styles, also called internal styles, are inserted within style tags in the head section of an .html page.

Inline styles are inserted in the opening tag using a style attribute.

Rules are also referred to as styles and consist of a selector and a set of one or more declarations.

A **selector** may "select" different areas in the html to style:

- An element name such as body or h1
- A class value. class="floatright" connects to the .floatright selector.
- An id value. id="outerwrapper" connects to the #outerwraper selector.
- Multiple items that are separated by commas. For example h1, h2, h3
- A descendant selector (for example, nav li) which selects only the li content within the nav tags.

A **declaration** (for example, color: #FFFFFF;) is made up of a CSS property followed by a colon : followed by the property value and ends with a semicolon ;

Inheritance means that CSS properties can be inherited from a parent container. For example, paragraphs and headings will inherit the font and color rules of the body selector. Properties that affect the placement of elements such as padding, borders, and margins are not inherited.

Specificity means that if the background-color property was applied to the body, p (paragraph), and #leftcolumn selectors in the same style sheet, the more specific selector wins. So the rule for the #leftcolumn selector would beat the p rule which would beat the body rule.

Specificity also means that that if two or more rules for the same property apply to the same content, the closer rule will win. For example, if the background-color property was created for the body selector in three different style sheets (inline, embedded, external), the inline style would beat the embedded style which would beat the external style.

The rules by which styles are applied help explain the "cascade" in cascading style sheets.

Figure 4–52

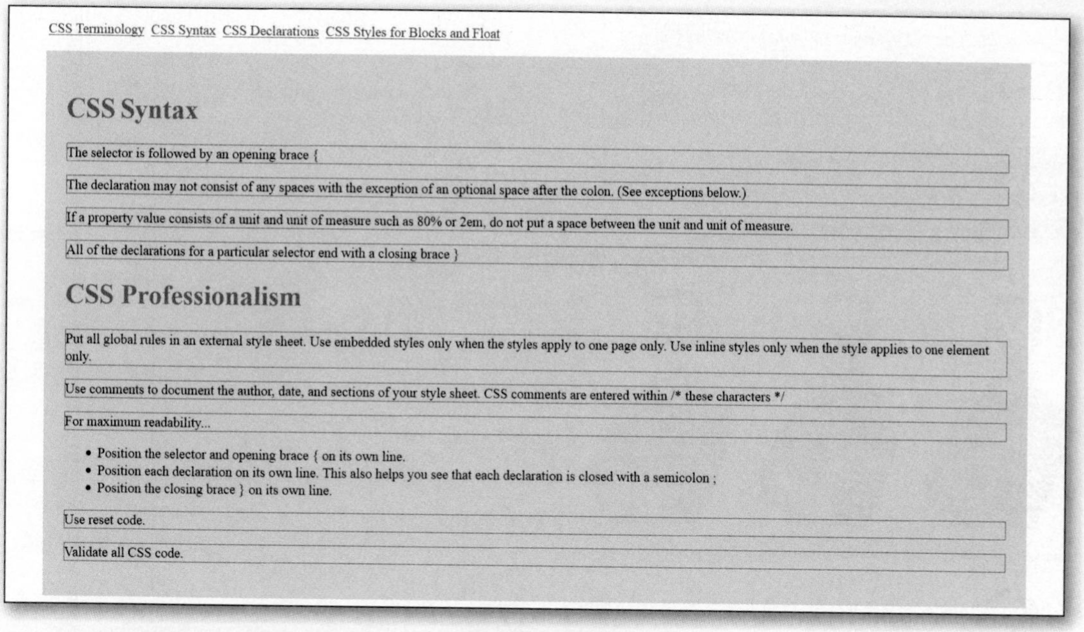

CSS Terminology CSS Syntax CSS Declarations CSS Styles for Blocks and Float

CSS Syntax

The selector is followed by an opening brace {

The declaration may not consist of any spaces with the exception of an optional space after the colon. (See exceptions below.)

If a property value consists of a unit and unit of measure such as 80% or 2em, do not put a space between the unit and unit of measure.

All of the declarations for a particular selector end with a closing brace }

CSS Professionalism

Put all global rules in an external style sheet. Use embedded styles only when the styles apply to one page only. Use inline styles only when the style applies to one element only.

Use comments to document the author, date, and sections of your style sheet. CSS comments are entered within /* these characters */

For maximum readability...

- Position the selector and opening brace { on its own line.
- Position each declaration on its own line. This also helps you see that each declaration is closed with a semicolon ;
- Position the closing brace } on its own line.

Use reset code.

Validate all CSS code.

Figure 4–53

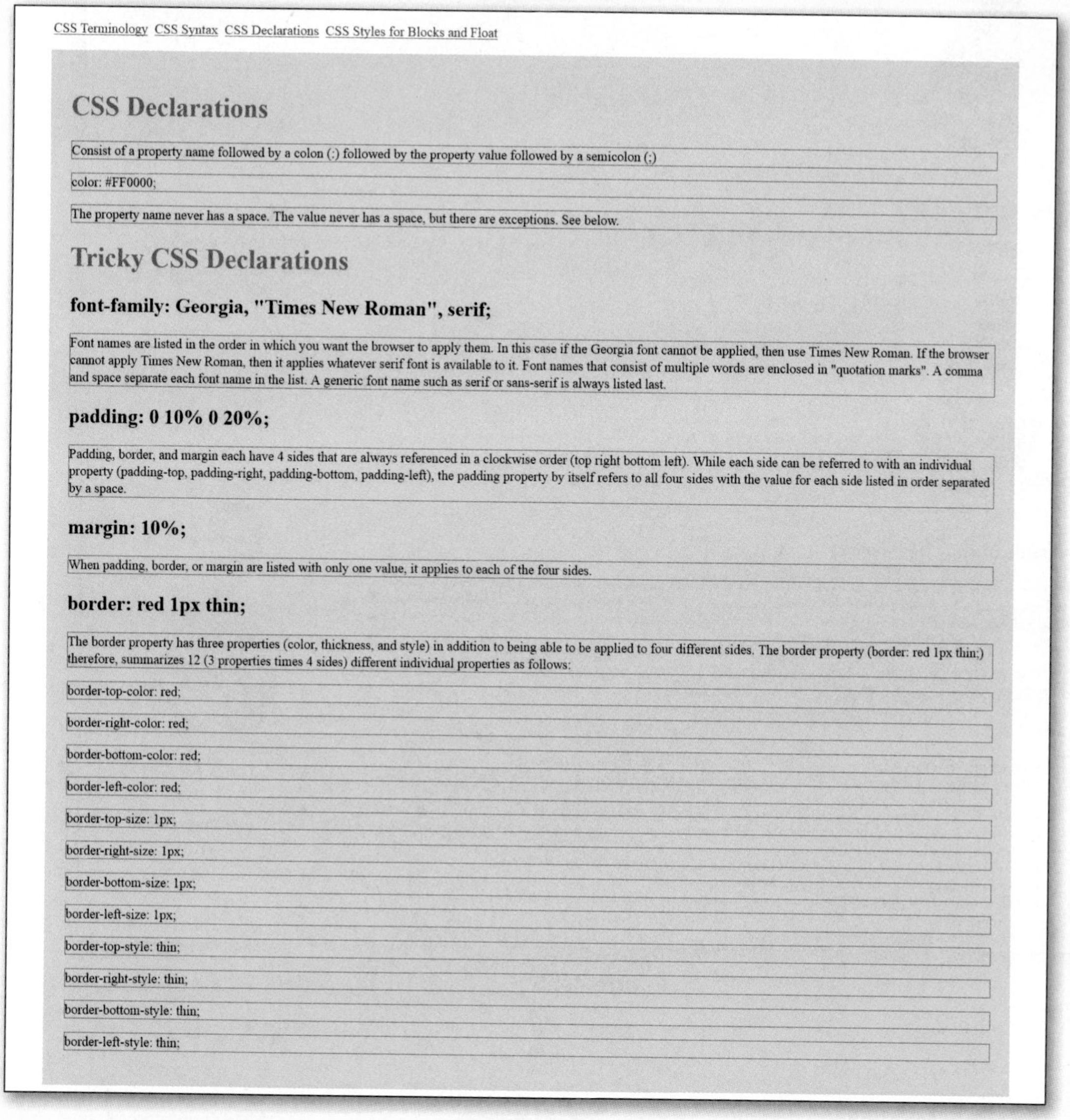

CSS Terminology CSS Syntax CSS Declarations CSS Styles for Blocks and Float

CSS Declarations

Consist of a property name followed by a colon (:) followed by the property value followed by a semicolon (;)

color: #FF0000;

The property name never has a space. The value never has a space, but there are exceptions. See below.

Tricky CSS Declarations

font-family: Georgia, "Times New Roman", serif;

Font names are listed in the order in which you want the browser to apply them. In this case if the Georgia font cannot be applied, then use Times New Roman. If the browser cannot apply Times New Roman, then it applies whatever serif font is available to it. Font names that consist of multiple words are enclosed in "quotation marks". A comma and space separate each font name in the list. A generic font name such as serif or sans-serif is always listed last.

padding: 0 10% 0 20%;

Padding, border, and margin each have 4 sides that are always referenced in a clockwise order (top right bottom left). While each side can be referred to with an individual property (padding-top, padding-right, padding-bottom, padding-left), the padding property by itself refers to all four sides with the value for each side listed in order separated by a space.

margin: 10%;

When padding, border, or margin are listed with only one value, it applies to each of the four sides.

border: red 1px thin;

The border property has three properties (color, thickness, and style) in addition to being able to be applied to four different sides. The border property (border: red 1px thin;) therefore, summarizes 12 (3 properties times 4 sides) different individual properties as follows:

border-top-color: red;

border-right-color: red;

border-bottom-color: red;

border-left-color: red;

border-top-size: 1px;

border-right-size: 1px;

border-bottom-size: 1px;

border-left-size: 1px;

border-top-style: thin;

border-right-style: thin;

border-bottom-style: thin;

border-left-style: thin;

Figure 4–54

STUDENT ASSIGNMENTS

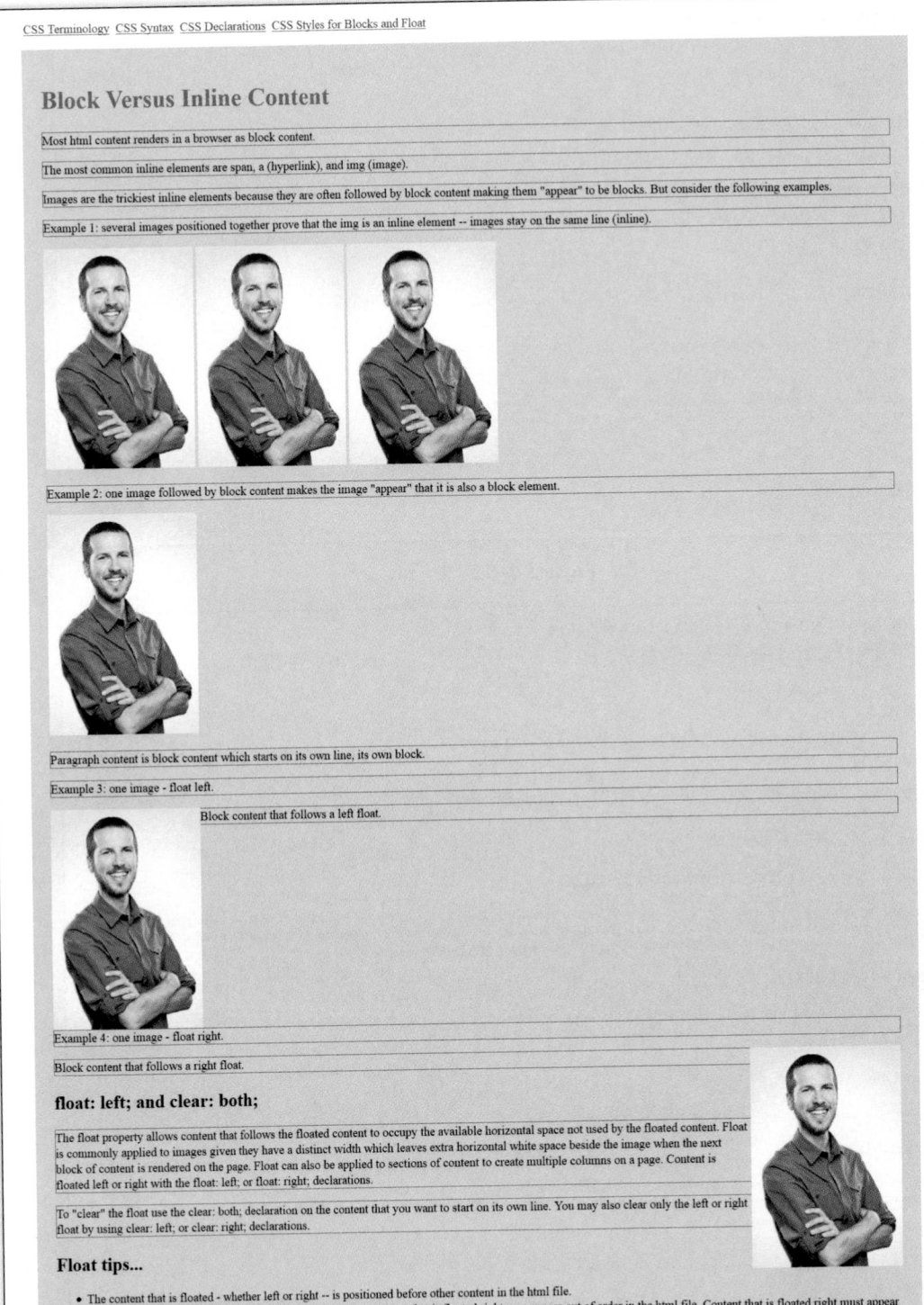

CSS Terminology CSS Syntax CSS Declarations CSS Styles for Blocks and Float

Block Versus Inline Content

Most html content renders in a browser as block content.

The most common inline elements are span, a (hyperlink), and img (image).

Images are the trickiest inline elements because they are often followed by block content making them "appear" to be blocks. But consider the following examples.

Example 1: several images positioned together prove that the img is an inline element -- images stay on the same line (inline).

Example 2: one image followed by block content makes the image "appear" that it is also a block element.

Paragraph content is block content which starts on its own line, its own block.

Example 3: one image - float left.

Block content that follows a left float.

Example 4: one image - float right.

Block content that follows a right float.

float: left; and clear: both;

The float property allows content that follows the floated content to occupy the available horizontal space not used by the floated content. Float is commonly applied to images given they have a distinct width which leaves extra horizontal white space beside the image when the next block of content is rendered on the page. Float can also be applied to sections of content to create multiple columns on a page. Content is floated left or right with the float: left; or float: right; declarations.

To "clear" the float use the clear: both; declaration on the content that you want to start on its own line. You may also clear only the left or right float by using clear: left; or clear: right; declarations.

Float tips...

- The content that is floated - whether left or right -- is positioned before other content in the html file.
- Because we read from left to right in the English language, content that is floated right may appear out of order in the html file. Content that is floated right must appear before other content in the html file.
- The "box" (margins, border, and padding) of content that follows a floated element behaves as if the floated element is not there.
- To clear a float which allows a block element to start on its own line, use the clear property. clear: both; is the most common declaration, but you can clear only a left or only a right float using clear: left; or clear: right;
- Textual content that is styled with a float should be given a width value. (Images have an inherent width.)
- It is not possible to float content in the center, only left or right.
- Floating content left or right shifts it to the left or right edge of the containing block.

Figure 4–55

© tommaso lizzul/Shutterstock.com

Instructions:

1. Open the `cssterminology04.html`, `csssyntax04.html`, `cssdeclarations04.html`, and `cssblock04.html` files in your HTML editor from the Data Files for Students and then modify the comment at the top of each of the four pages to include your name and today's date.

2. Enter `CSS terminology` within the <title> tags of cssterminology04.html, `CSS syntax` within the <title> tags of csssyntax04.html, `CSS declarations` within the <title> tags of the cssdeclarations04.html page, and `CSS block styles` within the <title> tags of the cssblock04.html page.

3. Open the cssterminology04.html page in the browser and read the page. Tap or click the links for the three other pages and read them as well. Note that the content goes "wall-to-wall" in your browser. To center the content within a small left and right margin, add padding between the content and border, and then change the background color to light gray. To do so, create an external style sheet with the following rules for the content marked up between <div id="main"> and </div> tags:

```
#main { width: 90%;
 margin: 0 auto 0 auto;
 padding: 2%;
 background-color: #D7D7D7;
 }
```

4. Save the file as `css04.css` in the same folder as the HTML webpages and then add a comment as the first line of the file with your name and the current date.

5. Link the css04.css stylesheet to each page by entering the following element to the <head> section in each page.

```
<link rel="stylesheet" href="css04.css">
```

6. Save and refresh your webpages after every step and tap or click each link to see the impact of each new set of rules on the four pages. Style <h1> content with a dark red text color by adding the following style to the external style sheet:

```
h1 { color: #CF0000; }
```

7. To study how borders are applied to block paragraph content, add the following rule to apply a blue, 1px, solid border to all sides of every paragraph:

```
p { border: blue 1px solid; }
```

Save your changes and then refresh your webpages and view the borders around the paragraphs.

8. To study how float is applied, you will work with the cssblock04.html page. Read the paragraphs that surround each example. Example 1 proves that when an image is followed by another image, they arrange themselves in a line, as inline content. Example 2 shows how a single image "appears" to be block content, but only because the content that follows the image is a block and thus starts on its own line.

You will modify the image after the Example 3 paragraph to float left. To do this, add `class="floatleft"` to the <img> tag that follows the Example 3 paragraph. (*Hint:* The order of attribute value pairs in an HTML tag is not technically significant, but it is common to put the most important attributes first. Typically class and id attribute values are listed early in the tag.)

Add the following rule to the external style sheet:

```
.floatleft { float: left; }
```

Save css04.css and cssblock04.html and then refresh the cssblock04.html page in the browser to observe how the image after the Example 3 paragraph floats left. Content that follows the floated image fills the space to the right of the floated image.

9. You want the Example 4 paragraph to start on its own line, so you need to clear the float at that point. To study how float is cleared, add `class="clearfloat"` to the opening <p> tag for the Example 4 paragraph. Add the following rule to the external style sheet:

`.clearfloat { clear: both; }`

Save the files and refresh the cssblock04.html page in the browser to observe how the Example 4 paragraph is "cleared of the float" and acts as normal block content again, starting on its own line.

10. You want the image after the Example 4 paragraph to float right. To do this, add `class="floatright"` to the <img> tag that follows the Example 4 paragraph. Add the following rule to the embedded style sheet:

`.floatright { float: right; }`

Save the files and refresh the cssblock04.html page in the browser to observe how the image following the Example 4 paragraph floats right. Floating content right can be tricky considering that people read English from left to right. Content that floats right is positioned before the content that flows next to it in the HTML file.

11. Change the existing navigation content into a horizontal navigation bar. To do this, first remove the bullets from the list items in the nav area. List item content naturally flows as block content, with each list item on its own line. To create a horizontal navigation system with each of the links on the same line, you also must add a rule to change the list item content from block to inline. To do this, add the following rules to the style sheet:

```
nav li { list-style-type: none;
  display: inline;
  }
```

Save the files and refresh the pages in the browser to observe the new horizontal navigation system.

12. Tap or click the CSS Terminology link to open the cssterminology.html page in the browser. This page lists several key CSS terms. You want to style the terms in bold. To do this, you will mark up the CSS key terms using the <span>...</span> tags. (The **span** element is an inline element that allows you to mark up and style content within a paragraph without creating a new line.) Mark up the following CSS terms using both the <span> tag and a `class="cssterm"` attribute in the opening <span> tag as follows: (*Hint:* Be careful to add only the opening and closing <span> tags and not change or delete any of the existing content or HTML code.)

`<span class="cssterm">`External styles`</span>` (first paragraph)

`<span class="cssterm">`Embedded styles`</span>` (second paragraph)

`<span class="cssterm">`Inline styles`</span>` (third paragraph)

`<span class="cssterm">`Rules`</span>` (fourth paragraph)

`<span class="cssterm">`selector`</span>` (fifth paragraph)

`<span class="cssterm">`declaration`</span>` (sixth paragraph)

`<span class="cssterm">`Inheritance`</span>` (seventh paragraph)

`<span class="cssterm">`Specificity`</span>` (eighth paragraph)

Add the following rule to the external style sheet to style the terms marked up by the `class="cssterm"` attribute value:

`.cssterm { font-weight: bold;}`

Save the files and refresh the pages in the browser to observe the new bold terms on the cssterminology04.html page.

13. Validate your HTML and CSS pages and fix any errors.

14. Submit your assignment in the format specified by your instructor.

15. ✸ Create a document with these four headings: Terminology, Syntax, Declarations, and Block Versus Inline. Reread cssterminology04.html webpage in your browser. After the Terminology heading in your document, write a sentence or two about something that you want to learn more about or still have questions about in regard to CSS terminology. Repeat this process for the other three pages in this exercise that discuss CSS syntax, CSS declarations, and CSS block versus inline styles. Your answers should prove that you have read the webpages. Save the file with the name `Chapter4Lab3CSS`.

Consider This: Your Turn

Apply your creative thinking and problem-solving skills to design and implement a solution.

1. Style Your Personal Portfolio Website

Personal

Part 1: In Chapter 3, you added content for your personal portfolio website on the `portfolio.html` webpage. In this exercise, you will update the page with an external style sheet that includes the following updates: (*Note:* Your instructor may want you to use the Data Files for Students provided for this exercise instead.)

1. Create an external style sheet with the name `portfoliostyles04.css` and save it in the `styles` folder within the your_turn_1 folder.

2. Add your name and the current date as a comment to the first line of the portfoliostyles04.css file.

3. Open your portfolio.html file in your HTML editor and float the image in the header section to the left by adding the attribute of `class="float-left"` to the <img> tag and a corresponding `.float-left {float: left;}` rule to the external style sheet.

4. Add a tag to the <head> section of the portfolio.html file to link the external style sheet to the portfolio.html page as follows:

`<link rel="stylesheet" href="styles/portfoliostyles04.css">`

Save both the CSS and HTML files, and open the portfolio.html file in your browser to make sure the style sheet is linked and the image is floating properly.

5. Add some space between the image and the content that is floated to the right by adding the following rule to the style sheet:

`img { margin-right: 3%; }`

Also remove the bullets on the list items within the nav section by adding the following rule to the style sheet:

`nav li { list-style-type: none; }`

6. Center the content on the page by containing all of the content within the `body` by surrounding it with `<div id="outerwrapper"> ... </div>` tags.

Add a comment after the closing </div> tag to identify that section as follows:

```
<!--end outerwrapper-->
```

Style the outerwrapper in the external style sheet to take up 70% of the available space on the screen and to center it within that space as follows:

```
#outerwrapper { width: 70%;
  margin: 0 auto 0 auto;
  }
```

7. To make sure the webpage will render successfully in all browsers, identify the main section using the <div id="main"> and </div> tags versus <main> and </main>, and include three pairs of <h2> tags in that section that mark up the headings of Strengths, Technologies, and Other.

8. Clear the float with the **main** content by adding the following style to the style sheet:

```
#main { clear: both; }
```

9. Push the content below the image by adding the following declaration to the **img** selector in the style sheet:

```
margin-bottom: 2%;
```

10. Style your name at the top of the webpage with a large Futura then Calibri then generic sans-serif font by adding the following class to the opening <p> tag that contains your name. **class="myname"** and by adding the following corresponding styles to the stylesheet:

```
.myname { font-family: Futura, Calibri, sans-serif;
  font-size: 2em;
  }
```

11. Add a light background color to the **#main** selector that goes well with the colors in your image.

12. Add styles for padding and a border with rounded corners to the **#main** selector as follows:

```
padding: 3%;
border: 2px black solid;
border-radius: 25px;
```

13. Link your style sheet to any other pages you have created in your portfolio website.

14. Add any other styles that you think would improve your portfolio webpages.

15. Validate and correct your HTML and CSS files, and then submit your assignment in the format specified by your instructor.

Part 2: ✳ Go to www.csszengarden.com and tap or click the style links to see how the single HTML file appears with different styles. The featured styles change, but at the time of this writing, the featured eight styles were named "Mid Century Modern," "Garments," "Steel," "Apothecary," "Screen Filler," "Fountain Kiss," "A Robot Named Jimmy," and "Verde Moderna." Be careful to tap or click the style names rather than the "by author's name" links to apply the new style to the webpage. Tapping or clicking the author's name links takes you to the home page for that author.

Explore the site to see how the location and appearance of the content changes from style to style. Locate the links to download the HTML file and CSS file. Download both files and open them in your HTML editor. After reviewing the code in each file, comment on what you learned or want to know more about.

2. Style the WebDevPros Webpages

Professional

Part 1: In Chapter 3, you added content within a wireframe and site map for the WebDevPros website. In this exercise, you will update the pages for that website with an external style sheet that includes the following updates: (*Note:* Your instructor may want you to use the Data Files for Students provided for this exercise instead.)

1. Create an external style sheet with the name `webdevstyles04.css` and save it in the `styles` folder within the your_turn_2 folder.

2. Add your name and the current date as a comment to the first line of the webdevstyles04.css file.

3. Open index.html and other files you created for WebDevPros in Chapter 3 in your HTML editor and float the images in the header section to the left or right by adding the attribute of `class="float-right"` or `class="float-left"` to the <img> tag and the corresponding `.float-right { float: right; }` or `.float-left { float: left; }` rules to the external style sheet. Make your decision on whether the image should float left or right based on how it looks best on the page.

4. Add a tag to the <head> section of the index.html file to link the external style sheet to the index.html page as follows:

   `<link rel="stylesheet" href="styles/webdevstyles04.css">`

   Save both the CSS and HTML file, and open the index.html file in your browser to make sure the style sheet is linked and the image is floating properly.

5. Add some space between the image and the content that is floated to the right by adding the following declaration and comment to the `.float-right` selector:

   `margin: 0 0 3% 3%; /* 0 top 0 right 3% bottom 3% left */`

   Add the following declaration and comment to the `.float-left` selector:

   `margin: 0 3% 3% 0; /* 0 top 3% right 3% bottom 0 left */`

6. Center the content on all of the pages by containing all of the content within the `body` by surrounding it with `<div id="outer-wrapper">` ... `</div>` tags.

   Add a comment after the closing </div> tag to identify that section as follows:

   `<!--end outer-wrapper-->`

   Then style the outer-wrapper section in the external style sheet to take up 80% of the available space on the screen and to center within that space as follows:

   `#outer-wrapper { width: 80%;`
   `  margin: 0 auto 0 auto;`
   `  }`

7. Add a style to clear the float as follows:

   `.clear-float { clear: both; }`

8. Add `class="clear-float"` to the first content tag following the <nav> section, which is probably the <div id="main"> tag unless you have modified your site beyond the previous chapter's instructions.

9. Add `class="webdev"` to the "WebDevPros" paragraph content at the top of each page. Style the class with a font face, font size, and font color as follows:

   `.webdev { font-family: "Mission Gothic", "Times New Roman", serif;`
   `  font-size: 3em;`
   `  color: #0033CC;`
   `  }`

10. Add a style to the style sheet to bold and change the font color of the <dt> content using the following style:

```
dt { font-weight: bold;
 color: #0033CC;
 }
```

11. Link your style sheet to any other pages you have created in your WebDevPros website.

12. Add any other styles that you think would improve your WebDevPros webpages.

13. Validate and correct your HTML and CSS files, and submit your assignment in the format specified by your instructor.

Part 2: ✺ You decide to add a horizontal navigation bar to the bottom of each page. Copy the <ul> content from the <nav> section and paste it inside <footer>…</footer> tags just before the closing </div> that closes the outer-wrapper section.

Add a style to your style sheet to remove the bullets from the <li> content in the <footer> section. (*Hint*: Use a `footer li` selector.) Also add a style to your style sheet to set the <li> content in the <footer> section inline.

Save and refresh all of your files. Why is it considered a good practice to add some sort of navigation bar to the bottom of webpages?

3. Styling the Dog Hall of Fame Webpages

Research and Collaboration

Part 1: In Chapter 3, you added content to the Dog Hall of Fame webpages. In this exercise, you will update those pages with an external style sheet that includes the following updates: (*Note:* Your instructor may want you to use the Data Files for Students provided for this exercise instead.)

1. Create an external style sheet with the name `dogstyles04.css` and save it in the `styles` folder within the your_turn_3 folder.

2. Add your name and the current date as a comment to the first line of the dogstyles04.css file.

3. Open the files you created for the Dog Hall of Fame in Chapter 3 in your HTML editor and float the images that do not span the page to the left or right by adding the attribute of `class="float-right"` or `class="float-left"` to the <img> tag and the corresponding `.float-right {float:right;}` or `.float-left {float:left;}` rules to the external style sheet. Make your decision on whether the image should float left or right based on what looks best on the page.

4. Add a 2% left and bottom margin style to the `.float-right` selector using the following declaration:

```
margin: 0 0 2% 2%;
```

Add a 2% right and bottom margin style to the `.float-left` selector using the following declaration:

```
margin: 0 2% 2% 0;
```

5. Add a tag to the <head> section of each page in the website to link the external style sheet to the dogfame04.html page as follows:

```
<link rel="stylesheet" href="styles/dogstyles04.css">
```

Save both the CSS and HTML files, and open the dogfame04.html file in your browser to make sure the style sheet is linked and the image is floating properly.

6. After viewing your pages, determine appropriate places for the float to be cleared. (For example, you probably want to clear the float when the new headings of "Working Dog" and "Companion Dog" are introduced.) Add a `class="clear-float"` to those tags in the HTML document and a corresponding `.clear-float { clear: both; }` rule to the CSS file.

7. Constrain the content to take 70% of the width of the page by inserting `<div id="page-wrapper">` after the opening <body> tag and closing the div with `</div> <!--close page-wrapper-->` before the closing </body> tag on each page.

   Then add a corresponding rule to set the page-wrapper content to 70% and centered in the page as follows:

```
#page-wrapper { width: 70%;
  margin: 0 auto; /* 0 top and bottom, auto left and right */
  }
```

8. Save and refresh your files.

9. Have each team member finish the style sheet using their own style decisions. Include styles for these elements:

   - Font color and font face for the body
   - Background color for the main content
   - Any other styles you deem important or appropriate to best display the content on the pages

   Use comments in your CSS file to document these styles.

10. Validate and correct your HTML and CSS files, and submit your assignment in the format specified by your instructor.

Part 2: ✳ As a group, share and compare how each of you styled the webpages. Discuss which features of each style sheet you liked the best. Together, build a final external style sheet that includes the best features from each member of your team. Note the features you chose from each member.

Appendix A
HTML Quick Reference

Common HTML Elements

HTML uses tags such as <h1> and <p> to structure content into headings, paragraphs, lists, hypertext links, and so on. Many HTML tags have attributes that further structure and describe the content of the element. For example, the height and width attributes in the <img> tag describe the size of the image.

The W3C continually updates the HTML specifications by adding, deleting, and replacing HTML tags and attributes. Table A–1 lists HTML tags and their associated attributes. The default value for each attribute is indicated by bold text in the Description column. The ⑤ icon indicates tags or attributes that are new with HTML5.

Global attributes can be used with most HTML tags. Table A–2 lists global attributes for HTML, including those new to HTML5.

As a web developer, you will most likely inherit a website developed by someone else. Carefully view the code to find **deprecated elements**, elements that are no longer supported in HTML5. Table A–3 lists deprecated elements. Attribute values in italic are value placeholders.

For a comprehensive list of HTML tags and attributes, more thorough descriptions, examples of HTML tags, and coding standards, visit the W3C website at w3.org.

Table A–1 Common HTML Elements and Attributes

New to HTML5	HTML Tags	Common Attributes	Values	Description
	<!DOCTYPE>	None		Indicates the version of HTML used
	<!-- Comments here -->	None		Inserts comments that are ignored by browsers
	<a> ... </a>	Global attributes		Anchor; creates a hyperlink or fragment identifier
⑤		download	*filename*	Sets the target to be downloaded
		href	*URL*	Hyperlink reference that specifies the target URL
		hreflang	*language_code*	Specifies the language of the linked document
⑤		media	*media_query*	Specifies the media or device the target URL is optimized for
		id	*text*	Specifies an id for enclosed text, allowing it to be the target of a hyperlink

HTML5 icon courtesy of W3.org

Table A–1 Common HTML Elements and Attributes *(continued)*

New to HTML5	HTML Tags	Common Attributes	Values	Description
		rel	alternate author bookmark help license next nofollow noreferrer prefetch prev search tag	Indicates the relationship from the current page to the target
		target	_blank _self _parent _top *framename*	Defines the name of the window or frame in which the linked resource will appear
		type	*media_type*	Specifies the media type of the target URL
	<abbr> …. </abbr>	Global attributes		Specifies an abbreviation or acronym
	<address> … </address>	Global attributes		Used for information such as author name, email address, or street address; enclosed text appears italicized and indented in some browsers
	<area> … </area>	Global attributes		Creates a hotspot (an area that can be tapped or clicked) on a client-side image map
		alt	*text*	Specifies alternate text for the area
		coords	*coordinates*	Specifies the coordinates that define the edges of the hotspot; a comma-delimited list of values
⑤		download	*filename*	Sets the target to be downloaded
		href	*URL*	Hyperlink reference that specifies the target URL
⑤		hreflang	*language_code*	Specifies the language of the target URL
⑤		media	*media query*	Specifies the media or device the target URL is optimized for
		rel	alternate author bookmark help license next nofollow noreferrer prefetch prev search tag	Specifies the relationship between the current page and the target URL

Table A–1 Common HTML Elements and Attributes *(continued)*

New to HTML5	HTML Tags	Common Attributes	Values	Description
		shape	default rect circle poly	Identifies the shape of the area
		target	_blank _self _parent _top *framename*	Defines the name of the window or frame in which the linked resource will appear
5		type	*media_type*	Specifies the media type of the target URL
5	\<article\> ... \</article\>	Global attributes		Defines an article
5	\<aside\> ... \</aside\>	Global attributes		Defines content aside from the main page content
5	\<audio\> ... \</audio\>			Defines sound content
		autoplay	autoplay	Specifies that the audio should start playing as soon as it is ready
		controls	controls	Specifies that playback controls should be displayed
		loop	loop	Specifies that the audio should start over when it is finished
		muted	muted	Specifies that the audio output should be muted
		preload	auto metadata none	Specifies whether the audio should be loaded when the page loads
		src	*URL*	Specifies the URL of the audio to play
	\<b\> ... \</b\>	Global attributes		Specifies text to appear in bold However, W3C recommends using CSS to bold text rather than using the \<b\> element
	\<base\>	Global attributes		Identifies the base in all relative URLs in the document Empty tag
		href	*URL*	Specifies the absolute URL used to resolve all relative URLs in the document
		target	_blank _self _parent _top *framename*	Defines the name for the default window (or frame*) in which the hyperlinked pages are displayed
	\<blockquote\> ... \</blockquote\>	Global attributes		Sets enclosed text to appear as a quotation, indented on the right and left
		cite	*URL*	Specifies the source of the quotation
	\<body\> ... \</body\>	Global attributes		Defines the start and end of the webpage content

Table A–1 Common HTML Elements and Attributes (*continued*)

New to HTML5	HTML Tags	Common Attributes	Values	Description
	` `	Global attributes		Inserts a line break Empty tag
5	`<canvas> ... </canvas>`	Global attributes		Defines graphics
		height	*pixels*	Specifies the height of the canvas
		width	*pixels*	Specifies the width of the canvas
	`<caption> ... </caption>`	Global attributes		Creates a caption for a table
	`<cite> ... </cite>`	Global attributes		Indicates that the enclosed text is a citation; text is usually displayed in italics
	`<code> ... </code>`	Global attributes		Indicates that the enclosed text is a code sample from a program; text is usually displayed in fixed-width font such as Courier
	`<col> ... </col>`	Global attributes		Organizes columns in a table into column groups to share attribute values
		span	*number*	Sets the number of columns that span the `<col>` element
	`<colgroup> ... </colgroup>`	Global attributes		Encloses a group of `<col>` tags and groups the columns to set properties
		span	*number*	Sets the number of columns the `<col>` element spans
5	`<datalist> ... </datalist>`	Global attributes		Defines a drop-down list
	`<dd> ... </dd>`	Global attributes		Indicates that the enclosed text is a definition in the definition list
5	`<details> ... </details>`	Global attributes		Defines details of an element
		open	open	Specifies that the details should be visible (open) to the user
5	`<dialog> .... </dialog>`	Global attributes		Specifies a dialog box
		open	open	Specifies that the dialog element is active and that the user can interact with it
	`<div> ... </div>`	Global attributes		Defines a block-level structure or division in the HTML document
	`<dl> ... </dl>`	Global attributes		Creates a definition list
	`<dt> ... </dt>`	Global attributes		Indicates that the enclosed text is a term in the definition list
	`<em> ... </em>`	Global attributes		Indicates that the enclosed text should be emphasized; usually appears in italics
5	`<embed> ... </embed>`	Global attributes		Defines external interactive content or plug-in
		height	*pixels*	Specifies the height of the embedded content
		src	*URL*	Specifies the URL of the embedded content

Table A–1 Common HTML Elements and Attributes (continued)

New to HTML5	HTML Tags	Common Attributes	Values	Description
		type	media_type	Specifies the media type of the embedded content
		width	pixels	Specifies the width of the embedded content
	<fieldset> ... </fieldset>	Global attributes		Groups related form controls and labels
		disabled	disabled	Specifies that a fieldset should be disabled
		form	form_id	Specifies one or more forms that a fieldset belongs to
		name	text	Specifies the name of the fieldset
5	<figcaption> ... </figcaption>	Global attributes		Defines the caption of a figure element
5	<figure> ... </figure>	Global attributes		Defines a group of media content and its caption
5	<footer> ... </footer>	Global attributes		Defines a footer for a section or page
	<form> ... </form>	Global attributes		Marks the start and end of a webpage form
		action	URL	Specifies the URL of the application that will process the form; required attribute
5		autocomplete	on off	Specifies whether the form should have autocomplete enabled
		enctype	encoding	Specifies how the form element values will be encoded
		method	get post	Specifies the method used to pass form parameters (data) to the server
		name= "form_name"		Specifies the name for a form
5		novalidate	novalidate	Indicates the form should not be validated when submitted
		target	_blank _self _parent _top framename	Specifies the frame or window that displays the form's results
	<head> ... </head>	Global attributes		Delimits the start and end of the HTML document's head
5	<header> ... </header>	Global attributes		Defines a header for a section or page
5	<hgroup> ... </hgroup>	Global attributes		Defines information about a section in a document
	<hn> ... </hn>	Global attributes		Defines a header level n, ranging from the largest (h1) to the smallest (h6)
	<hr>	Global attributes		Inserts a horizontal rule
	<html> ... </html>	Global attributes		Indicates the start and the end of the HTML document
5		manifest	URL	Specifies the URL of the document's cache manifest

Table A–1 Common HTML Elements and Attributes (continued)

New to HTML5	HTML Tags	Common Attributes	Values	Description
	<i> ... </i>	Global attributes		Sets enclosed text to appear in italics; W3C recommends using CSS to apply italic to text rather than using the <i> element
	<iframe> ... </iframe>	Global attributes		Creates an inline frame, also called a floating frame or subwindow, within an HTML document
		height	*pixels*	Sets the frame height to a value in pixels
		name	*text*	Specifies the name of the iframe
5		sandbox	allow-option	Specifies restrictions to the iframe content
5		seamless	seamless	Specifies that the iframe should be seamlessly integrated
		src	*URL*	Defines the URL of the source document displayed in the frame
5		srcdoc	*HTML_code*	Specifies the HTML code of the source document
		width	*pixels*	Sets the frame width to a value in pixels
	<img> ... </img>	Global attributes		Inserts an image into the current webpage
		alt	*text*	Provides a text description of an image if the browser cannot display the image; should always be used
		height	*pixels*	Sets the height of the image to a value in pixels (not percentages); should always be used
		src	*URL*	Specifies the URL of the image to be displayed; required
		usemap	*#mapname*	Specifies the map of coordinates and links that defines the href within this image
		width	*pixels*	Sets the width of the image to a value in pixels (not percentages); should always be used
	<input> ... </input>	Global attributes		Defines controls used in forms
		alt	*text*	Provides a short description of the control or image button
5		autocomplete	on off	Specifies whether the input field should display autocompletion options when a user starts to type in the field
5		autofocus	autofocus	Specifies that the input field should have focus on page load
		checked	checked	Sets option buttons and check boxes to the checked state
		disabled	disabled	Disables the control
5		form	*form_id*	Specifies one or more forms the input element belongs to

Table A–1 Common HTML Elements and Attributes *(continued)*

New to HTML5	HTML Tags	Common Attributes	Values	Description
5		formaction	*URL*	Overrides the form's action attribute; defines where to send the data when the form is submitted (for type="submit" and type="image")
5		formenctype	*encoding*	Overrides the form's enctype attribute; defines how form data should be encoded before sending it to the server (for type="submit" and type="image")
5		formmethod	get post	Overrides the form's method attribute; defines the HTTP method for sending data to the action URL (for type="submit" and type="image")
5		formnovalidate	formnovalidate	Overrides the form's novalidate attribute; defines that the input element should not be validated when submitted
		formtarget	_blank _self _parent _top *framename*	Overrides the form's target attribute; defines the target window to use when the form is submitted (for type="submit" and type="image")
5		height	*pixels*	Sets the height of an input element (for type="image")
5		list	*datalist_id*	Refers to a datalist that contains predefined options for the input element
5		max	*number* *date*	Specifies a maximum value for an input field
		maxlength	*number*	Sets a value for the maximum number of characters allowed as input for a text or password control
		multiple	*multiple*	Allows the user to enter more than one value
		name	*text*	Assigns a name to the control
5		pattern	*regexp*	Specifies a pattern or format for the input field's value
5		placeholder	*text*	Specifies a hint to help users fill out the input field
		readonly	readonly	Prevents changes to the control
5		required	required	Indicates that the input field's value is required in order to submit the form
		size	*number*	Sets the initial size of the control to a value in characters
5		step	*number*	Specifies the legal number of intervals for the input field
		src	*URL*	Identifies the location of the image if the control is set to an image
		type	*type*	Defines the type of control
		value	*value*	Sets the initial value of the control

Table A–1 Common HTML Elements and Attributes *(continued)*

New to HTML5	HTML Tags	Common Attributes	Values	Description
	\<ins\> ... \</ins\>	Global attributes		Identifies and displays text as having been inserted in the document in relation to a previous version
		cite	*URL*	Specifies the URL of a document that has more information on the inserted text
		datetime	*datetime*	Indicates the date and time of a change
	\<kbd\> ... \</kbd\>	Global attributes		Displays enclosed text as keyboard-like input
5	\<keygen\> ... \</keygen\>	Global attributes		Defines a generated key in a form
		autofocus	autofocus	Sets the focus on the input field on page load
		challenge	challenge	Specifies that the value of the keygen is set to be challenged when submitted
		disabled	disabled	Disables the keygen field
		form	*form_id*	Defines one or more forms the input field belongs to
		keytype	rsa dsa ec	Specifies the security algorithm of the key (for example, rsa generates an RSA key)
		name	*text*	Defines a unique name for the input element; the name attribute is used to collect the field's value when submitted
	\<label\> ... \</label\>	Global attributes		Creates a label for a form control
		for	*element_id*	Indicates the name or ID of the element to which the label is applied
		form	*form_id*	Specifies one or more forms the label field belongs to
	\<legend\> ... \</legend\>	Global attributes		Assigns a caption to a fieldset element, as defined by the \<fieldset\> tags
	\<li\> ... \</li\>	Global attributes		Defines the enclosed text as a list item in a list
		value	*value*	Inserts or restarts counting with value
	\<link\>	Global attributes		Establishes a link between the HTML document and another document, such as an external style sheet
		href	*URL*	Defines the URL of the linked document
		name	*text*	Names the current anchor so that it can be the destination for other links
		rel	*relationship*	Indicates the relationship from the current page to the target
5		sizes	any *heightxwidth*	Specifies sizes (height and width) of the linked resource
		type	*media_type*	Indicates the data or media type of the linked document
5	\<main\> ... \</main\>	Global attributes		Specifies the main content area of the page

Table A–1 Common HTML Elements and Attributes *(continued)*

New to HTML5	HTML Tags	Common Attributes	Values	Description
	`<map> ... </map>`	Global attributes		Specifies a client-side image map; must enclose `<area>` tags
		name	*text*	Assigns a name to the image map
5	`<mark> ... </mark>`	Global attributes		Defines marked text
	`<meta>`			Provides additional data (metadata) about an HTML document Empty tag
5		charset	*character_set*	Specifies the character encoding for the HTML document
		content	*text*	Specifies the value for the `<meta>` information; required
		http-equiv	*content-type* *default-style* *refresh*	Specifies the HTTP-equivalent name for metadata; tells the server to include that name and content in the HTTP header when the HTML document is sent to the client
		name	*text*	Assigns a name to metadata
5	`<meter> ... </meter>`	Global attributes		Defines measurement within a predefined range
		form	*form_id*	Specifies which form this meter belongs to
		high	*number*	Specifies at which point the measurement's value is considered a high value
		low	*number*	Specifies at which point the measurement's value is considered a low value
		max	*number*	Specifies the maximum value; default value is 1.0
		min	*number*	Specifies the minimum value; default value is 0
		optimum	*number*	Specifies which measurement's value is the best value
		value	*number*	Required; specifies the measurement's current or "measured" value
5	`<nav> ... </nav>`	Global attributes		Defines area for navigation links
	`<object> ... </object>`	Global attributes		Includes an external object in the HTML document such as an image, a Java applet, or other external object
		data	*URL*	Identifies the location of the object's data
5		form	*form_id*	Specifies one or more forms the object belongs to
		height	*pixels*	Sets the height of the object to a value in pixels
		name	*text*	Assigns a control name to the object for use in forms
		type	*media_type*	Specifies the content or media type of the object

Table A–1 Common HTML Elements and Attributes *(continued)*

New to HTML5	HTML Tags	Common Attributes	Values	Description
		usemap	#*mapname*	Associates an image map as defined by the <map> element
		width	*pixels*	Sets the width of the object to a value in pixels
	<ol> ... </ol>	Global attributes		Defines an ordered list that contains numbered list item elements (<li>)
5		reversed	reversed	Specifies that the list order should be descending
		start	*start*	Specifies the start value of an ordered list
		type	*option*	Sets or resets the numbering format for the list
5	<optgroup> ... </optgroup>	Global attributes		Defines an option group
		disabled	*disabled*	Specifies that an option group should be disabled
		label	*text*	Specifies a label for the option group
	<option> ... </option>	Global attributes		Defines individual options in a selection list, as defined by the <select> element
		disabled	disabled	Disables the option items
		label	*text*	Provides a shorter label for the option than that specified in its content
		selected	selected	Sets the option to be the default or the selected option in a list
		value	*text*	Sets a value returned to the server when the user selects the option
5	<output> ... </output>	Global attributes		Defines some types of output
		for	*element_id*	Specifies one or more elements the output field relates to
		form	*form_id*	Specifies one or more forms the output field belongs to
		name	*text*	Specifies a name for the object (to use when a form is submitted)
	<p> ... </p>	Global attributes		Delimits a paragraph; automatically inserts a blank line between text
	<param> ... </param>	Global attributes		Passes a parameter to an object or applet, as defined by the <object>
		name	*text*	Defines the name of the parameter required by an object
		value	*value*	Sets the value of the parameter
	<pre> ... </pre>	Global attributes		Preserves the original format of the enclosed text; keeps line breaks and spacing the same as the original
5	<progress> ... </progress>	Global attributes		Defines progress of a task of any kind
		max	*number*	Defines the value of completion

Table A–1 Common HTML Elements and Attributes *(continued)*

New to HTML5	HTML Tags	Common Attributes	Values	Description
		value	*number*	Defines the current value of the progress
	\<q\> ... \</q\>	Global attributes		Sets enclosed text as a short quotation
		cite	*URL*	Specifies the source URL of the quotation
5	\<rp\> ... \</rp\>	Global attributes		Used in ruby annotations to define what to show if a browser does not support the ruby element
5	\<rt\> ... \</rt\>	Global attributes		Defines explanation to ruby annotations
5	\<ruby\> ... \</ruby\>	Global attributes		Defines ruby annotations, which are used for East Asian typography
	\<s\> ... \</s\>	Global attributes		Defines text that is no longer correct, accurate, or relevant
	\<samp\> ... \</samp\>	Global attributes		Sets enclosed text to appear as sample output from a computer program or script; usually appears in a monospace font
	\<script\> ... \</script\>	Global attributes		Inserts a client-side script into an HTML document
5		async	async	Defines whether the script should be executed asynchronously
		charset	*charset*	Specifies the character encoding used in an external script file
		defer	defer	Indicates that the browser should defer executing the script
		src	*URL*	Identifies the location of an external script
		type	*media_type*	Specifies the media type of the script
5	\<section\> ... \</section\>	Global attributes		Defines a section
	\<select\> ... \</select\>	Global attributes		Defines a form control to create a multiple-choice menu or scrolling list; encloses a set of \<option\> tags to define one or more options
5		autofocus	autofocus	Sets the focus on the select field on page load
		disabled	disabled	Disables the selection list
		form	*form_id*	Defines one or more forms the select field belongs to
		multiple	multiple	Sets the list to allow multiple selections
		name	*text*	Assigns a name to the selection list
		size	*number*	Sets the number of visible options in the list
	\<small\> ... \</small\>	Global attributes		Sets enclosed text to appear in a smaller typeface
5	\<source\> ... \</source\>	Global attributes		Defines media resources
		media	*media_query* all	Specifies the media or device the media resource is optimized for; default value: all

Table A–1 Common HTML Elements and Attributes *(continued)*

New to HTML5	HTML Tags	Common Attributes	Values	Description
		src	*URL*	Specifies the URL of the media
		type	*media_type*	Specifies the media type of the media resource
	`<span>` ... `</span>`	Global attributes		Creates a user-defined container to add inline structure to the HTML document
	`<strong>` ... `</strong>`	Global attributes		Sets enclosed text to appear with strong emphasis; usually displayed as bold text W3C recommends using CSS instead of the `<strong>` element
	`<style>` ... `</style>`	Global attributes		Encloses embedded style sheet rules for use in the HTML document
		media	*media_query*	Identifies the intended medium of the style
5		scoped	*scoped*	Indicates the styles should only apply to this element's parent element and its child elements
		type	text/css	Specifies the media type of the style sheet
	`<sub>` ... `</sub>`	Global attributes		Sets enclosed text to appear in subscript
5	`<summary>` ... `</summary>`	Global attributes		Defines the header of a "detail" element
	`<sup>` ... `</sup>`	Global attributes		Sets enclosed text to appear in superscript
	`<table>` ... `</table>`	Global attributes		Marks the start and end of a data table
		sortable	sortable	Specifies that the table can be sorted
	`<tbody>` ... `</tbody>`	Global attributes		Defines a group of rows in a table body
	`<td>` ... `</td>`	Global attributes		Defines a data cell in a table; contents are left-aligned and normal text by default
		colspan	*number*	Defines the number of adjacent columns spanned by the cell
		headers	*header_id*	Defines the list of header cells for the current cell
		rowspan	*number*	Defines the number of adjacent rows spanned by the cell
	`<textarea>` ... `</textarea>`	Global attributes		Creates a multiline text input area within a form
5		autofocus	autofocus	Specifies that the text area field should have focus on page load
		cols	*number*	Defines the number of columns in the text input area
		disabled	disabled	Disables the element
5		form	*form_id*	Specifies one or more forms the text area belongs to
5		maxlength	*number*	Specifies the maximum number of characters allowed in the text area
		name	*text*	Assigns a name to the text area

Table A–1 Common HTML Elements and Attributes *(continued)*

New to HTML5	HTML Tags	Common Attributes	Values	Description
5		placeholder	*text*	Specifies a hint to help users fill out the input field
		readonly	readonly	Prevents the user from editing content in the text area
5		required	*required*	Indicates that the input field's value is required in order to submit the form
		rows	*number*	Defines the number of rows in the text input area
5		wrap	hard soft	Specifies how the text in the text area is wrapped, and if it should be wrapped when submitted in a form
	\<tfoot\> ... \</tfoot\>	Global attributes		Identifies and groups rows into a table footer
	\<th\> ... \</th\>	Global attributes		Defines a table header cell; contents are bold and center-aligned by default
		abbr	*text*	Specifies an abbreviated version of the content in a header cell
		colspan	*number*	Defines the number of adjacent columns spanned by the cell
5		headers	*header_id*	Specifies one or more header cells a cell is related to
		rowspan	*number*	Defines the number of adjacent rows spanned by the cell
		scope	col colgroup row rowgroup	Specifies whether a header cell is a header for a column, row, or group of columns or rows
	\<thead\> ... \</thead\>	Global attributes		Identifies and groups rows into a table header
5	\<time\> ... \</time\>	Global attributes		Defines a date or time
		datetime	*datetime*	Specifies the date or time for the \<time\> element; this attribute is used if no date or time is specified in the element's content
	\<title\> ... \</title\>	Global attributes		Defines the title for the HTML document; should always be used
	\<tr\> ... \</tr\>	Global attributes		Defines a row of cells within a table
	\<ul\> ... \</ul\>	Global attributes		Defines an unordered list that contains bulleted list item elements (\<li\>)
	\<var\> ... \</var\>	Global attributes		Indicates the enclosed text is a variable's name; used to mark up variables or program arguments
5	\<video\> ... \</video\>	Global attributes		Defines a video
		autoplay	autoplay	Sets the video to start playing as soon as it is ready
		controls	controls	Displays controls such as a play button
		height	*pixels*	Sets the height of the video player in pixels

Table A–1 Common HTML Elements and Attributes *(continued)*

New to HTML5	HTML Tags	Common Attributes	Values	Description
		loop	loop	Starts playing the video every time it is finished
		muted	muted	Specifies the default state of the audio; currently, only "muted" is allowed
		poster	*URL*	Specifies the URL of an image representing the video
		preload	auto metadata none	Specifies whether the video should be loaded when the page loads
		src	*URL*	Provides the URL of the video to play
		width	*pixels*	Sets the width of the video player in pixels
5	\<wbr\> ... \</wbr\>	Global attributes		Defines a possible line break

Table A–2 Global Attributes

New to HTML5	Attribute	Values	Example	Description
	accesskey	*character*	accesskey="s"	Specifies a shortcut key to access an element
	class	*classname*	class="intro"	Refers to a class specified in a style sheet
5	contenteditable	true false inherit	contenteditable= "false"	Specifies whether a user can edit the content of an element
5	contextmenu	*menu_id*	contextmenu= "mymenu"	Specifies a context menu for an element; the value must be the id of a \<menu\> element
	dir	ltr rtl auto	dir="rtl"	Specifies the text direction for the content in an element
5	draggable	true false auto	draggable="true"	Specifies whether a user is allowed to drag an element
5	dropzone	copy move link	dropzone="move"	Specifies what happens when dragged items/data are dropped in the element
5	hidden	hidden	hidden="hidden"	Specifies that an element should be hidden
	id	*id*	id="hoursOpen"	Specifies a unique id for an element
	lang	*language_code*	lang="en"	Specifies the language of the element's content
5	spellcheck	true false	spellcheck="false"	Specifies if the element must have its spelling and grammar checked
	style	*style_definitions*	style="color: red;"	Specifies an inline style for an element
	tabindex	*number*	tabindex="2"	Specifies the tab order of an element
	title	*text*	title="Product Information"	Specifies extra information about an element
5	translate	yes no	translate="no"	Specifies whether content should be translated

Table A–3 Deprecated Elements

Element	Replace with
<acronym>	<abbr>
<applet>	<object>
<basefront>	CSS style
<big>	CSS style
<center>	CSS style
<dir>	<ul>
<font>	CSS style
<frame>	no replacement
<frameset>	no replacement
<noframes>	no replacement
<s>	CSS style
<strike>	CSS style
<tt>	CSS style
<u>	CSS style
<xmp>	<pre>

Appendix B
CSS Quick Reference

This appendix provides a brief review of Cascading Style Sheets (CSS) concepts and terminology, and lists CSS level 1, 2, and 3 properties and values. CSS3 uses a modularized approach to style sheets, which allows CSS to be updated in a more timely and flexible manner. Many of the new properties are not supported by all modern browsers as of yet. Like HTML5, CSS3 is a moving target. Browsers adapt new properties on an ongoing basis and will continue to do so.

For a more comprehensive list of CSS properties and values, visit the World Wide Web Consortium at www.w3.org. In addition to an abundance of information about CSS levels 1 and 2, the W3C site also has extensive information about CSS3, from its history to its use with browsers today. The website also includes many online tutorials for learning CSS levels 1 and 2 as well as CSS3.

CSS Properties

Table B–1 shows units of measurement for web development. Tables B–2 through B–16 show the property names, descriptions, and valid values for various categories of CSS properties. Values listed in bold are the defaults.

Table B–1 Units of Measurement

Property Name	Description	Values
color	Keyword or a numerical hexadecimal, RGB, RGBA, HSL, or HSLA color specification	[keyword] [#rrggbb] [rgb(r,g,b)]
length	Indicates both relative (em, ex, px) and absolute (in, cm, mm, pt, pc) lengths	em — relative to size of capital M of browser default font ex — relative to small x of browser default font px — represents 1 pixel, smallest unit of measure in — 1 inch cm — 1 centimeter mm — 1 millimeter pt — 1/72 of an inch pc — 1/12 of an inch
percentage	Values are always relative to another value	percentage of width or height of parent element; if only one value is given, the second is set to "auto"

Table B–2 Animation Properties

Property Name	Description	Values	CSS
@keyframes	Specifies the animation	[animationname] [keyframes-selector] [css-styles]	3
animation	Shorthand property for all the other animation properties, except the animation-play-state property		3
animation-delay	Specifies when the animation starts	[time] initial inherit	3
animation-direction	Specifies whether the animation should play in reverse on alternate cycles	**normal** alternate	3
animation-duration	Specifies how many seconds or milliseconds an animation takes to complete one cycle	[time]	3
animation-fill-mode	Specifies values applied by the animation separate from the time it is executing	none forwards backwards both initial inherit	3
animation-iteration-count	Specifies the number of times an animation should be played	[n] infinite	3
animation-name	Specifies a name for the @keyframes animation	[keyframename] **none**	3
animation-play-state	Specifies whether the animation is running or paused	paused **running**	3
animation-timing-function	Specifies the speed curve of the animation	**ease** ease-in ease-out ease-in-out cubic-bezier linear	3

Table B–3 Background Properties

Property Name	Description	Values	CSS
background	Shorthand property for setting the individual background properties		1
background-attachment	Sets the background image to be fixed or to scroll with the page	scroll fixed	1
background-clip	Specifies the painting area of the background	border-box content-box padding-box	3
background-color	Sets the background color of an element	transparent [color]	1
background-image	Sets an image as the background	**none** [URL]	1
background-origin	Specifies the positioning area of the background images	border-box content-box padding-box	3

Table B–3 Background Properties *(continued)*

Property Name	Description	Values	CSS
background-position	Sets the starting position of a background image	[length] [percentage] bottom center left right top	1
background-repeat	Sets whether or how a background image is repeated	**repeat** repeat-x repeat-y no-repeat inherit	1
background-size	Specifies the size of the background images	auto contain cover length percentage	3

Table B–4 Border Properties

Property Name	Description	Values	CSS
border	Sets all the border properties in one declaration		1
border-color	Shorthand property for setting the color of the four borders in one declaration; can have from one to four colors	[color] transparent	1
border-top-color border-right-color border-bottom-color border-left-color	Sets the respective color of the top, right, bottom, and left borders individually	[color]	1
border-image	Shorthand property for setting all the border-image-*n* properties		3
border-image-outset	Specifies the amount by which the border image area extends beyond the border box	[length] [number]	3
border-image-repeat	Specifies whether the image-border should be repeated, rounded, or stretched	**stretch** repeat round	3
border-image-slice	Specifies the inward offsets of the image-border	[number] [percentage] fill	3
border-image-source	Specifies an image to be used as a border	**none** [image]	3
border-image-width	Specifies the widths of the image-border	[number] [percentage] auto	3
border-radius	Shorthand property for setting all the four border-*n*-radius properties		3
border-bottom-left-radius border-bottom-right-radius border-top-left-radius border-top-right-radius	Sets the shape of the border of the bottom-left, bottom-right, top-left, and top-right corners individually	[percentage] [length]	3

Table B–4 Border Properties *(continued)*

Property Name	Description	Values	CSS
border-style	Shorthand property for setting the style of the four borders in one declaration; can have from one to four styles	**none** dashed dotted double groove inset outset ridge solid	1
border-top-style border-right-style border-bottom-style border-left-style	Sets the respective style of the top, right, bottom, and left borders individually	**none** dashed dotted double groove inset outset ridge solid	1
border-width	Shorthand property for setting the width of the four borders in one declaration; can have from one to four values	**medium** [length] thick thin	1
border-top-width border-right-width border-bottom-width border-left-width	Sets the respective width of the top, right, bottom, and left borders individually	**medium** [length] thick thin	1

Table B–5 Basic Box Properties

Property Name	Description	Values	CSS
box-decoration-break	Sets the behavior of the background and border of an element at page-break, or at line-break for inline elements		3
box-shadow	Attaches one or more drop-shadows to the box	[h-shadow] [v-shadow] [blur] [spread] [color] inset none	3
overflow	Specifies what happens if content overflows into a box element's area	auto hidden scroll visible	2
overflow-x	Specifies whether to clip the left or right edges of the content, if it overflows the element's content area	**visible** hidden scroll auto no-display no-content	3
overflow-y	Specifies whether to clip the top or bottom edges of the content, if it overflows the element's content area	visible hidden scroll auto no-display no-content	3

Table B–6 Classification Properties

Property Name	Description	Values	CSS
display	Describes whether or how an element is displayed on the canvas, which may be on a printed page or a computer monitor, for example	block inline list-item none	1
white-space	Declares how white-space inside the element is handled: the 'normal' way (where white-space is collapsed), as pre (which behaves like the <pre> element in HTML) or as nowrap (where wrapping is done only through elements)	**normal** pre nowrap	1

Table B–7 Color Properties

Property Name	Description	Values	CSS
color	Sets the color of text	[value]	1
opacity	Sets the opacity level for an element	[value] inherit	3

Table B–8 Dimension Properties

Property Name	Description	Values	CSS
height	Sets the height of an element	**auto** [length] [percentage] inherit	1
max-height	Sets the maximum height of an element	**none** [length] [percentage] inherit	2
max-width	Sets the maximum width of an element	**none** [length] [percentage] inherit	2
min-height	Sets the minimum height of an element	[length] [percentage] inherit	2
min-width	Sets the minimum width of an element	[length] [percentage] inherit	2
width	Sets the width of an element	**auto** [length] [percentage] inherit	1

Table B–9 Flexible Box Properties

Property Name	Description	Values	CSS
align-content	Specifies alignment between lines inside flexible container when items do not use all available space	center flex-end flex-start space-around space-between stretch	3
align-items	Specifies alignment for items inside flexible container	baseline center flex-end flex-start stretch	3
align-self	Specifies alignment for specific elements inside flexible container	auto baseline center flex-end flex-start	3
flex	Specifies the length of an element, relative to the other elements	auto none	3
flex-basis	Specifies initial length of a flexible element	auto	3
flex-direction	Specifies direction of the flexible elements	column column-reverse row row-reverse	3
flex-flow	Shorthand property of flex-direction and flex-wrap properties		3
flex-grow	Specifies how much an element can grow relative to the other elements	[number]	3
flex-shrink	Specifies how much an element can shrink relative to the other elements	[number]	3
flex-wrap	Specifies whether flexible elements can wrap	nowrap wrap wrap-reverse	3
justify-content	Specifies the alignment between elements inside a flexible container when the elements do not use all available space	center flex-end flex-start space-around space-between	3
order	Sets the order of the flexible element, relative to the other elements	[number]	3

Table B–10 Font Properties

Property Name	Description	Values	CSS
font	Shorthand property for setting font properties		1
@font-face	Rule that allows websites to download and use fonts other than the "web-safe" fonts		3
font-family	Prioritized list of font-family names and/or generic family names for an element	[family-name] cursive fantasy monospace sans-serif serif	1

Table B–10 Font Properties *(continued)*

Property Name	Description	Values	CSS
font-size	Sets the size of a font	[length] [percentage] large larger **medium** small smaller x-large x-small xx-large xx-small inherit	1
font-size-adjust	Preserves the readability of text when font fallback occurs	[number] none inherit	3
font-stretch	Selects a normal, condensed, or expanded face from a font family		3
font-style	Sets the style of a font	**normal** italic oblique	1
font-variant	Displays text in a small-caps font or a normal font	**normal** small-caps	1
font-weight	Sets the weight of a font	**normal** bold bolder lighter	1

Table B–11 List Properties

Property Name	Description	Values	CSS
list-style	Shorthand property for setting list-style-image, list-style-position, and list-style-type in one declaration		1
list-style-image	Sets an image as the list-item marker	**none** [URL]	1
list-style-position	Indents or extends a list-item marker with respect to the item's content	**outside** inside	1
list-style-type	Sets the type of list-item marker	**disc** circle square decimal lower-alpha lower-roman upper-alpha upper-roman	1

Table B–12 Margin and Padding Properties

Property Name	Description	Values	CSS
margin	Shorthand property for setting margin properties		1
margin-top margin-right margin-bottom margin-left	Sets the top, right, bottom, and left margin of an element individually	[length] [percentage] auto inherit	1
padding	Shorthand property for setting padding properties in one declaration		1
padding-top padding-right padding-bottom padding-left	Sets the top, right, bottom, and left padding of an element individually	[length] [percentage] inherit	1

Table B–13 Positioning Properties

Property Name	Description	Values	CSS
bottom	Specifies the bottom position of a positioned element	**auto** [length] [percentage] inherit	2
clear	Specifies the sides of an element where other floating elements are not allowed	left right both **none** inherit	1
clip	Clips an absolutely positioned element	[shape] **auto** inherit	2
cursor	Specifies the type of cursor to display	[URL] auto crosshair default e-resize help move n-resize ne-resize nw-resize pointer progress s-resize se-resize sw-resize text w-resize wait inherit	2

Table B–13 Positioning Properties *(continued)*

Property Name	Description	Values	CSS
display	Specifies the type of box an element should generate	none block inline inline-block inline-table list-item run-in table table-caption table-cell table-column table-column-group table-footer-group table-header-group table-row table-row-group inherit	1
float	Specifies whether a box should float	left right **none** inherit	1
left	Specifies the left position of a positioned element	**auto** [length] [percentage] inherit	2
overflow	Specifies what happens if content overflows an element's box	**visible** hidden scroll auto inherit	2
position	Specifies the type of positioning method used for an element (static, relative, absolute, or fixed)	**static** absolute fixed relative inherit	2
right	Specifies the right position of a positioned element	**auto** [length] [percentage] inherit	2
top	Specifies the top position of a positioned element	auto [length] [percentage] inherit	2
visibility	Specifies whether an element is visible	visible hidden collapse inherit	2
z-index	Sets the stack order of a positioned element	auto [number] inherit	2

Table B–14 Table Properties

Property Name	Description	Values	CSS
border-collapse	Specifies whether table borders should be collapsed	collapse **separate** inherit	2
border-spacing	Specifies the distance between the borders of adjacent cells	[length] inherit	2
caption-side	Specifies the placement of a table caption	**top** bottom inherit	2
empty-cells	Specifies whether to display borders and background on empty cells in a table	hide **show** inherit	2
table-layout	Sets the layout algorithm to be used for a table	**auto** fixed inherit	2

Table B–15 Text Properties

Property Name	Description	Values	CSS
color	Sets the color of text	[color] inherit	1
direction	Specifies the text or writing direction	ltr rtl inherit	2
hanging-punctuation	Specifies whether a punctuation character may be placed outside the line box	none first last allow-end force-end	3
letter-spacing	Increases or decreases the space between characters	**normal** [length] inherit	1
line-height	Sets the line height	**normal** [length] [number] [percentage] inherit	1
punctuation-trim	Specifies whether a punctuation character should be trimmed	none start end allow-end adjacent	3
text-align	Specifies the horizontal alignment of text	left right center justify inherit	1
text-align-last	Describes how the last line of a block or a line right before a forced line break is aligned when text-align is "justify"		3
text-decoration	Adds decoration to text	**none** blink line-through overline underline inherit	1

Table B–15 Text Properties *(continued)*

Property Name	Description	Values	CSS
text-indent	Indents the first line of text in an element	[length] [percentage] inherit	1
text-justify	Specifies the justification method used when text-align is "justify"	auto interword interideograph intercluster distribute kashida none	3
text-overflow	Specifies what should happen when text overflows the containing element	clip ellipsis [string]	3
text-shadow	Adds shadow to text	[h-shadow] [v-shadow] [blur] [color]	3
text-transform	Controls text capitalization	**none** capitalize lowercase uppercase inherit	1
text-wrap	Specifies line breaking rules for text	normal none unrestricted suppress	3
vertical-align	Sets the vertical positioning of text	baseline [length] [percentage] bottom middle sub super text-bottom text-top top inherit	1
white-space	Specifies how white-space inside an element is handled	normal nowrap pre preline prewrap inherit	1
word-break	Specifies the line breaking rules for non-CJK scripts	normal break-all hyphenate	3
word-spacing	Increases or decreases the space between words	**normal** [length] inherit	1
word-wrap	Allows long, unbreakable words to be broken and wrap to the next line	normal break-word	3

Table B–16 Transition Properties

Property Name	Description	Values	CSS
transition	Shorthand property for setting the four transition properties		3
transition-delay	Specifies when the transition effect starts	[time]	3
transition-duration	Specifies how many seconds or milliseconds a transition effect takes to complete	[time]	3
transition-property	Specifies the name of the CSS property the transition effect is for	none **all** property	3
transition-timing-function	Specifies the speed curve of the transition effect	linear ease ease-in ease-in-out ease-out cubic-bezier	3

Appendix C
Color Reference Palette

Color Reference

Three hardware components help deliver color to a computer user: the processor, the video card, and the monitor. Because these components vary widely, the color quality that users see can vary. The software on a user's computer, specifically the web browser, also affects the way that color is displayed on a screen. It is very difficult, if not impossible, to plan for all possible color variations created by a web browser. In the past, web developers had to make sure that they used browser-safe colors. These browser-safe colors restricted the number of colors used on a webpage and minimized the impact of color variations. The trend for screens today is to display "true color," which means that any of 16 million colors can be displayed on the monitor. Few people use 8-bit monitors anymore, so you generally do not have to limit yourself to browser-safe colors.

A total of 216 browser-safe colors appear the same on different monitors, operating systems, and browsers — including Windows and Macintosh operating systems and Internet Explorer, Apple Safari, Google Chrome, and Mozilla Firefox browsers. When using color on your website, keep in mind that using only the 216 browser-safe colors can be very restrictive. On 8-bit monitors, only the browser-safe colors will be displayed. If you decide to use a non-browser-safe color, the browser will try to create the color by combining (a process called dithering) any number of the 216 acceptable colors. The resulting color could be slightly different from the color you had intended. Figure C–1 shows the original 216 browser-safe colors.

Figure C–1

000000	000033	000066	000099	0000CC	0000FF	003300	003333	003366	003399	0033CC	0033FF
006600	006633	006666	006699	0066CC	0066FF	009900	009933	009966	009999	0099CC	0099FF
00CC00	00CC33	00CC66	00CC99	00CCCC	00CCFF	00FF00	00FF33	00FF66	00FF99	00FFCC	00FFFF
330000	330033	330066	330099	3300CC	3300FF	333300	333333	333366	333399	3333CC	3333FF
336600	336633	336666	336699	3366CC	3366FF	339900	339933	339966	339999	3399CC	3399FF
33CC00	33CC33	33CC66	33CC99	33CCCC	33CCFF	33FF00	33FF33	33FF66	33FF99	33FFCC	33FFFF
660000	660033	660066	660099	6600CC	6600FF	663300	663333	663366	663399	6633CC	6633FF
666600	666633	666666	666699	6666CC	6666FF	669900	669933	669966	669999	6699CC	6699FF
66CC00	66CC33	66CC66	66CC99	66CCCC	66CCFF	66FF00	66FF33	66FF66	66FF99	66FFCC	66FFFF
990000	990033	990066	990099	9900CC	9900FF	993300	993333	993366	993399	9933CC	9933FF
996600	996633	996666	996699	9966CC	9966FF	999900	999933	999966	999999	9999CC	9999FF
99CC00	99CC33	99CC66	99CC99	99CCCC	99CCFF	99FF00	99FF33	99FF66	99FF99	99FFCC	99FFFF
CC0000	CC0033	CC0066	CC0099	CC00CC	CC00FF	CC3300	CC3333	CC3366	CC3399	CC33CC	CC33FF
CC6600	CC6633	CC6666	CC6699	CC66CC	CC66FF	CC9900	CC9933	CC9966	CC9999	CC99CC	CC99FF
CCCC00	CCCC33	CCCC66	CCCC99	CCCCCC	CCCCFF	CCFF00	CCFF33	CCFF66	CCFF99	CCFFCC	CCFFFF
FF0000	FF0033	FF0066	FF0099	FF00CC	FF00FF	FF3300	FF3333	FF3366	FF3399	FF33CC	FF33FF
FF6600	FF6633	FF6666	FF6699	FF66CC	FF66FF	FF9900	FF9933	FF9966	FF9999	FF99CC	FF99FF
FFCC00	FFCC33	FFCC66	FFCC99	FFCCCC	FFCCFF	FFFF00	FFFF33	FFFF66	FFFF99	FFFFCC	FFFFFF

© 2016 Cengage Learning

    With today's displays, you are not limited to these colors. To view additional color options, visit any of the following websites:

1. W3Schools: www.w3schools.com/tags/ref_colorpicker.asp
2. CSS Portal: www.cssportal.com/css3-color-names/
3. Color Picker: www.colorpicker.com/
4. HTML Color Codes: http://html-color-codes.info/

Appendix D
Accessibility Standards for Webpage Developers

Making the Web Accessible

According to the W3C, the goal of the web is to be accessible to all people, including those with a disability that limits their ability to perform computer tasks. The U.S. Congress passed the Rehabilitation Act in 1973, which prohibits discrimination for those with disabilities. In 1998, Congress amended this Act to reflect the latest changes in information technology. Section 508 requires that any electronic information developed, procured, maintained, or used by the federal government be accessible to people with disabilities. Disabilities that inhibit a person's ability to use the web fall into four main categories: visual, hearing, motor, and cognitive. This amendment has had a profound effect on how webpages are designed and developed.

The summary of Section 508 §1194.22 states, "The criteria for web-based technology and information are based on access guidelines developed by the Web Accessibility Initiative of the World Wide Web Consortium." The guidelines help to include everyone as a — potential user of your website, including those with disabilities. The Web Accessibility Initiative (WAI) develops guidelines and support materials for accessibility standards. These guidelines are known as the Web Content Accessibility Guidelines (WCAG) 2.0.

Section 508 Guidelines

Every federal government website must follow the Section 508 guidelines. Section 508 § 1194.22 refers to web-based intranet and internet information and applications and includes the following 16 rules.

- (a) A text equivalent for every non-text element shall be provided (e.g., via "alt," "longdesc," or in element content).
- (b) Equivalent alternatives for any multimedia presentation shall be synchronized with the presentation.
- (c) Web pages shall be designed so that all information conveyed with color is also available without color, for example from context or markup.
- (d) Documents shall be organized so they are readable without requiring an associated style sheet.
- (e) Redundant text links shall be provided for each active region of a server-side image map.
- (f) Client-side image maps shall be provided instead of server-side image maps except where the regions cannot be defined with an available geometric shape.
- (g) Row and column headers shall be identified for data tables.

(h) Markup shall be used to associate data cells and header cells for data tables that have two or more logical levels of row or column headers.

(i) Frames shall be titled with text that facilitates frame identification and navigation.

(j) Pages shall be designed to avoid causing the screen to flicker with a frequency greater than 2 Hz and lower than 55 Hz.

(k) A text-only page, with equivalent information or functionality, shall be provided to make a web site comply with the provisions of this part, when compliance cannot be accomplished in any other way. The content of the text-only page shall be updated whenever the primary page changes.

(l) When pages utilize scripting languages to display content, or to create interface elements, the information provided by the script shall be identified with functional text that can be read by assistive technology.

(m) When a web page requires that an applet, plug-in or other application be present on the client system to interpret page content, the page must provide a link to a plug-in or applet that complies with §1194.21(a) through (l).

(n) When electronic forms are designed to be completed on-line, the form shall allow people using assistive technology to access the information, field elements, and functionality required for completion and submission of the form, including all directions and cues.

(o) A method shall be provided that permits users to skip repetitive navigation links.

(p) When a timed response is required, the user shall be alerted and given sufficient time to indicate more time is required.

For more detailed information about these rules, please visit www.section508.gov.

Web Content Accessibility Guidelines

The WAI identifies 12 guidelines for web developers, known as Web Content Accessibility Guidelines (WCAG) 2.0. The WCAG specifies how to make web content more accessible to people with disabilities. **Web content** generally refers to the information in a web. Page or web application, including text, images, forms, and sounds. All web developers should review the information at the official website at w3.org/WAI/intro/wcag.php for complete information on these guidelines, and should apply the guidelines to their webpage development.

The 12 WCAG 2.0 guidelines are organized under four principles: perceivable, operable, understandable, and robust. Anyone who wants to use the web must have content that is:

Perceivable: Information and user interface components must be presentable to users in ways they can perceive. Users must be able to perceive the information being presented (it can't be invisible to all of their senses).

Operable: User interface components and navigation must be operable. Users must be able to operate the interface (the interface cannot require interaction that a user cannot perform).

Understandable: Information and the operation of the user interface must be understandable. Users must be able to understand the information as well as the operation of the user interface (the content or operation cannot be beyond their understanding).

Robust: Content must be robust enough that it can be interpreted reliably by a wide variety of user agents, including assistive technologies. Users must be able to access the content as technologies advance (as technologies and user agents evolve, the content should remain accessible).

If any of these are not true, users with disabilities will not be able to use the web.

For each guideline, there are testable success criteria, which are at three levels: A, AA, and AAA. In order for a web page to conform to WCAG 2.0, all of the following conformance requirements must be satisfied:

- **Level A:** For Level A conformance (the minimum level of conformance), the web page satisfies all the Level A Success Criteria, or a conforming alternate version is provided.

- **Level AA:** For Level AA conformance, the web page satisfies all the Level A and Level AA Success Criteria, or a Level AA conforming alternate version is provided.

- **Level AAA:** For Level AAA conformance, the web page satisfies all the Level A, Level AA, and Level AAA Success Criteria, or a Level AAA conforming alternate version is provided.

Table D–1 contains a summary of the WCAG 2.0 guidelines and the corresponding level of conformance.

Table D–1 WCAG 2.0 Guidelines

Item	Level
Principle 1: Perceivable — Information and user interface components must be presentable to users in ways they can perceive.	
Guideline 1.1 Text Alternatives: Provide text alternatives for any non-text content so that it can be changed into other forms people need, such as large print, braille, speech, symbols or simpler language.	
1.1.1 Nontext Content: All nontext content that is presented to the user has a text alternative that serves the equivalent purpose.	A
Guideline 1.2 Time Based Media: Provide alternatives for time-based media.	
1.2.1 Audio-only and Video-only (Prerecorded): An alternative for time-based media is provided that presents equivalent information for prerecorded audio-only or video-only content.	A
1.2.2 Captions (Prerecorded): Captions are provided for all prerecorded audio content in synchronized media, except when the media is a media alternative for text and is clearly labeled as such.	A
1.2.3 Audio Description or Media Alternative (Prerecorded): An alternative for time-based media or audio description of the prerecorded video content is provided for synchronized media, except when the media is a media alternative for text and is clearly labeled as such.	A
1.2.4 Captions (Live): Captions are provided for all live audio content in synchronized media.	AA
1.2.5 Audio Description (Prerecorded): Audio description is provided for all prerecorded video content in synchronized media.	AA
1.2.6 Sign Language (Prerecorded): Sign language interpretation is provided for all prerecorded audio content in synchronized media.	AAA
1.2.7 Extended Audio Description (Prerecorded): Where pauses in foreground audio are insufficient to allow audio descriptions to convey the sense of the video, extended audio description is provided for all prerecorded video content in synchronized media.	AAA

Table D–1 WCAG 2.0 Guidelines *(continued)*

Item	Level
1.2.8 Media Alternative (Prerecorded): An alternative for time-based media is provided for all prerecorded synchronized media and for all prerecorded video-only media.	AAA
1.2.9 Audio-only (Live): An alternative for time-based media that presents equivalent information for live audio-only content is provided.	AAA
Guideline 1.3 Adaptable: Create content that can be presented in different ways (for example simpler layout) without losing information or structure.	
1.3.1 Info and Relationships: Information, structure, and relationships conveyed through presentation can be programmatically determined or are available in text.	A
1.3.2 Meaningful Sequence: When the sequence in which content is presented affects its meaning, a correct reading sequence can be programmatically determined.	A
1.3.3 Sensory Characteristics: Instructions provided for understanding and operating content do not rely solely on sensory characteristics of components such as shape, size, visual location, orientation, or sound.	A
Guideline 1.4 Distinguishable: Make it easier for users to see and hear content including separating foreground from background.	
1.4.1 Use of Color: Color is not used as the only visual means of conveying information, indicating an action, prompting a response, or distinguishing a visual element.	A
1.4.2 Audio Control: If any audio on a web page plays automatically for more than 3 seconds, either a mechanism is available to pause or stop the audio, or a mechanism is available to control the audio volume independently from the overall system volume level.	A
1.4.3 Contrast (Minimum): The visual presentation of text and images of text has a contrast ratio of at least 4.5:1 (for specific exceptions, refer to w3.org/TR/WCAG).	AA
1.4.4 Resize text: Except for captions and images of text, text can be resized without assistive technology up to 200 percent without loss of content or functionality.	AA
1.4.5 Images of Text: If the technologies being used can achieve the visual presentation, text is used to convey information rather than images of (for specific exceptions, refer to w3.org/TR/WCAG).	AA
1.4.6 Contrast (Enhanced): The visual presentation of text and images of text has a contrast ratio of at least 7:1 (for specific exceptions, refer to w3.org/TR/WCAG).	AAA
1.4.7 Low or No Background Audio: For prerecorded audio-only content in which 1) the audio does not contain background sounds, 2) the background sounds can be turned off, or 3) the background sounds are at least 20 decibels lower than the foreground speech content.	AAA
1.4.8 Visual Presentation: For the visual presentation of blocks of text, a mechanism is available to manipulate the look of the page (e.g., background colors, text size) easily.	AAA
1.4.9 Images of Text (No Exception): Images of text are only used for pure decoration or where a particular presentation of text is essential to the information being conveyed.	AAA
Principle 2: Operable — User interface components and navigation must be operable.	
Guideline 2.1 Keyboard Accessible: Make all functionality available from the keyboard.	
2.1.1 Keyboard: All functionality of the content is operable through a keyboard interface without requiring specific timings for individual keystrokes, except where the underlying function requires input that depends on the path of the user's movement and not just the endpoints.	A
2.1.2 No Keyboard Trap: If keyboard focus can be moved to a component of the page using a keyboard interface, then focus can be moved away from that component using only a keyboard interface, and, if it requires more than unmodified arrow or tab keys or other standard exit methods, the user is advised of the method for moving focus away.	A
2.1.3 Keyboard (No Exception): All functionality of the content is operable through a keyboard interface without requiring specific timings for individual keystrokes.	AAA
Guideline 2.2 Enough Time: Provide users enough time to read and use content.	
2.2.1 Timing Adjustable: The user should be able to easily change each time limit that is set by the content.	A

Table D–1 WCAG 2.0 Guidelines *(continued)*

Item	Level
2.2.2 Pause, Stop, Hide: The user should be able to pause, stop, or hide moving, blinking, scrolling, or auto-updating information.	A
2.2.3 No Timing: Timing is not an essential part of the event or activity presented by the content, except for noninteractive synchronized media and real-time events.	AAA
2.2.4 Interruptions: Interruptions can be postponed or suppressed by the user, except interruptions involving an emergency.	AAA
2.2.5 Re-authenticating: When an authenticated session expires, the user can continue the activity without loss of data after re-authenticating.	AAA
Guideline 2.3 Seizures: Do not design content in a way that is known to cause seizures.	
2.3.1 Three Flashes or Below Threshold: web pages do not contain anything that flashes more than three times in any one second period, or the flash is below the general flash and red flash thresholds.	A
2.3.2 Three Flashes: web pages do not contain anything that flashes more than three times in any one second period.	AAA
Guideline 2.4 Navigable: Provide ways to help users navigate, find content, and determine where they are.	
2.4.1 Bypass Blocks: A mechanism is available to bypass blocks of content that are repeated on multiple web pages.	A
2.4.2 Page Titled: web pages have titles that describe topic or purpose.	A
2.4.3 Focus Order: If a web page can be navigated sequentially and the navigation sequences affect meaning or operation, focusable components receive focus in an order that preserves meaning and operability.	A
2.4.4 Link Purpose (In Context): The purpose of each link can be determined from the link text alone or from the link text together with its programmatically determined link context, except where the purpose of the link would be ambiguous to users in general.	A
2.4.5 Multiple Ways: More than one way is available to locate a web page within a set of web pages except where the web Page is the result of, or a step in, a process.	AA
2.4.6 Headings and Labels: Headings and labels describe topic or purpose.	AA
2.4.7 Focus Visible: Any keyboard operable user interface has a mode of operation where the keyboard focus indicator is visible.	AA
2.4.8 Location: Information about the user's location within a set of web pages is available.	AAA
2.4.9 Link Purpose (Link Only): A mechanism is available to allow the purpose of each link to be identified from link text alone, except where the purpose of the link would be ambiguous to users in general.	AAA
2.4.10 Section Headings: Section headings are used to organize the content.	AAA
Principle 3: Understandable—Information and the operation of user interface must be understandable.	
Guideline 3.1 Readable: Make text content readable and understandable.	
3.1.1 Language of Page: The default human language of each web page can be programmatically determined.	A
3.1.2 Language of Parts: The human language of each passage or phrase in the content can be programmatically determined except for proper names, technical terms, words of indeterminate language, and words or phrases that have become part of the vernacular of the immediately surrounding text.	AA
3.1.3 Unusual Words: A mechanism is available for identifying specific definitions of words or phrases used in an unusual or restricted way, including idioms and jargon.	AAA
3.1.4 Abbreviations: A mechanism for identifying the expanded form or meaning of abbreviations is available.	AAA

Table D–1 WCAG 2.0 Guidelines *(continued)*

Item	Level
3.1.5 Reading Level: When text requires reading ability more advanced than the lower secondary education level after removal of proper names and titles, supplemental content, or a version that does not require reading ability more advanced than the lower secondary education level, is available.	AAA
3.1.6 Pronunciation: A mechanism is available for identifying specific pronunciation of words where the meaning of the words, in context, is ambiguous without knowing the pronunciation.	AAA
Guideline 3.2 Predictable: Make web pages appear and operate in predictable ways.	
3.2.1 On Focus: When any component receives focus, it does not initiate a change of context.	A
3.2.2 On Input: Changing the setting of any user interface component does not automatically cause a change of context unless the user has been advised of the behavior before using the component.	A
3.2.3 Consistent Navigation: Navigational mechanisms that are repeated on multiple web pages within a set of web pages occur in the same relative order each time they are repeated, unless a change is initiated by the user.	AA
3.2.4 Consistent Identification: Components that have the same functionality within a set of web pages are identified consistently.	AA
3.2.5 Change on Request: Changes of context are initiated only by user request or a mechanism is available to turn off such changes.	AAA
Guideline 3.3 Input Assistance: Help users avoid and correct mistakes.	
3.3.1 Error Identification: If an input error is automatically detected, the item that is in error is identified and the error is described to the user in text.	A
3.3.2 Labels or Instructions: Labels or instructions are provided when content requires user input.	A
3.3.3 Error Suggestion: If an input error is automatically detected and suggestions for its correction are known, then the suggestions are provided to the user, unless it would jeopardize the security or purpose of the content.	AA
3.3.4 Error Prevention (Legal, Financial, Data): For web pages that cause legal commitments or financial transactions for the user to occur, that modify or delete user-controllable data in data storage systems, or that submit user test responses, a mechanism is available for reviewing, confirming, and correcting information before finalizing the submission.	AA
3.3.5 Help: Context-sensitive help is available.	AAA
3.3.6 Error Prevention (All): For web pages that require the user to submit information, a mechanism is available for reviewing, confirming, and correcting information before finalizing the submission.	AAA
Principle 4: Robust — Content must be robust enough that it can be interpreted reliably by a wide variety of user agents, including assistive technologies.	
Guideline 4.1 Compatible: Maximize compatibility with current and future user agents, including assistive technologies.	
4.1.1 Parsing: In content implemented using markup languages, elements have complete start and end tags, elements are nested according to their specifications, elements do not contain duplicate attributes, and any IDs are unique, except where the specifications allow these features.	A
4.1.2 Name, Role, Value: For all user interface components (including but not limited to: form elements, links, and components generated by scripts), the name and role can be programmatically determined; states, properties, and values that can be set by the user can be programmatically set; and notification of changes to these items is available to user agents, including assistive technologies.	A

Source of data: w3.org

Appendix E
Symbols and Characters Quick Reference

Using Symbols and Special Characters

At times you may want to insert a symbol such as an arrow or other symbol such as a copyright symbol — a character not found on most keyboards — on a webpage. These characters are called **character references** or **symbol entities** and are summarized in Tables E–1 through E–3.

The table references below are for English characters. If you need characters for other languages, visit the Unicode Consortium at unicode.org. The Unicode Consortium allows everyone around the world to use computers in their native language. You can visit their website to find characters for many languages. You can also search the web for many other Unicode character map resources.

Table E–1 Commonly Used Characters

Symbol	Character Reference	Description
&	&amp;	Ampersand
¦	&brvbar;	Broken vertical bar
¢	&cent;	Cent sign
©	&copy;	Copyright sign
¤	&curren;	Currency sign
†	&dagger;	Dagger
‡	&Dagger;	Double dagger
€	&euro;	Euro
>	&gt;	Greater-than sign
«	&laquo;	Left-pointing double angle quotation mark
<	&lt;	Less-than sign
—	&mdash;	Em dash
		Nonbreaking space
–	&ndash;	En dash
¬	&not;	Not sign
¶	&para;	Paragraph sign
£	&pound;	Pound
"	&quot;	Quotation mark = APL quote
®	&reg;	Registered mark sign
»	&raquo;	Right-pointing double angle quotation mark
§	&sect;	Section sign
™	&trade;	Trademark sign
¥	&yen;	Yen

Table E–2 Mathematical and Technical Characters

Symbol	Character Reference	Description
∧	&and;	Logical and
∠	&ang;	Angle
≈	&asymp;	Almost equal to
∩	&cap;	Intersection
∪	&cup;	Union
°	&deg;	Degree sign
÷	&divide;	Division sign
≡	&equiv;	Identical to
∃	&exist;	There exists
ƒ	&fnof;	Function
∀	&forall;	For all
½	&frac12;	Fraction one half
¼	&frac14;	Fraction one quarter
¾	&frac34;	Fraction three quarters
≥	&ge;	Greater-than or equal to
∞	&infin;	Infinity
∫	&int;	Integral
∈	&isin;	Element of
≤	&le;	Less-than or equal to
µ	&micro;	Micro sign
∇	&nabla;	Backward difference
≠	&ne;	Not equal to
∋	&ni;	Contains as a member
∂	&part;	Partial differential
⊥	&perp;	Perpendicular
±	&plusmn;	Plus-minus sign
∏	&prod;	n-ary product
∏	&prop;	Proportional to
√	&radic;	Square root
~	&sim;	Tilde
Σ	&sum;	n-ary summation
∴	&there4;	Therefore

Table E–3 Arrow Characters

Symbol	Character Reference	Description
↓	&darr;	Downward arrow
↔	&harr;	Left right arrow
←	&larr;	Leftward arrow
→	&rarr;	Rightward arrow
↑	&uarr;	Upward arrow